BlackBerry® Development Fundamentals

BlackBerry® Development Fundamentals

John M. Wargo

✦✦Addison-Wesley

Upper Saddle River, NJ • Boston • Indianapolis • San Francisco

New York • Toronto • Montreal • London • Munich • Paris • Madrid

Cape Town • Sydney • Tokyo • Singapore • Mexico City

Many of the designations used by manufacturers and sellers to distinguish their products are claimed as trademarks. Where those designations appear in this book, and the publisher was aware of a trademark claim, the designations have been printed with initial capital letters or in all capitals.

The author and publisher have taken care in the preparation of this book, but make no expressed or implied warranty of any kind and assume no responsibility for errors or omissions. No liability is assumed for incidental or consequential damages in connection with or arising out of the use of the information or programs contained herein.

The publisher offers excellent discounts on this book when ordered in quantity for bulk purchases or special sales, which may include electronic versions and/or custom covers and content particular to your business, training goals, marketing focus, and branding interests. For more information, please contact

U.S. Corporate and Government Sales
(800) 382-3419
corpsales@pearsontechgroup.com

For sales outside the United States, please contact

International Sales
international@pearson.com

Visit us on the web: informit.com/aw

Library of Congress Cataloging-in-Publication Data

Wargo, John M.

  BlackBerry development fundamentals / John M. Wargo.

    p. cm.

  ISBN 978-0-321-64742-9 (pbk. : alk. paper) 1. BlackBerry (Smartphone)--Programming. 2. Smartphones--Programming. 3. Application software--Development. I. Title.

  TK6570.M6W366 2009

  005.26--dc22

                                        2009034971

Copyright ©2010 Pearson Education, Inc.

All rights reserved. Printed in the United States of America. This publication is protected by copyright, and permission must be obtained from the publisher prior to any prohibited reproduction, storage in a retrieval system, or transmission in any form or by any means, electronic, mechanical, photocopying, recording, or likewise. For information regarding permissions, write to:

Pearson Education, Inc.
Rights and Contracts Department
501 Boylston Street, Suite 900
Boston, MA 02116
Fax (617) 671-3447

Portions of this material copyright AccuWeather, Inc. and are used with permission.

Portions of this material copyright Research In Motion Limited and are used with permission.

Portions of this material copyright dotMobi (mTLD Top Level Domain Ltd. d/b/a mobiThinking.com and mobiThinking.mobi) and used with permission.

ISBN-13: 978-0-321-64742-9
ISBN-10: 0-321-64742-4
Text printed in the United States on recycled paper at R.R. Donnelley in Crawfordsville, Indiana.
First printing November 2009

Editor-in-Chief
Mark Taub

Acquisitions Editor
Greg Doench

Development Editor
Michael Thurston

Managing Editor
Kristy Hart

Project Editor
Jovana San Nicolas-Shirley

Copy Editor
Sheri Cain

Indexer
Cheryl Lenser

Proofreader
Williams Woods Publishing Services

Publishing Coordinator
Michelle Housley

Cover Designer
Alan Clements

Compositor
Gloria Schurick

*This book is dedicated to my family, Anna, August, and Elizabeth
(even Buddy and Lucy, too), who waited patiently while I dedicated ten months
of my life to this project.*

Contents

Foreword

J ohn Wargo has been my friend and esteemed industry colleague for more than 21 years. To put things in perspective, that's longer than I've been married to my lovely wife, if only by a few months. Still, I was a bit hesitant when he asked me to review the chapters of his second book. You see, even though we've worked on exciting and challenging IT projects together all over the world—even launched a commercial software product together—we have very different skill sets. My expertise is generally in communication networks and project management (and, more recently, sales and marketing), and John is one of the most talented software developers I've ever met.

Anyone familiar with my work will tell you I haven't developed an application in at least 12 years, and I haven't developed a good application in closer to 15 years. Despite my own aversion to hands-on development, I really enjoyed *BlackBerry Development Fundamentals*. John approached the subject, as he does most everything in life, with a keen insight and common sense. The content is presented in a way that both the professional developer and his line of business manager or sponsoring executive can quickly grasp the key principles that they both have to understand to make good decisions and get on with the business at hand. To paraphrase one of the first managers that John and I both worked for, "John Wargo is a guy that is not just really technical, but also knows what a good sentence ought to look like," which is a lot less common than you might think.

As a road warrior and avid BlackBerry user, I hope that the developers who read this book will create amazing new applications. Applications that don't just enable businesses to be more efficient and profitable, but that, more importantly, make it possible for their users to attend more of their children's soccer games while still getting their work done in this increasingly demanding world—a sentiment that I'm sure John will both share and appreciate.

—David Via
Business Unit Executive, Worldwide Messaging and Collaboration Sales
IBM Software Group

Acknowledgments

Special thanks to my wife, Anna, for all of her support. In our almost nine years of marriage, I've had a lot of harebrained ideas, and she's supported every one of them with vigor. I now know why so many authors of technical books heap credit on their wives: There's no way any of these books could get written without their support.

I also want to thank the following:

Everyone from RIM who helped support the book, reviewed the manuscript, and steered me right when I occasionally went down the wrong path (apologies if I miss anyone): Prosanta Bhattacherjee, Jon Christiansen, Johnson Hsu, Mike Kirkup, Sanyu Kiruluta, Tim Neil, Joseph O'Leary, Mark Sohm, Paul Steel, Tariq Tahir, Brent Thornton, Mike Weitzel, and a host of behind-the-scenes reviewers.

David Via (IBM) for his help reviewing the chapters for readability and writing the Foreword.

Brian Reed (my boss) for being so supportive of my efforts.

Sam Hain for help with chapter flow and the content outline for the Java chapters.

The Pearson Education editorial staff: Greg Doench, Michelle Housley, and Michael Thurston.

About half of this book was written in room 443 at the Marriott Courtyard Columbia in Columbia, MD. Special thanks to Miss Janet, who made sure I had the same room every visit and a cold Dr. Pepper waiting for me every morning.

About the Author

John **Wargo** has been a professional software developer, educator, consultant, and presenter for more than 20 years.

As a subject matter expert (SME) on BlackBerry development platform and tools at Research In Motion (RIM), John was responsible for supporting a large U.S.-based carrier and its customers. He worked with key customers to help them design and build applications for their BlackBerry environments. He also created and delivered BlackBerry application developer training in cities across the United States.

Preface

Welcome to *BlackBerry Development Fundamentals*. I hope you enjoy reading this book and keep it on your bookshelf for a long time. After working for Research In Motion (RIM) and helping its customers understand their options for building custom applications for the BlackBerry platform, I knew the time was right for a book like this. Although the world is full of developers who know how to build applications for desktop, server, and even mobile platforms, many people building their first applications for BlackBerry just don't know where to start. The BlackBerry has so many interesting and unique capabilities, and the BlackBerry applications platform does so much for the developer that it's difficult to quickly learn everything you need to know to be productive.

Although a lot of information on the topic is available online, you'd have to do a lot of digging and searching to find everything you needed. Much of the information available assumes that you already kinda know how to do these things.[1] There is a lot of "how-to" information on the BlackBerry Developers website and elsewhere on the web, but I wrote this book to help provide some of the missing "how it works" and the "why's" that go along with it.

I spent many years of my career as an educator, teaching Lotus Notes/Domino Developer & Administrator courses, plus Novell NetWare Administrator courses full time. Because of this, I laid out the chapters and content in a way that lent itself to educating the reader rather than just dumping everything I know onto pages. Inside, you'll see chapters arranged like building blocks, covering topics and introducing concepts to make the content in later chapters easily digestible.

---

1. To see an example of what I mean by this, check out my posting here: www.johnwargo.com/index.php/blackberry/8-isinholster.

Who This Book Is For

This book is designed for software developers who are just getting started with BlackBerry development. You could be an experienced mobile developer who wants to know more about BlackBerry, or you could be an experienced application developer who is getting into mobile application development starting with BlackBerry. This book assumes that you have the basic concepts of application development covered and only deals with BlackBerry-specific topics beyond that. Microsoft Windows is key here because all the development tools RIM offers (each of which are free, by the way) only run on Windows (today, anyway).

If you're an experienced BlackBerry developer, this book is probably not for you, although I did learn and write about some things that I could not find documented anywhere on the BlackBerry Developer's website (www.blackberry.com/developers) or elsewhere on the Internet. You should still be able to find some interesting nuggets herein.

What This Book Covers

This book contains detailed descriptions of the application capabilities of the BlackBerry platform, information on how to use the tools that RIM provides and a discussion of specific application development features that are unique to BlackBerry. Where possible, I included sample code to illustrate many of the topics in this book. Where complete applications are needed to illustrate topics, I posted the applications (with detail about how the applications work) to the book's website.

Although the focus of this book is BlackBerry, you'll also find information that applies to other mobile platforms. The discussion of browser-based applications for BlackBerry and the Java discussion all include a conversation of cross-platform capabilities provided by these technologies.

This book contains the following chapters:

- Chapter 1, "Mobile Applications," provides a brief overview of mobile applications and the mobile application capabilities of the BlackBerry platform. This chapter illustrates the many types of applications and different application capabilities available to the BlackBerry developer.
- Chapter 2, "Determining the Best Approach," compares and contrasts the types of application technologies that can be used to build applications for the BlackBerry platform. This chapter helps you select the right starting point for your BlackBerry applications.

- Chapter 3, "The Connected BlackBerry," describes the available network connections a BlackBerry application can use to access network-based resources. Any network-aware BlackBerry application (even browser applications) will make heavy use of these connections, so it's important for a developer to understand the options and know when to use each.

- Chapter 4, "The BlackBerry Mobile Data System (MDS)," provides a detailed overview of the BlackBerry MDS. It describes how developers can use MDS to provide secure access to a corporation's internal resources from BlackBerry devices. It also describes the special optimizations it applies to all application traffic passed between a device and the server that processes the application's data.

- Chapter 5, "BlackBerry Application Data Push," provides an overview of the application data push capabilities of the BlackBerry platform and answers common questions asked by developers first learning about this technology.

- Chapter 6, "Pushing Data to Internal (BES) Users," explains how to build an application that pushes data to a BES-connected BlackBerry device. This chapter covers both RIM Push and PAP Push technologies.

- Chapter 7, "Pushing Data to External (BIS) Users," explains how to build an application that pushes data to a BIS-connected BlackBerry device. This chapter covers both BlackBerry Web Signals and the BlackBerry Push APIs.

- Chapter 8, "The BlackBerry Browser," describes the standard and non-standard capabilities of the BlackBerry browser. This chapter provides detailed information a developer needs to know regarding what can and cannot be done in the BlackBerry browser.

- Chapter 9, "Building BlackBerry Browser Applications," provides detailed information on how to build browser-based applications for the BlackBerry platform. This chapter covers how to build a website that provides the maximum performance and experience for BlackBerry users while leveraging some special features of the BlackBerry browser.

- Chapter 10, "Testing/Debugging BlackBerry Browser Applications," describes procedures and tools developers can use to test their BlackBerry browser applications before deploying them to end users. This chapter discusses how to use the BlackBerry Web Tools: the BlackBerry Plug-In for Visual Studio and the BlackBerry Web Development Plug-in for Eclipse.

- Chapter 11, "Building BlackBerry Java Applications," digs into the Java application capabilities available to BlackBerry developers. It addresses the unique capabilities RIM provides to allow developers to take advantage of special features of the BlackBerry platform.

- Chapter 12, "Getting Started with the BlackBerry Java Development Tools," provides developers with information they need to download and install the free BlackBerry Java development tools. It also contains information on how to use certain capabilities available to each of the tools (which are described in following chapters), including how to configure the BlackBerry Signing Keys and use the Java Preprocessor.

- Chapter 13, "Using the BlackBerry Java Development Environment (JDE)," contains information on how to use the BlackBerry JDE to build, test, and debug Java applications for the BlackBerry platform. Developers should read this chapter if they plan to use the JDE or want to learn more about this tool.

- Chapter 14, "Using the BlackBerry JDE Plug-In for Eclipse (eJDE)," contains information on how to use the BlackBerry JDE Plug-In for Eclipse to build, test, and debug Java applications for the BlackBerry platform. Developers should read this chapter if they plan to use the eJDE or want to learn more about the tool.

- Chapter 15, "Using the BlackBerry JDE Component Package Tools," contains information on how to use command-line tools included in the BlackBerry JDE Component Package to build, test, and debug Java applications for the BlackBerry platform. These tools are used with third-party development environments or as part of an automated build process.

- Chapter 16, "Deploying Java Applications," contains instructions that a developer can use to deploy BlackBerry Java applications to devices. It covers each way a developer can deploy applications, including pushing the application to target devices using the BES or posting information about an application online so interested users can download it.

- Chapter 17, "Using Additional BlackBerry Application Technologies," covers the topics that just didn't fit into any of the other chapters. It includes information on the Plazmic Content Development Kit, the e-Commerce Content Optimization Engine, using the BlackBerry Wallet in web applications, and the Sync Server SDK.

Inside This Book

Most of the device screen shots used in this book were taken on my BlackBerry Bold smartphone using the screen-capture capabilities in myBoxTone Expert from BoxTone, Inc.[2] This is a great application that allows you (and your application users) to obtain a wealth of information from a BlackBerry device. The screen-capture feature allowed me to open a screen that contained the information I wanted to highlight in the book and grab a screen shot and email it to myself for use later.

The reason I use a Bold and not the newer BlackBerry Storm or Tour smartphones is because, when I worked for RIM, I worked for RIM's AT&T Business Unit, and that's where my loyalties lie. That and the fact that nobody has given me a Storm to use!

In some cases, I used source-code examples from RIM knowledge base articles. In each case, I identified the article number for easy access.

At the end of each chapter, you can find a list of links to relevant external resources. Wherever I found an article on the web that helped me describe a topic, I added a link to the source article, page, or document to help provide you with as much information as possible. I even posted each link on this book's website (described next) to make it easier for you to access these resources.

When talking about the BlackBerry platform, I frequently refer to the BlackBerry Enterprise Server as the BES; it's not a "BES Server" because that would be redundant (BlackBerry Enterprise Server Server)—it's just like saying ATM Machine, NIC Card, VIN Number, and PIN Number. It's also not a B.E.S. (saying each letter separately), it's just a BES.

I originally intended on dedicating a portion of this book to the BlackBerry MDS Runtime technology I was very fond of. However, at the last minute, RIM announced end of life for the technology (MDS Runtime, MDS Studio, and the BlackBerry Plug-In for Microsoft Visual Studio versions 1.0 and 1.1) and encouraged me to omit the topic from the book. If you're using these technologies, you need to begin migrating existing applications to other technologies before new devices that don't support MDS Runtime start appearing in your organization.

---

2. I didn't create myBoxTone Expert, but I was involved in bringing it to market.

About This Book's Website

As I wrote this book, it quickly became clear that a lot of this book's content would be useful outside of these pages. As mentioned in the previous section, the links to additional resources included at the end of each chapter are more useful as actual links that you can access from a website.[3] Additionally, the complete applications I intended to include just didn't make sense as ink on a page; they needed to be available for download so developers can use them without retyping the code. Other useful materials on the website include two Appendices. Appendix A, "Using the BlackBerry Device Simulators," contains a detailed overview of BlackBerry device simulators. Appendix B, "Creating Application Icons," contains information on how to create icons for your BlackBerry applications. Finally, I wanted to write about BlackBerry Widgets, but the technology hadn't been released yet (nor had a device been released that could run them), so I needed a place to post additional content that couldn't make it into this book in time.

This book's website can be found at www.bbdevfundamentals.com. On the site, you can find all the content described in the previous paragraph, plus any additional information I come up with that I think will be useful. Be sure to bookmark this site in your browser so you have quick access to the additional resources links found at the end of each chapter.

I also publish BlackBerry development-related articles to my personal technical website (www.johnwargo.com). Check out the site periodically, because I post new content whenever I uncover anything interesting (which, so far, is pretty often).

---

3. Thank you, Sanyu, for suggesting this.

Mobile Applications

Before digging into the details of how to build mobile applications for the BlackBerry, it is important to be on the same page regarding what mobile applications are. This chapter describes the types of mobile applications and what they can do, how they can be built, where free applications can be found, where mobile applications can be purchased, and more.

1.1 The BlackBerry as an Application Platform

Many developers and business people think that the BlackBerry application platform is closed and that applications cannot be built for them. Some believe that the BlackBerry platform is proprietary, and you have to use special tools or technologies to build custom applications for it. Others believe that the only option for building BlackBerry applications is to build browser-based applications. The good news (and you probably already know this because you're reading the book) is that you can build different types of applications for the BlackBerry, and browser-based apps are not the only available option.

You've pretty much always been able to build applications for the BlackBerry. Early devices could run custom C++ applications and, when Research In Motion (RIM) migrated to the Java platform, you could also create Java applications for devices. The reason people think that you can't create custom applications for BlackBerry is that these devices normally come "feature complete" for most users—all the applications a mobile user needs are already on the device. It's this complete coverage of the standard applications a user needs that makes people think that's all there is.

BlackBerry applications became more powerful when RIM released the Black-Berry Mobile Data System (MDS), which is described in Chapter 4, "The Black-Berry Mobile Data System (MDS)." MDS gave mobile developers secure access to internal application servers and dramatically enhanced what mobile users can do while they are away from the office.

1.2 Why Mobile Applications Are So Important

It's necessary to understand why mobile applications are so important. Organizations and individual users often buy smartphones because they want to stay in touch via email and maintain their calendars and to-do lists while they're away from the office. Some enterprise customers and many consumers buy smartphones because they're cool, and they want to stay hooked into current technology. After you own a smartphone and get the value from the capabilities it provides, custom home-grown or third-party applications are an easy way to get even more value out of what you are already paying for. These applications only enhance the mobile user's experience.

The first question that must be answered is this: What type of mobile applications can be built for the BlackBerry platform? This is covered in the following sections.

1.3 Browser Applications

The most common type of mobile applications for BlackBerry are browser-based applications. Browser-based applications are built using HTML, XHTML, and other standard web technologies (JavaScript, Cascading Style Sheets [CSS] and others). Many people believe that you have to build mobile web applications using Wireless Application Protocol (WAP) and Wireless Markup Language (WML), but that's not true: Most modern smartphones support the standard web markup languages and more.

When you look at mobile browser applications, understand that they are simply websites or web pages accessed from a mobile device. The source for the browser application can be inside the company firewall (protected from the outside world and only available to "internal" users) or accessible by any device with a network connection. The application can be written specifically for the mobile platform (smaller versions of the desktop pages), or it can be the desktop version displayed on the mobile device (which may not render well on a small screen).

The browser application/site can provide static data (simple HTML pages), dynamic data (using technologies, such as Active Server Pages [ASP], Java Server Pages [JSP] or even PHP Hypertext Preprocessor [PHP]), and input forms that deliver data to backend data repositories. Special features of the BlackBerry platform even allow browser applications to access GPS location information on the device (described in Chapter 9, "Building BlackBerry Browser Applications") and browser applications to be pushed to one or more devices by the server through Push (described in Chapters 5, 6, and 7).

BlackBerry Widgets allow developers to package a web application into a Java application and deploy them to devices. These applications are built entirely using standard web technologies and can leverage both local and server-based content. The application sits on the BlackBerry home screen and is indistinguishable from other applications on the device. (As of this writing, the technology has not been released, so it will receive limited coverage in this book; additional information will be published to www.bbdevfundamentals.com when the technology becomes available.)

These browser applications are built using any of the web-development tools available in today's market. There's nothing special about these applications; they're just web pages formatted for a smaller screen and limited by the reduced capabilities of a mobile device (described in Chapters 8 and 9).

1.4 Rich Client Applications

You can build rich client applications for BlackBerry devices. Developers sometimes call them "native" applications, but that term doesn't really apply here. These applications look and feel like the applications created by RIM and pre-loaded on BlackBerry devices. Both of the options for rich client applications run within a runtime container on the device, so they're really not native applications.

Rich client applications can be built using Java, which also provides some cross-platform capabilities (explained in Chapter 2, "Determining the Best Approach"). Java applications have access to the full capabilities of the device, while browser applications cannot do as much on the device (although much of that changes with BlackBerry Widgets).

Rich client applications can do the following:

- Interact with a user in a more dynamic way than browser applications.
- Create email messages, manipulate existing messages, and interact with the contents of message folders.

- Place phone calls or act (do something) when a phone call is placed or received by a mobile user.
- Launch the browser or other local applications.
- Communicate with application servers by using any one of a number of standard and proprietary transport or communication protocols.
- Read, create, and modify data maintained by the internal Personal Information Management (PIM) applications.
- Access location information (where available; not all BlackBerry devices have built-in GPS capabilities).
- Store application data locally (either in device memory or on external storage).
- Communicate with external peripherals, typically Bluetooth or USB devices.
- Receive pushed data.
- Monitor device activity and register custom listeners.
- Register a custom rendering engine to allow a mobile user to view a file type not supported by the platform.
- Run at startup (launch when the device starts up and sit in the background to do something special, such as process pushed data or periodically check for new data on a server).
- Run in the background, which is something not all mobile devices can do (especially the iPhone and, until recently, Palm devices).
- Alert the user when any number of things happens.
- About anything else you can think of.

Although there are limitations on which application programming interfaces (APIs) are available to developers, many application capabilities are only limited by how hard it is for the developer to implement and how much time/resources the developer has at his disposal.

1.5 Targeting an Audience

Until the release of the BlackBerry Pearl 8100 in September of 2006, the Black-Berry smartphone had always been considered a device targeted at Enterprise (corporate) users. Although application capabilities had been a part of the Black-Berry platform for years, only enterprises really took advantage of them. With the Pearl, RIM started a big push into the consumer market and, therefore, the world has seen a corresponding increase in applications targeted at consumers (such as soccer moms, students, factory workers, and so on).

Both consumer and enterprise applications are used for many different activities. Some applications only interact with local data, such as a prescription medication database for physicians or a shopping-list application for consumers. Other applications gather data and submit it to a server somewhere. These might be survey applications, sports-scouting applications, network diagnostics or traffic analysis applications. Some applications interact directly with the data stored in one or more backend systems (for example, order lookup and order placement, patient records applications, or mobile banking).

Business applications typically interact with corporate data residing inside the corporate firewall, protected from external, nonemployee access. Many organizations all around the world have built applications that enable mobile workers to access most of the same customer or production data they can access from their desks. These applications enable mobile workers to spend more face time with their customers, suppliers, or partners, and can still be just as effective as they are in the office; in some cases, this eliminates the need and extra cost of a laptop.

With the proliferation of Service Oriented Architectures (SOA) and Web Services, many organizations find that their mobile applications can access both internal and external data at the same time while not sacrificing the security needed to protect the data during transmission.

Customer Example: Order Status and Delivery Confirmation

One customer I worked with learned about the application capabilities of the BlackBerry platform and then built some quick Web Services to access data maintained in JD Edwards, a popular Enterprise Resource Planning (ERP) software package. The company built and deployed four BlackBerry rich client applications in less than four months.

After it enabled the sales force to perform order status lookups from the team's BlackBerry devices, the sales representatives soon started asking for delivery confirmation. The developers quickly located an external Web Services that provided delivery confirmation information from both FedEx® and UPS® and added that to their application. Mobile users were accessing internal data regarding stock availability and order status and getting information on delivery status by using computer systems and Web Services provided by an external entity. In this case, access to the Web Services was free, but some services charge for access.

Organizations are building mobile applications to enable mobile workers to participate in many different types of business processes. Companies use mobile applications to support workflow and approval processes, field claims entry, mortgage or loan origination, monitor manufacturing facilities, order status, order entry, inventory lookup, and even proposal generation.

In many cases, the companies who develop and sell enterprise applications for the desktop have created versions of their applications specifically targeted at BlackBerry and other mobile platforms. Examples of these applications are SAP and salesforce.com; both organizations have made available mobile versions of their applications. These companies have also started to expose Web Services to allow developers to interact with their data in other ways.

As RIM's market share grew in the consumer smartphone market and with the release of the iPhone, Google Android and Palm Pre platforms, more and more applications are being created for consumers. The availability of browser applications for consumers changed dramatically—every major website in the market adjusted their sites to accommodate mobile users. The following list shows some examples of mobile-friendly websites available today:

- **Airlines:** Continental Airlines (www.continental.com), American Airlines (www.aa.com), Northwest Airlines (www.nwa.com), and United Airlines (www.united.com)
- **Entertainment:** YouTube (www.youtube.com) and MySpace (www.myspace.com)
- **Government:** Federal Emergency Management Agency (www.fema.gov)
- **News:** CNN (www.cnn.com), Fox News (www.foxnews.com), The New York Times (www.nyt.com), and The Wall Street Journal (www.wsj.com)
- **Search:** Google (www.google.com), Yahoo! (www.yahoo.com), and MSN (www.msn.com)
- **Shopping:** Amazon (www.amazon.com) and eBay (www.ebay.com)
- **Sports:** ESPN (www.espn.com), Major League Baseball (www.mlb.com), National Football League (www.nfl.com), National Hockey League (www.nhl.com), and National Basketball Association (www.nba.com)
- **Travel:** Federal Aviation Administration (www.faa.gov)
- **Weather:** Weather.com (www.weather.com), Weather Underground (www.weatherunderground.com), and AccuWeather (www.accuweather.com)

MLB even released an application it created that allows fans to "watch" a game in progress directly from their BlackBerry smartphones. Viewers don't get a video feed of the game, but they get a graphical representation of what is going on (through a picture of the field with indicators for which bases had men on). Using advanced browser capabilities (Asynchronous JavaScript and XML [AJAX] and XMLHTTPRequest), only changing data is sent to the mobile browser.

The Enterprise Pressure

The list of mobile-friendly consumer websites was added to this chapter to highlight that many of the sites consumers use on a daily basis have already been updated to support mobile devices.

Because these employees already use their mobile browsers to check movie times, purchase books, check-in for flights, check the weather, and track their favorite team's score in the big game, they're waiting for those business applications to also get mobilized. These employees understand the value of the things they can get done while mobile, and they want the same access to internal applications.

Many of these sites also offer a client-side application (usually written in Java) that sits as an icon on the BlackBerry home screen and, when opened, launches their site in the browser (Fox News, CNN, MLB teams, and more). RIM is calling these applications Web Icons. Other organizations offer special applications that allow mobile users to interact locally with data downloaded from their sites (The Wall Street Journal Mobile Reader and Ticketmaster).

Consumers also have access to rich content that can be delivered to mobile devices. Enterprises are also learning the value of these applications, and you can find many companies who deliver company-produced podcasts to mobile devices. RIM's recent acquisition of Chalk Media reinforces this point.

There are free local search applications, such as award-winning Poynt (www.mypoynt.com) and Google Local Search (www.google.com). There are Internet radio applications, such as Slacker (www.slacker.com) and XM Radio (www.xmradio.com), plus dynamic content-delivery systems, such as Viigo (www.viigo.com).

Another interesting category of mobile applications involves Location Based Services (LBS)—getting mobile users where they need to be or giving companies the capability to track mobile users so organizations know where their employees are. A popular option is TeleNav (www.telenav.com); it's an application that provides turn-by-turn directions anywhere in the U.S. and beyond. Many applications on the BlackBerry App World and in the BlackBerry Enterprise Solutions Catalog offer LBS capabilities. Consumers even have access to BlackBerry applications used to interact with social-networking sites, such as Facebook, MySpace, Flickr, and Twitter.

1.6 Push Instead of Pull

Another unique and interesting aspect of mobile applications on BlackBerry is the concept of Application Data Push. As previously mentioned, BlackBerry applications can receive data pushed to them from external data sources. This means that developers can build applications for both the enterprise and consumer space that receive their data via push rather than a manual or scheduled lookup from the device. With this feature, an application can receive data when it changes or when something important happens, rather than when the user looks for it. Data can be delivered to the device off hours, when the network is underutilized and the device is not busy doing other things, or whenever needed. Data can even be sent when the device is outside of wireless coverage and delivered when the device reappears. Chapters 5, 6, and 7 cover this topic in detail.

A good example of push is the BlackBerry Emergency Contact List (ECL) application that RIM offers as a free download from its website (www.blackberry.com/go/ecl). The application was built to allow organizations to deliver some data to devices that an organization needs to continue to function in a catastrophe. Through the application, a user can populate a list of a company's emergency contacts and click a button to push the data to any BlackBerry device in the organization. There is a version for Lotus Domino, Java, and .NET, and each version includes the source code you need to customize the application and understand how it works. Several companies have modified the application to create an executive contact list, department contact list, or even a rotating call schedule. Keep in mind that it's free and you get what you pay for, but this is an excellent way to see what can be done on a BlackBerry smartphone.

1.7 Finding Applications

How do users get these applications? People build them, pay someone to build them, or buy them from an Independent Software Vendor (ISV).

On the consumer side, there are many sources for BlackBerry applications. There are a lot of free and for-purchase applications available from developers and websites everywhere. A recent trend is for mobile handset manufacturers to build their own application storefront: Apple and Google both recently launched theirs, and RIM opened its application storefront called BlackBerry App World in spring 2009 (www.blackberry.com/appworld). App World offers both free and for-purchase BlackBerry applications and works by placing a Java application on a BlackBerry device; all purchasing and downloading of BlackBerry applications is performed through this client-side application.

Figure 1.1 shows the BlackBerry App World site from the desktop browser. From this page, you can provide an email address and have a link to the App World application sent to your BlackBerry.

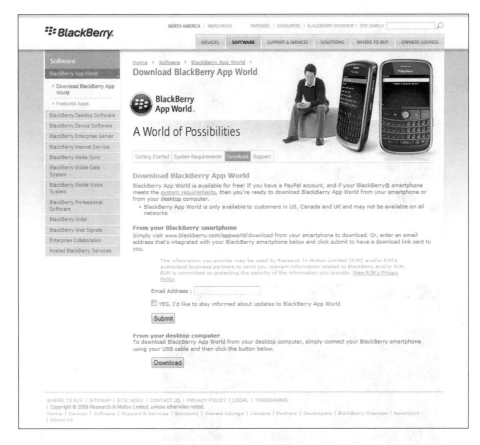

Figure 1.1 BlackBerry App World

After you download the BlackBerry App World application, it appears as an icon on your BlackBerry device, as shown in Figure 1.2. When you open the application, you can search for applications, see a list of the most popular applications, and download free or for-purchase applications to your device, as shown in Figure 1.3.

Figure 1.2   BlackBerry App World application icon

Figure 1.3   The BlackBerry App World application

RIM even created the Built for BlackBerry (www.builtforblackberry.com) website to boost awareness of consumer applications for BlackBerry.

You can also get help and download free mobile applications from RIM's Mobile Help website (mobile.blackberry.com). You must access the site from your BlackBerry device, as shown in Figure 1.4.

Figure 1.4   BlackBerry Mobile Help website

Online retailers, such as Handango (www.handango.com) and Handmark (www.handmark.com), maintain catalogs of BlackBerry applications available for sale. Handango even has a client-side application called Handango Inhand that allows you to browse for and purchase BlackBerry applications directly from the device. Even the wireless carriers are opening their own stores now. Expect that more and more sources for consumer and enterprise applications will become available over time.

The open source movement has even started producing enterprise applications and libraries for BlackBerry. Rhomobile has created an open source Rails platform for mobile devices (http://wiki.rhomobile.com/index.php/Rhodes) and PhoneGap (http://phonegap.com), which is an open source development tool for building mobile applications with JavaScript.

To help companies locate partners who offer enterprise applications for Black-Berry, RIM has created an online Enterprise Solutions Guide. This guide contains a listing for every application solution offered by RIM's ISV Alliance Partners. There is a link to the guide at the end of this chapter. Before you build an application, look at the guide to see if one already exists; buying is often easier than building.

1.8 Communicating with External Hardware

Developers should not limit themselves by thinking a mobile application can only work within the bounds of the mobile device. Most mobile devices and the mobile applications they run can interact with many different kinds of external hardware devices. Most external hardware for mobile devices communicates with the device using Bluetooth or even a physical cable connection.

A mobile device application often uses industry standards, such as the Bluetooth standard (through Java Specification Request [JSR] 82) to communicate with external devices. In other cases, the device manufacturer provides device drivers or other means for a mobile application to talk to the device.

Some companies manufacture keyboards, GPS receivers (for BlackBerry devices that don't include built-in GPS radios), digital pen and paper products, ruggedized cases, presentation and screen projection devices, and even printers. Using these, BlackBerry applications can capture signatures, print sales receipts, scan credit cards and fingerprints, project PowerPoint presentations without a laptop, and more.

1.9 Additional Resources

A complete listing of links to these resources is available online at www.bbdevfundamentals.com.

For free BlackBerry development tools, sample code, white papers, demonstration videos, and more, access the BlackBerry Developers website at www. blackberry.com/developers.

RIM offers a beginner's training course called Mobile Development 101. It can be accessed online from http://na.blackberry.com/eng/developers/started/mobiledev101.jsp.

To access the list of ISV solutions for BlackBerry, look at the BlackBerry Enterprise Solutions Guide at www.blackberrysolutionscatalog.com.

The BlackBerry App World home page is located at www.blackberry.com/appworld.

To browse listings of consumer applications for BlackBerry, go to www. builtforblackberry.com, www.handango.com/blackberry, and www.handmark.com.

Gartner Research recently released a report titled "Creating Persuasive Mobile Business Cases in a Recession" (document ID G00165062), which outlines some useful guidelines for making the business case for a mobile application. Even when not in a recession, the tips and guidelines in the document are relevant.

2

Determining the Best Approach

The remaining chapters of this book cover the capabilities of the BlackBerry application platform and then dig into each application development option in detail. Before any BlackBerry application development project begins, the developer must first make some decisions regarding the following:

- How the application will access server-based data
- Whether the application will manipulate a local copy of the data or access the data on the server
- Whether the application's data will be pushed to the application or pulled down from the server
- Whether the application should be purchased or built
- Which of the platform's supported application technologies will be used to build the application

This chapter covers the options that must be considered when addressing these questions

2.1   Local Versus Server-Based Data

The decision to store data on a device or access it all via a server is a decision that is made based on the needs of the application's users. At the same time, the developer must consider how this decision will affect the device's performance, battery life, and data plan usage.

The first portable devices (Palm Pilot, Windows CE, the Apple Newton, and others), didn't usually have any wireless network connectivity, unless the user added a Wi-Fi card to the device. For applications targeting these devices, developers usually built some mechanism to synchronize server-based data with the device while it was cradled (connected via cable to a desktop PC). Although this worked, there were issues related to how difficult it was to ensure that the mobile user had the most recent copy of the data. Additionally, it was painful to have two mobile users, with their own copy of the data, modify the same record before synchronizing it with the server. Although some users still own standalone mobile devices, the more common device is a network-connected smartphone that has more options available to it for sharing data with others.

An application running on a network-connected smartphone, such as the BlackBerry, can easily connect to a server to interact with data stored there, whether it's for a Customer Relationship Management (CRM) system, Enterprise Resource Planning (ERP) application, or any other type of client-server application. The standard mode for these applications, when interacting with corporate data, is for the data to be stored on a server, allowing multiple clients to access it simultaneously and ensure the users always have access to the most up-to-date data.

As good as the mobile networks are, there are still many situations where it makes sense to have the data local to the device. For mobile sales teams or service technicians that work in areas with limited wireless coverage, they might need to manipulate all or some of the application's data on the device and synchronize updates with the server when convenient.

In many cases, a hybrid approach is an appropriate option. With this approach, a database of relatively stable data, such as part numbers, store locations, zip/postal codes, or area/city codes, is stored on the device and rarely updated. More frequently updated data, such as sales orders, shipment status, invoices and customer contact information, is accessed from the server (over the wireless network) as needed. On the consumer side, a good example is Facebook—older messages never change and can be kept local to the device; friend information can always be retrieved from the network when needed.

With any network-connected application, a developer must consider the nature of the wireless network connection and check for connectivity before attempting any connection and recover gracefully when a connection is not available or terminates in the middle of a transmission. As a best practice, an application must be able to queue up any network request and deliver and/or retrieve data whenever the connection becomes available. In cases where the mobile user is not waiting for an update, the application should be able to reconnect and deliver the data without user intervention. The application can let the user know data has been queued, but it should not require that the user act to reestablish a connection that has been terminated.

The organization sponsoring the application will have a good understanding of the wireless network coverage options for its territories and decide on the best option for its users based on cost and performance.

2.2 Internal Versus External Access

What is the relationship between the owner of the application data and the mobile user accessing it? If the mobile user is part of the organization that owns the data, it's likely that the BlackBerry device's connection to the application server will be provided through the BlackBerry Mobile Data System (MDS) described in Chapter 4, "The BlackBerry Mobile Data System (MDS)."

If the mobile user is not part of the organization owning the data, it's likely that the data is provided as part of a subscription service or freely available on the Internet. With this option, the application accesses the server through an open firewall port through the organization's Internet connection.

In some cases, an application will use both connections, getting some data from an internal server and other data from an external data source. In this case, the application must keep track of multiple connections simultaneously. The best practice for this scenario is to let the internal application server connect to both internal and external data sources and reduce the load placed on the mobile device.

The options a developer might use for both internal and external network connections are described in detail in Chapter 3, "The Connected BlackBerry."

2.3 Pushing Versus Pulling the Data

Depending on how the application's users interact with the data or how often they need access to the data, it might be easier to just push updates to the application rather than forcing the user to periodically request updates from the server.

If the application's users interact with the server by performing just-in-time queries or lookups of data, the application must accommodate that requirement. On the other hand, if the application's user needs access to data that only changes periodically or changes on a triggered event (such as an order shipping or a back-ordered part becoming available), the application can minimize the load on the user (forcing him to periodically check for new data) and just push the data to the application behind the scenes when updates are available.

Fortunately, each of the BlackBerry application types (web and Java, enterprise and consumer) support push, so there is no limitation on which application type is used for the application. The options a developer can use to push data to device applications are described in Chapters 5, 6, and 7.

2.4 Building Versus Buying

For a developer, the decision to build or buy is sometimes difficult to make. Depending on the cost of a third-party solution, it might be less expensive to purchase a solution rather than build it.

Organizations build applications to help solve specific problems that the business faces. If the business problem the application is trying to solve is unique to your business, it is not likely that a solution will be available to purchase. If the business problem is a common problem encountered by many businesses, the likelihood that a third-party solution exists is much higher. Even if the target audience for an application is part of a niche or vertical market, if enough companies have the problem, there might be a solution available.

With third-party solutions, the responsibility for building, testing, and maintaining the application belongs to someone else. The organization purchasing the solution can use the application, knowing that someone else is responsible for it if it breaks. If a new version of the backend application server or mobile platform becomes available, it's the vendor's responsibility to build support for the new version. In the case of more sophisticated applications, because the cost of building the application is distributed across multiple customers, the overall entry cost for the application is low.

If the mobile application is communicating with a proprietary system that your company developed, it's likely that you have to build the solution yourself. If the business problem being solved is unique, but you're talking to an industry standard application platform (such as WebSphere, SAP, Remedy, PeopleSoft, and so on), you can likely leverage integration tools provided by RIM's ISV Alliance Partners to provide the connectivity; you would only be responsible for building the appropriate business logic.

For consumer applications, this is much simpler: It's just a question of the cost for the application (free is best, of course) versus how much is required to build the application yourself.

2.5 Selecting a Development Platform

The most important decision a mobile developer makes is the selection of the development platform/language to use for the application:

- The first thing to consider when selecting a platform is whether the client application already exists for another platform. If the application is already available for the desktop or another mobile platform, the developer will usually (but not always) use a similar technology to build the BlackBerry or mobile version.
- If the application is accessed today through a web browser, it's likely that BlackBerry users will also be able to use the browser. A browser-based application designed for a smaller screen should function just fine on the BlackBerry browser, as long as the application doesn't use ActiveX controls or Java applets. There are limitations on what a BlackBerry browser can and cannot do, which are covered in detail in Chapters 8 and 9.
- If an existing browser-based application runs on Google Gears, it should run on BlackBerry devices that support Gears (BlackBerry Device Software 5.0 and higher).
- If the application exists today as a rich client (non-browser) application, the situation is more difficult. If the existing application is written in Java, there is a chance that the application can be rewritten to run on the Black-Berry. If the existing application is written in Java Micro Edition (JME) and conforms to Mobile Information Device Profile (MIDP) and/or Connected Limited Device Configuration (CLDC) standards, it should run on the BlackBerry with limited modifications. (Chapter 11, "Building Black-Berry Java Applications," covers this in detail.) If the application was written for the Android platform (Android uses Java, but a different flavor of Java), the application must be rewritten for the BlackBerry platform. If the existing application was written in another technology, such as Delphi, any of the .NET languages, Objective-C (Mac OS, iPhone) and others, the application needs to be rewritten for the BlackBerry platform.
- If it's a new application or one created just for a BlackBerry device, select either of the available choices: either Browser or Java. We'll discuss these choices in the following sections.

2.5.1 Browser-Based Applications

Browser-based applications provide the best cross-platform option for mobile devices, and there is no shortage of developers/designers with the skills to build the applications. If the application will consist of static pages or the server-based data for the application can be easily served up through a browser interface, building the application in the browser is a good choice.

Browser-based applications are not the fastest option for mobile devices, so the developer needs to weigh the benefits of easy development against the performance issues inherent in the technology. Although the use of Asynchronous JavaScript and XML (AJAX) can reduce the amount of data delivered to the browser (by not requiring the entire page to update for a new request), in general, the browser is slower than other BlackBerry application technologies, even on high-speed third generation (3G) networks. This is because of the performance costs in setting up and tearing down a high speed connection to the server, and because a web page typically includes both content and layout information, more than just the displayed data is sent across the wireless network.

Build a browser-based application if the users are expecting to use the browser to access the application, if the developer's skills are limited to browser development and/or if the application must run on any mobile device without any additional work. Browser applications are also beneficial in that there is not a client application that must be deployed to mobile devices. With browser applications, the application can be updated at any time without impacting the application's users.

If the requirement is to build a browser application that interacts with local data (calendar, contacts, tasks, notes, and so on) on the BlackBerry device, the application should be created using BlackBerry Widgets or the Google Gears application platform.

Many existing web applications are built on a web services platform where the HTML delivered to the browser is created by applying an Extensible Stylesheet Language Transformation (XSLT) to the output from a web service. It may be possible, instead, to consume the service directly from a rich client application on the BlackBerry. This approach likely provides the mobile user with better performance for the application.

2.5.2 Java Applications

The developer that wants to provide the best possible experience for BlackBerry application users will, in most cases, develop the application using Java. The applications that BlackBerry owners use most often (Messaging, Calendar, Contacts, Tasks, Browser, Phone, Camera, and more) are all Java applications. Developers that want their applications to look, feel, and operate like the other applications on the BlackBerry will build their applications using Java. A Java application provides the most robust capabilities to the BlackBerry developer but, at the same time, is the most difficult application to build. Java applications are usually hand-crafted; there are not any graphical application builders for BlackBerry Java applications. Because of how robust and capable Java is, it usually takes a lot of code to accomplish many things that are easy to do in other languages.

Custom Java applications provide a rich client experience and have access to most, but not all, of the BlackBerry device's capabilities. RIM reserves some capabilities for its own use, but the list of restricted capabilities is relatively short compared to what else can be done on the device. Chapter 11 describes the Java application development options and capabilities.

2.5.3 MDS Runtime Applications

The MDS Runtime Environment was designed to allow nondevelopers to build rich client applications for the BlackBerry that look and feel like applications written in Java. For these applications, RIM created a special development environment that allows these applications to be built through a point and click, wizard-driven interface. The applications run in a special runtime environment that does not have access to the full suite of Java API's. The applications are much easier to build than Java applications but cannot provide all the functionality that Java applications can.

RIM announced end of life for MDS Runtime and the associated development tools (MDS Studio and the BlackBerry Plug-In for Microsoft Visual Studio versions 1.0 and 1.1) for December 31, 2009. For that reason, MDS Runtime applications and the tools used to build MDS Runtime applications will not be discussed in this book.

2.6 Choosing the Right Tools

When it comes to building mobile applications for BlackBerry, the required tools are readily available. For browser-based applications, you can continue to use the tools currently being used to build the pages. The only difference for the developer is the size and capabilities of the pages being built, the technologies behind them (HTML, XHTML, XML, CSS, and JavaScript, for example) stay the same. RIM recently announced development tools that allow developers to build and test mobile web applications in both Microsoft Visual Studio and Eclipse.

For building rich client applications for BlackBerry, all the tools you need are freely available from RIM. The tools, all of which only run under Microsoft Windows, are free downloads from the BlackBerry Developer's website (www.blackberry.com/developers), as shown in Figure 2.1. Developers can build and test Browser and Java applications using the Eclipse Integrated Development Environment (IDE) and browser applications using Microsoft Visual Studio. These tools and how they're used are described in subsequent chapters.

Figure 2.1   BlackBerry Developer's website

Some Java developers are only comfortable with the IDE they have been working in for years. Java developers who do not like Eclipse and do not want to use the RIM JDE can still develop applications for BlackBerry using the Java IDE of their choice. The BlackBerry JDE Component Package can be integrated with other IDEs to build and test BlackBerry applications.

2.7 Additional Resources

A link to the following resource is available at www.bbdevfundamentals.com.

To highlight some of the choices an organization makes when deciding to build mobile applications, RIM published a guide called *Developing an Application Mobilization Plan for your Business*, located at http://na.blackberry.com/eng/services/Developing_an_Application_Mobilization_Plan_for_your_Business.pdf.

3

The Connected
BlackBerry

The wireless network connection used by a BlackBerry smartphone is what makes the majority of mobile applications useful. Unfortunately, a developer building a network-connected mobile application cannot simply open a connection to any server; it is more complicated than that. An application can use different paths to reach a server, and the developer has to understand which connection to use depending on the situation. Although a developer can develop BlackBerry applications without knowing about all the connectivity options available to BlackBerry smartphones, it's likely he will make decisions differently after he knows what's available. The BlackBerry platform offers developers special abilities, ones that are not available with other platforms. This makes it easy for a BlackBerry smartphone to connect to any of the data it needs (provided that the user has wireless coverage and the necessary credentials, of course).

This chapter's purpose is to define the different connection paths available to a BlackBerry smartphone and demonstrate how to use them. This chapter also describes the benefits and limitations of each connection type and recommends which connection to use depending on the availability of network connectivity.

3.1 Data-Connected Devices

An unconnected BlackBerry smartphone has interesting and useful features, but it is not using its full potential. You can maintain your calendar, to-do lists and address book, take notes, and, with the appropriate calling plan, make and receive phone calls. You can play games and install third-party applications on the device. You would be, however, limited to applications that don't rely on a connection to an external server for its data. You could send and receive Short Message Service (SMS) messages, because SMS makes its connection through a channel on the voice network instead of the data network. If you installed the BlackBerry Desktop Manager software package, you could synchronize your Personal Information Management (PIM) data (calendar, to-do, address book, and note data) with one or more Personal Information Management (PIM) applications on your Windows-based or Apple PC.

You would certainly receive benefits from its capabilities, but you'd be challenged by your need to physically connect (via USB cable or Bluetooth) with a PC to make the data available somewhere else besides on your smartphone.

The difference between a phone and a smartphone is the applications the phone runs. Modern mobile phones include applications; the difference is the complexity of the applications and the type of user for which the applications are designed. Smartphones typically include a host of personal productivity applications that make the mobile user's life easier. Along with those smartphone capabilities, and the true reason why people purchase smartphones, is the benefit the mobile user receives from the connectivity that comes with the smartphone and its corresponding data plan. People purchase smartphones because of their application capability, but that capability is enhanced dramatically through the connection the smartphone has to data residing somewhere else.

With a data plan enabled smartphone, not only can a mobile user do all the things he can do with an unconnected smartphone, he can also use other features that enhance the value of the device. Data-connected BlackBerry smartphones can

- Wirelessly send and receive email messages.
- Wirelessly synchronize calendar, to-do lists, notes, address book data, and more (enterprise-activated devices only).
- Browse the Internet or even the company Intranet.
- Receive application data pushed from a server.
- Install applications by downloading them from a server or receive applications pushed to them from the server.

- Wirelessly upgrade the BlackBerry device software running on the device (provided that the carrier supports it and the device is running a supported version of the BlackBerry Device Software).
- Use Location Based Services (LBS) to access information, services, and coupons relevant to where the mobile user is currently located and provide turn by turn directions to a destination.
- Synchronize data with an external database/database server (through the BlackBerry Synchronization Service and Sync Server SDK).

And much, much more—this is in no way a complete list.

3.2 Connecting Through the Firewall

On a typical smartphone, the mobile user can use Wireless Access Protocol (WAP) or Transmission Control Protocol/Internet Protocol (TCP/IP) to access network resources from the browser or a custom application. If the data the device needs to access is located behind a corporate firewall, the organization's network administrators must open the firewall ports to provide access to the data from mobile devices. It's important to understand that there are risks involved when opening firewall ports to enable users to access data normally only available to resources located inside the firewall.

On the other hand, the BlackBerry has the same connectivity typical smartphones have, plus additional ones provided by the BlackBerry Infrastructure.[1] BlackBerry devices activated in an enterprise have access to internal (inside the firewall) resources without the need to open up additional firewall ports. Chapter 4, "The BlackBerry Mobile Data System (MDS)," covers this in detail.

Although a developer could use an Internet connection to provide BlackBerry smartphones with access to data, the security and performance issues inherent in that option make it a dangerous choice. If the data the user needs to access resides inside the corporate firewall, opening firewall ports to enable the mobile user with access only opens up another area for hackers. When a government agency, a medical organization governed by HIPAA (U.S. Government Health Insurance Portability and Accountability Act) or an organization that processes credit cards for Visa or MasterCard opens up a firewall port, it has to have a good reason for doing so.

---

1. The BlackBerry Infrastructure consists of special software running in the RIM Network Operations Center (NOC), plus network connections and the necessary service agreements with each Wireless Carrier that supports the BlackBerry platform.

3.3 Service Books

Before we talk about the available connections, it's important to understand how those connections are configured on the BlackBerry. Many of the connectivity options available to BlackBerry devices are controlled by Service Books. Service Books tell the BlackBerry what connectivity options are available and how to reach the appropriate gateway servicing that connection. When a wireless carrier provisions a BlackBerry smartphone with a data plan or when a BlackBerry activates against a BlackBerry Enterprise Server, the required Service Books are delivered to the device, thereby enabling connectivity through the connections described in the Service Book. Each carrier can configure its Service Books in different ways, and Enterprise BlackBerry administrators can control what connections are or are not allowed, even to the point of being able to disable something that the carrier has enabled.

Figure 3.1 shows an example of a BlackBerry Service Book from a BlackBerry Bold smartphone running on the AT&T wireless network. It describes the settings for WAP connections (explained later in this chapter). The gateway is provided by the Wireless Carrier (WAP 2.0, in this case). If the Service Book were missing, the device would be unable to connect via WAP 2.0.

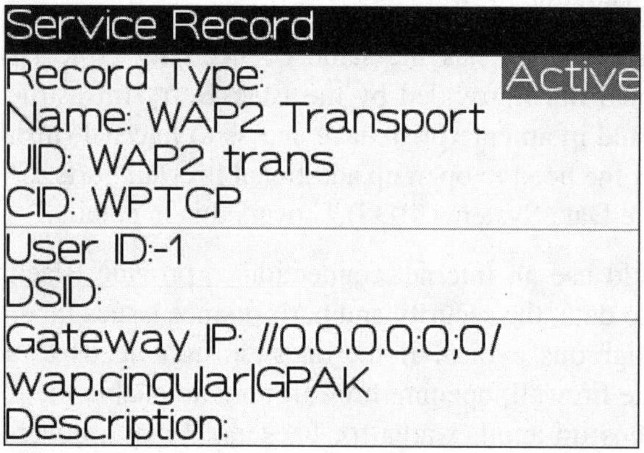

```
Service Record
Record Type:                  Active
Name: WAP2 Transport
UID: WAP2 trans
CID: WPTCP
User ID:-1
DSID:
Gateway IP: //0.0.0.0:0;0/
wap.cingular|GPAK
Description:
```

Figure 3.1   WAP Service Book entry

Figure 3.2 shows the MDS Service Book. This Service Book is provisioned by the BES during enterprise activation. If the Service Book were not on the device, the mobile user would not be able to communicate through MDS to internal resources.

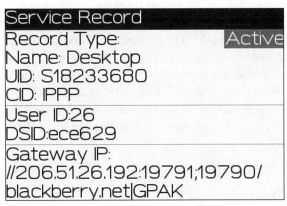

Figure 3.2 Desktop MDS Service Book

The default applications on the BlackBerry smartphone (such as the browser and email client) are already coded to look for the appropriate Service Book before attempting an activity enabled by a Service Book. When building Java applications for the BlackBerry platform, in most cases, the developer must first determine if the appropriate Service Book is available before attempting a connection. RIM includes an application programming interface (API) that developers can use to easily locate a particular Service Book and retrieve configuration values from within an application (net.rim.device.api.servicebook). Sample code for searching for and retrieving information from Service Books is provided in Chapter 11, "Building BlackBerry Java Applications."

3.4 Connection Paths

A BlackBerry smartphone application has multiple paths that it can use to access data located outside of the device (most likely on a server somewhere). A path is the route the request (and corresponding response) takes to get from the device to the server and back. The BlackBerry browser (described in Chapter 8, "The BlackBerry Browser") and BlackBerry Java applications (described in Chapter 11) can access servers using any of the paths. The options are

- Wireless Application Protocol (WAP)
- Direct TCP
- BlackBerry Internet Service (BIS)
- BlackBerry Mobile Data System (MDS)
- Wi-Fi

A good understanding of connections is important because application developers often need to decide which path to use to get to their data and write the code that the connection needs to use that path. When a developer doesn't understand all the available options, the option selected might not be the best one for the application or the mobile user, and the application might not work if the wrong connection path is used. When building applications, RIM recommends a different prioritization of transports, depending on the intended audience for the application. Applications should try the first transport and move down the list until a connection can be made.

For Enterprise applications, RIM recommends the following prioritization:

1. BlackBerry Mobile Data System (MDS)
2. Wi-Fi
3. Wireless Application Protocol (WAP) 2.0
4. BlackBerry Internet Service (BIS)
5. Direct TCP
6. WAP 1.0/1.1

For consumer applications, RIM recommends the following prioritization:

1. Wi-Fi
2. Wireless Application Protocol (WAP) 2.0
3. BlackBerry Internet Service (BIS)
4. BlackBerry Mobile Data System (MDS)
5. Direct TCP
6. WAP 1.0/1.1

The following sections cover the various connection paths and highlight the strengths and limitations of each.

3.4.1 Wireless Application Protocol (WAP) Connection

Before smartphones, back in the days of the early feature phones, carriers wanted to provide their customers with access to Internet-based resources. Because of the limitations of these devices (processing power, browser capabilities, and network bandwidth) a special protocol was created to provide a subset of typical desktop web-browsing capabilities to mobile devices. This protocol, WAP, required special gateways provided by the wireless carriers and used a special, reduced capability mobile page markup language called Wireless Markup Language (WML).

WAP used to be the most consistent way to access the Internet from mobile phones—both smartphones and regular mobile phones supported the protocol. Today, WAP gateways are still provided by carriers and there are a lot of services still offered via WAP.

When you open a WAP connection, either through a URL opened in the WAP browser or through a connection from a Java application, the request takes a special route through the WAP gateway provided by your wireless carrier. As shown in Figure 3.3, a WAP request travels from the BlackBerry device (1) to the carrier's WAP gateway (2), and then out to the public Internet (3). As with all the connections discussed in this chapter, the response from the server follows the same path only in reverse order. The WAP gateway acts as a proxy for the requests made by the device and can reformat the data (convert HTML to WML, for example) returned to the requesting application.

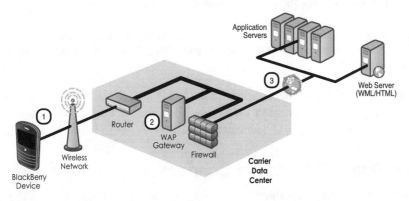

Figure 3.3 WAP request path

When connecting via WAP from a Java application, the way it's done varies depending on which version of WAP you use. With WAP 2.0, your application must append the unique ID (UID) of the WAP 2.0 Service Book to the `Connector.open` command. To implement this, your application must first locate the WAP 2.0 Service Book, then retrieve the UID for the Service Book (shown in Figure 3.1) and include it as a parameter in the call to `Connector.open`:

```
HttpConnection conn = (HttpConnection)Connector.open(
  "http://somewapsite.com;ConnectionUID=WAP2 trans");
```

You can't just assume the name of the UID; you must look up the WAP 2.0 Service Book on every device your application runs on, unless your application is only targeted to a single carrier's customers and you are comfortable hard-coding it in your application. Although it might look like you can make an assumption about the UID for the Service Book, it is possible that the carrier will use a different value in the Service Book it pushes to a device. Additionally, Service Book settings can change at any time and be pushed to the device, so it is risky to hard-code the Service Book information.

Note:
On the BlackBerry, the implementation of WAP 2.0 is just a Service Book-based TCP connection.

If your application is using a WAP 1.0 or WAP 1.1 connection, you must append the Access Point Name[2] (APN) provided by the carrier for the WAP connection. In the following sample Java code, both `WAPGatewayAPN` and `WAPGatewayIP` are required parameters for the call to `Connector.open`:

```
HttpConnection conn = (HttpConnection)Connector.open(
"http://somewapsite.com;WapGatewayIP=0.0.0.0;WapGatewayAPN=
apn_name");
```

As with the WAP 2.0 connection, to use the WAP 1.0/1.1 connection provided by the carrier, you need to locate the Service Book for the connection and retrieve the values for `WAPGatewayAPN` and `WAPGatewayIP` to use in your application.

3.4.2 Direct TCP Internet Connection

Another way to access the Internet from either a browser or Java application is to use an Internet connection using Transmission Control Protocol (TCP), called Direct TCP. The Direct TCP request takes a route from the BlackBerry device (1) through an Internet gateway provided by the carrier (2) to the server processing the request (3), as shown in Figure 3.4. The path is similar to the one shown in Figure 3.3, except that the request is delivered through an Internet gateway located at the carrier data center rather than a WAP gateway. The Internet gateway does not perform any reformatting of the data as it is returned to the application requesting the data.

---

2. An Access Point Name describes the gateway server that the device uses for its connection.

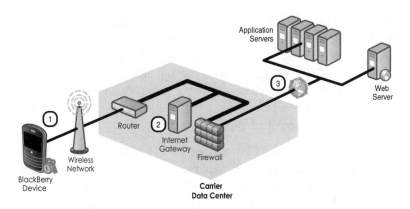

Figure 3.4 Direct TCP Internet request path

When opening a connection using Direct TCP, the application must use the APN for the particular device's current wireless carrier. The easiest way to do this is to direct the BlackBerry to select the APN automatically as shown in the following Java code:

```
HttpConnection conn = (HttpConnection)Connector.open(
"http://www.somesite.com;deviceside=true");
```

In this example, the `deviceside=true` parameter tells the device to manage the connection rather than directing it through MDS (described next) or through a specific APN (either provided by the user or the carrier). In many cases, the device will not be provisioned by the carrier with the information the device needs to determine the APN, and the connection will fail.

You can specify the specific APN to use for the connection, as follows:

```
HttpConnection conn = (HttpConnection)Connector.open(
"http://www.somesite.com;deviceside=true;apn=apn_name");
```

This might be problematic because you need the user to provide the name of the carrier's APN or you have to build logic into your application to know the APNs for every carrier network you support with your application.

Some APNs require that credentials are provided when the connection is made. The credentials are appended to the URL string passed to `Connector.open`, as shown here:

```
HttpConnection conn = (HttpConnection)Connector.open(
"http://www.blackberry.com;deviceside=true;
apn=wap.cingular; TunnelAuthUsername=some_username;
TunellAuthPassword=some_password");
```

3.4.3 BlackBerry Internet Service Connection

The BlackBerry Internet Service (BIS) is a special service that BlackBerry users can subscribe to from their carriers to provide Internet access to BlackBerry smartphones. In most cases, enterprise-activated BlackBerry devices already have this capability (BIS is included with most, if not all, BES plans), but consumers purchasing BlackBerry devices must be provisioned for BIS to be able to access their mail (up to ten personal mail accounts) on the device, browse the Internet, and run Internet-enabled applications.

One of the issues with Direct TCP connections to Internet-based servers is that an application might not be sure whether the connection parameters have been set or set correctly or, if not set, what they might be. RIM created a special connection type called BlackBerry Internet Service – Browser (BIS-B), which eliminates the carrier dependencies inherent in making connections.

BIS-B routes the request from the BlackBerry smartphone (1) through the carrier's network (2) to the BlackBerry infrastructure (3) to the destination server (4), as shown in Figure 3.5. It eliminates any requirement for the device to understand anything about the carrier's connection to the Internet. Unfortunately, today, this option is only available to ISV Alliance Partners, but RIM has stated that it might open this to other developers in the future.

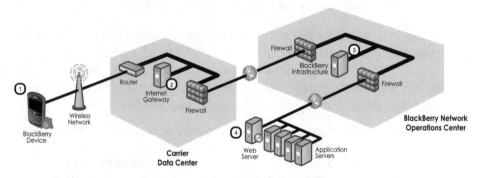

Figure 3.5   BIS-B request path

When using this connection type, be careful how much data you send across it. Because the connection goes through the BlackBerry infrastructure, it is possible that RIM will restrict how much data you send through this connection. Contact RIM for information about how to become a member of the ISV Alliance Program.

3.4.4 Mobile Data Service Connection

Applications running on BlackBerry smartphones activated against the Black-Berry Enterprise Server have an extra connection not available to consumer (BIS) devices. A component of the BlackBerry Enterprise platform, called Mobile Data System (MDS), provides applications with a connection to internal network resources. These enterprise applications can open network connections to internal (inside the corporate firewall) application servers and securely access the data.

Figure 3.6 shows the path that a request takes to its destination. The request routes from the BlackBerry smartphone (1) through the carrier's network (2) to the BlackBerry infrastructure (3) to the BlackBerry Enterprise Server running MDS (4), and then to the destination server (5).

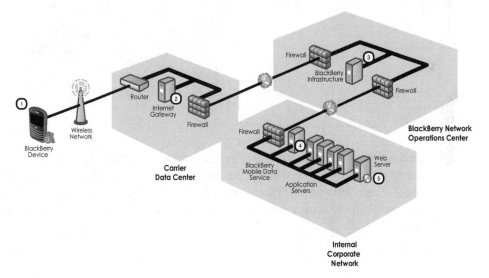

Figure 3.6 Intranet request path

It's possible for a BES administrator to configure the company's BlackBerry devices so every request from a device to an Internet site must first route through the company's MDS server (as shown in Figure 3.7). In this case, the request routes from the BlackBerry smartphone (1) through the carrier's network (2) to the BlackBerry infrastructure (3) to the BlackBerry Enterprise Server running MDS (4), and then out through the company firewall to the destination server (5).

An organization would use this approach to enable IT to log every request (both internal and/or external) made by a mobile device or use a proxy server to restrict access to certain Internet sites. As companies are restricted more and more by government or industry regulations, this option has become a more common configuration.

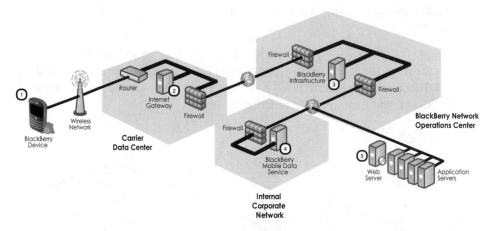

Figure 3.7   Internet request path through MDS

All BES-activated BlackBerry devices except for the BlackBerry 6500 series and the BlackBerry 7500 series devices use the BlackBerry MDS connection if available. (The 6500 and 7500 series uses Direct TCP by default.) If you need to open a connection to an internal resource, you must force the MDS connection so your application can easily support all device models without additional coding. This sample Java code illustrates how to open this connection:

```
(HttpConnection)Connector.open("http://www.somesite.com;
deviceside=false");
```

The `Deviceside=false` parameter tells the device to use the MDS connection. If the application wants to connect directly to the server, bypassing MDS, it should try to force the device (not MDS) managed connection by using

```
(HttpConnection)Connector.open("http://www.somesite.com;
deviceside=true");
```

When using MDS, all communication between the device application and any internal resources is always compressed and encrypted. Chapter 4 describes MDS and the capabilities it provides in detail; for now, it is just important to highlight the connection provided by this service.

3.4.5 Wi-Fi Connection

Beginning with the BlackBerry 8820, RIM began adding Wi-Fi capabilities to most device models. The first Wi-Fi device offered by RIM was the BlackBerry 7270 smartphone, but it was not available from carriers. These newer Wi-Fi–enabled devices use either the carrier's network or a Wi-Fi connection for data transmission. When a Wi-Fi access point is in range, an application can use the Wi-Fi network instead of the carrier's network; it's cheaper and faster for the mobile user, and it doesn't consume the carrier's network bandwidth.

When using a Wi-Fi connection, the data can either connect directly to the destination server (if allowed by the carrier) or connect through the BlackBerry infrastructure, as shown in Figure 3.8. As shown in the figure, the request begins at the BlackBerry device (1), travels through the BlackBerry infrastructure (2) to the corporation's MDS server (3), and on to the appropriate server (4).

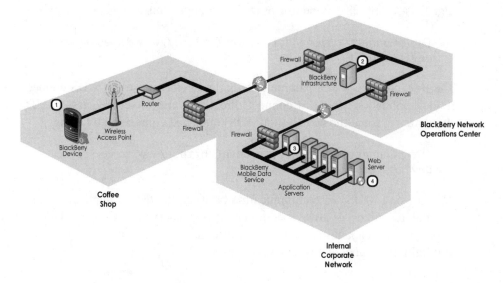

Figure 3.8   Wi-Fi connection path

As discussed previously, when using WAP or a Direct TCP connection, the data path runs through the carrier's network (refer to Figure 3.4). When developing applications that use either of these connections plus Wi-Fi, the developer must manually switch the data connection from the carrier's network to Wi-Fi (and back) when needed. This restriction exists because the device network stack does not know how to switch automatically between the networks.

To detect the availability of the Wi-Fi connection, Java developers can use the BlackBerry WLANInfo class (added with the BlackBerry 4.3 device software) to register a WLANConnectionListener. This listener allows applications to receive notifications whenever the device connects or disconnects to/from a wireless access point.

To force a data connection to use a Wi-Fi connection, you must append interface=wifi to the Connector.open method call in your application, as follows:

```
(HttpConnection)Connector.open("http://www.somesite.com;
interface=wifi");
```

Before you attempt the Wi-Fi connection, however, check to see if Wi-Fi is enabled by using the following code:

```
public static boolean isWiFiActive() {
    return (RadioInfo.getActiveWAFs() & RadioInfo.WAF_WLAN)!=0;
}
```

If your application will be running on BlackBerry smartphones running Device Software 4.3 or higher, you can also check to see if the device is connected to a Wi-Fi network by using the following code:

```
public static boolean isWiFiActive() {
    return WLANInfo.getWLANState()==
    WLANInfo.WLAN_STATE_CONNECTED;
}
```

Data connections using BIS-B and MDS are handled differently. Both of these connections route data traffic through the BlackBerry infrastructure and support seamless routing across networks. Because of this ability, the network connection libraries that contain the special programming logic needed to switch networks automatically include the ability to switch from a carrier network to a Wi-Fi connection. What this means for the developer is that, if you're using BIS-B or MDS connections, your data communication will automatically switch to Wi-Fi when a Wi-Fi connection is available; there is nothing your application needs to do to detect or act upon the availability or loss or the Wi-Fi connection. Table 3.1 summarizes the Wi-Fi connection options that are available to a developer.

Table 3.1 Wi-Fi Connection Options

Connection Path	Switch to Wi-Fi	Notes
WAP	Manual	Developer must watch for availability of the Wi-Fi connection and switch over (and back, if needed) manually.
Direct TCP	Manual	
BIS-B	Automatic	The BlackBerry device network software automatically detects the presence of the Wi-Fi connection and automatically routes data traffic over Wi-Fi if the connection is available and switches back to the carrier network when the device loses its connection to the Wi-Fi access point.
MDS	Automatic	

A Wi-Fi–connected BlackBerry smartphone can also connect to internal network resources via a Virtual Private Network (VPN) connection, as shown in Figure 3.9. For this connection, the VPN connection specifics are handled by the VPN software running on the device; the application does not need to worry about setting up the connection parameters. The request begins with the BlackBerry device (1), travels through a secure VPN connection to the MDS server (2), and on to the destination server (3).

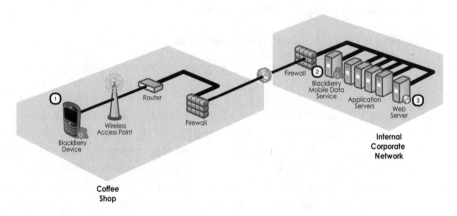

Figure 3.9   Wi-Fi VPN connection path

3.5 Roaming Across Networks

Direct TCP and WAP connections provide your applications only limited support for roaming. When using a network connection to route data to/from a server, note that when a device roams from one network to another, it's possible that you might lose your connection to the server. It's not that these technologies can't handle roaming; it is just that the ability to continue data communication while roaming can be restricted by the scope of any roaming agreements your primary carrier has with the carrier on whose network you are roaming. Roaming agreements usually provide support for phone calls, so it's reasonable to assume that you can make phone calls while roaming. If the agreement between the carriers also supports data communication when roaming, you might also be able to maintain the data connection when roaming.

When connecting through MDS or BIS-B, any carrier that supports BlackBerry and has the appropriate data-roaming agreements in place automatically routes the traffic to the BlackBerry infrastructure (which then sends the data to its destination). This is just a function of the relationship and agreements the carriers have with each other and RIM.

3.6 Service Routing

The ServiceRouting API, added to the BlackBerry in Device Software 4.1, allows an application to determine when a device is on a least cost routing connection (connected to a PC via USB cable or Bluetooth) and, therefore, can afford large data transfers (backend database updates). This API does a lot of heavy lifting for the developer. Unfortunately, the API does not (as of Black-Berry Device Software version 4.7) support Wi-Fi as part of its determination.

When your application has a lot of updates to make or if the server has told your application that there's a large update available, you can check the Service Route to determine whether it's a good time to transmit or request data. Additionally, you can register a Service Routing Listener so your program is notified when a low-cost connection is available, then perform the update only when practical. You can even notify the user that there's a large update available and let her decide whether to wait for low-cost connection or to go ahead and immediately use the mobile network.

3.7 Coverage Info API

Your application can keep a handle on the available network connectivity by using the CoverageInfo API included on the BlackBerry beginning with Black-Berry Device Software version 4.2. Using this API, developers can check the availability of data network connectivity before attempting a connection to a server.

BlackBerry applications need to be smart about the way they use the network connection to reduce battery consumption and avoid potential airtime charges. As good as carrier networks are today and with the prevalence of Wi-Fi network options available to the mobile user, there are still times when the device might not have network connectivity. Your application should never try to send data when the connection is unavailable and can even register network connectivity listeners and be notified by the device whenever the availability of data network connectivity changes (goes up or down).

3.8 Connection Security

In an application opening a secure connection to a backend data source, a Black-Berry device can use Secure Sockets Layer (SSL) or the updated Transport Layer Security (TLS) to encrypt the data across the connection. Because TLS is merely an updated version of SSL, both are treated as one in this section. The BlackBerry platform supports these two options for SSL:

- **Proxy SSL Mode:** The SSL connection is made between the MDS Connection Service (MDS-CS) and the backend data source. The data between the device and MDS-CS is still encrypted using Triple-DES or AES, but the data is converted to SSL before it's placed on the internal network.

  With this option, there is a brief moment in time where the data resides on the MDS server in an unencrypted state. This option is useful when you trust the integrity of the MDS server.

- **End-to-End SSL:** The SSL connection is made from the BlackBerry device all the way through to the backend server with which the application is communicating. This option eliminates the period where the data is temporarily unencrypted during conversion performed by MDS-CS in Proxy SSL mode. Use this option when the only trusted entities in a transaction are the BlackBerry device application and the backend server to which the device is connecting.

  Using this option places a greater load on the BlackBerry device and degrades the device's performance and battery life.

The options described can be set by either the BlackBerry device user (through a configuration setting in Options, Security) or by the programmer when he opens an HTTPS connection. Note that an application can never request a less secure connection type than the user has configured in the device's Security options.

To use Proxy SSL mode, the developer doesn't need to do anything; when you open an HTTPS connection using `Connector.open`, the mode is selected by default. When enabling End-to-End SSL, the developer can use one of the following options:

- **EndtoEndDesired:** Specifies that an End-to-End SSL/TLS connection should be used from the device to the server, if the BlackBerry Device Software supports it. If handheld does not support this option, and the device configuration supports proxy SSL/TLS, a proxy connection is set up.

- **EndtoEndRequired:** Specifies that End-to-End SSL/TLS must be used from the BlackBerry device to the server. If handheld does not support SSL/TLS, the connection is closed.

To open an HTTPS connection requiring that an End-to-End SSL/TLS connection be used, use the following Java code:

```
(HttpConnection)Connector.open("https://www.somesite.com;
EndToEndRequired");
```

To open an HTTPS connection with an optional but preferred End-to-End SSL/TLS connection, use the following Java code:

```
(HttpConnection)Connector.open("https://www.somesite.com;
EndToEndDesired");
```

3.9 Providing Seamless Connection Paths

Because of the complexities of Direct TCP connections and the WAP protocol stack, when you build your Java applications for BlackBerry, try to make use of the MDS connection (to internal resources) and BIS-B Internet connection (consumer applications or enterprise applications that access information residing outside of the firewall). These connections offer seamless roaming to your application. When your users leave one network for another, they will be able to reliably (as long as they have coverage) communicate with your server as long as they're on a network that supports BlackBerry data communication.

Although WAP and Direct TCP provide some support for roaming data connections, there is no guarantee that your user will get to the data they need when using these communication paths. What this issue demonstrates is one of the huge benefits of the BlackBerry platform: the ability to have the complexities of negotiating different carrier networks taken completely off of your plate when building your applications.

Table 3.2 lists the pros and cons of the different connection paths available to the BlackBerry developer. Use this table to help select the right path to use for your application. In many cases, the best practice is to build logic into your application that tries each connection in order of preference until a connection to the server can be made.

Table 3.2 Summary of Connection Paths

Connection Path	Pros	Cons
WAP	Well established, time-tested protocol. Support for older devices, older networks, and non-BlackBerry devices.	Limited support for roaming. Must open firewall ports to enable access to data sitting inside of the corporate firewall.
Direct TIP	Simple, direct path to the data residing on a server.	Limited support for roaming. Requires that the user or developer know the APN for the connection. Must open firewall ports to enable access to data sitting inside of the corporate firewall.
BIS-B	Seamless roaming. Eliminates the complexity of setting up the connection (APN information).	Only available to BlackBerry ISV Alliances members today, but expected to be publically available in the future.
MDS	Seamless roaming. Safe access to corporate data residing inside the firewall.	Requires the BlackBerry Enterprise Server.
Wi-Fi	Seamless roaming. Free. Does not use the carrier data plan. Automatic switch to Wi-Fi for both BIS-B and MDS connections.	If using WAP or Direct TCP Connection, will have to manually switch to Wi-Fi when available for data connection.

3.10 Additional Resources

A complete listing of links to these resources is available at www.bbdevfundamentals.com.

RIM's "What Is: Different Ways to Make an HTTP or Socket Connection" knowledge base article contains information on how to open different HTTP connections from a Java application. Access the developer knowledge base from www.blackberry.com/developers and search for article number DB-00396.

For a description of security options provided via HTTP connections, see "What Is: BlackBerry Support for HTTPS Connection," by searching the BlackBerry Developer's knowledge base for article number DB-00423.

For a great article describing the tasks a developer must perform to create a network connection in a Java application and to learn more about the BlackBerry Network Diagnostic Tool, see "What Is: Network Diagnostic Tool," by searching the BlackBerry Developer's knowledge base for article number DB-00684.

The Network Transports video from the BlackBerry Developers Video Library (www. blackberry.com/DevMediaLibrary/view.do?name=NetworkingTransports) contains more information on the topics covered in this chapter.

For information on BlackBerry Service Books, see the "What Is a Service Book" knowledge base article. Access the BlackBerry knowledge base from www.blackberry.com and search for article number KB03151.

For additional information on the options available for using Wi-Fi connections, see http://na.blackberry.com/eng/deliverables/7693/WiFi_connections_509011_ 11.jsp.

4

The BlackBerry Mobile Data System (MDS)

As explained in Chapter 3, "The Connected BlackBerry," BlackBerry applications can use different paths to the servers hosting the data they need. What's special about the BlackBerry platform's capabilities for Enterprise Applications is that, with BlackBerry, you can access your company's internal applications on your BlackBerry devices without unnecessarily exposing components of your environment to security risks from the Internet or malicious users. This capability, the BlackBerry Enterprise Applications special sauce, is provided by the BlackBerry Mobile Data System (MDS) and is the topic for this chapter.[1]

4.1 The BlackBerry Enterprise Server

MDS is a component of the BlackBerry Enterprise Server (BES), so before we dig into MDS, let's talk about the BES. The BES is a server solution that sits inside an organization's firewall and provides a secure conduit for the exchange of mail and Personal Information Manager (PIM) data between BlackBerry devices and the organization's mail server. There are versions of the BES for IBM Lotus Domino®, Novell GroupWise®, and Microsoft Exchange mail servers.

---

1. Many BlackBerry users, administrators, and even developers think that any application running on a BlackBerry device or accessing internal (inside of the firewall) data is an "MDS application," but this is not true. There is MDS (a component of the BES) and BlackBerry applications—there's no such thing as an MDS application.

When a new mail message appears in a mobile user's inbox, the BES picks it up and wirelessly delivers it to the user's device. If the user's device is not within wireless coverage, the message is queued up and delivered when possible. When the mobile user reads the message (either on the desktop mail client or on the BlackBerry), the BES can synchronize read status between the two entities. When the mobile user sends an email message from a device, the BES receives it, delivers it to the mail server, and places it into the user's sent mail folder. When the mobile user replies to an email message, the device records the user's response and sends the response to the BES, the BES appends the content of the original message (no need to do this on the device—too much extra work) and forwards it to its destination(s).

When the mobile user creates, edits, or accepts a calendar entry, the BES makes sure that the information is accurately synchronized between the device and the mail account. The same is true for contacts in the address book, to-do list, and even notes (through the BlackBerry MemoPad application). Changes made in any of these applications on the desktop or the BlackBerry are automatically synchronized by the BES.

For security, the BES has multiple components working together to make the BlackBerry solution the most secure mobile platform on the market. To begin with, all communication between a BlackBerry device and the BES is encrypted using either Advanced Encryption Standard (AES) or Triple Data Encryption Standard (Triple DES), which are two strong standards for encryption in the market today. When a BlackBerry device and the BES "connect" for the first time during the Enterprise Activation (EA) process, the parties negotiate a set of encryption keys that encrypt all communication between them. Even though all the data passes through the RIM Network Operations Center (NOC), because access to the keys is restricted to only those two entities, there is no way for anyone but the device and the BES to see the data sent between them. Additionally, to protect against prying eyes, the keys are periodically renegotiated to keep the encryption fresh.

The second layer of security applies at the organization's firewall. With many server-based solutions, access to the server from external mobile devices is typically provided through open ports on the company's firewall. For most non-BlackBerry solutions, when a mobile user uses the web browser to access an internal website, firewall administrators must open the necessary ports (port 80 in the case of HTTP, 443 for HTTPS) to allow access. In some cases, organizations use a nonstandard port for this access, hoping to thwart the bad guys, but that doesn't protect them from hackers trying any available port just to find an opening.

Contrary to what many people believe, when you deploy the BlackBerry solution to your enterprise, you're not exposing any part of your organization to outside parties. With the BlackBerry Enterprise Solution, administrators must open only one port in the firewall (port 3101), and it's open as an outbound initiated port only. This means that while the port is open, it is open outbound only—anyone trying to connect through the port from outside the firewall won't gain access to the environment.

When the BES starts up, it opens up a connection to the infrastructure using a proprietary protocol called Server Routing Protocol (SRP). All communication between the BES and the NOC is transmitted securely over this SRP connection. Because the connection is initiated by the BES, it uses an outbound connection through the firewall and does not expose any open ports to the outside world. In no situation does the NOC ever initiate a connection to the BES; it communicates with the BES using the bidirectional connection created by the BES.

The BlackBerry solution tries to be as secure as possible and, at the same time, do what it can to conserve battery life on the device. Every bit of data transmitted over the wireless network to or from a BlackBerry device impacts its battery life. Therefore, not only is the data between the BES and device encrypted, it is compressed first. By automatically compressing all transmitted data, the BlackBerry solution reduces the amount of work a device needs to do to communicate with the server and, therefore, achieves battery life unlike any other device on the market.

In addition to the security features just described, the BES provides additional capabilities, such as the following:

- Support for more than 450 over the air (OTA) wireless IT policies that give a BES administrator control over the features and capabilities of the device
- Remote wipe and locking, which protects an organization when a device is lost or stolen
- OTA backup and restore of device data, which provides an easy way to get a device back up and running after being replaced
- OTA deployment of BlackBerry applications
- Integration with Enterprise instant messaging systems, such as IBM Lotus SameTime® and Microsoft Office Communication Server (OCS)

As an example, Figure 4.1 shows a typical Enterprise BlackBerry environment. The BES is sitting inside the firewall and has ready access to the organization's mail servers. As previously mentioned, the firewall has only one port opened to support the BlackBerry platform, and it is open as an outbound initiated connection. The BES is connected to the BlackBerry NOC, as are the BlackBerry devices. The NOC is in constant connection with the BES though the SRP connection initiated by the BES on startup. The NOC is also in constant connection with BlackBerry devices through an efficient heartbeat connection maintained with the device.

Whenever the BES has data for a device, it sends it to the NOC for delivery. Whenever a device has data for the BES, it sends it to the NOC across the carrier's network (or through a Wi-Fi connection if available), and the NOC sends the data to the BES over its SRP connection. The BES also supports the queuing of requests when the device is out of coverage; it holds onto messages destined for the device and purges them after seven days (for more information, refer to BlackBerry Knowledge Base article #KB01868).

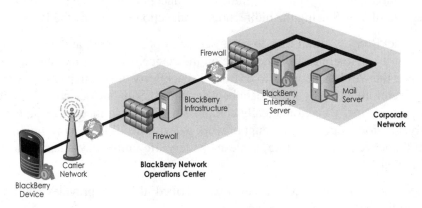

Figure 4.1   Typical BlackBerry architecture

4.2 BlackBerry MDS Overview

The BlackBerry MDS is an Enterprise Application gateway for BlackBerry. It is included as a free component of the BES and is typically installed on the same physical server as the BES. As an organization's BlackBerry application adoption increases, it might make sense, for performance reasons, to move the MDS components onto a separate server.

Figure 4.2 shows a typical BlackBerry environment with a single server running the BES and MDS. The role of MDS in a BlackBerry environment is to act as a gateway between BlackBerry applications and the web and application servers inside the firewall that contain the data the device needs.

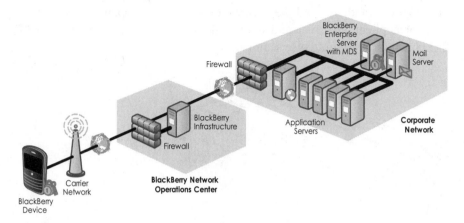

Figure 4.2 BlackBerry architecture with MDS

For devices activated against a BES, PIM data is synchronized with the device through the Synchronization Service and other parts of the BES. The browser and custom applications requesting corporate data (data residing inside the firewall) from a server get access to its data through MDS. You can open the necessary firewall ports and access the data bypassing MDS, but as you will soon see, that is a much less efficient way to do it, and it unnecessarily opens an organization to greater security risks.

When an application requests data from an application server, the request makes its way to MDS, and MDS retrieves the data on the behalf of the device. From the application server standpoint, all requests from BlackBerry devices appear as if they were made by the server running MDS (they come from the MDS server's IP address, after all) rather than the individual BlackBerry devices.

MDS even performs some optimization on the data it receives from the application server before sending it to the destination device. This is done to minimize utilization of the wireless network and reduce the work required on the device to receive and process the data. The optimizations that MDS performs are described in detail later.

For the developer, it looks like the BlackBerry application is connecting directly with the server that contains the data, as shown in Figure 4.3. Developers do not need to concern themselves with any of the components of MDS; from the developer's standpoint, all the application has to do is open a connection to the web or application server and request the data it needs. The NOC, BES, and MDS handle everything else seamlessly.

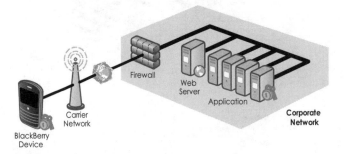

Figure 4.3   Developer's view of server connectivity

Remember that, although the BES and MDS are RIM proprietary software components that perform special tasks, developers need to disregard these components and develop the applications they need by using open, industry standards for application development. There is nothing proprietary about the applications you build for a BlackBerry device. Many of the open standards in place for mobile development apply well to BlackBerry applications.

Don't forget that all the data transmitted between the BES and a BlackBerry device is encrypted using keys that only the BES and the device know. Additionally, all data sent between a device and the BES is also compressed. The seamless, secure access to corporate data and the optimization of data before transmission to a device allows MDS to simplify and accelerate development of Enterprise Applications for BlackBerry, because much of the network complexity a developer has to deal with when building mobile applications is no longer an issue.

4.3 MDS Components

MDS consists primarily of two components: the MDS Connection Service (MDS-CS) and the MDS Integration Service (MDS-IS). Both components help extend enterprise systems (and corporate data) to BlackBerry devices. You might have heard the components called MDS Services and MDS Connection Services, but the name for MDS Services was changed in BES 4.1.6.

Administrators have the option to install the MDS components on the same server as the BES or on a separate system. An organization would split the MDS components off onto a separate system to minimize the impact on BES performance while MDS processes content requests. Note, however, that for many organizations, the BES attachment rendering service usually places a higher load on the BES than the MDS components.

4.3.1 MDS Connection Service

The BlackBerry MDS-CS proxies any TCP or HTTP requests between a BlackBerry application and backend application servers. Any TCP or HTTP (and HTTPS) connection opened by either the browser or a custom Java application is managed by MDS-CS. The service submits the request to the application server and optimizes the results before delivering them across the wireless network.

4.3.2 MDS Integration Service

The BlackBerry MDS-IS manages all the application connectivity and data optimizations for MDS Runtime applications. This means that MDS-IS acts as a proxy for any web-services requests and directs database access requests from a MDS Runtime application. When an MDS Runtime application requests data via an XML web service (using SOAP over HTTP, for example) or when it issues a database query through the MDS Runtime database connectors, MDS-IS makes the request on behalf of the user and optimizes the data returned to the requesting application.

4.4 MDS Functions

Components of MDS-CS optimize any data before sending it to the requesting application. This data optimization is important because it reduces the amount of work a BlackBerry device must do to receive and process the data. By optimizing the data before placing it on the network, MDS helps application data communication appear faster than on other types of devices and helps dramatically increase the device' battery life.

MDS performs some optimizations that apply to all application traffic. As previously mentioned, all the data transmitted between the device and the BES (MDS, too) is encrypted and compressed. Additionally, all XML content is converted to WAP Binary XML (WBXML), which is a binary representation of XML. WBXML allows XML data to be transmitted across the wireless network in a compact format.

4.4.1   Browser Optimizations

For the BlackBerry browser (Chapter 8, "The BlackBerry Browser," describes the different browsers), MDS-CS provides an encrypted connection between the device browser and the BES. The encryption is provided through the same mechanism that encrypts all mail and PIM data communication between the device and the BES.

When a browser requests a typical desktop browser web page, the computer has to do a lot of work before it can get a page back from the server. It has to open a network connection and locate the server hosting the page being requested (typically through a DNS lookup). After it's located the server, it has to connect to the server and request the page. If the server is down, or if there are network issues between the requestor and the server, the system must wait a reasonable time for a response and then either try again or report an error to the user. When the page finally comes back from the server, the browser has to retrieve any images, style sheets, and other media that are a part of the page being requested. After the data gets to the browser, it must render everything and process any client-side scripting included on the page.

When the BlackBerry browser requests a page from the web server, the request is sent to MDS-CS, and it requests the page on the behalf of the BlackBerry browser. This proxying of the request dramatically reduces the load placed on the device to retrieve the page. MDS-CS does all the work to locate the web server via a DNS lookup, connect to the server, retry any connections, and request the page. All the BlackBerry browser does is send off the request and wait for something to come back (either the requested page or an error).

Before MDS-CS delivers the results of the request to the BlackBerry, it processes the data returned from the server (the web page, any style sheets, included files, images, and other media) to allow it to be more efficiently transmitted across the wireless network to the requesting device. It doesn't reformat the page for better rendering on the BlackBerry's small screen (see the sidebar, "What MDS Doesn't Do for Browser Requests," for more information); it allows it to be transmitted to the device as efficiently as possible.

This processing includes several steps:

- Converts data to a tokenized format
- Removes unsupported/unneeded HTML tags, white space, and erroneous JavaScript
- Compresses the data[2]

---

2. This is actually performed by the Dispatcher, which is another component of the BES.

After this optimization, the data is encrypted and sent to the device.

Regarding removing unsupported and unneeded content from the page: What gets removed is comments, extra white space (extra spaces, line breaks, and so on) and any HTML tags that MDS knows the BlackBerry device won't recognize.

Unwanted Side Effect of Browser Optimization

The process of stripping HTML tags has a side effect that can affect your applications. If you think about how MDS-CS knows which tags to remove from the page, it bases its actions on what it knows about the capabilities of the BlackBerry browser available at the time it was released. So, if the version of MDS-CS you're running knows that the browser doesn't support a particular markup tag that your page contains, it strips it—even though your device might be running a later version of the browser that does support the particular tag.

I was working with a customer mobilizing an internal web application specifically for the BlackBerry. He had done all the work to convert the pages to a format that rendered well on the device's smaller screen and within the limitations of the BlackBerry browser (discussed in Chapter 8). In the middle of testing the application, the customer noticed that the tables he used on the pages weren't rendering properly. He double-checked the browser to make sure tables were a supported feature, but it still wouldn't work.

After doing some research, I determined that, although the browser supported HTML Table tags, the BES actually removed them before sending the pages to the browser. What happened was that the company was part of a larger organization that was late in upgrading its BES to the latest version. The devices were running BlackBerry Device Software 4.1, but the BES was running an older version, 4.0. When the BES 4.0 software was released, the BlackBerry Device Software 4.0 Browser didn't support tables. Because the company was still running this older BES, MDS assumed that all devices couldn't handle tables, so it stripped them from the HTML on the way out to the device. The only options available to this customer were to build the pages without tables or wait to roll the application out until after the company upgraded to BES 4.1.

MDS also retrieves images referenced on the page while processing HTML and XHTML pages. This allows the server to do some work in parallel so it can deliver all of the data as quickly as possible. When MDS receives the images, it optimizes them before sending them on to the device. It

- Converts the images in Joint Photographic Experts Group (.JPEG), Graphics Interchange Format (.GIF), Portable Pixel Map (.PPM), and Portable Anymap (.PNM) formats to Portable Network Graphics (.PNG) files for better rendering on the device
- Resizes the images to fit the screen resolution of the destination device

MDS resizes images to the device screen so that they render more efficiently when the web page is first rendered on the device. Imagine a mobile user accessing a product image that is sized for the desktop browser; what benefit is there delivering an image at 1024 by 768 pixels resolution to a device with a screen sized at 320 by 240 pixels? The user is unable to really look at the picture on such a small screen; she could view it, but she would have to pan around to see the entire image. By reducing the image to the device screen resolution, it allows the mobile user to view the entire image immediately and dramatically reduces the amount of data sent across the wireless network. If a user wants to view the entire image, she can click on the device's menu button and select Full Image to download the image at full resolution. This way, the user only downloads what she needs to be able see what the picture is before deciding to consume the necessary time, bandwidth and battery life to get the entire picture on the device.

Slipstream Acquisition

In the middle of 2006, RIM made an acquisition that allowed the BlackBerry platform to further optimize images delivered to the BlackBerry browser. The acquisition, a small company called Slipstream, created the content optimization technology that helped give NetZero customers a performance boost over other dial-up networks. The integration of the Slipstream technology into the BlackBerry platform allowed images to be reduced in size even more before being sent across the wireless network to the browser.

As previously mentioned, because MDS-CS is brokering all HTTP requests from the device, all BlackBerry browser requests appear to the web server that they're coming from the MDS server. Even though the requests are coming from external devices, the requests all seem like they're coming from an internal IP address; this is a side effect of the work the BES is doing and the fact that nobody is opening firewall ports to provide access to these applications.

MDS can be configured to store browser cookies on MDS rather than on the BlackBerry device. This further reduces the amount of data sent between MDS and the BlackBerry device.

What MDS Doesn't Do for Browser Requests

When people hear about or read the descriptions of the MDS components, they often misunderstand what is really happening when MDS optimizes content. The BlackBerry Mobile Data System Technical Overview (there's a reference to it at the end of this chapter) says this:

> Both the BlackBerry MDS Connection Service and the BlackBerry MDS Integration Service convert server-side content and data into a format that is optimized for efficient wireless transmission and for use on wireless smartphones.

Many people think this means that MDS-CS reformats a page so it looks better on the Black-Berry screen—that's not what happens.

This quoted text says that the data is reformatted into a format that is optimized for efficient transmission across the wireless network and processing on the device. MDS-CS helps reduce the load on the BlackBerry device by reducing the amount of data sent across the network—even removing some data that it knows the device can never use. It does not make any decisions about the content; it just makes sure that it's formatted and transmitted in a manner that sends as little data across the network as possible and puts as small of a strain as possible on the device.

Any optimization that converts desktop-sized HTML pages to render on a mobile device on the fly needs to understand a fair amount about the page layout before it can do this reliably. RIM can do this, but not through MDS. RIM offers its partners special tools to do some of this optimization through the e-Commerce Content Optimization Service, which is described in Chapter 17, "Using Additional BlackBerry Application Technologies." It isn't done on the fly; it's done through a manual analysis of the page and the manual creation of a special tag file that instructs the BlackBerry infrastructure how to adjust the content on the way to a custom browser application running on the device.

4.4.2 Java Application Optimizations

BlackBerry applications written in Java can do just about anything. To support these applications and provide access to application servers and resources inside the corporate firewall, MDS-CS acts as a proxy for any connections from Black-Berry devices. When a connection is opened from a device and a server, MDS-CS acts as a gateway that provides the connection with access to the corporate network.

When MDS-CS receives data to deliver to a BlackBerry application, it compresses and encrypts the data before sending it across the wireless network to the requesting application.

4.5 Knowing That Your Data Is Being Securely Transmitted

Because MDS proxies all the application data requests made by device-side applications, and an organization isn't exposing any firewall ports to enable BlackBerry applications, BlackBerry devices look and feel to the network like PCs sitting inside the firewall. Existing authentication mechanisms for internal systems can still apply to mobile devices without worrying about malicious attackers having more access to your internal environment than they did before the BlackBerry devices came along.

Because of this, there is no need to implement a Virtual Private Network (VPN) to provide these mobile devices with access to internal applications. This capability is already baked into the solution—a sort of pseudo-VPN. The internal resources BlackBerry applications need to connect to are already available to applications the moment you enable MDS. Adding a VPN on top of this secure connection to internal resources provided by MDS is just extra work that the device has to do for little value and decreases the performance of the application (because it takes more time to encrypt the data a second time for the VPN connection) and reduces the device's overall battery life.

If your organization is worried about what these mobile devices are doing, your BlackBerry administrators can lock down the devices so they can't access any servers outside of your firewall (block all external sites).They can lock down the connections so any request has to come through MDS before it routes to the external network and can even block access to certain internal servers. This allows an organization to monitor all traffic (both internal and external) and block access to sites that should not be accessed. All of this capability is provided through components of the BlackBerry Enterprise Solution.

Raising Security Concerns

I attended a meeting with the BES administrators for a national retailer. I spent an hour talking about MDS, the free development tools, and the benefits they can provide the organization. The administrators listened politely and we all agreed that they'd let me know when they needed to dig deeper into the topic.

A few days later, I received a call from one of the administrators. He said he had a security person on the line and he wanted to talk about BlackBerry security. At the start of the call, he told me that security had an issue with all this access MDS was providing BlackBerry users. He said, "So, a BlackBerry device has access to any internal resource inside our firewall," and I told him that it was true, what MDS could see, devices could also see. If they wanted to protect certain resources (servers), they needed to isolate the system running MDS from the network segments that housed the servers in question.

The response from the security guy was, "Well, we can't have that!" I asked him to explain, and what I heard was that, because the company processed transactions with Visa and MasterCard, it had to conform to standards that would prohibit these devices from accessing the network.[3] I explained to him that I was sure that the major credit-card companies were using BlackBerry devices and that it would be OK. I pointed him to www.blackberry.com/security to find more details on how to ensure the company's BlackBerry environment was as secure as it needed to be.

---

3. Retailers who process above a certain amount of transactions must conform to an industry standard for security called Payment Card Industry Data Security Standard (PCI DSS) that affects how data is transmitted and maintained on a company's network.

4.6 Using the BlackBerry MDS Simulator

The BlackBerry MDS simulator provides developers with a local copy of the BlackBerry MDS service the BlackBerry device simulators[5] can use to connect to local and network resources. With MDS running, the BlackBerry device simulator can connect to resources running on the local system (such as local web servers or other application servers) and any remote network resources accessible from the system.

Most versions of the BlackBerry development tools include the MDS simulator; the only exception was the 4.2.0 and 4.2.1 JDE. The only time you need to download it separately is if you're testing applications in the simulator outside of one of the development tools or working with the specified versions of the JDE. If needed, you can download it from the BlackBerry Developer's website at http://na.blackberry.com/eng/developers/browserdev/devtoolsdownloads.jsp. After you download the simulator, launch the file to begin the installation and just accept all the default options. After installation, start the MDS simulator by opening the Windows Start menu and navigating to Programs, Research In Motion, BlackBerry Email and MDS Services Simulators 4.1.2, then clicking the icon labeled MDS.

When the simulator opens, there is no interface for the developer to interact with; it displays inside of a simple DOS console window, as shown in Figure 4.4. Whenever the MDS simulator receives a request from or returns data to the BlackBerry device simulator, the console updates to show the activity. You can use this display to verify that the device simulator is talking to the network and receiving a response.

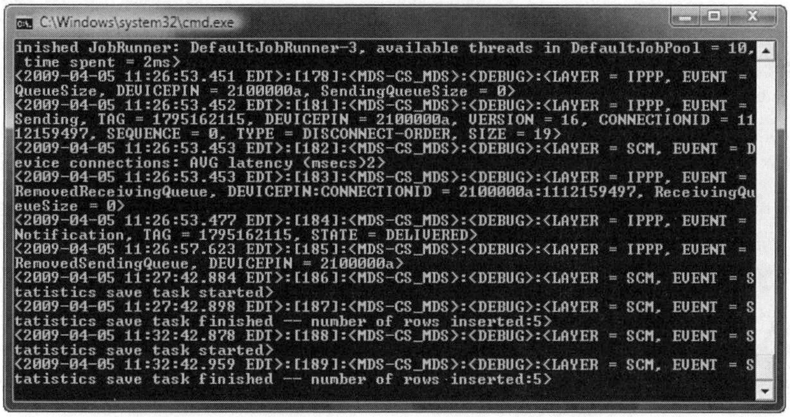

Figure 4.4 BlackBerry MDS simulator window

To close the MDS simulator, click the red X in the upper-right corner of the window.

---

5. Blackberry device similators are described in Appendix A, "Using the BlackBerry Devices Simulators," located at www.bbdevfundamentals.com.

4.7 Configuring MDS

You can use some special configuration settings to help you better troubleshoot your applications and allow you to verify the identity of a BlackBerry application user without having to prompt the user for credentials. This section discusses how to enable these features and use them to make your life easier.

To modify the MDS configuration, you make changes to a text file called `rimpublic.properties` installed with MDS. Settings can be modified using the administrator tools RIM provides, or it can be manually edited. Ask an administrator for help making any changes.

To edit the file, look for it in the `config` folder underneath the folder where MDS is installed. The location of this folder varies, depending on whether you're looking at MDS running on a server or an instance of MDS installed on your development workstation. Figure 4.5 shows the location of the folder when the Email and MDS simulator package was installed. If you are working with MDS running on a server, the BES/MDS installation places the `config` folder in C:\Program Files\Research In Motion\BlackBerry Enterprise Server\MDS\ servers\[BlackBerry Enterprise Server Name]\Config, where [BlackBerry Enterprise Server Name] refers to the BES name.

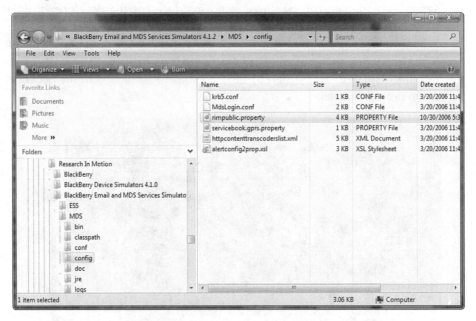

Figure 4.5   MDS config folder

The rimpublic.properties file is a simple text file that can be modified using any standard text editor. Be sure that your text editor doesn't add a txt to the filename when writing your changes back out to the file. A sample rimpublic.properties is shown here for your reference. In the file, section titles are delimited by square brackets ([and]) and comment lines begin with the pound (#) sign:

```
[Logging]
Logging.level=4
Logging.console.log.level=4

[WebServer]
WebServer.Tomcat.transcoding=false
WebServer.listen.host=localhost
WebServer.listen.port=8080
WebServer.listen.sslport=8443
WebServer.servlet.push.port=81
WebServer.servlet.push.host=localhost
WebServer.servlet.sb.ssl=false
WebServer.servlet.sb.authentication=false

[IPPP]
IPPP.push.listen.tcp.port=81
IPPP.connection.MaxNumberOfKBytesToSend=256
IPPP.queue.flowcontrol.window.size=-1
IPPP.queue.flowcontrol.timeout=600000
IPPP.logging=true

[UDP]
UDP.receive.port=19781
UDP.send.default=19780
UDP.send.host=localhost
UDP.logging=false

[HTTP HANDLER]
application.handler.http.logging=true
application.handler.http.logging.verbose=true
application.handler.http.CookieSupport=true
application.handler.http.AuthenticationSupport=true
application.handler.http.AuthenticationTimeout=3600000
application.handler.http.device.connection.timeout=120000
application.handler.http.server.connection.timeout=120000

[HTTPS HANDLER]
application.handler.https.allowUntrustedServer=false

[TLS HANDLER]
application.handler.tls.allowUntrustedServer=false
application.handler.tls.logging=true
```

```
[OCSP HANDLER]
application.handler.ocsp.StatusProviders=
net.rim.protocol.iplayer.connection.handler.device.ocsp.
OCSPProvider
application.handler.StatusProviders.OCSP.PrimaryResponderRank=
Default
application.handler.StatusProviders.OCSP.Responder.Default=
http://somemachine.rim.net/ocsp
application.handler.StatusProviders.OCSP.UseDeviceResponders
=yes
application.handler.StatusProviders.OCSP.UseCertResponders
=yes
application.handler.ocsp.DebugLogging=no

[LDAP HANDLER]
application.handler.ldap.DEFAULT_SERVER=dhobbs-wnt
application.handler.ldap.DEFAULT_PORT=389
application.handler.ldap.DEFAULT_QUERY=ou=people, o=rim.net
application.handler.ldap.DEFAULT_LIMIT=20
application.handler.ldap.COMPRESSION=true
application.handler.ldap.logging =false

[Database]
MDSName=MDS

[Simulator]
#[CDK_MODIFICATIONS for Running Multiple Simulators]
#Each simulator instance must have a unique IPPP port assignment
#ie. Simulator fledge.exe command lines must have:
#       /ignore-data-port-conflicts /app-param=IPPPSourcePort:
<port>
Simulator.2100000a=MDS,simulator@pushme.com
Simulator.2100000b=MDS,user2100000b@pushme.com
Simulator.2100000c=MDS,user2100000c@pushme.com
Simulator.2100000d=MDS,user2100000d@pushme.com
Simulator.2100000e=MDS,user2100000e@pushme.com
Simulator.2100000f=MDS,user2100000f@pushme.com

[ACL]
ACL.Authorization.Datastore=net.rim.shared.service.
authorization.JDBCAuthorizationDatastore

[Java Security Property]
networkaddress.cache.ttl=0

[Email]
#Email.mode=standalone
#Email.mode=connect
Email.mode=none
```

```
#Common settings for both standalone and connect mode
Email.personal=Test User
Email.address=myemail@mycompany.com
Email.deviceId=2100000a

#Connect mode settings
Email.pop3Server=popServer
Email.smtpServer=smtpServer
Email.smtpPort=25
Email.pop3Port=110
Email.userId=popUser
Email.password=popPassword
Email.pollInterval=30

[SRPH]
SRPH.AuthenticationString=lsfjdnflownenlgfnp
SRPH.UID=S 00005
SRPH.listen.port=3200

#FS.sourceDir=mobitex_simulator
#FSLayer.logging=true
#push.application.reliable.ports=100
```

4.7.1 Logging HTTP Requests

When debugging a web application or a JME application that uses HTTP, you can increase the amount of information MDS logs as it processes the requests from the device application. This allows the application developer to see everything that transpires as MDS receives requests, connects to the server to retrieve the data, and optimizes the results before sending them to the device. This enhanced logging is enabled by enabling HTTP logging and setting verbose mode.

To enable HTTP verbose logging, locate the [HTTP HANDLER] section in the rimpublic.properties file and add the following two lines to the section:

```
application.handler.http.logging=true
application.handler.http.logging.verbose=true
```

When you enable application.handler.http.logging, HTTP transactions appear in the MDS logs. When you enable application.handler.http.logging.verbose, MDS logs the contents of web pages accessed by the BlackBerry Browser. This generates a large amount of data, so be sure to disable this setting when it is no longer needed.

Note: Restart MDS after you complete the necessary changes.

4.7.2 Adding PIN or Email to the HTTP Request Headers

There are times when a developer needs to validate the identity of a mobile user without prompting them to provide a username and password. You can do this by configuring MDS to include a BlackBerry smartphone PIN and/or email address in the HTTP header for all requests originating from MDS. When your application receives the request, it can perform a reverse lookup against the SQL tables maintained by the BES or against LDAP, Active Directory, or some other up-to-date source of user information. Although this is not a secure option, because all requests from a BlackBerry device activated against a BES and MDS look like they come from inside the firewall, it might be acceptable for some situations.

To enable these options, locate the [HTTP HANDLER] section of the `rimpublic.properties` file and add the appropriate value listed here:

- `application.handler.http.header=pin`. Adds the header value `Rim-device-id: <PIN>` to the HTTP header for the request
- `application.handler.http.header=email`. Adds the header value `Rim-device-email: <user_name>@acme.com` to the HTTP header for the request
- `application.handler.http.header=email,pin`. Adds both `Rim-device-id: <PIN>` and `Rim-device-email: <user_name>@acme.com` to the HTTP header for the request

You can also restrict the addition of these header values to specific domains by adding the following to the [HTTP HANDLER] section of the `rimpublic.properties` file:

```
application.handler.http.header.domain=
```

This option allows you to keep the PIN and email address private except for the domain(s) listed.

When you add this line, you must include the domains for which you want the header values included. To add header values for only the somecompany.com domain, the `rimpublic.properties` line looks like this:

```
application.handler.http.header.domain= somecompany\.com;.+\.
somecompany\.com
```

The entry `somecompany\.com` covers the root domain while `.+\.somecompany\.com` covers any subdomain name that ends with somecompany.com (i.e. server1.somecompany.com).

To add additional domains, append the domain designators to the end of the line by using the same format shown for each additional domain.

 Note: The ability for MDS to include the email address in the HTTP headers is based on a reverse lookup of device PIN against the SQL tables maintained by the BES. To keep the PIN-to-email address mapping, you must ensure that the Black-Berry Database Consistency Service is running on the BES.

4.8 Additional Resources

A complete listing of links to these resources is available online at www. bbdevfundamentals.com.

To learn more about the BlackBerry MDS, see the *BlackBerry Mobile Data System Technical Overview* located at www.blackberry.com/knowledgecenterpublic/livelink.exe?func=ll&objId=1406098&objAction=browse&sort=name.

RIM published an interesting white paper, "Troubleshooting the BlackBerry MDS Service," that provides detailed information about the log lines created by MDS. It is located at www.blackberry.com/btsc/articles/KSM/Technical Documentation/Technical%20Advisories/Troubleshooting%20the% 20BlackBerry%20Mobile%20Data%20Service.pdf.

For more information on web services, refer to the Wikipedia definition of Web Services, located at http://en.wikipedia.org/wiki/Web_service, and the Web Services Tutorial, located at http://www.w3schools.com/webservices/default.asp.

5

BlackBerry Application
Data Push

Developers have the ability to push data to BlackBerry devices in several ways. While not unique to the BlackBerry platform, Research In Motion's (RIM) support for push is thorough and manifests itself in several ways. Although detailed information on the different types of push is provided in Chapters 6 and 7, this chapter provides background information about the application data push capabilities provided by the BlackBerry platform.

5.1 Why Push Is Important to BlackBerry Developers

Chapter 4, "The BlackBerry Mobile Data System (MDS)," discussed how the BlackBerry Enterprise Server (BES) synchronized email and Personal Information Manager (PIM) data with the device. BlackBerry users are familiar with and comfortable knowing that, when they need their data, it is available on their device. With third-party or enterprise applications, mobile users are used to opening an application, entering some information on screen, and clicking a button to make the device connect to one or more servers to retrieve the requested data.

For mobile users who need access to a large amount of data to work with locally (on the device), companies have used the BlackBerry Desktop application programming interface (API) to create the conduit device an application needs to synchronize data to a device connected to the network using the BlackBerry

Desktop Manager. To perform a similar synchronization over the air, developers can use the BlackBerry Sync Server SDK to create a connector that synchronizes data with a device application through the Synchronization Service on the BES.

The game-changing feature of the BlackBerry platform is the ability the BES has to push application data to any device application. For a mobile application, instead of having a user open an application and request the data or building the application so it schedules a periodic pull of data (even when new data might not be available) from a server, the application receives its data by having it pushed directly to the application when it becomes available.

Both BlackBerry application types (Browser and Java) can receive data via push.

The ability to push data directly to BlackBerry applications has many dramatic and powerful effects:

- Data can be sent to devices only when there is new data available, rather than requiring that the user check for new data or having the application pull data on a schedule.
- Data can be sent to the device off-hours, on a schedule maintained by the server application or even configured by the user. This allows a server to distribute the load over time and, therefore, eliminates most peak loads on an application server and BES. By sending the data off-hours, there is no disruption of the other tasks the user might be performing on the device.
- Because the data is only sent when there's new data to send, the device is not connecting to the server repeatedly looking for new data. This reduces the amount of data the device transmits, receives, and processes.
- Because the device does less work (sending less data across the network), a user gets greater life out of a battery charge.

There is no reason that an application can't also request data on demand when the users want it. In this case, push can populate background information or data that the application knows the mobile user needs. The application can still request additional information when the data it needs is not on the device.

5.2 How the Application Data Push Process Works

Although each push option works in a slightly different manner, Figure 5.1 shows the data push process at a high level.

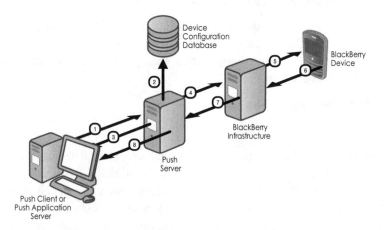

Figure 5.1 BlackBerry application data push process

To push data to a BlackBerry application, the following steps are performed:

1. An application creates the data that needs to be pushed to one or more devices and then sends the data to a server. The server can be inside or outside the firewall, depending on the push option being used.
2. The server verifies the identity of the target recipients.
3. The server notifies the push application that the data has been accepted.
4. The server sends the data to the BlackBerry infrastructure.
5. The BlackBerry infrastructure delivers the data to the device.
6. The device receives the pushed data and returns an acknowledgment that it received the data.
7. The BlackBerry infrastructure receives the notification from the device and forwards it to the push server.
8. The push server returns the notification to the push application.

If the mobile user is out of coverage, the data might still be delivered when the device reappears, as long as it is within certain defined time limits. (Chapters 6 and 7 discuss these limits.) The BlackBerry infrastructure queues requests for a limited amount of time and delivers them when the device returns to coverage. When building a push application, developers must take into account that the device might not be available when the push is sent. The push request can be set up so the push application is notified when the data arrives on the device, and the push application can push the data again if the notification is not received within an expected amount of time.

5.3 Common Questions About Push

The concept of true application data push is unique to the BlackBerry platform; it's not a common capability found on mobile devices. When many developers are first exposed to the BlackBerry application data push, some common questions seem to pop up every time:

Where does the push application run?

The push application can run anywhere.

Regardless of whether you're pushing to internal or external users, the only requirements are that the system running the push application has access to the data it needs to send and that it has the ability to communicate over the network (via HTTP) with the server that is processing the push request (the BES or the RIM Push Infrastructure). The application can run on a desktop computer sitting under a developer's desk, or it can run on an application server sitting in a corporate data center. The push application can, although it's not recommended, run on a BlackBerry, Windows Mobile device, or even an iPhone.

For enterprise push applications, the push application also should not be installed on the BES. It sends data to the BES, but it should not be running on the BES or servers hosting any components of the BES or MDS.

What programming languages can I use to write push applications?

Any development language can be used.

Push applications can be written in any computer language, as long as the language supports the technologies required for push. As you'll see later, the only requirement for a push application is that it is able to communicate with a server via HTTP. There are push applications deployed that are written in PHP, ASP.NET, Python, Java, Visual Basic, C#, and even Delphi.

When should the data be sent to target devices?

Anytime that is appropriate for the target audience.

It's up to the developer writing the push application to decide when the pushed data should be sent to target devices. Data is typically sent based on a schedule or trigger defined by the business requirements for the application. The data can be sent on schedule; every morning at 7:00 A.M., for example. The data can be sent on a trigger—data can be sent whenever specific changes are made to the data or a specific event occurs.

All that matters is that the developer is careful about how often the data is pushed. Although push typically reduces the amount of data sent to/from a device by removing the need for the application to periodically check for updates, you can still reduce battery performance or increase data plan usage if data is pushed more often than needed. Send the data only when it's important to send it and try to batch updates to minimize how often data is sent.

If the application is pushing data to a Java application running on the destination device, the push application can just push new or updated data rather than the full data set with every push. The client-side application or application user can be responsible for purging older data.

Can pushed content be customized per destination user or group of users?

Yes. The push application is created based on the needs of the application user. Whether the pushed data is customized for every recipient or the same data is sent to everyone, it is a decision the developer makes when building the push application.

If the information is general and applicable to an entire team (sales promotions, business unit performance against a quota, industry news), send the same data to everyone. If the data being sent is relevant to a single user or group of users, the push application must build a set of data for them and push it before building the data for the next set of users.

5.4 Pushing to Internal Versus External Users

Chapters 6 and 7 cover the options for pushing to both internal and external push recipients. The two types of recipients (target devices) differ in how the push application can reach them.

Internal recipients are BlackBerry users whose device has been activated against a corporate BES. The devices have a BlackBerry Enterprise data plan from their wireless carrier, get corporate email and other PIM data synchronized wirelessly via the BES and have access to internal systems via MDS.

Until recently, data push was only available to internal recipients. RIM recently released products that support pushing data to external recipients (either personal or consumer devices) through *Web Signals* and the *Java Push APIs*.

External recipients refer to users whose BlackBerry devices are not under the direct control of the organization pushing the data. They might be BES connected users, but they would be connected to a BES located inside some other corporation's firewall. The external user definition also covers mobile, BlackBerry-carrying users who might only use their device to access personal email accounts and web browsing through the BlackBerry Internet Service (BIS).

5.5 Additional Resources

A complete listing of links to these resources is available online at www. bbdevfundamentals.com.

For information on how to use the BlackBerry Desktop API to synchronize back-end data with a BlackBerry device through the BlackBerry Desktop Manager application, refer to the *BlackBerry Desktop API Reference Guide*, located at http://na.blackberry.com/eng/deliverables/1093/Desktop_API_Reference_Guide_46.pdf.

For information on how to use the BlackBerry Sync Server API to synchronize data to an application using the BlackBerry Sync Server service, refer to the *Synchronization Server SDK - Development Guide*, located at http://na. blackberry.com/eng/deliverables/2233/Synchronization%20Server%20SDK %20 Development%20Guide.pdf.

The BlackBerry Java Development Environment (JDE) contains sample code that demonstrates the use of these APIs.

6

Pushing Data to Internal (BES) Users

As mentioned in Chapter 5, "BlackBerry Application Data Push," each Black-Berry application type supports push. When pushing to the BlackBerry browser or to Java applications, the push process is almost exactly the same. The only difference between the two is the port number on the device on which the destination application is listening.

To push data to a BlackBerry Enterprise Server (BES) connected BlackBerry device, you must write an application to perform the push for you. Your application connects to MDS (via HTTP) and delivers the data you want pushed. MDS works with the BES to locate the user and push the data to the specified application (via a port number specified in the push request). Depending on parameters included with the push request, the push application can receive notification of push success (or failure) in several ways. This is discussed in detail later in this chapter.

When pushing data, the push destination can be identified using the mobile user's corporate email address or the device's PIN. The push application can also specify multiple destinations in a single push request. The application can even push data to groups of users defined on the BES.

When developers first hear about this push capability, many think that the application pushing data to internal users must need to be installed on the BES for this to work. The opposite is actually true—never install any application on a BES unless the application is a BES add-in that was designed to integrate with the BES. The BES should run on a dedicated system, and no other software (unless it's BES related) should be installed there. You don't want a potential bug in your push application to bring down the BES and halt message delivery to senior executives and field personnel.

This chapter describes each of the push options supported by the BlackBerry platform and the process a developer must implement in his applications to push data to BlackBerry devices.

6.1 Browser Push

The BlackBerry browser is a supported target for pushed data. A typical browser (be it desktop or mobile) is normally used to request pages or content from a server, review the content, and submit information back to a server. It is a simple process.

Most mainstream browsers provide support for subscribing to RSS feeds. Because of its name, many users believe the data is fed into the browser. What happens with RSS is that the browser periodically checks the feed for new data and downloads new articles that have become available since the last check.

For the BlackBerry Browser Push, it's slightly different. An application is not pushing data to the browser, what the application does is push content to the device that, when accessed, is opened in the BlackBerry browser. There are three types of Browser Pushes you can perform to a device: Channel Push, Message Push, and Cache Push. You can also delete a Browser Channel by using the Browser Channel Delete operation. Table 6.1 summarizes these options, which are described in detail in the following sections.

Table 6.1 Comparison of Browser Push Types

	Custom Icon	User Notification	Destination	Content Types	Subsequent Push Overrides
Channel	Yes	Yes	Home Screen	HTML and URL	Yes
Message	No	Yes	Messages Application	HTML and URL	No
Cache	N/A	No	Browser Cache	Any web content	Yes

The best part about browser push is that, unlike any other mobile application, when you build browser push applications for BlackBerry, you are building applications without writing any program code for the mobile device. Except for the content, the HTML pages, or other content being delivered to the browser, all the development for this process is done in the backend push application, not on the target device.

When building browser push applications, a developer can use any development language he wants because the push process doesn't involve code that runs on the BlackBerry. The push process happens in the background, between the push application and BES components; there is no user's involvement or intervention in the process. With this technology, an organization can leverage existing development skills the company has without ever having to learn how to write applications for a mobile device.

6.1.1 Channel Push

With Channel Push, the push application pushes a web page or the page's URL to the device. The page appears as an icon on the BlackBerry Home Screen.[1] When the mobile user clicks the icon or opens the channel, the browser opens and displays the page. It's better to push a page rather than a URL so the page is stored on the device and available even if the device has gone out of network coverage. See the later section, "Storing the Page," for more information on the limitations of this option.

The Power in Channel Icons

A developer can do some interesting things with the icon that is pushed with the channel. When a Channel Push is sent to a device, the push request includes the URLs for two icons associated with the channel. The icons are Read and Unread[2] icons and the device uses them to indicate when there has been new data pushed to the channel. As soon as the channel has been received by the device, the browser accesses each icon's URL to retrieve the icons from a server. When a channel first appears on a device, the icons take a while to appear on the screen; a default browser icon is used until the channel's icons are retrieved from the server by the browser. You can use Cache Push (described later) to deliver the icons to the device cache in advance of the Channel Push, but that is likely not worth the effort because the icons will appear moments after the pushed content is delivered to the device.

---

1. You might hear people (including me) refer to the Home Screen as the "ribbon."
2. If you happen to be a Notes/Domino developer, this should sound familiar; it's similar to the Unread Marks that Notes allows you to display in a view.

The Unread icon displays until the mobile user opens the channel; as soon as the channel is opened, the icon switches to the Read icon. This gives the user a visual indication whether new data is available in the channel, which is similar to what the user can do with the Messages application.

These icons can impart some information about the nature of the data behind the channel. Rather than use two static icons for the channel, because you can push new icon URLs with each push request, you can use icons that represent the state of the data in the channel with every push.

Here are some examples of how Channel Push can be used:

- **Sales Management:** A company might use a sales-management application that pushes regular updates on progress toward quota. The data might be pushed via a Browser Channel and the employee's progress toward quota represented in the icon. The application might use a red icon when the sales numbers are below quota and a green icon when the sales person has exceeded the daily quota. It can even show the percentage against quota as a number within the icon. The sales people can pull the device out of the holster, take a quick glance at the screen, and know where they stand, without ever opening the application.

- **Brewery:** For a brewery that wants to keep the Brewmaster informed on the status of his brew vats, assuming vat temperatures were maintained in a relational database. The typical approach might be to build a client application that periodically queried the database. With Channel Push, updating the Brewmaster could happen automatically. A triggered procedure could run when any of the temperatures goes above or below pre-defined thresholds. When the temperatures change, an application can build a summary of the vat temperatures in HTML format and push the page to any interested party. The channel's icon can indicate whether there is a problem or not: red if any of the temperatures are too high, blue if any of the temperatures are too low, and a frothy yellow color when the temperatures are just right!

- **IT Management:** An IT organization can use push to deliver a summary of current issues within the environment. Instead of filling everyone's inbox with alerts and alert cancelation messages, a channel can list a summary of the current conditions. The channel's icon can use color to indicate alert level and show the number of critical alerts on the icon.

How Push Changes the Way You Think about Mobile Applications

The brewery concept came from a sales contest RIM sponsored for one of the U.S. wireless carriers. We were promoting mobile applications and asked them to create a proposal for that scenario. Being smart people, they immediately started thinking about the middleware they might need to connect to the database and what type of rich client application was needed for the device. The solution I described here, however, allowed a solution to be developed without any middleware (except for MDS, of course, but an organization would already have that) and without any client application code being developed for the BlackBerry device. The organization could use the skills it already had in-house to build a simple web page (using HTML) that was pushed to the device. Because the channel icon imparts information to the user, the application doesn't even have to be opened to see how things are doing back at the brewery.

To see how channel icons can look on a device, look at Figure 6.1 and Figure 6.2. Figure 6.1 shows an unread icon, which is an icon indicating that there is new data behind the channel. Figure 6.2 shows the read icon for the same channel, which indicates that the channel has been opened since the data was pushed.

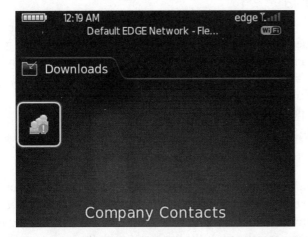

Figure 6.1   Sample Browser Channel unread icon

Figure 6.2   Sample Browser Channel read icon

As you'll see when we talk about Web Signals in Chapter 7, "Pushing Data to External (BIS) Users," a Browser Channel can display a completely different icon depending on the data included with the push. The AccuWeather Web Signal icon shows the weather conditions for the location being monitored. The icon shows a sunny sky when it's sunny outside, rain clouds when it's raining, and snow through most of the winter. This is just another example of how the channel icon can impart information.

If you push a Browser Channel and don't specify a read and/or unread icon for the channel, the BlackBerry uses a default, generic icon for the channel included with the device theme.

Overwriting Pushed Data

When pushing data to a channel, any new push to the channel overwrites the previous channel data—there is no history maintained on the device. If a push application is pushing new data but there's also some legacy information that needs to be included as well (data from a previous push, for example), the push application must push all of the data every time, both the old and the new. Because complete web pages are being pushed, the developer cannot expect that new data just appends to the end of what is already there.

Pointing to the Portal

Many organizations use Browser Channels as a way to place an icon for the company's portal on every BlackBerry device. In this case, they simply push the URL for the portal down once and it's there any time the user needs it. If the portal URL ever changes, they merely rerun the push and push the new portal location to the channel. Another option is to build and deploy a simple Java application that launches the portal URL when opened.

Storing the Page

When you push a channel to a device, you must store the HTML page on a web server so it can be accessed by the device when needed. By default, the Black-Berry browser only stores information in its cache for a limited amount of time (approximately 12 hours, but that's no guarantee). If the device's internal routines that manage memory determine that it needs the memory being used to store your page for a more important purpose, the local copy of the page may be deleted. If the page is purged from the device, the BlackBerry browser just goes to the web server and retrieves a new copy of the page when it needs it.

A push application can set an extended expiration date for the content when the content is pushed to the device; this is detailed in the section, "RIM Push

Parameters." There is still no guarantee that the data remains if the device truly needs the memory for something more important or if the user clears the cache.

Number of Channels

A device can support many channels. There is likely a limit to the number of channels you can have on a device, but if you bump up against the limit, the user probably already has other problems. When organizations start deploying channels, they must think carefully about the impact on mobile users. If a user is monitoring one, two, or even up to about five channels, it's probably not too difficult for the user to pay attention to. But, if the user has to manage the contents of her inbox plus deal with many separate channels, it quickly becomes more difficult. You might end up losing the benefits you could be getting from this feature by overloading the user with channels.

Notifying the User

The question that mobile developers ask most often is, "Can I notify the user when there's new data?" The answer is yes, and the user even gets to decide how he is notified. If you look at a BlackBerry device, there is an application icon somewhere labeled Profiles. On the BlackBerry Bold Smartphone, it's a speaker icon in the upper-left corner of the screen, as shown in Figure 6.3.

Figure 6.3 BlackBerry device Profiles

When you open the Profiles application, a menu appears that lists the profiles currently defined on the device. Each profile defines a series of alert settings for each of the possible alerting applications running on the device. Scroll to the bottom of the list and highlight the item labeled Advanced, as shown in Figure 6.4. Click the trackball or press the Enter key to open the item, and a screen appears that shows another list of the profiles.

Figure 6.4   BlackBerry Profiles menu

Select one of the profiles (it doesn't matter which), click the BlackBerry menu button, and select Edit from the menu that appears, as shown in Figure 6.5.

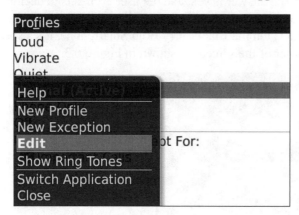

Figure 6.5   Edit Profile

Figure 6.6 shows the different options for the selected profile. Select the option labeled Browser, as shown in Figure 6.6. This alert gets triggered when pushed browser data is received by the device.

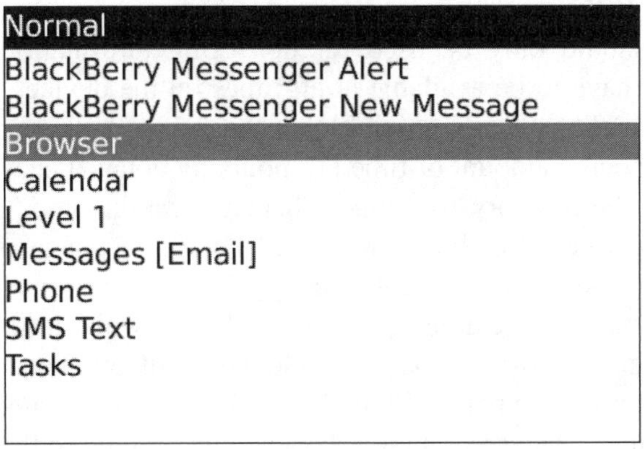

```
Normal
BlackBerry Messenger Alert
BlackBerry Messenger New Message
Browser
Calendar
Level 1
Messages [Email]
Phone
SMS Text
Tasks
```

Figure 6.6   Selecting Profile Option to Modify

In Figure 6.7, you see the options available to configure this profile for how the user will be alerted. You can define options for when the device is holstered and when it's out of the holster. You can have a tone played, have the device vibrate, or both. You can even specify the volume and number of beeps and/or vibrations for the alert.

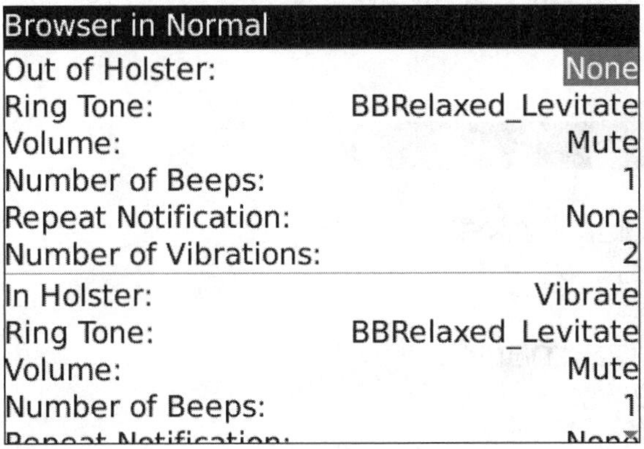

```
Browser in Normal
Out of Holster:                        None
Ring Tone:            BBRelaxed_Levitate
Volume:                                Mute
Number of Beeps:                          1
Repeat Notification:                   None
Number of Vibrations:                     2
In Holster:                          Vibrate
Ring Tone:            BBRelaxed_Levitate
Volume:                                Mute
Number of Beeps:                          1
Repeat Notification:                   None
```

Figure 6.7   Profile option in Edit mode

When you finish making changes, press the BlackBerry menu button, select Save to save your changes, and close the Profile Editor.

Limitations of Channel Push

Browser Channel Push should only be used for delivering information to a BlackBerry that does not have to be available at all times on the device. When you push a web page to a channel, it's possible that the device will purge the page from cache after a specific amount of time (12 hours by default) or if there is some critical need for the memory for some other application. This isn't a problem for most channels because the browser will access the page on the server if the copy it needs is no longer available locally. If the application's target users need to have access to the page at all times and if they're without network connectivity or if the server that hosts the page is no longer available (because of some catastrophe, for example), the page will not be available. If the pushed data must be available at all times, push the data to a Java application instead, as discussed shortly.

Removing Browser Channels

It is possible to delete a channel from the device when the mobile user no longer wants to receive the information or when the channel is no longer being pushed. To delete the channel, open the browser and access the Bookmarks page, as shown in Figure 6.8. At the bottom of the list is an expandable section called Browser Channels. When this section is expanded, a list of all the channels is displayed.

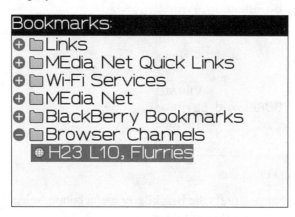

Figure 6.8 Browser Channel listing in Browser Bookmarks

Highlight the channel you want to delete (shown in Figure 6.8 as a local weather report) and press the BlackBerry Menu button. From the menu that appears (see Figure 6.9), select Delete Channel, and the channel is removed from your device.

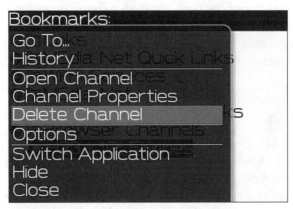

Figure 6.9 Deleting a Browser Channel

With BlackBerry Device Software version 4.6 and beyond, the channel can be deleted directly from the BlackBerry Home Screen. To do this, highlight the channel, press the BlackBerry menu button, and select Delete Channel from the menu that appears, as shown in Figure 6.10.

Figure 6.10 Deleting a channel directly from the Home Screen

 Note: If you delete the channel but if the channel data is still being periodically delivered to your device by a push application, the channel will reappear the next time a push occurs for that channel. Be sure to unsubscribe from any active channels before you delete them.

The developer can make unsubscribing from the push easy by including an X-RIM-PUSH-DELETE-URL parameter with the push request. This URL is triggered when the user deletes the channel icon from her device. Developers should create code to automatically delete the user from the push application when the URL is triggered.

6.1.2 Message Push

Message Push works just like Channel Push except that, instead of the page appearing as a separate icon on the ribbon, the pushed web page or URL appears as a message in the device's Messages application, as shown in Figure 6.11. The message has a special globe icon to indicate that it's pointing to a browser URL. When the user opens the message, the browser opens and renders the page.

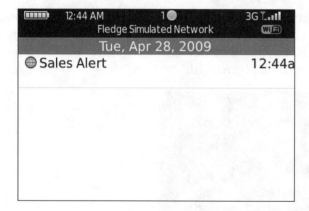

Figure 6.11   Messages application showing a pushed message

 Note: With Message Push, the messages only appear in your BlackBerry Messages application; they do not appear in your desktop messaging system inbox.

Message pushes are different than Channel Pushes because, with Channel Push, any subsequent push overwrites the previous push, but with Message Push, each subsequent push becomes a separate icon in the Messages application.

Use Message Push when you want to deliver pushed data to a BlackBerry device only, and you have some interest in being able to continue to see the content pushed previously. Imagine, for example, if you were working with a group of service technicians or delivery personnel: These users might not have corporate email accounts (but likely personal ones) on their BlackBerry devices, but you could dispatch them to new service calls or package pickups via message push.

6.1.3 Cache Push

Cache Push allows browser content (web pages, input forms, graphics, style sheets, JavaScript files, and more) to be pushed to the device's browser cache without the user's knowledge; the content will be there whenever the user needs it. The difference between this and Channel Push is that, for Cache Push, the user is not alerted when the content appears on the device, and the cached page does not automatically get represented as an icon on the ribbon. This option allows content to be available when the device is not within wireless coverage or to save retrieving data for review or a form for data entry.

A good use for Cache Push is for pushing the ancillary files a Channel Push needs (channel icon, CSS, JavaScript libraries, image files, and so on) onto the device so they won't have to be retrieved from the network when the channel is opened.

 Note: When pushing an HTML page to the browser cache, only the HTML data gets pushed to cache. If the HTML page contains references to external resources, such as images, style sheets, and JavaScript files, your push application needs to parse the source HTML page looking for any linked references and separate content pushes for each additional resource.

6.2 Pushing to a Java Application

Data can be pushed to BlackBerry client applications written in Java. The push process is primarily the same as the previous examples in this chapter; the major difference is that, instead of pushing an HTML page, the application pushes data in whatever format the destination application supports. The application can push HTML or XML data to the client application, but extra markup information would be delivered that likely wouldn't be used in a Java application. Another difference is that, when pushing to a Java application, most of the push parameters used to support Browser Push are not used.

On the client side of this push option is a custom Java application that must be created and deployed to receive the pushed content. This application, the push listener or receiver, must perform the following functions:

- Register as a startup application on the BlackBerry so it will be ready to receive pushed content without the user's intervention. This ensures the data is as accurate as possible because the application always listens for data while the device is on.
- Open a new thread for processing the data sent by the push application.

- Store the data locally (so it can be viewed by the mobile user).
- Render the data in a way easily processed by the user of the application.

You can have the user execute the program when needed, but that eliminates much of the benefit you get from push and requires coordination between the mobile user and the push process. If the push receiver isn't running when the pushed data arrives, it will not be processed by the application.

Each push listener listens on a particular port on the destination device. Pushed content is targeted at a particular client application on the destination device through the port number the application is listening on. When the push request is sent to the server for the device, the push application includes the port number with the request so the device knows where to deliver the data once it arrives.

Use this push option if you want to send data to a device application and have the ability to work with the data even when the device is outside of network coverage (a wireless dead zone or on an airplane). Because the listener application has the ability to store the data locally and manipulate it any way it wants, this option provides more flexibility and potential for a better user experience.

For an example for how this could be used, imagine a sales representative who frequently enters areas where network coverage is not available. A backend push application might be used to push sales data, customer order information, special promotions, or even inventory numbers to a rich client running on the device. The sales rep can review information, take orders, inform the customer of delivery estimates—all without having network coverage. The sales rep can even take orders when there's no network coverage; she can have inventory information on the device (albeit a bit dated) and any orders can be queued up, delivered, and validated later when the device goes back into coverage.

This is a powerful capability that is not available on any other mobile platform. To learn how to build a push listener application in Java, analyze the source code from the BlackBerry Emergency Contact List (ECL) application available at www.blackberry.com/go/ecl.

6.3 The Enterprise Push Process

The push process begins with an application running on a desktop or server somewhere. The application can be written in any development language that supports HTTP. The application can do its push any time it wants: randomly, on a schedule or on a trigger. Both the BES and MDS will be involved in getting the push content delivered to the device.

To push data to BlackBerry devices, the BlackBerry environment must be running BES for Exchange 3.5 or higher or BES for Domino version 2.2 or higher.

Additionally, the MDS Connection Service must be installed and enabled in the environment.

Figure 6.12 illustrates the push process, which consists of the following steps:

1. The push application builds a push request (including destination addresses, data, and push settings) and sends the request to the MDS server.

2. MDS-CS validates the recipients against the BlackBerry Configuration Database on the BES.

3. If the recipients are provisioned on the BES, an acknowledgment is returned to the push application.

4. MDS reformats the request and delivers the pushed content across the wireless network to the destination device or devices.

5. The device sends an acknowledgment to MDS, indicating that it has received the data.

6. (Optional) MDS notifies the push application that the push has been received.

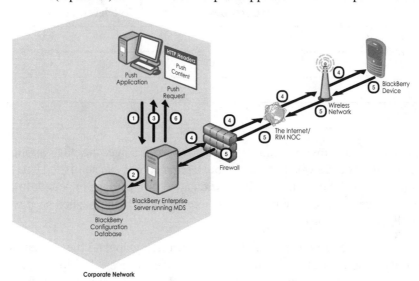

Figure 6.12   Enterprise push process

The destination device can be identified through the email address or PIN associated with the device. If PIN is used, there will need to be some way to keep the PIN list updated when users change devices. Because users frequently upgrade their devices, the most reliable way to identify users is via their email address.

If a push recipient is not within wireless coverage and, therefore, not able to receive the pushed data, MDS only holds onto the push request for a limited amount of time[3] before discarding the request. When you build your push application, take

_____

3. This is controlled by the Flow Control Timeout as configured on the BES. The default value is 10 minutes.

advantage of the push feature `X-RIM-PUSH-NOTIFYURL` that allows your application to receive a notification when the pushed data arrives on the device. If the data is important, push the data again if you don't receive confirmation that the data was delivered successfully.

A former colleague once said, "I'd recommend developers assume the data won't get there so they are ready to handle situations where a device is out of coverage (battery dead, user on a flight, etc.)." There's just no guarantee the data will be delivered to the device.

The pushed content can get to a device in different ways. In most cases, the pushed content is delivered to the device with the initial push request but, in other cases, it can be retrieved later. Table 6.2 summarizes the available options.

Table 6.2 Pushed Content Delivery Options

	Pushed Data Included in Push Request	Push Data Can Be Retrieved Later
Browser Channel	X	X
Browser Message	X	X
Browser Cache	X	
Java Listener	X	

When sending a Browser Channel or a Browser Message, the push application can either include the web page in the push request or it can send the URL to the content and it will be retrieved when the channel or message is opened. In either case, the page must be stored on a web server before being pushed so it will be available if it is ever needed.

To push the page or content with the request, merely append the content to the end of the push request. To have the content retrieved later, the push application should leave the push request empty and include the URL pointing to the stored page in the `Content-Location` HTTP header.

For Cache Push and pushes to a custom Java listener application, the pushed content must be included with the request.

6.4 Controlling Access to Push

By default, anyone can push data to any BlackBerry device as long as he has access to the user's BES. All the push capabilities described in this chapter are available to anyone who has the necessary information. The BES administrator can, and should, configure the BES so each push request can only be performed when the appropriate credentials (username and password) are provided.

The credentials sent to MDS-CS for authentication are sent in HTTP Basic Authentication format. To use this feature, the push application must add the credentials for the push user to the request HTTP headers. The credentials are passed as a Base64 encoded combination of the username and password (username:pswd). To perform this operation in Java, use the following code:

```
String auth = "Basic " + new BASE64Encoder().encode((username +
  ":" + pswd).getBytes());
mdsConn.setRequestProperty("Authorization", auth);
```

6.5 Locating Internal Push Recipients

Depending on the configuration of an organization's BlackBerry environment, it might be difficult to locate the recipient for a push request. If the BES environment is configured with a single BES domain and a central push server (see Figure 6.13), the application can submit the push request to the central push server and it will locate the recipient's BES and deliver the data.

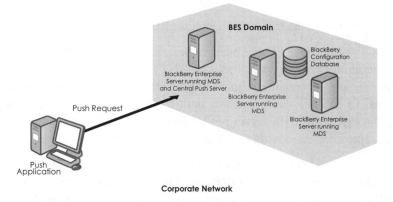

Figure 6.13   Locating push recipients in a single BES domain

If the BES environment is configured with multiple BES domains or a single domain without a central push server, as shown in Figure 6.14, the task is more difficult. In this scenario, the push application has to maintain a list of all the valid MDS servers in the environment (in a single domain or multiple domains, it doesn't matter—the MDS server is not aware of the other MDS servers) and push to each MDS server until the server accepts the push request.

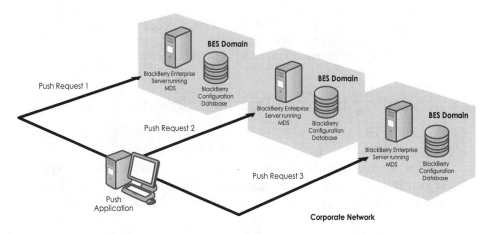

Figure 6.14 Locating push recipients in a multiple BES domain environment

When the MDS server receives the push request, it validates the user against the BES Configuration Database. MDS returns a HTTP result code of 200 when it locates the user and accepts the push. It returns an HTTP result code 403 if the email address or PIN for the recipient cannot be located. The push application must loop through each MDS server until it receives confirmation that the push has been accepted before moving to the next push recipient.

When developers first learn about this feature, their first inclination is to modify the table containing push recipient information to include the MDS server information. When the push application retrieves recipient information from the table, it also retrieves the MDS server information. The problem with this approach is that users sometimes switch BES. Because of this, as soon as this table is created, it is out of date.

6.6 Push Request Formats

The BlackBerry platform supports two push request formats. The first option is RIM Push, which is a proprietary push format that RIM created to support pushing data through the BES. RIM later joined the WAP Forum's definition of a push standard called Push Access Protocol (PAP). It doesn't matter which method you pick; in both cases, the data gets to the same place at the same time. With both types, the push request is bundled up in a HTTP POST and sent to MDS-CS. The difference is the format of the data included in the POST.

One of the benefits of PAP push is that it supports some additional features over RIM Push. PAP Push allows the push application to

- Check the status of a push request
- Cancel a push request
- Specify additional parameters around when a push request would be delivered (deliver-before and deliver-after timestamps sent with the push request)

RIM Push is the push option of choice for most developers. The push application defines the push request, sets parameters in the HTTP headers, and stores the pushed content in the body. PAP Push, on the other hand, is more complicated, difficult to implement, and sensitive to the format of the push request. Use RIM Push unless your push application needs to be able to push to both BlackBerry and other devices that support PAP.

6.6.1 RIM Push

To implement RIM Push, an HTTP POST request is created and sent to MDS-CS. The POST URL identifies the push recipients and listener port for the destination application. Figure 6.15 illustrates the components of the RIM Push request. Parameters that instruct the push server and push recipient on how to process the pushed data are added to the request via HTTP header values. The body of the push request contains the data being pushed to the device. Each option is described in detail later, and some code samples that illustrate the different types of RIM Push are available on this book's website (www.bbdevfundamentals.com).

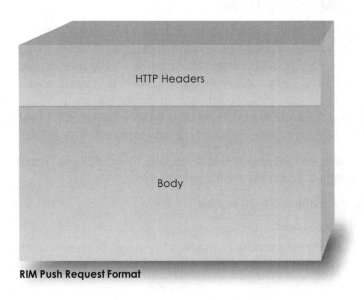

RIM Push Request Format

Figure 6.15   RIM Push request format

RIM Push URL

For RIM Push, the URL used to initiate that the push has several components. In the following example, the options for the URL are enclosed in square brackets:

```
http://[mds_server]:[mds_port]/push?DESTINATION=[destination]&
PORT=[listen_port]&REQUESTURI=/
```

Table 6.3 describes each option for the RIM Push URL.

Table 6.3 RIM Push URL Components

URL Component	Description
mds_server	The hostname for the MDS server that processes the request. The push application should include a fully qualified domain name (FQDN) for the server address, if uncertain whether DNS will properly resolve the name.
mds_port	Specifies the port number that the MDS server is listening on for push requests. This value is set by the BES administrators when the BES software is installed. For current versions of the BES, MDS listens by default on port 8080. For older BES, on the Exchange BES, the MDS server listened on port 8300 and, for both the MDS Simulator and IBM Domino BES, MDS listened on port 8080. Developers should check with their BES administrators to determine the correct value for this parameter before pushing any data.

Table 6.3 RIM Push URL Components

URL Component	Description
Destination	Specifies the destination device or devices for the push. This parameter should include either the email address or PINs for the destination devices. Refer to the section, "Pushing to Multiple Recipients," for information on how to specify multiple recipients in a single push request.
listen_port	Specifies the port number used by the BlackBerry client application to receive pushes. The BlackBerry browser listens on port 7874 (used for any Channel Push, Message Push, and Cache Push); if you're pushing to the browser, you must push to this port. When pushing to a custom listener in Java, specify the port number the application has been coded to listen on.

Each URL option listed in Table 6.3 is required; there are no default settings.

If you're performing Browser Channel Push to a Domino BES running on bes1.somecompany.com and sending the channel to the BlackBerry device used by some.user@somecompany.com, the push request will look something like this:

```
http://bes1.somecompany.com:8080/push?DESTINATION=
some.user@somecompany.com&PORT=7874&REQUESTURI=/
```

If you're pushing data to a custom listener application (listening on port 1199) via an Exchange BES bes2.anothercompany.com, the push URL will look something like this:

```
http://bes2.anothercompany.com:8080/push?DESTINATION=
another.user@anothercompany.com&PORT=1199&REQUESTURI=/
```

To push to a device using the PIN instead of the email address, the push URL will look like this:

```
http://bes1.somecompany.com:8080/push?DESTINATION=2086dbf4&
PORT=7874&REQUESTURI=/
```

 Note: Don't forget that the user's PIN changes every time the user switches devices, so you need to have a reliable way to know what the current PIN is for the user.

There is a limitation on how large the push URL and push headers combined can be. Because of a limitation in the Apache server included with MDS, in certain versions of MDS, the limit is 3 kilobytes. To ensure that your pushes are delivered reliably, split your pushes into multiple requests if you think you're going to approach the limit, or use PAP push instead. (PAP pushes do not have the size limitation because the URL for PAP pushes is simple.)

Pushing to Multiple Recipients

You can push to multiple recipients by specifying multiple DESTINATION parameters in your push request URL; just be sure to use the ampersand (&) between each one:

```
http://bes1.somecompany.com:8080/push?DESTINATION=
juser1@somecompany.com&DESTINATION=1user2@somecompany.com&
PORT=7874&REQUESTURI=/
```

Pushing to Groups

To push to BlackBerry groups (groups defined on the BES via BlackBerry manager), you must designate that you're pushing to a group by preceding the group name with a $. Because a dollar sign ($) is a valid character in a URL, the $ in a group name is encoded to a hexadecimal representation (%24) to avoid ambiguity. To push a Browser Channel to a BES Group called Sales, use the following format:

```
http://bes1.yetanothercompany.com:8080/push?DESTINATION=
%24Sales&PORT=7874&REQUESTURI=/
```

RIM Push Parameters

After the push URL is defined, the application must set the appropriate values in one or more HTTP headers included with the push request.

The following tables list the push request header options and their usage. Some headers control how MDS pushes the content to the destination, while others control what happens on the device after the pushed data has been received. Most of the header values apply to browser pushes only, mostly channels. Table 6.4 lists the minimum required parameters for each push type.

Table 6.4 Minimum Required Push Parameters

Push Type	Minimum Required Header Parameters
Browser Cache	X-RIM-PUSH-TYPE
Browser Channel	X-RIM-PUSH-CHANNEL-ID X-RIM-PUSH-TITLE X-RIM-PUSH-TYPE
Browser Channel Delete	X-RIM-PUSH-CHANNEL-ID X-RIM-PUSH-TYPE

Table 6.4 Minimum Required Push Parameters

Push Type	Minimum Required Header Parameters
Browser Message	X-RIM-PUSH-TITLE X-RIM-PUSH-TYPE
Custom Listener (client-side Java application)	None

Table 6.5 lists the supported RIM Push header parameters.

Table 6.5 5RIM Push Header Parameters

Push Type	Description
Cache-Control	Possible values are `no-cache`, `max-age`, and `must-revalidate`. Controls how the browser treats the pushed content. Although the `Expires` header value is used to try to get the device to keep the content in the cache longer (or shorter) than the default 12 hours, this parameter controls how long the browser trusts the content stored in its cache. Value of `no-cache` tells the browser not to even store the page in the cache. The `max-age` value specifies the number of seconds before the content is considered invalid. The `must-revalidate` option forces the browser to always get a fresh copy of the page whenever it's requested, even if the user accesses the page via the browser's history.
Content-Location	Specifies the URL from where the content is downloaded if the content is not included with the push request. This applies only to browser push request. If the push content is not included with the push request, the browser retrieves a new copy of the page when the channel is opened. This is a standard HTTP header value; it is not specific to RIM Push.
Content-Type	Allows you to specify a list of MIME types that can be included with the pushed content. The list of MIME types is included in this parameter as a comma-separated list of types.
Expires	Specifies the amount of time the pushed content is stored in the device's cache memory. The format of this value is GMT Time (Fri 06 Feb 2009 12:00:00 GMT). When using this parameter, don't forget that, if the device decides it needs the memory for something else, it's possible that the content will be purged sooner than you expect.
X-RIM-PUSH-CHANNEL-ID	Unique text identifier for the push. Include the name for your push, the server or application name, or something to help differentiate this push from all others on the device. This ID is used when deleting the push later. See the description for X-RIM-PUSH-TYPE for information about browser-channel-delete.

Continues

Table 6.5 5RIM Push Header Parameters *(Continued)*

Push Type	Description
X-RIM-PUSH-DELETE-URL	Specifies the URL activated/triggered when the user deletes a Browser Channel from his device. (See the section, "Removing Browser Channels," for information on how to manually delete a channel and trigger this URL). This allows the push application to know when the user has acted to remove the content. You could use this URL to trigger pushing the channel back to the device (not allow the user to delete the channel), or you could use it to automatically unsubscribe the user from the channel because he clearly doesn't want it anymore. The device does not deliver any information about the channel when it triggers this URL, so the URL must include some identifying information about the channel, such as Channel ID and PIN in the URL, so you can identify the source of the deletion.
X-RIM-PUSH-DELIVER-BEFORE	Specifies an expiration date and time for the push request. If the push is not completed by the specified date, it is removed from the push queue. The format for the parameter is GMT Time (Fri 06 Feb 2009 12:00:00 GMT).
X-RIM-PUSH-DESCRIPTION	Brief description of the push. This value is displayed when the user views the properties of a channel on the device (within browser bookmarks).
X-RIM-PUSH-ID	Unique ID associated with the push. When using PAP, every push ID must be unique or MDS does not accept the push request. This ID is returned with the delivered/failed push acknowledgment sent from MDS to the push application. It allows a push application to track its pushes and know if they were delivered or not.
X-RIM-PUSH-NOTIFYURL	Specifies the URL that's accessed/triggered when the push is received. Allows a push application to receive external notification when the content arrives.
X-RIM-PUSH-PRIORITY	Specifies how the user is notified when the push is received on the device. This parameter supports four possible options: **High:** The user is notified via the alert specified for browser messages, the unread icon is displayed on the BlackBerry Home Screen for the channel, and a dialog box is displayed that tells the user new data has been pushed to the channel. **Medium:** The user is notified via the alert specified for browser messages and the unread icon is displayed on the BlackBerry Home Screen for the channel. **Low:** The user is notified via the alert specified for browser messages and the unread icon is displayed on the BlackBerry Home Screen for the channel. **None:** The unread icon is displayed on the BlackBerry Home Screen for the Channel. The default value for this property is Medium.

Table 6.5 5RIM Push Header Parameters *(Continued)*

X-RIM-PUSH-READ-ICON-URL	A URL pointing to the icon file used to identify when the pushed content has been viewed (opened) by the mobile user. A Browser Channel displays the unread icon until the user opens the channel; after the channel is opened, the icon switches to the Read icon. With this parameter, the icon is not pushed to the device with the pushed content. The device downloads the icon file after the pushed content has been received on the device.
X-RIM-PUSH-RELIABILITY	Push Reliability defines how the receiving device notifies the push application that the content has been received. Because the capabilities for this option changed with BlackBerry Device Software 4.0, you need to use a special compatibility option when pushing to a mixed audience (devices running BlackBerry Device Software below, equal, and greater than 4.0). **Transport:** A message is sent from the device when the content is received. This option is supported on all BlackBerry Device Software versions. **Application:** A message is sent from the device once the content has been delivered to the destination application. This option is only supported on devices running BlackBerry Device Software version 4.0 and greater. **Application-Preferred:** (Compatibility Mode) On devices running BlackBerry Device Software version 4.0 and greater sends an acknowledgment message when the push content has been delivered to the destination application. For devices running BlackBerry Device Software earlier than version 4.0, it sends an acknowledgment when content is received by the device. The default option for this property is Transport.
X-RIM-PUSH-RIBBON-POSITION	An integer value that instructs the device where to place a Browser Channel icon on the BlackBerry ribbon. This parameter does not function reliably; apparently, there are issues where the active theme on the device might override the specified ribbon position. You can use this parameter in your push application, but chances are it will not provide any value to your push recipients.
X-RIM-PUSH-TITLE	A descriptive name for the pushed content. For Browser Channels, the string value provided here is displayed on the device's Home Screen when the Channel icon is selected. For Browser Messages, the title is displayed in the message list as the subject for the message.

Continues

Table 6.5 5RIM Push Header Parameters *(Continued)*

X-RIM-PUSH-TRANSCODE-CONTENT	Possible values: */*, none, or a list of MIME types. Specifies which types of content are transcoded by MDS before being delivered to the destination device. A value of */* indicates that all content is transcoded. A value of none tells MDS not to transcode any content. This is used to optimize pushed content for viewing on the BlackBerry. If the push application is pushing a large image that needs to be viewed in its native format, you might not want to not have MDS transcode it. The push application needs to enable this option to enable the pushing of nonweb content that the browser can display (such as a PDF or PowerPoint Presentation). If you're not sure, it's best to specify */*. To specify one or more MIME types to be transcoded, specify them in a comma separated list of MIME types.
X-RIM-PUSH-TYPE	Possible values: `browser-message`, `browser-content`, `browser-channel`, and `browser-channel-delete`. Used for browser pushes to identify the type of push being performed. Most of these options were described in detail earlier: **Browser-Message:** The pushed content appears in the Messages application with a special icon to indicate that it's a browser message. **Browser-Content:** The pushed content is a Cache Push; the content is stored in the device's content cache until needed. **Browser-Channel:** The pushed content should appear on the device Home Screen. **Browser-Channel Delete:** The specified Browser Channel should be removed from the device. The Browser Channel to delete is identified by the unique channel ID (`X-RIM-PUSH-CHANNEL-ID`) used when the channel was first sent to the device.
X-RIM-PUSH-UNREAD-ICON-URL	A URL pointing to the icon file used to identify when there is new pushed content available on a Browser Channel. A Browser Channel displays the Unread icon until the user opens the channel; after the channel is opened, the icon switches to the Read icon. With this parameter, the icon is not pushed to the device with the pushed content. The device downloads the icon file after the pushed content has been received on the device.

Table 6.5 5RIM Push Header Parameters *(Continued)*

X-RIM-PUSH-USE-COVERAGE	Possible values: `true` and `false`. Allows a push application to notify MDS that it does not want the push request queued up if the mobile user is not within wireless coverage. A push application can specify a value of `true` in the `X-Rim-Push-Use-Coverage` header in the push request to receive network coverage information from BlackBerry MDS. This information can determine whether to submit push messages to a particular device. When the header is enabled, the push response sent by BlackBerry MDS also includes an `X-Rim-Device-State` header. This header has a value of `true` if the destination device is in network coverage or `false` if it is not. If BlackBerry MDS detects that a device is out of coverage, the push connection is terminated (if one was created), regardless of whether a deliver-before-time has been reached. A result notification indicates that the push was not successful and that the destination device is out of coverage: `X-Rim-Device-State: false`. When the device comes into coverage, BlackBerry MDS sends an additional result notification with an `X-Rim-Device-State` header that has a value of `true`, which indicates that the device is in coverage. The push initiator can continue pushing to the device.

As a slight variation on Channel Pushes, if you push a Cache Push and include an `X-RIM-PUSH-CHANNEL-ID`, the pushed content is added to the channel and the user is not notified. If the Channel ID is not included, the content is just added to the cache.

RIM Push Content

For each RIM Push type, the body of the POST message contains the content being delivered to the device. For Browser Pushes, the body of the POST message is the web page being delivered to the browser. For content pushed to a custom listener (Java push listener), the body of the POST message contains the data being pushed in whatever format is required for your listener application.

RIM Push Response Codes

When a push request has been accepted by MDS, the server returns a result code indicating the status of the request. A result code of 200 indicates that the push request has been accepted and is being processed. Any other response indicates that there was a problem with the push request, either an improperly formatted push request ror an error with the data in the request. A complete list of HTTP Push Request Response codes can be found in the BlackBerry Developer Knowledge Base article, "What Is: RIM Push Request Response Codes." To access this article, go to www.blackberry.com/developers and search the developer's knowledge base for article DB-00502.

6.6.2 Push Access Protocol (PAP) Push

PAP Push is similar to RIM Push in that the push request is delivered via HTTP. The format of the push request, however, is very different. Although PAP Push uses the same push parameters as RIM Push (refer to Table 6.5), they're sent to MDS in a different part of the message. Instead of RIM Push, which has one push request type and uses parameters to define what happens with the push, PAP push supports three different types of requests/messages. Each message format is described later in this section, and code samples illustrating the different types of PAP Push requests are available on this book's website (www. bbdevfundamentals.com).

The PAP Push URL

For PAP push, the push URL is very simple:

```
http://[mds_server]:[mds_port]/pap
```

Table 6.6 describes each option for the PAP Push URL.

Table 6.6 PAP Push URL Components

URL Component	Description
mds_server	The hostname for the MDS server that processes the request. The push application should include a fully qualified domain name (FQDN) for the server address if uncertain whether DNS will properly resolve the name.
mds_port	Specifies the port number that the MDS server is listening on for push requests. This value is set by the BES administrators when the BES software is installed. For current versions of the BES, MDS listens by default on port 8080. For older BES, on the Exchange BES, the MDS server listened on port 8300 and, for both the MDS Simulator and IBM Domino BES, MDS listened on port 8080. Developers need to check with their BES administrators to determine the correct value for this parameter before pushing any data.

If an application is performing a PAP Push to a BES running on bes1.somecompany. com, the default push request URL looks like

```
http://bes1.somecompany.com:8080/pap
```

Push Message Format and Content

The content included with the push request differs, depending on which push message the application is sending to MDS. PAP push supports three different push messages: `push-message`, `cancel-message` and `statusquery-message`. Each option is described in the following sections.

PAP Push-Message

The `push-message` message is the most complicated message for PAP push. Because the push request body contains push parameters and the push content, the message body is sent as a MIME Multipart message, as shown in Figure 6.16.

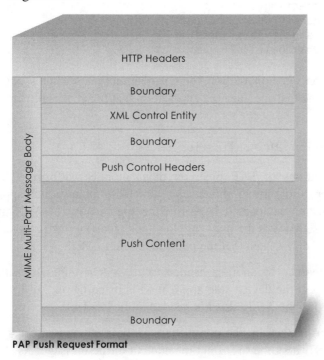

PAP Push Request Format

Figure 6.16 PAP Push request format

The MIME message contains an XML document that describes the push (the control entity) and any push headers and the data that will be pushed to the destination device(s).

The Push Control Headers and the Push Content sections shown in Figure 6.16 are just the push request content used in RIM Push. This means that the PAP request is just a MIME multipart message containing a XML Control Entity, plus the content that is submitted to a server via RIM Push. This is one of the reasons it's just simpler to use RIM Push over PAP Push. PAP just adds additional overhead to the push process.

The boundary is just a random series of characters that may not be included as part of the message content. It distinguishes between the different parts of the MIME Multipart message. When sending a push message, an application must first set the `Content-Type` HTTP Request header to tell the receiving service the format of the HTTP POST:

```
Content-Type:multipart/related; type="application/xml";
 boundary=jausyhstaositate
```

In Java, the header can be set using the following code:

```
HttpURLConnection mdsConn = (HttpURLConnection)
mdsUrl.openConnection();
mdsConn.setRequestProperty( "Content-Type",
"multipart/related;type=\"application/xml\";
boundary=jausyhstaositate" );
```

In Research In Motion's documentation, there's mention that you can specify an additional header value that specifies the application that the push will be routed through:

```
X-WAP-Application-ID: Application_ID
```

In other implementations of PAP push on other mobile platforms (Nokia, Microsoft, and other third parties), this header value determines which application receives the pushed payload. It is part of the specification so MDS must include it, but because MDS is the only "application" receiving the payload, the developer can just specify /, such that the payload is sent to MDS.

There is also a reference to another header value, `X-Rim-Push-Dest-Port`, which specifies the port the device side application is listening on, but for PAP, because it's specified in the XML, it is not needed in the header.

After the application has set up the connection so the receiving server knows how to read the POST, it's time to format the content of the message. As shown in Figure 6.16, the first component of the push request is an XML control entity that describes the push request. A simple push-message control entity is shown in the following example:

```
<pap>
 <push-message push-id="UniquePushID">
  <address address-value=
    "WAPPUSH=someuser%40somecompany.com%3A7874/
    TYPE=USER@rim.net" />
 </push-message>
</pap>
```

The application can also specify additional (optional) elements and attributes in the control entity, as shown in the following example:

```
<pap product-name="My first Sample PAP Push Application">
 <push-message push-id="UniquePushID" ppg-notify-requested-to=
"someurl" deliver-after-timestamp="2009-10-16T12:00:00Z"
deliver-before-timestamp="2009-10-17T12:00:00Z" >
   <address address-value=
     "WAPPUSH=someuser%40somecompany.com%3A7874/
     TYPE=USER@rim.net" />
   <address address-value=
     "WAPPUSH=anotheruser%40somecompany.com%3A7874/
     TYPE=USER@rim.net" />
   <quality-of-service delivery-method="confirmed" />
 </push-message>
</pap>
```

The supported attributes for the `push-message` control entity elements are defined in Table 6.7.

Table 6.7 Elements and Attributes of a PAP Push Push-Message Control Entity

Element	Attributes
\<pap\>	**product-name:** Identifies the name of the application that submitted the push request.
\<push-message\>	**push-id**: A unique ID associated with this particular push request. The ID must be provided with any subsequent requests cancelling or requesting the status of the push request. **ppg-notify-requested-to**: Specifies the URL that will be triggered when the push request has been completed by MDS. The notification is from MDS directly to the push initiator via this URL; the URL does not need to point to the same system as the push initiator. **deliver-after-timestamp**: Specifies the date and time that the push must be delivered after. The value provided here must be in Coordinated Universal Time (UTC). Example: '2009-02-11T12:00:00Z' where the 'Z' at the end of the string indicates UTC. **deliver-before-timestamp: Content that has not been sent by this date is not delivered. The value provided here must be in Coordinated Universal Time (UTC). Example: '2009-02-11T11:00:00Z' where the 'Z' at the end of the string indicates UTC.**
\<address\>	address-value: Specifies the address of one or more destination devices. Address can be device PIN, email address, or BlackBerry group name. The complete address includes the destination port for the push content listener and a type parameter. This format is necessary to conform to WAP-PAP 2.0 addressing standards. Any nonalphanumeric characters in the email address portion mush be encoded into their hexadecimal values indicated by the percent sign (%) and the numeric values that follow. An @ is represented by %40 and a colon (:) by %3A.

Element	Attributes
<quality-of-service>	**delivery-method**: Specifies how the destination device provides an acknowledgment that the pushed content has been received and processed. Options: **unconfirmed**: Default: A message is sent from the device when the content is received. This option is supported on all BlackBerry Device Software versions. **confirmed**: A message is sent from the device once the content has been delivered to the destination application. This option is only supported on devices running Black-Berry Device Software version 4.0 and greater. preferconfirmed: (Compatibility mode) On devices running BlackBerry Device Software version 4.0 and greater, sends an acknowledgment message when the push content has been delivered to the destination application. For devices running BlackBerry Device Software earlier than version 4.0, sends an acknowledgment when content is received by the device.

Now that all the options for the PAP push-message have been discussed, let's look at an example of what this push message looks like when sent to MDS:

```
--jausyhstaositate
Content-Type: application/xml; charset=UTF-8

<?xml version="1.0"?>
<!DOCTYPE pap PUBLIC "-//WAPFORUM//DTD PAP 2.0//EN"
  "http://www.wapforum.org/DTD/pap_2.0.dtd"
  [<?wap-pap-ver supported-versions="2.0,1.*"?>]>
<pap>
  <push-message push-id="UniquePushID">
    <address address-value=
    "WAPPUSH=someuser%40somecompany.com%3A7874/
    TYPE=USER@rim.net" />
  </push-message>
</pap>
--jausyhstaositate
X-RIM-PUSH-CHANNEL-ID:Push1092817
X-RIM-PUSH-TITLE:My First Channel Push
X-RIM-PUSH-TYPE:Browser-Channel
X-RIM-PUSH-UNREAD-ICON-URL:
http://someserver.somecompany.com/icons/unread.png
X-RIM-PUSH-READ-ICON-URL:
http://someserver.somecompany.com/icons/read.png

<!DOCTYPE html PUBLIC "-//W3C//DTD XHTML 1.0 Transitional//EN"
"http://www.w3.org/TR/xhtml1/DTD/xhtml1-transitional.dtd">
<html xmlns="http://www.w3.org/1999/xhtml">
<head>
<meta http-equiv="Content-Type" content="text/html;
 charset=iso-8859-1" />
```

```
<title>Sample Channel Push</title>
</head>
<body>
<h1>Welcome</h1>
<p>What do you think of my cool new Channel Push?</p>
</body>
</html>
--jausyhstaositate-
```

The blank lines between sections of this request are deliberate. The format of multipart MIME messages requires Carriage Return/Line Feed combinations (CR/LF) between certain parts of the message. Refer to RFC 1341 for additional information on this requirement (www.w3.org/Protocols/rfc1341/7_2_Multipart.html).

When MDS receives and processes the push request, it returns an HTTP status code indicating whether the message was processed successfully. The server returns either a 200 (OK) or a 202 (Accepted); any other status code indicates that there was a problem with the push.

The server also returns an XML document in the body of the HTTP response containing information about the push. The push application should parse the XML to obtain additional information about the status of the push request. For a Browser Channel Push, the XML response looks like the following:

```
<?xml version="1.0" encoding="UTF-8" standalone="no"?>
<!DOCTYPE pap PUBLIC "-//WAPFORUM//DTD PAP 2.0//EN"
"http://www.wapforum.org/DTD/pap_2.0.dtd" [<?wap-pap-ver
supported-versions="2.0"?>]>
<pap product-name="Research In Motion Ltd. Mobile Data
➥Service">
  <push-response reply-time="2009-04-27T01:50:46Z"
sender-name="MDS" sender-address="http://127.0.0.1:8080/pap"
push-id="my_push_app_128852706442332210">
    <response-result code="1001" />
  </push-response>
</pap>
```

Table 6.8 lists the elements and attributes included in the response.

Table 6.8 Elements and Attributes of a PAP Push Push-Message Control Entity

Element	Attributes
Pap	Product-Name: Identifies the product name for the application that sent the response.
Push-response	**Reply-Time**: Indicates the date and time that the response was sent. **Sender-Name**: The short name of the server sending the response. **Sender-Address**: The URL for the server sending the response. **Push-ID:** The Push-ID included with the push request. This ID needs to be included with any subsequent requests sent to the server related to this push request.
Response-result	Code: Status code indicating the result of the push operation. The list of the most common status codes is provided in Table 6.9.

Table 6.9 PAP Response Status Codes

Status Code	Description
1000	The request succeeded.
1001	The request has been accepted for processing.
2000	The request is invalid (malformed syntax).
2001	The requested action is forbidden or the request was refused.
2002	The specified PIN is not recognized.
2003	Address not found.
2004	Push ID not found.
2005	Capabilities mismatch.
2006	Required capabilities not supported by client.
2007	Duplicate Push ID.
2008	Cancellation not possible.
3000	Internal server error.
3001	The server does not support the requested operation.
3002	Version not supported.
3003	The action is not possible because the message is no longer available.
3006	Transformation failure.
3007	Specified delivery method not possible.
4000	Service failure.
4001	Service unavailable.
5xxx	The mobile client aborted the operation.

The HTTP result code merely indicates that the request has been accepted, the push application must parse the resulting XML to understand what really happened with the push.

Checking the Status of a Push Request and Cancelling a Push Request

The PAP `statusquery-message` and `cancel-message` messages are formatted differently than push-message messages, because there isn't any pushed content included with the request. For both, the request contains just the XML control entity needed to define the parameters for the request, as shown in Figure 6.17.

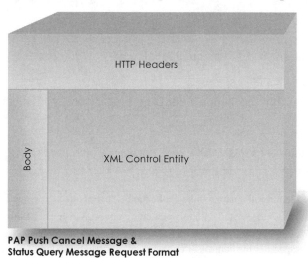

**PAP Push Cancel Message &
Status Query Message Request Format**

Figure 6.17 PAP Push cancel-message and statusquery-message format

When sending one of these messages, a push application must first set the Content-Type HTTP Request header to tell the receiving service the format of the HTTP POST:

```
Content-Type: application/xml
```

In Java, the header can be set using the following code:

```
HttpURLConnection mdsConn = (HttpURLConnection)
➥mdsUrl.openConnection();
mdsConn.setRequestProperty( "Content-Type", "application/xml"
➥);
```

Cancel-Message Control Entity Format The `cancel-message` control entity cancels a push request for all or some push destinations. This is used when the data being sent has changed since it was pushed, and the application does not want the original content delivered. A simple `cancel-message` control entity for a specific user is shown in the following example:

```
<pap>
 <cancel-message push-id="UniquePushID">
  <address address-value=
```

```
    "WAPPUSH=someuser%40somecompany.com%3A7874/
➥TYPE=USER@rim.net" />
</cancel-message>
</pap>
```

A `cancel-message` control entity that cancels a push for all destinations looks like this:

```
<pap>
 <cancel-message push-id="UniquePushID" />
</pap>
```

The supported attributes for the `cancel-message` control entity elements are defined in Table 6.10.

Table 6.10 Elements and Attributes of a PAP Push Cancel-Message Control Entity

Element	Attributes
<pap>	**roduct-name:** Identifies the name of the application that submitted the request.
<cancel-mes-sage>	**push-id:** A unique ID associated with this particular request. This must be the same ID used to submit the push.
<address>	**address-value**: Specifies the address of one or more destination devices. Use this attribute to define the list of destinations for which the push should be canceled. This allows you to cancel the push request only for certain destinations. If no addresses are included with the `cancel-message`, the push is cancelled for all recipients of the specified push. Address can be device PIN, email address, or BlackBerry group name. The complete address includes the destination port for the push content listener and a type parameter. The type parameter shown is necessary to conform to WAP-PAP 2.0 addressing standards. Any nonalphanumeric characters in the email address portion mush be encoded into their hexadecimal values indicated by the percent sign (%) and the numeric values that follow. An @ is represented by %40 and a colon (:) by %3A.

Now that all the options for the PAP `cancel-message` are covered, let's look at an example of what this push message looks like when sent to MDS:

```
<?xml version="1.0"?>
<!DOCTYPE pap PUBLIC "-//WAPFORUM//DTD PAP 2.0//EN"
  "http://www.wapforum.org/DTD/pap_2.0.dtd"
  [<?wap-pap-ver supported-versions="2.0,1.*"?>]>
<pap>
   <cancel-message push-id="UniquePushID">
     <address address-value=
      "WAPPUSH=someuser%40somecompany.com%3A7874/
      TYPE=USER@rim.net" />
   </cancel-message>
</pap>
```

statusquery-message Control Entity Format A `statusquery-message` control entity queries the status of a push request for one or all push destinations. A simple `statusquery-message` control entity is shown in the following example:

```
<pap>
 <statusquery-message push-id="UniquePushID">
  <address address-value=
     "WAPPUSH=someuser%40somecompany.com%3A7874/
➥TYPE=USER@rim.net" />
 </statusquery-message>
</pap>
```

The supported attributes for the `statusquery-message` control entity elements are defined in Table 6.11.

Table 6.11 Elements and Attributes of a PAP Push Statusquery-Message Control Entity

Element	Attributes
<pap>	**product-name:** Identifies the name of the application that submitted the request.
<statusquery-message>	**push-id:** The unique ID of the request for which you want to query the status. This must be the same ID used to submit the push.
<address>	**address-value:** Specifies the address of one or more destination devices. Use this attribute to define the list of destinations for which the request is being queried. Addresses can be device PIN, email address, or BlackBerry group name. The complete address includes the destination port for the push content listener and a type parameter. The type parameter shown is necessary to conform to WAP-PAP 2.0 addressing standards. If no addresses are included with the message, the status is returned for all recipients of the specified push. Any nonalphanumeric characters in the email address portion mush be encoded into their hexadecimal values indicated by the percent sign (%) and the numeric values that follow. An @ is represented by %40 and a colon (:) by %3A.

Now that all the options for the PAP statusquery-message message have been covered, let's look at an example of what this message would look like when sent to MDS:

```
<?xml version="1.0"?>
<!DOCTYPE pap PUBLIC "-//WAPFORUM//DTD PAP 2.0//EN"
   "http://www.wapforum.org/DTD/pap_2.0.dtd"
   [<?wap-pap-ver supported-versions="2.0,1.*"?>]>
<pap>
   <statusquery-message push-id="UniquePushID">
     <address address-value=
        "WAPPUSH=someuser%40somecompeny.com%3A7874/
        TYPE=USER@rim.net" />
   </statusquery-message>
</pap>
```

When MDS receives and processes the request, it returns an XML document that contains the status for the push request for the specified (or all) recipient devices. The push application can parse the document to determine the status of the push request for each recipient. Refer to the PAP standard for additional information about the elements and attributes included in the document.

6.7 Sample Push Applications

If you would rather work with a completed push application and tear into the source code, there are several sample push applications you can use. These samples are fully functional push applications designed to get functional push applications into customer's hands so they can immediately see the benefits rather than to help developers understand how to use push:

- **Emergency Contact List (ECL):** Designed to allow you to push a list of emergency contacts to multiple BlackBerry devices. You populate a database with contact information and run an application to perform the push. It was created to help several U.S. Government agencies deal with a natural disaster.

  Three versions of the application are available for download: IBM Lotus Domino, Microsoft .NET, and Java, and the source code is included with each. They include pushing to Browser Channel but also include the source code for a Java listener application. A free copy of the application can be downloaded from www.blackberry.com/go/ecl.

- **JDE Samples:** The BlackBerry Java development tools (described in Chapter 12, "Getting Started with the BlackBerry Java Development Tools") include the source code for several sample push applications. The tools can be downloaded from www.blackberry.com/developers.

With each application, keep in mind that they are free and you get what you pay for. If you want additional functionality in these applications, dig into the source code and make the changes you want.

6.8 Additional Resources

A complete listing of links to these resources is available online at www.bbdevfundamentals.com.

The best source for detailed information on how push works is the browser-development guides, located at http://na.blackberry.com/eng/support/docs/subcategories/?userType=21&category=BlackBerry+Browser.

Another interesting reference on push is the white paper, "Developing Browser Push Applications," located at www.blackberry.com/knowledgecenterpublic/livelink.exe?func=ll&objId=832210&objAction=browse&sort=name.

The BlackBerry Developer's knowledge base (www.blackberry.com/developers) has several interesting articles on push. For information on how to push data to a device only when it is in wireless coverage, search for article number DB-00519. For more information on how to push to multiple devices in the same push request, search for article number DB-00517. For additional information on the Push Notification format, search for article number DB-00395.

You can find a complete list of the HTTP Push Request Response codes in a BlackBerry Developer knowledge base article, "What Is: RIM Push Request Response Codes." To access this article, go to www.blackberry.com/developers and search for article DB-00502.

Research In Motion has published a series of developer labs: There is a lab exercise on Browser push, located at http://na.blackberry.com/eng/developers/resources/developer_labs.jsp#tab_tab_browser. It contains different versions of a sample push application and a brief set of instructions for how to use the samples.

For information on PAP, the WAP Forum publishes a PAP specification document at www.wapforum.org/what/technical_1_2.htm and www.openmobilealliance.org/tech/affiliates/LicenseAgreement.asp?DocName=/wap/wap-247-pap-20010429-a.pdf.

7

Pushing Data to External (BIS) Users

There are situations when an organization might want to make data available to customers or other interested parties external to their organization. Because these devices are not connected to a BlackBerry Enterprise Server (BES) controlled by the organization pushing the data, other push mechanisms were needed. The available options for consumer (non-Enterprise or BIS-connected) devices are Web Signals[1] and the BlackBerry Push APIs. Both options are only available to RIM ISV Alliance members.

Web Signals are similar to the Browser Channel push discussed in Chapter 6, "Pushing Data to Internal (BES) Users," although more limited in capability. A developer can select Web Signals if the content accessed by the end user was entirely web-based and the user only needed to be notified when new data was available.

The BlackBerry Push APIs are similar to using PAP to push data to a Java application running on the device. A developer can select the BlackBerry Push APIs when pushing data to a device where the data will be manipulated client-side by a push receiver application.

Both Web Signals and the BlackBerry Push APIs require specific procedures to be followed (and confirmed by the BlackBerry user) before any data can be pushed to a device. This chapter outlines the process a mobile user must follow to use one of these services and describes the process a developer follows to build an application that uses these services.

---

1. The service was originally called PushMarks, which is a more descriptive name for what the service does.

7.1 Web Signals

Web Signals is a service that provides organizations with the ability to push a URL for a target web page and two icons (a read icon and an unread icon) to a BlackBerry device. This is similar to the way Browser Channels work, but a limited version. As described in Chapter 6, with Browser Channels, developers have control over many of the options for the channel, but Web Signals can only push a URL and two icons to the destination device—nothing more. Where an application uses HTTP headers to deliver a Browser Channel parameters to a device, with Web Signals, it's done through parameters included in the push URL.

In practical use, a developer is likely not going to change the URL being pushed to a subscriber. If the Web Signal is architected correctly, the information that the backend system needs to render the correct information for the subscriber should be built into the URL. Rather than sending a custom URL with every push, craft the URL carefully (with all the information needed to generate custom content for the subscriber), and then just generate the content as needed on the backend, leaving the URL static. In this case, subsequent push requests merely notify the user that there is new data available for the Web Signal. The Web Signal can send different icons periodically, but it would likely not push a different URL every time.

Some examples of how this technology could be used are

- **Weather:** An organization providing weather forecasts could build a Web Signal and periodically push a weather icon to subscribers. The signal's icon would show graphically what the current weather conditions are for the registered location.

- **Stocks:** A financial management service could create a Web Signal that allowed a subscriber to register for the stocks they were interested in monitoring. It would deliver an icon that indicated by color or some other mechanism (such as a plus/minus or up/down arrow), indicating the current value of the stock being monitored.

- **News:** A news aggregator service could offer a Web Signal that allowed subscribers to define search terms they were interested in. The Web Signal would push an alert when any related items were published online. The icon for the Web Signal could be just the icon for the news service or could indicate visually for example the priority of the items in the current update (high, medium, or low, based on source or date).

To see a listing of the available Web Signals, go to RIM's Web Signals website at http://na.blackberry.com/eng/services/websignals/. Figure 7.1 shows the site.

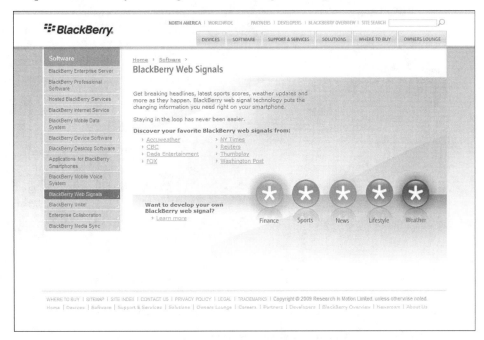

Figure 7.1 BlackBerry Web Signals website

7.1.1 How Web Signals Work

This section uses one of the public Web Signals to demonstrate how a Web Signal works from the end user's perspective. Subsequent sections discuss how each step would be performed by a push application.

The first Web Signal announced by RIM was a free weather service provided by AccuWeather (www.accuweather.com). Subscribers register for the Web Signal and identify the location for which they are interested in receiving weather reports. Figure 7.2 shows the AccuWeather Web Signals page.

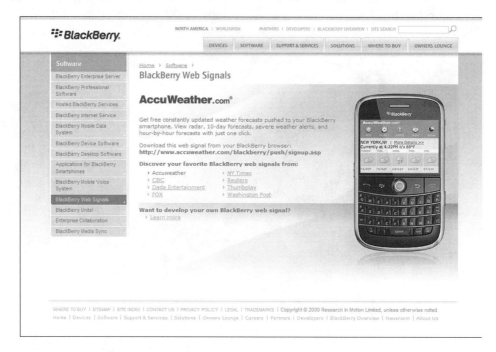

Figure 7.2   AccuWeather Web Signals page

To register for the Web Signal, the subscriber must access the signal's registration page at www.accuweather.com/blackberry/push/signup.asp from a BlackBerry device. Because Web Signals push data using the BIS service rather than the BES, the Internet browser (discussed in Chapter 8, "The BlackBerry Browser") must be used to access the registration site. On the site, the first thing the subscriber sees is a page describing the service and a link for them to use to subscribe to the service, as shown in Figure 7.3.

Figure 7.3   AccuWeather Web Signals information page

The subscriber is presented with information about the service and might need to agree to the terms and conditions for the service before he can continue. After the user indicates that he wants to use the service, he is directed to the RIM's website, where he must agree to RIM's terms, as shown in Figure 7.4.

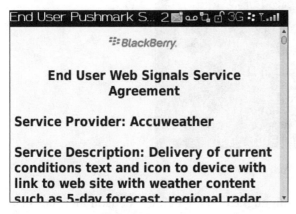

Figure 7.4   BlackBerry Web Signals service agreement page

After the subscriber accepts RIM's agreement, he is directed to a page where he can configure the location for which he will receive weather alerts, as shown in Figure 7.5.

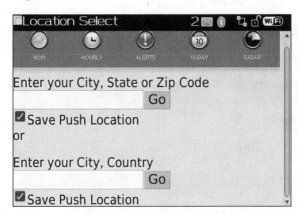

Figure 7.5   AccuWeather Web Signals preferences page

Some time after you complete the registration process, the first weather Web Signal is delivered to the device, as shown in Figure 7.6.

Figure 7.6   AccuWeather Web Signals icon

The AccuWeather icon is highlighted in the figure. The icon indicates that snow flurries are currently falling and the title of the Web Signal (shown at the bottom of the screen) indicates that the projected high temperature is 23 degrees and the projected low is 10 degrees.

When the Web Signal is opened, the browser opens and displays the weather report for the specified location, as shown in Figure 7.7.

Figure 7.7   AccuWeather Weather Forecast page

Having the weather pushed to a device periodically is useful. The subscriber can tell at a glance what the weather is without ever opening the application.

7.1.2 Signing Up for Web Signals

Before any data can be pushed through a Web Signal, an organization must first register with RIM to obtain the credentials needed to communicate with the RIM Push Infrastructure. Information on Web Signals and a link to the registration page is available at http://na.blackberry.com/eng/developers/browserdev/websignals.jsp. Click the Request a Web Signal for Your Application link to register for Web Signals. Most of the fields on the registration form should be self-explanatory; Table 7.1 lists the values that might require some explanation.

Table 7.1 Web Signals Registration Information

Registration Field	Value
Describe product or service Web Signals is to be used for	Briefly describe the push service. Be brief, but as clear as possible.
Source IP address for pushes	Identifies the IP address of the computer system that will perform pushes. The system must have a static, public IP address assigned to it.
How many subscribers will register to Web Signals (Total)	Used by RIM to help understand the projected audience for the Web Signal. This value, along with pushes per day (defined next), is likely to be used by RIM to define a quota in pushes per day to associate with this Web Signal. Be sure to accommodate for projected growth for your service when you set this number; you don't want to set it too low and constantly negotiate with RIM to increase the number of allowed subscribers.
Pushes per day, per subscriber	Used by RIM to help understand the scope of the Web Signal's projected daily activity to help estimate pricing for the service.
Which URL is used for a successful subscription	When the subscriber agrees to RIM's terms and conditions for the Web Signal, the user is redirected to this URL. Use this URL to allow subscriber to define preferences or settings for their subscription.
Which URL is used for an unsuccessful subscription	If the subscriber does not agree to RIM's terms and conditions for the Web Signal, he is redirected to the URL provided here. Use the page behind this URL to inform the subscriber that he will not receive the Web Signal because he did not accept all the terms of service or there was an error.
Which region will this service mainly be offered	This value is likely used to identify the RIM Network Operations Center (NOC) that is responsible for handling most of the load for this Web Signal.
Will the Web Signals have a specific enablement date	Identifies when the Web Signal service is expected to be available to subscribers.

After an organization submits the registration form and the Web Signal has been approved, RIM sends an email notification containing the information needed to be able to begin accepting subscriptions and delivering data to subscribers. Table 7.2 lists the credentials that are used by Web Signals.

Table 7.2 Web Signals Registration Credentials

Registration Item	Description
Service Identifier (SID)	A unique identifier for the Web Signal. The SID is not case sensitive and is restricted to both upper and lower alpha-numeric characters (A-z and 0-9), plus bang (!) and the dash (-) character. It cannot contain any spaces and can have a maximum length of 20 bytes. The ID is generated by RIM based on the information provided during registration.
Content Provider ID	A unique identifier for the Web Signal content provider. This value is not case sensitive and is restricted to both upper and lower alpha-numeric characters (A-z and 0-9), plus the !, -, @, ., and _ characters. It can contain internal spaces (leading and trailing spaces are removed) and can have a maximum length of 20 bytes.
SID Description	Assigned by RIM, contains a description of the Web Signal. The description can have a maximum length of 256 bytes and is not case sensitive. The value is restricted to both upper and lower alpha-numeric characters (A-z and 0-9), plus the !, -, @, ., and _ characters. It can contain internal spaces (leading and trailing spaces are removed) and have a maximum length of 20 bytes.
SID Password	The password associated with the Web Signal SID. Assignment of the password is managed by the Web Signals Coordinator. The password must be between 8 and 24 characters in length and can consist of any printable characters in the 7.bit ASCII character set with the exception of single quotation marks ('), double quotation marks ("), backslash (\), and spaces. Any leading or trailing spaces should be removed. To make the password more difficult to guess, the password cannot contain the word "password" or the signal's SID.
Quota per day	Assigned by RIM, this value specifies the maximum number of pushes allowed for this Web Signal per day.
Quota per hour	Assigned by RIM, this value specifies the maximum number of pushes allowed for this Web Signal per hour.
Priority	Specifies the priority associated with a push request. In the initial implementation of Web Signals, RIM has only exposed the option of Bulk Priority to content providers. Bulk Priority means that RIM only attempts to deliver the push content once and therefore delivery is not guaranteed.
Expiration Date	An expiration date might be assigned to your Web Signal by RIM. The expiration date is currently not used, but that could change in the future.

7.1.3 Building a Web Signal

After the Web Signal has been registered and RIM has provided the information needed to deliver content to devices, it's time to build the system to manage push subscriptions. The push application needs a database and a processing system to manage any interaction with subscribers and to manage delivery of the content to subscribers through the RIM Push Infrastructure. When it comes to pushing the content to subscribers, any sort of scheduled or triggered process works; the option selected depends on the nature of the service being provided and how often new data is available.

The database is used to maintain a table of subscriber information. At a minimum, each subscriber needs to have a unique ID assigned to them by the push application; through this ID, RIM can identify a push recipient for the Web Signal. An application can create its own IDs for subscribers, but it's probably easiest to just use the subscriber's email address because they're already unique by their very nature.

The database can store additional information, such as the subscriber's preferences for the service and any other information needed to manage delivery of content to the subscriber. If subscribers are being charged for the service, this is also probably where the application would maintain information about the subscriber's subscription expiration, renewal date, and so on.

Web Signal Domains

Throughout the remainder of the Web Signals discussion, the examples reference the Web Signals domain to use in the URLs the push application should use to interact with the system. The push application should use the appropriate domain, based on the location where the push is being performed. RIM has implemented regional Network Operations Centers worldwide, and through these regional centers, pushed content is processed. Because of this regionalization, the push application should use the correct domain information when submitting any request. RIM currently supports three regions; Table 7.3 describes the scope of each region and lists the appropriate domain to use for each.

Table 7.3 Web Signals Production Domain Regions

Region	Scope	Web Signals Domain
na	North America, Latin America, South America, and Africa	push.na.blackberry.com
eu	Europe	push.eu.blackberry.com
ap	Asia-Pacific	push.ap.blackberry.com

RIM allows developers to use a test domain when building and debugging their push applications. The application needs to transition to one of the production domains when ready to roll out a version of the service to subscribers. The domain information for the test domains is provided when partners are approved for the service.

Web Signal Subscriber Registration

The first step in the process to create a Web Signal is to implement the registration process required by RIM. There's no reason the push application can't expand on the concepts explained here, but at a minimum, the application must complete the steps outlined in this section.

As previously shown, the Web Signals registration process consists of several actions on the part of the subscriber. The subscriber first requests access to the service, and then confirms their acceptance of RIM's terms and conditions for Web Signals before they can participate.

The starting point for this is typically a link from a web page or even a registration form located on a website. On the push application's Web Signal's registration form, the application should gather whatever information is needed regarding the user—it could be as much as their contact information or as little as nothing. If the application will assign a unique Push User ID (PUID) to every subscriber, there might not be any information that needs to be collected. The email address is a useful value to collect from a subscriber. It's useful because it's a unique identifier that can be used to identify the subscriber, but also because it provides a reliable way to communicate with the subscriber outside of the Web Signal push process. For the AccuWeather service, the PUID is assigned automatically in the URL used to register for the service.

The subscriber can begin the registration process from a desktop browser, but it must be completed from the device browser, so the Web Signals infrastructure can obtain the information it needs to be able to correctly identify the subscriber's device. If a push application allows subscribers to register for the service using a desktop browser, the subscriber is sent a link they can activate from their BlackBerry browser on the device to complete the process.

The link that completes the process is the link to the End User Web Signals Service Agreement. The application does this by redirecting them to a special URL in the following format:

```
https://[push-domain]/mss/PM_subReg?puid=[puid-value]&
sid=[sid-value]
```

The values in brackets refer to values that need to be replaced with the specific options for the particular request, as defined in Table 7.4.

Table 7.4 Web Signals Registration URL Components

Parameter	Value
Push-Domain	The regional domain that the push recipient resides in. Refer to Table 7.3 for the possible values for this parameter.
PUID-Value	A unique Push User ID (PUID) that you have assigned to this subscriber. RIM uses this identifier to identify this subscriber for all subsequent activities related to the Web Signal.
SID-Value	The Service ID (SID) assigned to this Web Signal by RIM.

For example, if an application with a SID of MyWebSignal was registering a North American subscriber and assigned a Push User ID (PUID) of someuser@somedomain.com, the registration URL would look like this:

```
https://push.na.blackberry.com/mss/PM_subReg?
puid=someuser@somecompany.com&sid=mywebsignal
```

At this point, the mobile user is presented with the page shown in Figure 7.4. If the subscriber accepts the agreement, the Success URL provided during registration (described in Table 7.1) is triggered with the PUID appended to the end of the URL. For example, if, during registration, an organization provided a success URL of

```
https://ws1.someserver.com/s_registration
```

at the conclusion of a successful registration for the Web Signal, the following URL would be triggered by the RIM Push Infrastructure:

```
https://ws1.someserver.com/s_registration?
puid=someuser@somecompany.com
```

If the subscriber does not accept the agreement, the Failure URL provided during registration (described in Table 7.1) is triggered with the PUID appended to the end of the URL. For example, if during registration an organization provided a failure URL of

```
https://ws1.someserver.com/f_registration
```

at the conclusion of a failed registration for the Web Signal, the following URL would be triggered by the RIM Push Infrastructure:

```
https://ws1.someserver.com/f_registration?
puid=someuser@somecompany.com&rc=[response-code]
```

The options for response-code are defined in Table 7.5. When the registration process fails, it is the responsibility of the push application to process the response code and display a useful page for subscribers so they can tell what to do next.

Table 7.5 Web Signals Registration Response Codes

Response Code	Description
0100	A SID was not provided in the registration URL.
0101	The subscriber did not accept the terms of RIM's end user agreement.
0102	The PUID was not provided in the registration URL.
0103	The specified PUID has already been registered for the Web Signal associated with the SID.
0104	The SID included in the request has expired or is not valid.
0105	The PUID included in the request is not valid (contains invalid characters, is too long, and so on).
1000	The Web Signals service is currently not available.

Pushing Data to Subscribers

To push data to one or more subscribers, the push application must build an HTTP POST request that contains all the information needed for the push and deliver it to the same server described above. The POST URL contains all the information passed to the RIM Push Infrastructure; the body of the POST is not used to deliver any information.

The Push URL is formatted with the following information:

```
https://[push-domain]/mss/PM_submitJob?sid=[SID]
&pass=[SID-Password]&validfor=[expiration]&title=[title]
&readiconURL=[Read-Icon]&unreadiconURL=[Unread-Icon]&
contentURL=[Content-URL]&puids=[PUID-List]
```

HTTPS protects the contents of the SID and SID password when delivered in the URL.

Table 7.6 provides a description for each of the push URL parameters.

Table 7.6 Web Signal Push Request URL Parameters

Push Parameter	Description
Push-Domain	The regional domain that the push recipient resides in. Refer to Table 7.3 for the possible values for this parameter.
SID	The Service ID (SID) assigned to this Web Signal by RIM.
SID-Password	The password associated with the SID.

Push Parameter	Description
Expiration	The time, in seconds, that the push request is valid. The minimum value is 7,200 seconds (2 hours) and the maximum value is 86,400 seconds (24 hours).
Title	Specifies the title that appears on the BlackBerry Home Screen for the Web Signal. The push application uses this value to identify the Web Signal on the device, but can also use it to provide some information about the contents of the signal. (Refer to Figure 7.6 for an example of how this is used by AccuWeather in their service.) The title must be in English and can be of a maximum length of 256 bytes. Valid characters for the title are both upper and lower alphanumeric characters (A-z and 0-9), plus the !, -, @, ., and _ characters. It can contain internal spaces, but both leading and trailing spaces are removed.
Read-Icon	Specifies the absolute URL for the icon file (in PNG format) displayed after the mobile user opens the signal after a successful push. The icon file must conform to the standards for BlackBerry application icons and the URL accessible by external (outside the firewall) resources.
Unread-Icon	Specifies the absolute URL for the icon file (in PNG format) displayed until the mobile user has openeds the signal after a successful push. The icon file must conform to the standards for BlackBerry application icons and the URL accessible by external (outside the firewall) resources.
Content -URL	Specifies the absolute URL for content being pushed to the device. The URL provided here will be opened in the browser when the user opens the Web Signal. The URL can be up to 2,048 bytes in length.
PUID-List	Comma-separated list of subscriber PUIDs to which the content will be delivered. The push application can push to all subscribers for the SID by using ALL_USERS for this parameter.

The requirement for Icon URLs to be absolute URLs pointing to the icon file is based on the fact that the BlackBerry device retrieves the icons separately after the push request has been received. The BlackBerry Device Software has to know exactly where to locate the file and has to be able to access the file from outside the company's firewall. The icon URL can be up to 2,048 bytes in length. For information on how to create icons for the BlackBerry home screen, see Appendix B, "Creating Application Icons," located on the book's website at www.bbdevfundamentals.com.

Assuming email address is used for the PUID, to push content to a North American subscriber, the push URL would look like this:

```
https://push.na.blackberry.com/mss/PM_submitJob?
sid=mywebsignal&pass=mypassword&validfor=86400&title=
```

```
My%20Web%20Signal&readiconURL=http://ws.someserver.com/
read.png&unreadiconURL
=http://ws.someserver.com/unread.png&contentURL=
ws.someserver.com/signal&puid=someuser@somecompany.com
```

Because spaces are not valid characters in Internet URLs, the example used %20 to encode any spaces in the URL provided.

If the push application needed to push to more than one subscriber, the push URL would look like this:

```
https://push.na.blackberry.com/mss/PM_
submitJob?sid=mywebsignal
&pass=mypassword&validfor=86400&title=My%20Web%20Signal
&readiconURL=http://ws.someserver.com/read.png
&unreadiconURL=http://ws.someserver.com/unread.png
&contentURL=ws.someserver.com/signal
&puid=someuser@somecompany.com,anotheruser@abc.com,
yetanotheruser@def.com
```

If the push application wanted to push to all subscribers of the service, a sample push URL would be

```
https://push.na.blackberry.com/mss/PM_
submitJob?sid=mywebsignal
&pass=mypassword&validfor=86400&title=My%20Web%20Signal
&readiconURL=http://ws.someserver.com/read.png
&unreadiconURL=http://ws.someserver.com/unread.png
&contentURL=ws.someserver.com/signal&puid=ALL_USERS
```

For a successful push request, the push server responds with a JobID. The job ID identifies the push request for debugging purposes or if the content provider needs to open an investigation with RIM. For unsuccessful requests, the server returns rc=*some-value*, where *some-value* is one of the response codes listed in Table 7.7.

Table 7.7 Web Signals Subscriber Registration Response Codes

Response Code	Description
0500	A SID was not included in the push request URL.
0501	A SID password was not included in the push request URL.
0502	A PUID was not included in the push request URL.
0503	Authentication failed.
0504	A title was not included in the push request.
0505	A read icon URL was not included in the push request.
0506	An unread icon URL was not included in the push request.

Continues

Table 7.7 Web Signals Subscriber Registration Response Codes *(Continued)*

Response Code	Description
0507	A content URL was not included in the push request.
0508	The push expiration (`validFor`) parameter was not included in the push request.
0509	Invalid title.
0510	The read icon URL is not a valid URL.
0511	The unread icon URL is not a valid URL.
0512	The content URL is not a valid URL.
0513	The `validFor` parameter is not valid.
0514	The value for `validFor` parameter is not between the minimum and maximum allowed values (7200 < value < 86400).
0515	The SID has expired or is not active.
0516	The SID has exceeded the daily limit for push requests.
1000	The system is currently unavailable.

Requesting the Status of a Subscription

A Web Signal can check the subscription status for subscribers by using the following URL:

```
https://[push-domain]/mss/PM_sidUserStatus?sid=[SID]
&pass=[SID-Password]&puids=[PUID-List]
```

Table 7.8 provides a description for each of the status URL parameters.

Table 7.8 Web Signals Push Status Request Parameters

Push Parameter	Description
Push-Domain	The regional domain that the push recipient resides in. Refer to Table 7.3 for the possible values for this parameter.
SID	The Service ID (SID) assigned to this Web Signal by RIM.
SID-Password	The password associated with the SID.
PUID-List	Comma-separated list of subscriber PUIDs to which the content is delivered. The push application can query the status for all subscribers for the SID by using 'ALL_USERS' for this parameter.

If the request is successful, the server returns a comma-separated list of status values in the following format:

```
puid1=[status],puid2=[status],puid3=[status]
```

The possible [status] values are defined in Table 7.9.

Table 7.9 Web Signals Push Status Request Status Values

Status	Description
A	The user is subscribed to the Web Signal.
C	The user has been unsubscribed from the Web Signal by the content provider.
S	The user has unsubscribed from the Web Signal.
I	The PUID is invalid or does not exist.

If the system is unable to process the request, the server returns `rc=some-value`, where *some-value* is one of the response codes described in Table 7.10.

Table 7.10 Web Signals Status Request Response Codes

Response Code	Description
0300	A SID has not been provided.
0301	A SID password has not been provided.
0302	The request does not contain at least one PUID.
0303	Authentication failed.
0304	The specified SID does not have any subscribers.
0305	The SID has expired or is not active.
1000	The system is currently unavailable.

To check the status of a single North American PUID, the push application would use the following URL:

```
https://push.na.blackberry.com/mss/PM_siduersStatus?
sid=mywebsignal&pass=mypassword&puids=someuser@somecompany.com
```

A successful response from the server would look like the following, indicating that the user is an active (a) subscriber:

```
puid1=a
```

If the push application does not use email address for the PUID, but some internal ID (such as `PR0192JHSKJ`), the URL would look like this:

```
https://push.na.blackberry.com/mss/PM_siduersStatus?
sid=mywebsignal&pass=mypassword&puids=PR0192JHSKJ
```

To check the status of multiple push subscribers, the push application would use the following URL:

```
https://push.na.blackberry.com/mss/PM_siduersStatus?
sid=mywebsignal&pass=mypassword&puids=someuser@somecompany.com,
anotheruser@abc.com,yetanotheruser@def.com
```

A successful response from the server would look like the following, indicating that `puid1` and `puid2` are currently subscribed, but `puid3` has been unsubscribed:

```
puid1=a,puid2=a,puid3=s
```

To check the status of all push subscribers, the push application would use the following URL:

```
https://push.na.blackberry.com/mss/PM_siduersStatus?
sid=mywebsignal&pass=mypassword&puids=ALL_USERS
```

Unsubscribing from a Subscription

There are two ways a subscriber can unsubscribe from a Web Signal. The subscription service can provide them with a link on a website that allows them to unsubscribe, or the service can provide them with a link to the RIM's Web Signals site to see a list of all of their subscriptions and they can unsubscribe from there.

To give subscribers access to a link that allows them to see all of the Web Signals they're subscribed to, use the following URL:

```
http://[push-domain]/mss/PM_sublist
```

As an example, for a North American subscriber, you would use

```
http://push.na.blackberry.com/mss/PM_subList
```

Because RIM uses information provided by the device browser to identify the mobile user, the URL must be accessed from the user's BlackBerry device. Figure 7.8 shows the subscriptions list for the particular device.

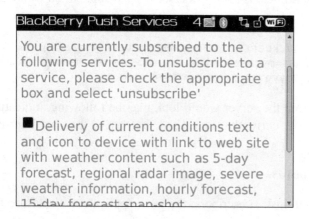

Figure 7.8   Web Signals subscription list page

 Note: The subscriber list URL is case sensitive. It must be entered exactly as shown to view the list of Web Signals to which the device is subscribed.

To unsubscribe a subscriber from a Web Signal, the push application must provide subscribers with the means to request to be removed from the subscriber list. After the push application receives the notification from the subscriber, it would submit the POST request to the RIM Push Infrastructure with the following URL:

```
https://[push-domain]/mss/PM_puidDereg?sid=[SID]&
pass=[SID-Password]&puids=[PUID-List]
```

More than one subscriber can be unsubscribed at a time, so it might be best to accept unsubscription requests from subscribers then submit the list to RIM in a batch periodically via the Deregistration request. Table 7.11 provides a description for each of the parameters for the unsubscribe URL.

Table 7.11 Web Signals Deregistration Request URL Parameters

Parameter	Description
Push-Domain	The regional domain that the push recipient resides in. Refer to Table 7.3 for the possible values for this parameter.
SID	The Service ID (SID) assigned to this Web Signal by RIM.
SID Password	The password associated with the SID.
PUID-List	Comma-separated list of subscriber PUIDs to which the content is delivered. The push application can unsubscribe all users by using ALL_USERS for this parameter.

For a North American subscriber to the `mywebsignal` Web Signal, the unsubscribe URL would be

```
https://push.na.blackberry.com/mss/PMpuidDereg
?sid=mywebsignal&pass=mypassword
&puids=someuser@somecompany.com
```

To unsubscribe a batch of subscribers, include each subscriber in a comma-separated list:

```
https://push.na.blackberry.com/mss/PM_puidDereg
?sid=mywebsignal&pass=mypassword
&puids=someuser@somecompany.com,
anotheruser@abc.com,yetanotheruser@def.com
```

All subscribers can be unsubscribed using the following URL:

```
https://push.na.blackberry.com/mss/PM_puidDereg
?sid=mywebsignal&pass=mypassword
&puids=ALL_USERS
```

It is hard to think of a reason why a subscription service would want to unsubscribe all users unless the service were being shut down or was in beta mode and wanted to start over, but the capability is there.

If the RIM push infrastructure is able to successfully process an unsubscription request, the server responds with a JobID—an ID that uniquely identified the request. The job ID identifies the push request for debugging purposes or if the content provider needs to open an investigation with RIM. If the request is unsuccessful, the system returns `rc=`*some-value*, where *some-value* is one of the response codes listed in Table 7.12.

Table 7.12 Web Signals Deregistration Request Response Codes

Response Code	Description
0400	A SID was not provided in the request.
0401	A SID Password was not provided in the request.
0402	The request does not contain at least one PUID.
0403	Authentication failed.
0404	The specified SID does not have any subscribers, so there is nobody to unsubscribe.
0405	The SID has expired or is not active.
1000	The system is currently unavailable.

7.2 BlackBerry Push APIs

The BlackBerry Push APIs allow a content provider to push content, any content as long as it conforms to RIM's guidelines, to any BlackBerry device. Instead of pushing to the browser like Web Signals does, the content is pushed to a custom Java application (a push listener) that the content provider creates and distributes to subscribers. The only requirements for the subscriber are that the target device is running BlackBerry Device Software version 4.2 or higher and that the device is provisioned on the BlackBerry Internet Service (BIS).

Some examples of how this technology can be used are

- **Professional sports team:** The organization could allow subscribers to subscribe to updates on the team status, rankings, and other topics. This avoids having the subscriber access a website to look up the information; it could be pushed to a Java application running on the device whenever new information was available.
- **Stocks:** A financial-management service could create a service that allowed subscribers to register for the stocks they are interested in and deliver performance reports on a regular basis to a device application.
- **News:** A news aggregator service could offer a service that allowed subscribers to define search terms they were interested in and push results when any related items were published online.

As a content provider, a push application can provide a service for free or can charge a subscription fee. The push application can push content daily, weekly, monthly, or on some trigger either controlled by the service or defined by subscribers. Push requests are limited to 8 kilobytes (8192 bytes) of payload per request and is constrained by any pushes per day (PPD) limitations RIM may impose on the service. There are also costs associated with the Push APIs. RIM charges organizations a setup fee and a usage fee for the service.

7.2.1 BlackBerry Push API Subscription Process

The BlackBerry Push APIs differ from Web Signals in that the registration process happens within a client-side Java application rather than through the browser. Figure 7.9 illustrates the registration process that must be completed before the application can receive data pushed from the content provider.

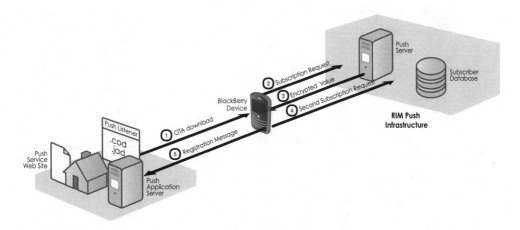

Figure 7.9   BlackBerry Push APIs push subscription process

The subscriber visits websites or an online application repository and downloads an application (1) designed to be the receiver for the pushed data the site offers. When the application is installed on the device and runs for the first time, a registration process begins that sends a request to the RIM Push Infrastructure requesting access to the service (2). The Push Infrastructure validates information in the registration request and returns an encrypted value to the application (3). The application submits a second registration request and includes the encrypted value it received from the first request (4). If everything is good with this second request, the RIM Push Infrastructure returns a status code, indicating the status of the registration process to the application. At this point, the client-side application should submit a registration to the push application (5), indicating that it's configured and ready to receive pushed content.

7.2.2 Signing Up to Use the BlackBerry Push APIs

Before the push application can push any data using the BlackBerry Push APIs, the application must be registered with RIM to obtain the credentials needed to push data to subscribers. Information on the Push APIs and a link to the registration page is available at http://na.blackberry.com/eng/developers/javaappdev/pushapi.jsp. The BlackBerry Push API website is shown in Figure 7.10.

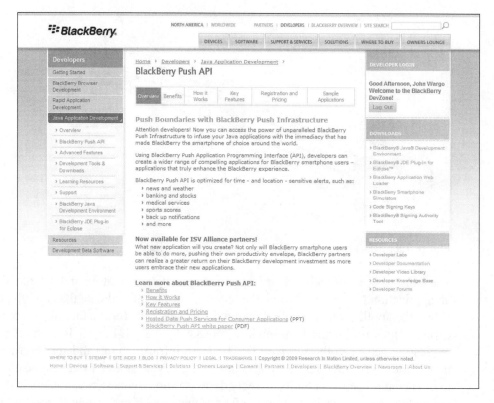

Figure 7.10 BlackBerry Push API developer website

When registering to use the BlackBerry Push APIs, the fields required for registration are basically the same as shown in Table 7.1. The listen port the push listener listens on is assigned by RIM after the services have been accepted into the program.

After the registration form has been submitted and the service has been approved, RIM sends a response containing the information the application needs to be able to begin accepting subscriptions and delivering data to subscribers.

7.2.3 Building an Application that Uses the BlackBerry Push APIs

Now, it's time to build the applications needed for your service. The service needs both a client application and a server-based application. RIM provides approved content providers with sample client and server applications that can be studied and used as a base for the applications created for a service. These applications can be downloaded from the BlackBerry Alliance Partner Portal: BlackBerry Universe for Partners.

The client application is called a Push Receiver or Push Listener Application and acts as a listener for the pushed data sent by the service. It registers as a Black-Berry startup application and listens on a particular port (defined when the service was registered) for data pushed to it from the RIM Push Infrastructure. When it receives a push, the application is responsible for processing the data, storing it somewhere so it can be rendered on the screen when the subscriber wants to view it, and (optionally) notifying the user that new data has arrived. If the data is important enough, the push receiver application could repeatedly notify the user until the application is opened. To learn how to build a push listener application in Java, analyze the source code provided to partners when they are approved to use the service or from the BlackBerry Emergency Contact List (ECL) sample application available at www.blackberry.com/go/ecl.

The server-based application is responsible for managing everything related to push subscriptions. The service needs a database and a processing system to manage interaction with subscribers and to manage delivery of the content to subscribers through the RIM Push Infrastructure. When it comes to pushing the content to subscribers, any sort of scheduled or triggered process works; the selected option depends on the nature of the service being provided and how often the data changes.

The database maintains a table of subscriber information. For each subscriber, the application needs to at least store the device PIN associated with the subscription. The database can store additional information, such as the subscriber's preferences for the service and any other information needed to manage delivery of content to the subscriber. If there is a fee to access the service, this is also probably where information about the subscriber's subscription expiration, renewal date, and so on would be stored.

BlackBerry Push API Domains

Throughout the remainder of this chapter, the examples make reference to the Push Infrastructure domain to use in the URLs used to interact with the system.

The Push application must use the appropriate domain based on where a subscriber is located in the world. RIM has implemented regional Network Operations Centers worldwide, and through these regional centers, data is pushed. Because of this regionalization, the push application must ensure it uses the correct domain information when submitting any request. RIM currently supports three regions; Table 7.13 describes the scope of each region and lists the appropriate domain to use for each.

Table 7.13 BlackBerry Push API Production Domain Regions

Region	Scope	Web Signals Domain
na	North America, Latin America, South America, and Africa	pushapi.na.blackberry.com
eu	Europe	pushapi.eu.blackberry.com
ap	Asia-Pacific	pushapi.ap.blackberry.com

For all BlackBerry Push APIs registration requests to the push infrastructure, HTTPS is used rather than HTTP. This allows the content provider credentials to be included in the POST without being visible to prying eyes.

Subscriber Registration

Registering a subscriber is a multipart process involving multiple connections to the RIM Push Infrastructure plus a connection to the content provider's backend push application. The registration process takes place inside the custom device-side Java application created for the service.

The first step in the process involves an initial registration with the RIM Push Infrastructure. In this step, the client-side application submits an HTTP POST request to the RIM Push Infrastructure using the following URL:

```
https://[push-domain]/mss/PD_subReg?serviceid=[service-ID]&
osversion=[device-OS-version]&model=[device-model]
```

The push parameters are described in Table 7.14.

Table 7.14 BlackBerry Push API Registration URL Parameters

Registration Parameter	Description
Push-Domain	The regional domain that the push recipient resides in. Refer to Table 7.13 for the possible values for this parameter.
Service-ID	The unique ID for the push service; this value is provided during registration for the service.
Device-OS-Version	The version of the BlackBerry Device Software platform used by the device requesting access to the service. The value can be retrieved by calling the `DeviceInfo.getPlatformVersion()` method in Java.
Device-Model	The model number for the device requesting access to the service. The value can be retrieved by calling the `DeviceInfo.getDeviceName()` method in Java.

For a North American subscriber on a BlackBerry 9000 running BlackBerry Device Software 4.6, the URL would look like this:

```
https://pushapi.na.blackberry.com/mss/PD_subReg?
serviceid=myAppName&osversion=4.0.0.183&model=9000
```

Note: You might notice that, although the device is running Device Software 4.6, the platform version is actually 4.0. This is not a bug; it's merely the way RIM handles versioning of the different components of the handheld operating system and device applications. The OS version is 4.0.x, while the BlackBerry Device Software version is 4.6.x.

The RIM Push infrastructure responds with a string of encrypted data that the application must return (within a certain timeframe) to the RIM Push infrastructure for the registration to complete successfully. The return URL looks similar to the previous URL except for the addition of the encrypted data to the end of the URL. The follow-up registration URL is performed via another HTTP POST and is in the following format, where *[Encrypted-Data]* is replaced with the content received from the server on the first request:

```
https://[push-domain]/mss/PD_subReg?serviceid=[service-ID]&
osversion=[device-OS-version]&model=[device-model]&
[Encrypted-data]
```

If the RIM Push Infrastructure returned `someencryptedvalue` from the initial registration request, the subsequent POST URL looks like this:

```
https://pushapi.na.blackberry.com/mss/PD_subReg?
serviceid=myAppName&osversion=4.0.0.183&model=9000&
someencryptedvalue
```

The RIM Push Infrastructure returns a response code, indicating the status of the request in the format of `rc=some-value`, where *some-value* is one of the response codes listed in Table 7.15.

Table 7.15 BlackBerry Push API Registration Result Codes

Response Code	Description
200	Registration successful.
10001	The BlackBerry device PIN is missing or invalid.
10002	The PSID is missing or invalid, or the push service is inactive.
10003	The specified PIN is already subscribed to the push service.
10004	The specified PIN has already been unsubscribed by the user.
10005	The specified PIN has already been unsubscribed by the content provider.
10006	The subscription status was set to an invalid value.
10007	The specified PIN could not be found.
10009	The subscription request failed because the access code was incorrect or an invalid number of parameters were passed.
10010	The subscription request failed because the content provider already has the maximum number of subscribers.
10011	A required parameter was missing from the subscription request.
-9999	A system error occurred.

If the application is pushing the same content to every subscriber, the registration process is complete; when the application wants to push data to subscribers, it uses the `push_all` attribute for the `<address>` element in the push request. Refer to the section, "Pushing Data to a Subscriber," for additional information on this option.

If the application is pushing customized content to every subscriber or wishes to push to individual device PINs, there's one more step in this process. After the push listener application has successfully registered with the RIM Push infrastructure, the client application must notify the backend push application that the particular device has completed the subscription process and is ready to receive pushed data. The format of this notification is not defined; the application submits the notification request in whatever manner and format suits the requirements for the application or the preference of the developer creating the application. All that matters is that the Push application has access to the registered device PIN because that is how the subscriber device is identified in push requests. If this step is not completed, a subscriber has a registered device that is never sent any data by the Push application.

For a sample application that demonstrates this registration process, refer to the sample application code provided by RIM.

Unsubscribing From the Push System

When a subscriber no longer wants to receive content from the service, the device-side application must notify the RIM Push Infrastructure and, if the listener application registered with the push application, notify the push application as well. To unsubscribe with the RIM Push Infrastructure, the following URL must be used:

```
https://[push-domain]/mss/PD_subDereg?serviceid=[service-ID]
```

The push parameters are described in Table 7.16.

Table 7.16 BlackBerry Push API Deregistration URL Parameters

Registration Parameter	Description
Push-Domain	The regional domain that the push recipient resides in. Refer to Table 7.13 for the possible values for this parameter.
Service-ID	The unique ID for the push service; this value will be provided during registration of the service.

For a North American subscriber, the POST URL would look something like this:

```
https://pushapi.na.blackberry.com/mss/PD_subDereg?
serviceid=myAppName
```

The RIM Push Infrastructure responds with a string of encrypted data that the application must return (within a certain timeframe) to the RIM Push Infrastructure for the deregistration process to complete successfully. The return URL looks similar to the previous one except for the addition of the encrypted data to the end of the URL. The follow-up registration URL is performed via another HTTP POST and is in the following format, where *[Encrypted-Data]* is replaced with the content received from the server on the first request:

```
https://[push-domain]/mss/PD_subDereg?serviceid=[service-ID]
&[Encrypted-data]
```

If the RIM Push Infrastructure returned `someencryptedvalue` from the initial registration request, the subsequent POST URL looks like this:

```
https://pushapi.na.blackberry.com/mss/PD_subDereg?
serviceid=myAppName&someencryptedvalue
```

The RIM Push Infrastructure returns a response code, indicating the status of the request in the format of `rc=some-value`, where *some-value* is one of the response codes listed in Table 7.17.

Table 7.17 BlackBerry Push API Deregistration Request Result Codes

Response Code	Description
200	The deregistration was completed successfully.
10004	The deregistration process has already been completed by the user.
10005	The deregistration process has already been completed by the service provider.

The device-side application is also responsible for notifying the content provider service of the unsubscribe using whatever mechanism is appropriate for the application.

This concludes the discussion of the push receiver, device-side application. The remaining activities related to the BlackBerry Push APIs are all performed from the backend push application.

Pushing Data to a Subscriber

When the push application is ready to send data to one or more subscriber devices, the application must submit a push request to the RIM Push Infrastructure containing the data being delivered. The push request is a simple PAP request, similar to the ones described in Chapter 6. Because the application merely pushes data to a destination application, the format of the push request is much simpler because many of the push parameters used for browser push described in Chapter 6 don't apply and are, therefore, not needed.

For a PAP push request, the message body is sent as a MIME multipart message, as shown in Figure 7.11. The MIME message contains an XML document that describes the push (the control entity), plus the data that is pushed to the destination device(s). The boundary shown in the figure is just a random series of characters that is not included anywhere as part of the message content. It distinguishes between the different parts of the MIME multipart message.

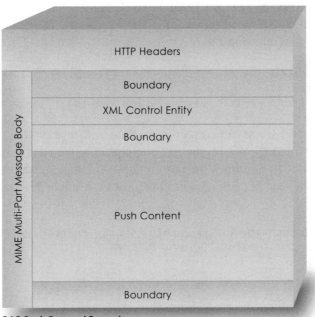

Figure 7.11   PAP Push Request Format

When pushing data to a subscriber, the push application uses the following URL for the HTTP POST request sent to the RIM Push infrastructure, where `push-domain` refers to one of domains listed in Table 7.13:

```
http://[push-domain]/mss/PD_pushRequest
```

The HTTP POST request must contain two header values: `Content-Type` and `Authorization`. The push application must set the `Content-Type` HTTP request header to tell the receiving service the format of the request. In the `Content-Type` header, the application can use any boundary string, as long as it is unique (not used anywhere else in the message). The following example just uses some random characters typed on the keyboard:

```
Content-Type:multipart/related; type="application/xml";
boundary=jausyhstaositate
```

In Java, the header can be set using the following code:

```
HttpURLConnection psConn =
  (HttpURLConnection)psUrl.openConnection();
psConn.setRequestProperty( "Content-Type", "multipart/related;
 type=\"application/xml\"; boundary=jausyhstaositate" );
```

The application delivers the credentials for the push request in the `Authorization` header. The credentials are passed as a Base64 encoded combination of the provider's push service ID (PSID) and password (PSID:Password). To perform this operation in Java, use the following code:

```
String auth = "Basic " + new BASE64Encoder().encode((psid + ":"
+ pswd).getBytes());
psConn.setRequestProperty("Authorization", auth);
```

After the request headers are set up correctly, it's time to format the content of the message. As shown in Figure 7.11, the first component of the push request is an XML control entity that describes the push request. A simple push-message control entity is shown here that defines a push request for a single device PIN:

```
<pap>
  <push-message push-id="UniquePushID" source-reference="PSID">
    <address address-value="DevicePIN1" />
  </push-message>
</pap>
```

To push to multiple devices, the push request would contain multiple address elements, as shown here:

```
<pap>
  <push-message push-id="UniquePushID" source-reference="PSID">
    <address address-value="DevicePIN1" />
    <address address-value="DevicePIN2" />
    <address address-value="DevicePIN3" />
  </push-message>
</pap>
```

If the application needed to push to all subscribers, the push request would look similar to the one shown here:

```
<pap>
  <push-message push-id="UniquePushID" source-reference="PSID">
    <address address-value="push_all" />
  </push-message>
</pap>
```

The application can specify additional (optional) elements/attributes in the control entity, as shown here:

```
<pap>
  <push-message push-id="UniquePushID" source-reference="PSID"
    ppg-notify-requested-to="someurl"
```

```
      deliver-before-timestamp="sometime" >
      <address address-value="DevicePIN1" />
      <quality-of-service delivery-method="confirmed" />
    </push-message>
  </pap>
```

The supported attributes for the `push-message` control entity elements are defined in Table 7.18.

Table 7.18 PAP Push Push-Message Control Entity Elements/Attributes

Element	Attributes
`<push-message>`	**push-id:** A unique ID associated with this particular push request. The ID must be provided with any subsequent requests cancelling or requesting the status of the push request. The push application is responsible for generating this unique push-id. This is a required attribute for the push-message element. **source-reference:** The unique Push Service ID (PSID) assigned to the push service when it was registered with the RIM Push Infrastructure. The ID identifies the push content provider, the push application, and the port number the data is delivered to on the destination device. This is a required attribute for the push-message element. **ppg-notify-requested-to:** Specifies the URL that is triggered by the RIM Push Infrastructure when the push request has been processed. This is an optional attribute for the push-message element; if no value is provided, the push application is not notified when the pushed content has been delivered. **deliver-before-timestamp:** Specifies the date and time that the push must be delivered before. If the content is not delivered by this date/time, it is discarded by the RIM Push Infrastructure. The value provided here must be in Coordinated Universal Time (UTC). Example: '2009-02-11T11:00:00Z' where the Z at the end of the string indicates UTC. This is a required attribute for the push-message element.
`<address>`	**address-value:** Specifies the address of one or more destination devices. The address-value must be a valid device PIN that has already been registered in the RIM Push Infrastructure for this push application. This is a required element for the push request.
`<quality-of-service>`	**delivery-method:** Specifies the delivery reliability for the push message. The attribute values defined below here define criteria for determining successful delivery of the push content. Possible values are: **confirmed:** A message is considered delivered when the content has been delivered to the destination application on the device. **notspecified, preferconfirmed, or unconfirmed:** A message is considered delivered when the content has been delivered to the destination device. In order to have a delivery notification sent to the push application, the request must also enable the ppg-notify-requested-to attribute defined above.

The following is an example of what the push message would look like when sent to the RIM Push Infrastructure:

```
--jausyhstaositate
Content-Type: application/xml; charset=UTF-8

<?xml version="1.0"?>
<!DOCTYPE pap PUBLIC "-//WAPFORUM//DTD PAP 1.0//EN"
  "http://www.openmobilealliance.org/DTD/pap_1.0.dtd"
  [<?wap-pap-ver supported-versions="2.0,1.*"?>]>
<pap>
  <push-message push-id="UniquePushID" source-reference="PSID">
    <address address-value="DevicePIN1" />
  </push-message>
</pap>
--jausyhstaositate
CouponTitle="Really Great Deal"
CouponExpiry="September 12, 2009"
CouponDetails="Act now to receive 20% off on all products"
--jausyhstaositate
```

When the RIM Push Infrastructure has processed the push request, it returns an HTTP result code and an XML document containing information about the results of the request. The server returns either a 200 (OK) or a 202 (Accepted); any other status code indicates that there was a problem with the push. A sample of the XML document returned is shown in the following example:

```
Content-Type: application/xml
<?xml version="1.0"?>
<!DOCTYPE pap PUBLIC "-//WAPFORUM//DTD PAP 1.0//EN"
"http://www.openmobilealliance.org/tech/DTD/pap_1.0.dtd">
<pap>
  <push-response push-id="UniquePushID"
    sender-address=" http://ws1.someserver.com/push_app"
    sender-name="RIM Push-Data"
    reply-time="2009-09-12T13:00:00Z">
    <response-result code="status-code" desc="Description" />
  </push-message>
</pap>
```

Table 7.19 lists the elements and the attribute values associated with each element in the response message.

Table 7.19 PAP Push Response Elements/Attributes

Element	Attribute/Description
<push-response>	**Push-ID:** The unique Push ID associated with the push request **Sender-Address:** The name of the server sending the response **Reply-Time:** The date and time (in Coordinated Universal Time [UTC]) that the reply was sent
<response-result>	**Code:** One of the status codes listed in Table 7.20 **Desc:** The description for the status code

Table 7.20 contains the list of PAP response status codes used by the push-response message and other response messages from the RIM push infrastructure.

Table 7.20 PAP Response Status Codes

Status Code	Description
1000	The request succeeded (the data reached the destination device).
1001	The request has been accepted for processing (the push request has been accepted by the server but has not been validated for delivery to the destination device).
2000	The request is invalid (malformed syntax).
2001	The requested action is forbidden or the request was refused.
2002	The specified PIN is not recognized.
2003	Address not found.
2004	The Push ID specified was not found for the provided push service.
2005	Capabilities mismatch.
2006	Required capabilities not supported by client.
2007	The Push ID specified is not unique.
2008	The Push ID was located, but cancellation is not possible.
3000	Internal server error.
3001	The server does not support the requested operation.
3002	Version not supported.
3003	The action is not possible because the message is no longer available.
3006	Transformation failure.
3007	Specified delivery method not possible.
4000	Service failure.
4001	Service unavailable.
4500	The request has expired.
4501	The request failed.
4502	The push request failed because the BlackBerry device listen port was closed.
5xxx	The mobile client aborted the operation.

The push application must parse the response message to determine the results of the push request. The application can also receive a notification when the data actually arrives on the device by specifying a URL in the `ppg-notify-requested-to` attribute of the push-message element in the push request.

When the application specifies a `ppg-notify-requested-to` URL in the push request, depending on the quality of service defined in the request, the RIM Push Infrastructure triggers the URL when the data arrives on the device (`quality-of-service` confirmed) or when the data arrives at the destination application (all other options for `quality-of-service`). Additionally, the PAP specification indicates that this mechanism can also notify when an error has occurred. Because there's no guarantee that the RIM Push Infrastructure is able to deliver the push, the push application should use this mechanism to detect whether the push was delivered and, if the data is important enough to the subscriber, push the data again if it wasn't delivered.

The response from the RIM Push Infrastructure is delivered in the form of a Result Notification Response message. This message is an XML control entity containing information about the status of the push message. The PAP specification indicates that the result message could be a MIME multipart message containing XML control entities from both the push service and the device, but RIM does not seem to support that option. A sample result notification message is shown here:

```
<?xml version="1.0"?>
<!DOCTYPE pap PUBLIC "-//WAPFORUM//DTD PAP 1.0//EN"
"http://www.openmobilealliance.org/
tech/DTD/pap_1.0.dtd">
<pap>
  <resultnotification-message push-id="UniquePushID"
    sender-address="https://www.pushdatadomain/paprequestpage"
    sender-name="RIM Push-Data"
    message-state="Message State"
    code="1000"
    desc="OK">
    <address address-value="DevicePIN1" />
  </resultnotification-message>
</pap>
```

Table 7.21 lists the possible elements and attributes for the response message.

Table 7.21 PAP Resultnotification-Message Elements/Attributes

Element	Attribute/Description
\<resultnotification-message\>	**Push-ID:** The unique Push ID associated with the push request. **Sender-Address:** The URL for the server sending the response. **Sender-Name:** A descriptive name for the response sender. **Message-State:** One of the Message state options listed in Table 7.22. **Code:** One of the status codes listed in Table 7.20. **Desc:** The description for the status code. **Received-Time:** The date and time (in Coordinated Universal Time [UTC]) when the push request was received by the RIM Push Infrastructure. **Event-Time:** The date and time (in Coordinated Universal Time [UTC]) that the push request reached its completed state.
\<Address\>	**Address-Value:** The device PIN for which the response is associated.
\<quality-of-service\>	**Delivery-Method:** If a quality of service element was included in the original push request, it is included in the response.

Table 7.22 contains the list of possible Message State attributes for the response message.

Table 7.22 Message State Options

Message State	Description
Aborted	The destination BlackBerry device aborted the delivery process.
Cancelled	The push message was cancelled by the content provider before the content was delivered to the destination BlackBerry device.
Delivered	The push content was successfully delivered to the destination BlackBerry device.
Expired	The push message reached its maximum age (defined in seconds in the push request) before it could be delivered by the RIM Push Infrastructure.
Pending	The push message is still in queue, it has not been processed yet.
Rejected	The push message was not accepted for delivery by the RIM Push Infrastructure.
Timeout	The delivery process timed-out.
Undeliverable	The push message cannot be delivered to the destination BlackBerry device.
Unknown	An unknown error has occurred.

The push application is responsible for responding to the RIM Push Infrastructure acknowledging receipt of the result notification. A sample `resultnotification-response` message is shown here:

```
<?xml version="1.0"?>
<!DOCTYPE pap PUBLIC "-//WAPFORUM//DTD PAP 1.0//EN"
"http://www.openmobilealliance.org/tech/DTD/pap_1.0.dtd">
<pap>
   <resultnotification-response push-id="UniquePushID"
     code="1000" desc="OK" />
</pap>
```

Table 7.23 contains a listing of the possible attributes for the `resultnotification-response` element in the Result Notification Response message.

Table 7.23 PAP Push Resultnotification-Response Element Attributes

Attribute	Description
Push-id	A unique ID associated with a particular push request. The push application is responsible for generating this unique push-id and including it with the initial push request.
Code	One of the result codes listed in Table 7.20.
Desc	The textual description for the result code.

It's likely that the push application would always respond with a `1000`, indicating that the response was received successfully.

Checking the Status of a Push Request and Cancelling a Push Request

The push application can check the status of a push request by sending a `statusquery-message` control entity to the RIM Push Infrastructure and can cancel a push request by sending a `cancel-message` control entity. Because neither request types contain content being pushed to devices, these requests use a slightly modified version of the push request. For both, the request sent to the RIM push infrastructure contains just the XML control entity needed to define the parameters for the request, as shown in Figure 7.12.

PAP Cancel Message & Status Query Message Request Format

Figure 7.12 PAP cancel-message and statusquery-message format

For these requests, the push application uses the same URL used when pushing data to a subscriber, where [push-domain] refers to one of the domains listed in Table 7.13:

```
https://[push-domain]/mss/PD_pushRequest
```

When sending one of these messages, the application must set the Content-Type HTTP request header to tell the receiving service the format of the request.

```
Content-Type: application/xml
```

In Java, the header can be set using the following code:

```
HttpURLConnection mdsConn =
(HttpURLConnection)mdsUrl.openConnection();
mdsConn.setRequestProperty( "Content-Type", "application/xml"
);
```

Note: The documentation does not indicate that the PSID or credentials are included with either the cancel-message and statusquery-message requests, but it would seem that the RIM Push Infrastructure would need to have those values to identify the push service being updated.

Cancelling a Push Request The cancel-message control entity cancels a push request for all or some push destinations. The RIM Push Infrastructure is only able to cancel a push request if the original push request is still pending (the data has not yet been delivered). A simple cancel-message control entity is shown here; in this example, the cancellation request being made only for a single device:

```
<pap>
  <cancel-message push-id="UniquePushID">
    <address address-value="DevicePIN1" />
  </cancel-message>
</pap>
```

A `cancel-message` control entity that cancels a push for all destinations would look like the following:

```
<pap>
  <cancel-message push-id="UniquePushID">
    <address />
  </cancel-message>
</pap>
```

The supported attributes for the `cancel-message` control entity elements are defined in Table 7.24.

Table 7.24 PAP Cancel-Message Control Entity Elements/Attributes

Element	Attributes
<cancel-message>	**push-id:** A unique ID associated with this particular request. This must be the same the ID used when the push request was submitted.
<address>	**address-value:** Specifies the device PIN for one or more destination devices. Use this attribute to define the list of destinations for which the push should be canceled. This allows you to cancel the push request only for certain destinations. If no addresses are included with the cancel-message, the push is cancelled for all recipients of the specified push.

A sample `cancel-message` request is shown here:

```
<?xml version="1.0"?>
<!DOCTYPE pap PUBLIC "-//WAPFORUM//DTD PAP 1.0//EN"
  "http://www.openmobilealliance.org/DTD/pap_1.0.dtd"
<pap>
  <cancel-message push-id="UniquePushID">
    <address address-value="DevicePIN1" />
  </cancel-message>
</pap>
```

When the RIM Push Infrastructure has processed the cancellation request, it returns an XML document that containing the results of the request, as shown here:

```
Content-Type: application/xml
<?xml version="1.0"?>
<!DOCTYPE pap PUBLIC "-//WAPFORUM//DTD PAP 1.0//EN"
"http://www.openmobilealliance.org/tech/DTD/pap_1.0.dtd">
<pap>
  <cancel-response push-id="UniquePushID">
    <cancel-result code="status-code" desc="Description" />
  </cancel-response>
</pap>
```

Table 7.25 lists the elements and the attribute values associated with each element in the `cancel-response` message.

Table 7.25 PAP Cancel-Response Elements/Attributes

Element	Attribute/Description
<cancel -response>	**Push-ID:** the unique Push ID associated with the push request.
<cancel -result>	**Code:** One of the status codes listed in Table 7.20. **Desc:** The description for the status code.

Checking the Status of a Push Request The push application can check the status of any push request by sending a request containing a `statusquery-message` control entity to the RIM Push Infrastructure. The request must be submitted within 24 hours of the original push request. A simple `statusquery-message` control entity is shown here:

```
<pap>
  <statusquery-message push-id="UniquePushID">
    <address address-value="DevicePIN" />
  </statusquery-message>
</pap>
```

The supported attributes for the `statusquery-message` control entity elements are defined in Table 7.26.

Table 7.26 PAP Statusquery-Message Control Entity Elements/Attributes

Element	Attributes
\<statusquery-message>	**push-id:** The unique ID of the request being queried for status. This must be same the ID used to submit the push.
\<address>	**address-value:** The device PIN for one or more destination devices.

To query the status for every device listed in the original push request, submit the `statusquery-message` control entity without specifying an `address` element, as shown in the following example:

```
<pap>
  <statusquery-message push-id="UniquePushID" />
</pap>
```

A sample `statusquery-message` request for a single device is shown here:

```
Content-Type: application/xml
<?xml version="1.0"?>
<!DOCTYPE pap PUBLIC "-//WAPFORUM//DTD PAP 1.0//EN"
"http://www.openmobilealliance.org/tech/DTD/pap_1.0.dtd">
<pap>
  <statusquery-message push-id="UniquePushID">
    <address address-value="DevicePIN1" />
  </statusquery-message>
</pap>
```

When the RIM Push Infrastructure has received and processed the request, it returns an XML document containing the status for the push request for the specified (or all) recipient devices, as shown here:

```
<?xml version="1.0"?>
<!DOCTYPE pap PUBLIC "-//WAPFORUM//DTD PAP 2.0//EN"
"http://www.openmobilealliance.org/tech/DTD/pap_2.0.dtd">
<pap>
  <statusquery-response push-id="UniquePushID">
    <statusquery-result
      event-time="2009-03-05T20:51:05Z"
      message-state="pending"
      code="status-code"
      desc="the request has been accepted for processing.">
      <address address-value="somePIN" />
    </statusquery-result>
  </statusquery-response>
</pap>
```

The supported attributes for the `statusquery-response` control entity elements are defined in Table 7.27.

Table 7.27 PAP Statusquery-Message Response Address Attributes

Address Attribute	Description/Possible Values
Message-state	One of the Message state options listed in Table 7.22.
code	A list of status codes is provided in Table 7.20.
Desc	A description of the result code.

7.3 Additional Resources

A complete listing of links to these resources is available online at www.bbdevfundamentals.com.

Detailed information and sample code for Web Signals can be found on the Web Signals website, located at http://na.blackberry.com/eng/services/websignals/.

Detailed information, documentation, and sample code for the BlackBerry Push APIs can be found on the Push API's website, located at http://na.blackberry.com/eng/developers/javaappdev/pushapi.jsp.

For information on how to create icons for the BlackBerry Home Screen, see Appendix B or the RIM developers knowledge base article, "How To: Create an Icon for an Application." The article is on the BlackBerry developer's website (www.blackberry.com/developers); search for knowledge base article DB-00126.

The complete WAP Forum (Open Mobile Alliance) PAP 2.2 Specification can be found at www.openmobilealliance.org/technical/release_program/docs/copyrightclick.aspx?pck=Push&file=V2_2-20071002-C/OMA-WAP-TS-PAP-V2_2-20071002-C.pdf.

8

The BlackBerry Browser

Y̲ou are assigned the task of building a new web-based product for BlackBerry devices. What do you do?

Depending on how much experience you have with BlackBerry or mobile development platform, you probably have at least two different thoughts about the project. You can think that, because the BlackBerry is a unique animal in the mobile space, there's probably some weird things you have to do to make your site work on the BlackBerry. You might also think that, because the BlackBerry is a standards-based platform and because the site should be using standard web technologies, you could probably just do all of your work using the technologies with which you're already familiar. If you read all the way through this book up to this point, you already know that the second option is the one that applies to you and your mobilization efforts.

The BlackBerry browser is a standards-based browser. Most of the technologies in use on the Web today are supported in the browser. There are some limitations in the BlackBerry browser, and there are some special considerations to keep in mind when building your site, but in general, the BlackBerry browser works just like most other mobile browsers. This chapter discusses the capabilities of the BlackBerry browser and some special things it can do that no other browser can.

8.1 The BlackBerry Browsers

On many BlackBerry devices, there can be several browser icons on the BlackBerry Home Screen. This is often confusing for users; they just don't know which one to use. If they are only signed up for the BIS service, they see two browser icons: one called the Internet Browser and another called the WAP browser. If they are activated against a BES, they see those two browser icons listed, plus another one called BlackBerry Browser. The difference between the browsers is the path the request takes to get to the server hosting the pages being viewed. A description of each of the browser paths is provided in the following list:

- **BlackBerry Browser:** Uses the MDS Connection Service (MDS-CS, which is described in Chapter 4, "The BlackBerry Mobile Data System (MDS)") to access web servers inside the corporate firewall. This option is only available when the device is activated against a BES.

- **Internet Browser:** Uses a wireless carrier's gateway to access websites using HTTP. This option is described in Chapter 3, "The Connected Black-Berry."

- **WAP Browser:** Uses a wireless carrier's WAP gateway to access sites using WAP. The gateway converts HTML pages to WML on the way to the browser. This option is described in Chapter 3.

- **Hotspot Browser:** Uses a device's Wi-Fi connection to connect to a local hotspot for connection to the Internet. This browser type adds an additional interface (and supporting software) to manage authenticating to a secure hotspot (subscription service in a public location, for example).

What appear to be multiple browsers is really a single browser rendering engine using different transports to access websites. Beginning with BlackBerry Device Software 4.2, RIM reduced the number of browser icons on the device. The BlackBerry browser and the Internet browser have been consolidated into a single icon called Browser, as shown in Figure 8.1 on the BlackBerry Bold smartphone.

Figure 8.1   Consolidated browser icon

On the Bold and many other devices, the WAP browser is still a separate icon, mostly because of the carrier's branding of the services it provides. The icon and the name associated with the browser are defined by the carrier and the currently selected theme on the device. Figure 8.2 shows the icon for the WAP browser; it's called MEdia Net on the AT&T network.

Figure 8.2 WAP browser icon

When RIM changed the way the browser icons worked, it also changed the way the user determined the path to use for web page requests. First, the BlackBerry user sets the default browser to use for all requests. If he later wants to access a site using a different path (switching from the Internet browser to the WAP browser), he must change the default browser type before requesting the new page.

The reason this is important is because, when a developer builds browser-based applications, the browser the application audience uses affects whether it can access the site or not. If the default browser is set to the Internet browser and the site is sitting inside the company firewall not visible to the outside world, the user won't be able to access the site using that browser. If the default browser is set to the BlackBerry browser and the site is on the public Internet, the user won't be able to access the site unless the BES Administrator allows external connections through MDS. When troubleshooting connection issues, one of the first questions to ask is which browser is being used.

To set the default browser, open the browser, press the menu button, and select Options from the menu that appears. Figure 8.3 shows the screen that appears in BlackBerry Device Software 4.6.

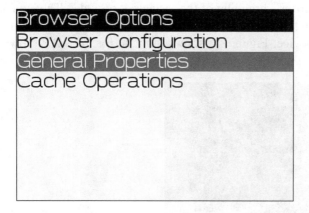

Figure 8.3   Browser Options

Select General Properties from the menu screen, and a screen similar to the one shown in Figure 8.4 is displayed. On this screen, the default browser can be set for the device and some other display-related options.

Figure 8.4   Browser General Options

If your user needs to access your site from a different browser than the one he has set as the default, he needs to switch to the browser the application requires, then access the application with that browser set as the default. After the application is opened, he clicks the menu button to add a bookmark for your application, as shown in Figure 8.5.

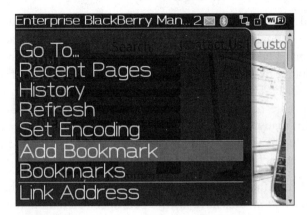

Figure 8.5 Browser Add Bookmark menu

In the dialog used to define parameters for the saved bookmark (shown in Figure 8.6), the user must ensure that the correct browser is selected (it should be by default) and click the Add button to save the bookmark. After the bookmark is saved, the user can return to Browser Options and reset the default browser to his preference.

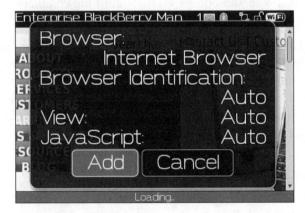

Figure 8.6 Add Bookmark dialog

Another option for this scenario is to build a Web Icon for your site. A Web Icon is a simple Java application that launches a particular browser to access a URL embedded in the program. Many companies use this method to put an icon for their portal or company website right on the device home screen for easy access.

This process becomes easier if the site can be accessed from any browser, but a particular browser should be used for regular access. In this case, the user can access the application from whichever browser is set as the default and change the browser used for subsequent access when saving the bookmark.

8.2 BlackBerry Browser Capabilities

As previously mentioned, the BlackBerry browser is a standards-based browser. The browser supports the standard web markup languages and many of the additional technologies that make up the World Wide Web. What's important to note, however, is that even though the BlackBerry supports these technologies, there might be limitations in RIM's implementation of the standards. In most cases, these limitations are not there because of any shortcomings of the BlackBerry platform, they're there, in many cases, because of a conscious decision by the BlackBerry product development teams to adopt certain technologies but, at the same time, minimize any impact on the mobile user.

The reason this is important is that the engineers at RIM who created the Black-Berry and designed subsequent models have always paid special attention to performance, battery life, and industry standards. Wherever RIM could adopt a standard, it did. On the browser capabilities, it adopted many of the standards in the market, but implemented, in some cases, a subset of features either because some of the features perhaps didn't apply to a mobile device or because of limitations due to processor capability, memory capacity, or the potential impact on performance and/or battery life. In many cases, a portion of a standard made it into the browser for a specific BlackBerry Device Software version, and then additional features were added in subsequent versions until the complete standard was implemented.

For every release of the BlackBerry Device Software, RIM publishes documentation for the browser that describes all the browser features provided in the release. The following sections highlight the different browser technologies and how they're implemented in the BlackBerry browser. Chapter 9, "Building BlackBerry Browser Applications," covers how to work within these limitations when building web applications for the BlackBerry.

8.2.1 Markup Languages

RIM has regularly kept up with the standards in browser technologies. The BlackBerry browser supports the following markup languages:

- Hypertext Markup Language (HTML) version 4.01
- Compact HTML (cHTML)
- XHTML Mobile Profile (XHTML-MP) (subset of XHTML 1.1)
- Wireless Markup Language (WML) version 1.3

The supported options and standard version vary depending on BlackBerry Device Software version.

This means that a developer can use any of the markup language standards for both the desktop and mobile browsers. Chapter 9 discusses how to select which markup language to use, but for now, realize that unless the application is targeting both mobile phones and smartphones, it should use standard HTML (or XHTML, if needed) to build sites. With this approach, developers can code once and run on both desktop and mobile platforms using a single markup language.

What's interesting about this is that the much ballyhooed iPhone does not support any mobile markup languages. Apple created a small desktop browser rather than a browser that supported both desktop and mobile markup languages. What this means for the user is that any of the special considerations a developer puts in place to accommodate a mobile browser (described in Chapter 9) don't work for the iPhone—that the full desktop version of any web application is downloaded across the wireless network at the cost of slow performance, reduced battery life, and increased network utilization.

8.2.2 HTML Framesets

Frames are supported in the BlackBerry browser, but it wasn't until BlackBerry Device Software 4.2 that it became useful and not until 4.6 did full support become available. In versions of the BlackBerry Device Software prior to 4.2, a developer could use frames, but not in an expected way. Until the 4.2 browser, when a page was opened that contained a Frameset definition, the user would see a screen similar to the one shown in Figure 8.7. The browser would prompt the user to select which portion of the frameset would load and only show that part of the page in the browser.

Figure 8.7 Frameset displayed in the 4.1 browser

What was wrong with this scenario was that the user would get to see the page, but not any of the navigation and other content shown in the other frames. Additionally, many systems blocked users from being able to access frame components directly, so they would lose the ability to create a bookmark that pointed to the content they wanted to see. Often, the names for the frames were non-descriptive and therefore useless for the user; users were unable to determine the frame to use based on the name.

With the 4.2 browser, the support for framesets got better. In 4.2 up to 4.6, the browser would display all the frames, but it would stack them on top of each other in order left to right, top to bottom. This means that if a user loaded the page shown in Figure 8.7 on the 4.2 browser, the browser would load the top frame, then the main frame followed by the right frame. The user would see the entire frameset, but not in the way the web designer planed.

Beginning with the BlackBerry 4.6 browser, RIM implemented a full feature set for HTML and associated technologies. This new and improved browser has the ability to function more like a desktop browser; it can render frames in the full layout intended by the developer who created the page.

8.2.3 HTML Tables

Tables have been around in the BlackBerry browser for a while. The documentation says they were implemented in BlackBerry Device Software 3.8,[1] but as described in Chapter 4, there were some limitations. It wasn't until BlackBerry Device Software 4.1 that tables really worked in the expected way. Chapter 9 covers tables and highlights some of the reasons why developers might not want to use them in their browser applications.

The most important thing to remember about tables from this chapter is that, although the BlackBerry browser supports them, they can be turned off in Browser Options. (In many versions, they're turned off by default.) So, even though the browser can support tables, they might just not work depending on how the user (or the BES administrator) has the browser configured. This was changed beginning with the browser in BlackBerry Device Software 4.6 and above; tables are no longer a configuration option, they are enabled by default within the browser.

---

1. The BlackBerry Browser Guides and HTML Guides contradict each other when it comes to tables. The browser guide says tables were added with BlackBerry Device Software 3.8 and the HTML guide says they made it into BlackBerry Device Software 4.0. Actually, they're both correct—the issue is related to how RIM named the versions. BlackBerry Device Software 3.8 launched before BES 4.0 but then RIM started calling it BlackBerry Device Software 4.0 after the launch.

8.2.4 Cascading Style Sheets (CSS)

Cascading Style Sheets (CSS) have been supported in the BlackBerry browser for some time. The browser supports both the World Wide Web Consortium (W3C) CSS standard and WAP CSS.

There are two important things to remember about style sheets from this chapter. First, although the BlackBerry browser supports them, they can be turned off in Browser Options. (In many versions, they're turned off by default.) Even though the browser can support style sheets, they might just not work depending on how the user (or the BES administrator) has the browser configured. This was changed beginning with the browser in BlackBerry Device Software 4.6 and above; style sheets are no longer a configuration option, they are enabled by default within the browser.

Second, even though style sheets give the browser developer all sorts of great capabilities, it doesn't mean all of them make sense on a device with a screen resolution of 240 by 260 pixels (like the BlackBerry Pearl 8100 smartphone). (See the sidebar for additional information about this limitation.)

Example of an Inappropriate Use of Style Sheets

I was working with a local regional bank to help them figure out a problem with their portal. The bank had created a portal using Domino and WebSphere, and they were having trouble getting it to work correctly on the BlackBerry browser. As you'll see later in this chapter, I'm not a big fan of looking for the problem in the BlackBerry browser first; I think the source of most BlackBerry rendering problems can actually be located somewhere else. Nevertheless, I compared the bank's portal in the desktop browser with the same page on the BlackBerry browser.

As illustrated in Figure 8.8, the desktop version showed a header and some navigation elements on the top and some deeper navigation on the left side of the page. The remainder of the page was dedicated to content with an image taking up the lower-right corner of the page. However, the BlackBerry browser contained just the image, nothing else.

The bank used CSS to lay out the different parts of the page and position the graphic in the lower-right corner. The BlackBerry browser had dutifully rendered the top navigation, side navigation, and all the remaining content of the page, then positioned the image in the lower-right corner of the page as instructed. But, because the image just happened to be about the same size as the BlackBerry screen (320 pixels by 240 pixels), when viewed on a BlackBerry 8800 or 8300, all you saw was the image, it covered the entire page's other content.

It didn't take me long to explain this to the customer, who quickly implemented a fix for the problem by removing the image for the mobile version. The moral of this story is that just because you can use CSS to set the absolute or relative position of a page element doesn't mean you should on a mobile device, because the screens are so small.

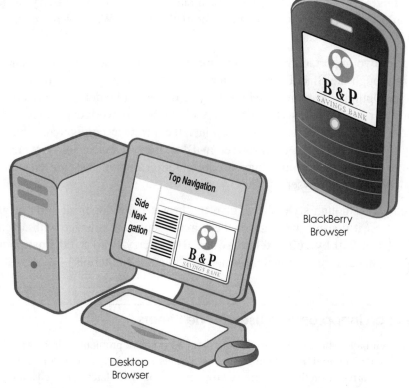

Figure 8.8   Sample portal pages

8.2.5 JavaScript

The BlackBerry browser has supported JavaScript for some time. In general, older devices support JavaScript 1.3 plus a subset of the functionality provided in JavaScript 1.4 and 1.5. With BlackBerry Device Software 4.6, RIM added full support for JavaScript 1.5.

Until BlackBerry Device Software 4.6, the JavaScript Document Object Model (DOM), the in memory, object-based representation of the browser page being displayed, was read-only. Developers could read the page's objects via the DOM, but couldn't make any changes to it. Prior to BlackBerry Device Software 4.6, even though a page contained JavaScript, anything that ran while the user interacted with the page did not execute. The browser would draw the page and stop executing any script in the background. Event-driven script behind buttons and drop-down lists would still execute, but not much else. What this did was prevent the BlackBerry browser from rendering much of the dynamic content available on the Web, including JavaScript menu systems, hovers, mouseovers, and so on.

With BlackBerry Device Software 4.6 and beyond, RIM has implemented a full-service DOM (read-write). Developers can use JavaScript and the DOM to manipulate the contents of the page in real time. This opened up all sorts of capabilities to the mobile user including dynamic menus, interactive web pages and more.

This is covered in detail in the next chapter, but there are two important things to remember about JavaScript from this chapter. First, although the BlackBerry browser supports the technology, it is turned off by default and, if set to on by an administrator, could still be turned off by the user in Browser Options. Second, even though JavaScript provides all sorts of cool capabilities for a web page, it's still a mobile browser, and developers will want to send as little data across the wireless network as possible. The best practice is to use JavaScript only where it adds value to the application such as client-side email address validation.

All this changes, of course, with the high-speed third generation (3G) wireless networks and faster processors on the Bold, Storm, and beyond, but it never hurts to pay attention to how an application affects download and render times for users. A lightweight site always loads faster than a heavy one, no matter what the network speed is.

8.2.6 Asynchronous JavaScript and XML (AJAX)

Beginning with BlackBerry Device Software 4.6, the BlackBerry browser implemented support for AJAX. There was not a way to do this before 4.6 because the JavaScript DOM was read-only and the implementation of JavaScript didn't provide support for the XMLHttpRequest object.

8.2.7 Dynamic Content

One of the questions developers ask is, "Does the BlackBerry browser support X?," where X could be Active Server Pages (ASP), Java Server Pages (JSP),

PHP Hypertext Preprocessor (PHP), or any other dynamic content generators for the Web. Each of those technologies is a backend server technology used to generate web content using a scripting language embedded in the page. The server loads the page, processes the script, and replaces it with the output from the script and sends the resulting HTML (or whatever) to the destination browser. Considering how this works, there's really not anything the BlackBerry needs to do in the process. Because the output of the process is content the device will be rendering, as long as the output is in a markup language the BlackBerry browser supports, it will work just fine.

8.2.8   Java Applets

Even though the BlackBerry device is a Java device, it cannot run Java applets. The BlackBerry browser does not offer the framework/container for these applets to run under. If a browser application requires the use of Java applets, it cannot run on a BlackBerry.

Java Applets Versus Java Applications

It's important to draw a clear distinction between Java applets and Java applications. Many developers I worked with would use the two terms interchangeably and they're really different things.

Java applications are just that: full grown applications written in the Java language. Java applets, on the other hand, are also written in Java, but they run inside the context of a browser. They're designed to be small gadgets that originally provided functionality that just wasn't available in the browser. The capabilities of web browsers has dramatically improved so applets are not used much on the Internet anymore; their functionality has been replaced by JavaScript and other technologies.

8.2.9   ActiveX Controls

ActiveX Controls are a proprietary type of application plug-in that only runs in Microsoft Internet Explorer. ActiveX Controls are not supported in the BlackBerry browser. If a browser application requires the use of ActiveX Controls, it will not run on a BlackBerry.

8.2.10   Adobe Flash

As of this writing, Adobe Flash it is not supported on BlackBerry devices. Instead, RIM offers the Plazmic Content Development kit (described in Chapter

17, "Using Additional BlackBerry Application Technologies"), which allows developers to create rich media files for BlackBerry and includes a Flash-to-Plazmic conversion utility that can convert simple Flash content for display on BlackBerry devices.

8.2.11 Streaming Media

The ability to stream media files (audio and video) is controlled by both server-side and client-side components. The BlackBerry browser can play these files; which file formats are supported is a function of the version of the BlackBerry Device Software the device is running and the BES or Carrier Internet Gateway being used. The gateway (either BES or the carrier's gateway) processes media files on the way to the browser to convert them or optimize them for playback on the BlackBerry.

Refer to the BlackBerry Device Software or BES software documentation to determine if the media file the application delivers is supported. In general, the device can play most popular file formats, but it's best to check before committing to a particular format for an application.

For a complete list of the supported media types, refer to the BlackBerry knowledge base article KB05482, "Media Types Supported on the BlackBerry Smartphone." To access the article, go to www.blackberry.com and access the Support and Services area of the site. Search for Media Types to locate the article.[2]

8.2.12 Browser Authentication

For authentication, the BlackBerry browser works just like the desktop browser. If a web application requires authentication, the browser prompts the user for credentials and passes them on to the web server for authentication. The BlackBerry browser supports industry standard authentication mechanisms: HTTP Basic Authentication, Lightweight Third-Party Authentication (LTPA), NT LAN Manager (NTLM), and Kerberos.™

What's missing today but expected in some future release of the BES is the ability for a user to authenticate against a Windows Domain (Active Directory for example) and have those credentials validate against any other server in the domain without user interaction. With desktop browsers, after users log into Windows, their domain credentials get them into almost any server they need. With the BlackBerry browser, users would have to authenticate against each

---

2. For some reason, you can't search directly for KB articles.

server as they switch from application to application unless special Single Sign-On (SSO) systems are put into place.

Prior to BlackBerry Device Software 4.2, a user could configure the browser to cache both the username and password. With this version, users can only save their user name; they must provide their password every time they access a restricted site. This feature was likely implemented (or removed, depending on how you look at things) for one or more new security certifications RIM received for the platform.

There is a way to allow users to access internal systems without direct authentication (prompting for user name and password). As mentioned in Chapter 4, administrators can configure MDS to include the device PIN and/or email address in the HTTP Headers for a request. An application can retrieve one of these values and perform a reverse lookup to validate that the user (or at least the user's device) has the right to access the system.

8.2.13   RSS Feeds

Beginning with BlackBerry Device Software 4.2, the BlackBerry Browser added support for web feed formats:

- RSS 0.9, 1.0, and 2.0
- Atom

The browser lists feed items by date and marks unread items in bold. When the user opens an item, the feed content appears in a new page. The BlackBerry Browser does not act as an aggregator, and it does not store web feed content (except as cached content after it has been opened). Because the feed is just a URL, users can add web feeds to the bookmark list the same way they add any other bookmark.

With BlackBerry Device Software 4.2.2 or later, the BlackBerry Browser added support for RSS enclosures, designed to provide users with access to media files that are located at the URLs specified in the `<enclosure>` tag. In earlier versions, these links were ignored by the browser. To access the media file, users can click the link in the web feed content.

Troubleshooting Browser Problems

Troubleshooting browser problems is covered in Chapter 10, "Testing/Debugging BlackBerry Browser Applications," but it makes sense to cover some of this topic now. Knowing what has already been discussed about the BlackBerry browser, what are the chances that problems with a web page rendering are caused by the BlackBerry browser? Remember, the BlackBerry browser is a standards-based browser—it renders whatever it is told to render. It might not look right, but if a page contains HTML, XHTML, cHTML, WML, whatever supported markup language is used, the BlackBerry browser renders it.

In every case where I've been brought in to look at a problem with a web page rendering on the BlackBerry browser, the problem has been related to the technology used to build the page or something the web server does to the data before sending it to the browser. If the site relies on Java applets or ActiveX Controls, it's just not going to work on the BlackBerry. If the site relies on a heavy implementation of JavaScript to make the application dance, it's not going to run properly on any device running BlackBerry Device Software prior to 4.6; the read-only DOM available to JavaScript won't allow it to run dynamic web applications.

In many cases, the web server detects that the user agent (through the USER-AGENT header value) is not from a recognizable browser. Because it doesn't recognize the browser, in many cases, it just sends nothing or sends an error message. In either case, the BlackBerry browser is blamed and that's not a fair assessment.

When you troubleshoot a problem on the BlackBerry browser, one of the first things you should do is look at the page source being sent to the browser. When you see a blank page or missing or extra content on your page, look at the source to see what's actually being returned by the web server before you try to blame it on the BlackBerry. To view the page source—and I know this tip is going to make it worth the purchase price of the book—hold the device's ALT key and type 'rbvs' before releasing the Alt key. The BlackBerry browser opens a viewer and shows you the source code for the page it's rendering.

By the way, if you're looking for an easy way to remember this key combination, I'm pretty sure it stands for RIM BlackBerry View Source. Enjoy!

8.3 Special Features of the BlackBerry Browser

This section describes the special things that the BlackBerry browser does that are unique to the BlackBerry platform.

8.3.1 Receiving Pushed Data

Just in case you jumped to this chapter without reading from the beginning of the book, the BlackBerry browser can receive data pushed to it from an application running on another system. For more information on this topic, read Chapters 5, 6, and 7.

8.3.2   Opening Links to Files in the Browser

When a user clicks a link to a file from the desktop browser, the server determines whether it can support the file type. If the file type is recognized, the server processes and delivers it to the device. If the browser indicates it can support the file type (through the contents of the HTTP Accepts header value), the file is delivered to the browser for processing.

In the BlackBerry browser, it's handled differently. When a BlackBerry user clicks a link to a file on a website, the BlackBerry Attachment Service renders the file and streams it to the device for viewing. The file doesn't actually reside on the device; the content from the file is streamed to a viewer on the BlackBerry device. If the attachment service doesn't know how to render the file, an error is sent to the browser.

By design, the BlackBerry device doesn't usually work directly with attachments. Only more recent versions of the BlackBerry Device Software (4.3 and beyond) allow attachments to be downloaded directly to the device. When users open a file in the browser, they can choose to download the file or open it in the file viewer application. With the file open in the file viewer, the user can press the menu button and select Download File to save a copy of the file on the device, as shown in Figure 8.9. The browser prompts for the location to save the file and proceeds with the download to the specified location.

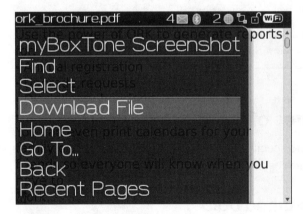

Figure 8.9   Download file

Beginning with BlackBerry Device Software 4.5, RIM licensed software products by DataViz called *Documents To Go*®, which allows users to create and edit Microsoft Office files on the device. When a supported file is opened in the browser, the user can choose to open it for editing in Documents To Go or open it in the BlackBerry file viewer.

8.3.3 Browser Identification

Experienced BlackBerry users might have noticed the setting in Browser Options called Browser Identification, shown in Figure 8.10 (called Browser Emulation in older browsers). Many people incorrectly think it's a way to make the browser emulate a different browser. What it really does is change the way the BlackBerry identifies itself to a web server. The possible values for this setting are BlackBerry, Firefox, and Internet Explorer.

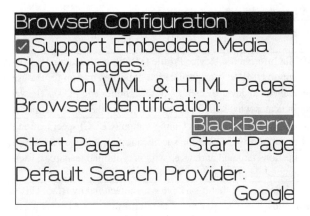

Figure 8.10   Browser Identification

When any browser submits a request to a web server, it delivers with the request a series of request header values (or properties) that the server can use to determine things about the client requesting a resource. There's a particular header value called USER-AGENT that identifies the agent application (the browser) making the request.

By default, the BlackBerry browser populates this header value with the following, where the values in brackets represent values that vary from device to device:

```
BlackBerry[Model Number]/[BlackBerry Device Software Version]
Profile/[MIDP Profile] Configuration/[CLDC Version] VendorID/
[Vendor ID]
```

Each value is described in Table 8.1. For the BlackBerry Bold smartphone, the USER-AGENT header value contains:

```
BlackBerry9000/4.6.0.92 Profile/MIDP-2.0 Configuration/CLDC-
1.1 VendorID/1
```

Table 8.1 BlackBerry User Agent Parameters

Value	Description
Model Number	The model number (numeric only, no product names, like 'Bold' or 'Storm') for the device.
BlackBerry Device Software Version	The BlackBerry Device Software version running on the device.
MIDP Profile	The Mobile Information Device Profile (MIDP) specification version the device supports. MIDP is a specification published by Sun for the use of Java on embedded devices, such as mobile phones and PDAs. The version number indicates what MIDP related capabilities the device supports.
CLDC Version	The Connected Limited Device Configuration (CLDC) specification that the device supports. CLDC is the specification for a framework for Java ME applications targeted at devices with very limited resources, such as pagers and mobile phones.
Vendor ID	Usually, '1' indicating that it's a device manufactured by RIM. This value is here to allow a server application to tell the difference between a device manufactured by RIM and a licensed device manufactured by another vendor under the BlackBerry Built-In® program.

When the value for Browser Identification is changed on a BlackBerry Bold smartphone, a different value is set for USER-AGENT, based on which identification has been selected.

For Firefox, it looks like this:

```
Mozilla/5.0 (Windows: U; Windows NT 5.1; rv:1.8.1.14) Gecko/
20080404 Firefox/2.0.0.14
```

For Internet Explorer, it looks like this:

```
Mozilla/4.0 (compatible; MDIS 6.0; Windows NT 5.1; SV1; .NET CLR
2.0.50727)
```

Header Dump Application

To help test this and see what header values are delivered by the BlackBerry browser, I built a Domino application that parses all the header values and returns them to the browser. The application is shown in Figure 8.11, and the source code is available on the book's website (www.bbdevfundamentals.com), if you want to run something like this for yourself. Domino stores the USER-AGENT value in a field called HTTP_USER_AGENT, so that is why the figure looks different than expected.

You can easily do the same thing in JSP, ASP, PHP, or another web server technology.

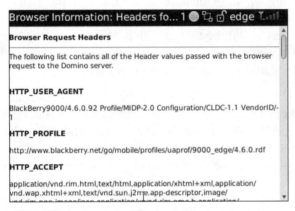

Figure 8.11 Browser Header values

The first question most users ask is, "Why would someone want to change the browser identification?" Many websites or web applications use the value in USER-AGENT to determine what content should be delivered to the agent. In some cases, the site might only support Microsoft Internet Explorer (IE); when a user tries to access the site from the BlackBerry browser, even though it would likely work (it is a standard browser after all), the server would return an error and the user wouldn't be able to access the site. By switching the browser identification to Internet Explorer, the server no longer thinks the request agent is a BlackBerry and delivers the site as expected. Don't forget that the BlackBerry browser doesn't support ActiveX controls, so a site using ActiveX and other proprietary Microsoft features won't work on a BlackBerry.

Where this backfires is for sites that have been optimized for the mobile browser. A site optimized for a mobile device (described in Chapter 9) won't look right when you turn off the mechanism the web server uses to determine if the agent is a mobile device. Most commercial websites and many enterprise web applications detect whether the agent is a mobile device and deliver content formatted in such a way as to make best use of the limited screen real estate, reduced browser capabilities, and available wireless network bandwidth. When they do this, they reduce the size or use of images, lay content out in a vertical rather than a horizontal layout, and simplify the site as much as possible. When browser identification is changed, the browser detection the site might be doing is short-circuited. In this case, the user likely ends up with the full desktop website trying to fit on a BlackBerry screen. Chances are, it won't look very good.

The recommended approach is to use BlackBerry browser identification unless the site requires otherwise. If the user is using a device running BlackBerry Device Software 4.6 or higher, the enhanced capabilities of the BlackBerry browser allow them to leave browser identification on Internet Explorer or Firefox full time—as long as they're willing to deal with the extra steps it requires to zoom into the portion of a web page they want to view. See the section, "Page Versus Column Mode," for additional information on this topic.

The next question developers ask is, "So, when the device identification is changed by the user, is there a way I can still tell if the agent is a BlackBerry?" The answer is, of course, yes! Look at Figure 8.11; there's another HTTP Header value shown called PROFILE, which contains a URL pointing to a Resource Description Framework (RDF) file on the blackberry.net website. The URL in the figure is

```
http://www.blackberry.net/go/mobile/profiles/uaprof/9000_edge/
4.6.0.rdf
```

In general, it suffices to parse the URL to determine the model number and BlackBerry Device Software version for the target device. If more detailed information is needed, the application should query the RDF file for device configuration information. A sample of the RDF file pointed to by this URL is shown in Figure 8.12.

```
<?xml version="1.0" encoding="utf-8"?>
<!--
 *
 * (c) 2009 Research In Motion Ltd.,
 * 295 Phillip Street
 * Waterloo, Ontario, Canada
 * N2L 3W8
 *
 * Version: 2
 * Created: Thu Feb 19 09:41:01 EST 2009
 *
 * Notes:
 *     Elements that are not required by RIM Browser have been omitted from this template.
 *     Any elements that are defined in the UAProf specification may be added to this document.
 *
 *
 * Revision History:
 * 1: Initial Version
 * 2: XSLT'd Files
 * 3: New models
 *
 *
 -->
<rdf:RDF xmlns:rdf="http://www.w3.org/1999/02/22-rdf-syntax-ns#" xmlns:rdfs="http://www.w3.org/2000/01/rdf-schema#" xmlns:prf="http://www.o
    <rdf:Description rdf:ID="DeviceProfile">
<!-- Hardware Platform Description -->
        <prf:component>
            <rdf:Description rdf:ID="HardwarePlatform">
                <rdf:type rdf:resource="http://www.openmobilealliance.org/tech/profiles/UAPROF/ccppschema-20021212#HardwarePlatform"/>
                <prf:BluetoothProfile>
                    <rdf:Bag>
                        <rdf:li>Headset Profile</rdf:li>
                        <rdf:li>Handsfree Profile</rdf:li>
                        <rdf:li>Serial Port Profile</rdf:li>
                        <rdf:li>Dial-Up Networking Profile</rdf:li>
                        <rdf:li>Phone Book Access Profile</rdf:li>
                    </rdf:Bag>
                </prf:BluetoothProfile>
                <prf:BitsPerPixel>16</prf:BitsPerPixel>
                <prf:ColorCapable>Yes</prf:ColorCapable>
                <prf:CPU>XScale</prf:CPU>
```

Figure 8.12   Device RDF file contents

The Open Mobile Alliance has defined standards for the User Agent Profile [UAPROF] and the RDF file is an XML document that describes the software and hardware capabilities of a mobile device. RIM provides a link to this file in the HTTP headers to make it easy for a web application to easily determine the complete set of capabilities for the device requesting the page.

If an application is looking at a USER-AGENT value that says the agent is running Firefox or Internet Explorer, it can look for the PROFILE header to determine whether it's really a BlackBerry impersonating another browser.

If a developer needs to know about every possible feature and/or capability of any BlackBerry device, he can grab the appropriate RDF file for the device and dig through it. The URL follows a standard format:

```
http://www.blackberry.net/go/mobile/profiles/uaprof/
[BlackBerry-model]/ [software-version].rdf
```

Replace *[BlackBerry-model]* and *[software-version]* with the appropriate values for the device.

If the application needs to generate custom content for each device, say for example, the application needs to display content in a graphic sized for the resolution of the device, the application can retrieve the RDF file, determine the exact resolution of the screen, and create the necessary graphic to return to the device. In the Browser Content Developer's Guides for BlackBerry Device Software 4.2 and 4.3, sample code uses the URL from the PROFILE header to determine whether the destination device can display black and white or color images.

8.3.4 Determining the Request Path

An application can also determine the path a request took to get to a web server. The BlackBerry device adds an HTTP header value called via to every HTTP request. The header identifies the gateway used to process the HTTP request and the version of the gateway software. For the Internet browser connecting through a carrier Internet gateway, the header looks like this:

```
Via: BISB_3.3.0.45, 1.1 pmds51.bisb1.blackberry:3128 (squid/
2.5.STABLE12)
```

For the BlackBerry Browser connecting through MDS version 4.1.2, the header looks like

```
Via: MDS_4.1.2.17
```

For the WAP browser connecting through a carrier WAP gateway, the header looks like

```
Via: 1.1 to5magproxy1.int.gprs.carrier_name.com
```

The BlackBerry Hotspot Browser does not set the value for the via header.

A developer might use this value to determine whether to redirect a non-MDS connection through an HTTPS connection or might reduce the number of images or rich media on a page for users who are connecting through a WAP gateway.

8.3.5 Page Versus Column View

Beginning with the 4.5 browser, RIM enhanced the browser to support different ways to render the contents of a web page: Column View and Page View. Column View is how the BlackBerry browser worked before the addition of Page View. In Column View, the web page is rendered directly in the browser; the content on the page renders from top left to bottom right and anything that goes off the right border of the screen is wrapped to the left side on the next line. A sample from my personal blog (www.johnwargo.com) in Column View is shown in Figure 8.13. In this mode, the cursor is used to scroll up and down within the page.

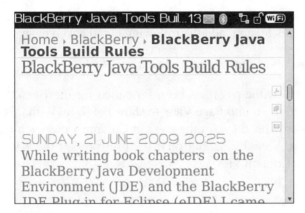

Figure 8.13   Web page in Column View

In Page View, the browser zooms back and displays the page in the way it would look in the desktop browser. The cursor switches to a magnifying glass indicating that the user can click on a portion of the page to zoom in and view just that part of the page. A sample of the same web page from Figure 8.13 is shown in Figure 8.14 in Page View.

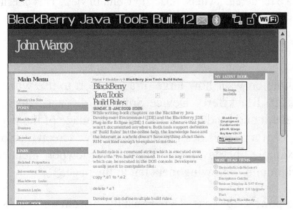

Figure 8.14   Web page in Page View

The Page View feature was added in preparation for the higher resolution screens and enhanced browser capabilities of devices running BlackBerry Device Software 4.6 and beyond. With those devices, RIM produced the first devices capable of displaying a desktop-like version of the page, so the browser was updated to accommodate.

If you are looking at a page and want to switch between Column and Page View, press the z key on the BlackBerry keyboard. To switch back, press the z key again.

A developer can override Page View by adding the HandheldFriendly meta tag to a web page. To enable this feature, add the following tag to a web page:

```
<meta name="HandheldFriendly" content="true" />
```

The tag tells the browser that the page has been formatted for the BlackBerry screen, and there's no need to go into Page View to show the page. With this tag present on the page, the browser displays the page in Column view, even if the browser is set to use Page View by default or if the user presses the z key to switch to Page View from Column View.

An Accidental Feature

I found this feature by accident. I was checking my wife's BlackBerry Curve 8310 smartphone to see if Page View was supported in BlackBerry Device Software 4.5 and brought up the CNN website to test it. The browser was set up for Column View and I pressed the z key to switch to page view.

What happened perplexed me until I did some research on the feature: The browser switched to Page View then, as soon as the page rendered, switched back to Column view. This doesn't happen in BlackBerry Device Software 4.6; when I try to switch to Page View, nothing happens. I'm assuming this is an anomaly in BlackBerry Device Software 4.5.

A developer can also tell the browser how large of a viewport to use when rendering the page. By default, BlackBerry Device Software 4.6 and later opens pages in Page View by default and renders the zoomed-out image of the page on a 1024 by 768 pixel canvas. If a page is designed for a smaller screen resolution, 800 by 600 pixels, for example, the developer can use the viewport meta tag to inform the browser by adding the following meta tag to the page:

```
<meta name = "viewport" content="width=800, height=600" />
```

For width, the default value is 1024 and for height the default is 768. The device-width and device-height parameters instruct the browser to use the device width and height for the viewport, as shown in the following example:

```
<meta name = "viewport" content="width=device-width,
height=device-height" />
```

8.3.6 Offline Form Submission

When a developer begins building a browser-based data entry application, he knows that as good as the mobile networks are today, there's still a chance that the mobile user will try to submit data when the device is not in wireless coverage. Rather than letting the POST time out and frustrate the user, there is a better way to handle this. The developer could use a Java application to perform the data entry, but because the application is already designed for the browser it doesn't make sense to create a separate application for the mobile device.

The BlackBerry browser supports a special feature that allows a web developer to define one or more Form Submission Queues to temporarily store form data until the device can deliver it to the server. If the device is within wireless coverage, the data goes into the queue then right out again to be delivered to the server. If the device is not within coverage, the data is held in the queue until the device reenters coverage. This amazing piece of technology takes a minimum of one code line to implement.

The way this feature works is through special meta tags a developer adds to the input form. The tags tell the browser how to handle submission of the form's data; there's one required tag and some additional tags the application can use to further refine how this feature works. The tags are used by the BlackBerry browser and ignored by the desktop browser. The options for this feature are described in Table 8.2.

Table 8.2 Offline Forms Queue Fields

Field	Description
x-rim-queue-id	Required. Specifies the Offline Form Queue to which any GET or POST requests from form submissions on this page should go. The value can be any text string.
x-rim-next-target	Specifies the next page to load after sending any GET or POST requests resulting from this page to the Offline Form Queue. The value can be any valid URL.
x-rim-request-title	Specifies the label used to identify this request in the Queue view page. The value can be any text string. By default, the request is identified using the title of the page.
x-rim-request-id	Specifies whether the browser will generates a unique ID and add it as an HTTP header for every offline request resulting from this page. The value can be a Boolean True or False. By default, this value is True.
x-rim-request-date	Specifies whether the browser will generate a time stamp and add it as an HTTP header for every offline request resulting from this page. The value can be a Boolean True or False. By default, this value is True.

This feature can be implemented in two ways. For one option, the parameters that control the offline queue are stored in a header property file and the web server is configured to include the headers in the appropriate forms. Because most developers are not going to be able to modify the server's configuration to support this feature, it is not covered here. For more information on this approach, refer to the appropriate BlackBerry Browser Content Development Guide for the version of BlackBerry Device Software your target devices are running.

The other option is to add the appropriate tags to the input form directly. For forms, the meta tags are added as hidden input fields on the page. If, for example, the application uses an input form similar to the one shown here:

```html
<!DOCTYPE HTML PUBLIC "-//W3C//DTD HTML 4.01 Transitional//EN">
<HTML>
<HEAD>
<TITLE>Sample Form Submission</TITLE>
</HEAD>
<BODY>
  <FORM name="input" action="" method="get">
    First name: <INPUT type="text" name="firstname"><BR>
    Last name:<INPUT type="text" name="lastname">
    <INPUT type="submit" value="Submit">
  </FORM>
</BODY>
</HTML>
```

To configure the form to use an offline queue called My Form Queue, the form would be modified to look like this:

```html
<!DOCTYPE html public "-//W3C//DTD HTML 4.01 Transitional//EN">
<HTML>
<HEAD>
<TITLE>Sample Form Submission</TITLE>
</HEAD>
<BODY>
  <FORM name="input" action="" method="get">
    <INPUT type="hidden" name="x-rim-queue-id"
      value="My Form Queue">
    First name: <INPUT type="text" name="firstname"><BR>
    Last name:<INPUT type="text" name="lastname">
    <INPUT type="submit" value="Submit">
  </FORM>
</BODY>
</HTML>
```

When the user clicks the submit button, the form is stored in the queue for delivery whenever possible. To make use of any of the other options for the offline queue, add additional parameters as additional hidden fields on the form, as shown in the following example:

```
<!DOCTYPE html public "-//W3C//DTD HTML 4.01 Transitional//EN">
<HTML>
<HEAD>
<TITLE>Sample Form Submission</TITLE>
</HEAD>
<BODY>
  <FORM name="input" action="" method="get">
    <INPUT type="hidden" name="x-rim-queue-id"
      value="My Form Queue">
    <INPUT type="hidden" name="x-rim-request-title"
      value="Sample">
    <INPUT type="hidden" name="x-rim-next-target"
      value="success_page.html">
    First name: <INPUT type="text" name="firstname"><BR>
    Last name:<INPUT type="text" name="lastname">
    <INPUT type="submit" value="Submit">
  </FORM>
</BODY>
</HTML>
```

In this case, not only is the form created, but the title for the submission (just in case multiple forms are using the same queue) is set to Sample and, after the form is submitted, a page called success_page.html is loaded into the browser.

 Note: It appears that this feature did not make it into BlackBerry Device Software 4.6 and 4.7. It should be available again in a future release.

One of the questions developers often ask at this point is, "How do you get the form onto the device so it's available even when the device is out of coverage?" The developer could use browser Cache Push to get a page or a form on the device's cache behind the scenes.

8.3.7 Save Browser Request

There are times when a user tries to access a website and the page does not come up fast enough or he needs to do something else on the device while he waits for the page to load. There are other times where a user might want to look at something on multiples pages, and the BlackBerry browser doesn't support tabs. With the BlackBerry browser, a user can save page requests for viewing later. When opening a web page in the browser, the user can press the BlackBerry menu button and select Save Request from the menu that appears, as shown in Figure 8.15.

Figure 8.15   Browser Save Request option

The user can then leave the browser and do something else on the device or open another page and repeat the process. The browser continues to receive the page and stores a link to the page in the Messages application to be opened later. Figure 8.16 shows the BlackBerry Messages application with two saved page requests. Also, notice the globe icon at the top of the screen with the number 2 next to it. The icon indicates that there are two saved web requests waiting to be opened.

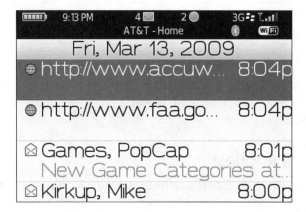

Figure 8.16   Browser Save Request results

When the user opens the saved page request from the Messages application, the browser opens and displays the locally cached version of the page.

8.3.8 Location-Based Services

It's not something you would normally think of, but the BlackBerry browser can access location information on devices that have built-in GPS capabilities. The JavaScript engine in the browser exposes a Location object that can be used to access location information and use it in your application. Chapter 9 contains additional information about this feature.

8.4 Coming Soon

Developers should expect that the BlackBerry platform will continue to evolve and new features will be added regularly. RIM recently announced new features that were not available on devices while this book was being written, but they should be available by the time you're reading this.

8.4.1 Google Gears

RIM recently announced that BlackBerry Device Software 5.0 would provide support for Google Gears. Gears is an open source project that enhances a browser by providing additional capabilities, such as a local database repository, a local web server, parallel execution of JavaScript code, and more. Gears enhances a browser application's capabilities but, through the local database and web server, also allows the application to run even when the device is not connected to a wireless network.

8.4.2 SQLite

At the same time, RIM announced support for SQLite: This is another open source project that provides a relational database engine. Although SQLite doesn't really belong in a chapter on the BlackBerry browser, it's important because it is a component of Gears support; it's easy to see why RIM announced support for it.

But, there's another reason why this is important: For years, BlackBerry developers have been clamoring to have a relational database engine available on the BlackBerry platform. Although there are ways to store application data on a device, there's never been a database that can be queried using Structured Query Language (SQL) commands. This has been a regular feature on Windows mobile devices for some time, and it's nice to see it becoming available on the BlackBerry platform.

8.5 Additional Resources

A complete listing of links to these resources is available online at www. bbdevfundamentals.com.

The best place to find detailed documentation on the capabilities of the Black-Berry browser is to go to the BlackBerry Browser documentation area of the BlackBerry developer's website at http://na.blackberry.com/eng/support/docs/subcategories/?userType=21&category=BlackBerry+Browser.

Several interesting knowledge base articles are related to concepts in this chapter:

- How To: Retrieve Information About the BlackBerry Browser (Article # DB-00435)
- How To: Create a Web Icon (Article #DB-00709)

To access the articles, go to www.blackberry.com/developers and search for the relevant knowledge base article.

The World Wide Web Consortium (W3C) has published some interesting guide-lines for mobile web development. The Mobile Web Application Best Practices guide can be found at http://www.w3.org/TR/mwabp/U. and the Mobile Web Best Practices guide can be found at http://www.w3.org/TR/mobile-bp/U.

Building BlackBerry Browser Applications

Chapter 8, "The BlackBerry Browser," covered the capabilities of the BlackBerry browser; the supported standard browser features, some of the limitations, and the special features that are unique to the BlackBerry platform. If you jumped ahead to this chapter because you want to know how to build browser-based applications for the BlackBerry browser, you might want to go back and read Chapter 8 before you continue.

This chapter discusses how to build a mobile web application for the BlackBerry browser. We start by talking about what you need to know about your target audience, then dig into some guidelines to use when building your web application. This chapter is not going to teach you anything about HTML, WML, or any other web technologies; it focuses on the things developers need to know to build websites compatible with BlackBerry smartphones.

9.1 Optimizing Your Application

Let's start with some guiding principles to apply to any efforts building a mobile web application for the BlackBerry browser. For any mobile browser application, the developer must do some optimization of the content in the application for the target device and target user. mobiThinking (http://mobithinking.com) said it best in 'Ten Tips for Making a Great Mobile Web' site from its free eBook called *Marketing Your Small Business on the Mobile Web* (only the first five are shown):

1. Think about the mobile device. Recognize its limitations (small screen, no mouse), but also think about its extra capabilities (it's a phone, a camera, a text device…).

2. Think about the mobile user. Think "fast access to short bits of content."

3. Keep it simple. Use short, direct sentences. Make navigation easy. Don't expect people to fill out long forms. Let people find things with as few clicks as possible.

4. Keep it fast. Lots of video, animation, or large image files slow down your site. Keep them to a minimum.

5. Make it useful. Don't just think about your business and your goals; think about your audience and what they really need, especially when they're on the go.

To say it another way, a developer must optimize the application's content because it is displayed on devices that have limitations caused by screen size, processor speed, device memory, network bandwidth and availability, plus battery life. The goal should always be for the user to have the best experience possible.

9.2 Understanding the Application's Audience

Before beginning any web application, the developer must know a bit about the target audience for the application. The target device or devices for the application controls most of the decisions made while building the application.

9.2.1 Selecting a Markup Language

In the early days of web-enabled mobile phones or smartphones, the browsers had limited capabilities, and the options for building your application were limited as well. In general, developers could build the site using Wireless Markup Language (WML) or they could…well, could build the application using WML. There weren't really any other options. As phones became smarter, they began supporting more advanced web technologies, such as HTML and later XHTML Mobile Profile (XHTML MP), Compact HTML (cHTML), and others.

The trick then is to select a markup language (and other web technologies) that allows the application to reach the majority of the target devices. If the application is targeted at both mobile phones and smartphones, a markup language (such as WML) must be selected that works on both device types. If the application is targeted at only smartphones, WML should be skipped and HTML and the other variants of the technology should be used for the application.

A Popular Mobile Device with a Non-Mobile Browser

As mentioned in Chapter 8, the iPhone is an interesting animal when it comes to markup language support. When Apple created the iPhone, it deliberately omitted any mobile markup languages. So, if you decide your target audience includes both web-enabled phones and smartphones, and you select WML as your markup language, you deny iPhone users access to your application.

Nowadays, developers really don't have to worry too much about markup language. Unless you're certain that the target device only supports WML, the application can probably be built using HTML. The beauty of using HTML for the application is that the selected technology works for most browsers. Rather than creating a mobile version using a mobile markup language and a separate desktop version using a desktop markup language, the application can use the same technology for both.

9.2.2 Selecting Features

After the markup language is selected for the application, developers must start thinking about the capabilities of the target browser. For the BlackBerry platform, it's complicated in two ways:

- The standard features of the mobile web have been added not all at once, but over time, in different BlackBerry Device Software versions.
- The enhanced browser available beginning with BlackBerry Device Software 4.6 dramatically enhanced the capabilities of the BlackBerry browser.

This means that the developer must understand even more carefully which browser the target devices are likely to use. If the client browser is running BlackBerry Device Software 4.5 or earlier, most of the web technologies are supported, but likely with some limitations. As mentioned in Chapter 8, features such as JavaScript, tables, CSS, and others might be supported by the browser, but could be disabled by default.

With BlackBerry Device Software 4.6 and higher, many of the limitations are removed, and there are so many enhancements added to the browser that the application will be able to do so much more than on other devices. Unless the application uses standard browser features, features available across every version of the BlackBerry browser, the developer will have to make very sure the application knows whether the features are supported. Unless every device accessing the application is running BlackBerry Device Software 4.6 or higher, there might need to be two "versions" of the application: one for older devices and one for newer ones. Don't panic; I'm not suggesting you build two sites, but I do suggest that you detect the target device and adjust the site accordingly. This is why dynamic web technologies, such as JSP, ASP, PHP, Lotus Domino and so on, exist.

9.2.3 Knowing the Application's Impact

A developer building a mobile web application has to make a deliberate choice when it comes to the amount and types of content that get delivered to the mobile browser. The developer can

- Use all the possible bells and whistles supported by the browser
- Use a simple approach and use as few bells and whistles as needed to make the site useful
- Find some happy medium between the other options

The reason this becomes so important is because a careful mobile developer has to constantly decide whether a particular simple feature or cooler, flashy feature is worth the price the mobile user pays (battery life, load time, performance) when using the application. With mobile devices, every aspect of a web application, every markup tag, every image file, and every chunk of JavaScript affects the performance of the application. As described in Chapter 4, "The BlackBerry Mobile Data System (MDS)," the BlackBerry MDS and the carrier's BIS Internet gateways optimize the web pages and its supporting content before sending them to the browser. Although this extra work is done for your users, the application must always be considerate of the mobile user.

Impacting Battery Life

When a mobile user accesses the application, every byte of data transmitted to or from the mobile device drains the battery—there's just no getting around it. Every video or audio file played has a similar effect. Developers must make sure the feature added to the site is worth the drain on the life of the destination device's battery.

Minimizing Client-Side Processing

Although this applies more to Java applications, a developer must also concern himself with how much client-side processing is done on the device. Running a bunch of JavaScript in the background, making heavy use of XMLHTTPRequest to retrieve content, or streaming a media file to the device puts a load on the limited network bandwidth, battery life, and processor capacity of the device.

This is why the iPhone takes a hit on battery life, and Apple is so concerned about enabling background applications. Because the iPhone doesn't support any mobile markup languages, and there aren't Internet gateways involved to optimize content transferred to the mobile device, the iPhone is regularly accessing sites that were optimized for the desktop browser with no concern for network bandwidth utilization and the corresponding impact on battery life and client-side processing.

Exceeding Data Plan Limits

Mobile users in the United States are spoiled when it comes to wireless carrier data plans. Most users have unlimited data plans (although, for some carriers, an unlimited data plan doesn't actually mean unlimited), so BlackBerry users can send and receive as much data as they want. In other countries, there are no unlimited data plans, or the unlimited data plans allow a measly 4MB of traffic per month. If the web application is heavy on the graphics or streaming media, it might push the user over their monthly data plan limits and cause extra usage charges. Granted, the wide adoption of Wi-Fi enabled devices helps mitigate this concern; the web applications of today cannot tell whether the user is using a cellular or Wi-Fi connection.

The Dramatic Effect of a Simple Design

I was working with a customer to mobilize a desktop browser-based web application for use on the BlackBerry and other platforms. They had done a really good job of dynamically converting the pages (through the use of ASP.NET) for the mobile browser, and I had only a few suggestions. They also had questions about things they were considering changing.

The application contained a rather long page containing information about everything the customer had ever purchased from the company. The content was poured into a long series of tables, one for every order, and looked pretty clean. They were thinking of making each column header a clickable link that would sort the tables on the page by the selected column. I suggested they not do this and explained that, by adding links to every column on each table, they would at least double and possibly (depending on the length of the link URL) triple the amount of content sent to the browser for the page. Look at the following HTML defining a simple table on a web page:

```
<!DOCTYPE HTML PUBLIC "-//W3C//DTD HTML 4.01 Transitional//EN">
<html>
<head>
<title>Sample Table 1</title>
</head>
<body>
<table border="1" cellspacing="2" cellpadding="2">
<tr>
<th>Column 1</th>
<th>Column 2</th>
```

```
<th>Column 3</th>
<th>Column 4</th>
</tr>
<tr>
<td>Row Value 1-1</td>
<td>Row Value 1-2</td>
<td>Row Value 1-3</td>
<td>Row Value 1-4</td>
</tr>
<tr>
<td>Row Value 2-1</td>
<td>Row Value 2-2</td>
<td>Row Value 2-3</td>
<td>Row Value 2-4</td>
</tr>
<tr>
<td>Row Value 3-1</td>
<td>Row Value 3-2</td>
<td>Row Value 3-3</td>
<td>Row Value 3-4</td>
</tr>
<tr>
<td>Row Value 4-1</td>
<td>Row Value 4-2</td>
<td>Row Value 4-3</td>
<td>Row Value 4-4</td>
</tr>
</table>
</body>
</html>
```

When you add the Anchor tags to make the column headings clickable to change the sort order and add a sort icon image to the cell, the table code looks like this:

```
<!DOCTYPE HTML PUBLIC "-//W3C//DTD HTML 4.01 Transitional//EN">
<html>
<head>
<title>Sample Table 2</title></head>
<body>
<table border="1" cellspacing="2" cellpadding="2">
<tr><th>
<a href="http://www.somesite.com/app_name/page_name&
sort=col1">Column 1<img src=
"http://www.somesite.com/images/sorticon.gif"
alt="Sort Icon" border="0" align="left"></a>
</th><th>
<a href="http://www.somesite.com/app_name/page_name&
sort=col1">Column 1<img src=
"http://www.somesite.com/images/sorticon.gif" alt="Sort Icon" border="0"
align="left"></a>
</th><th>
<a href="http://www.somesite.com/app_name/page_name&
sort=col1">Column 1<img src=
"http://www.somesite.com/images/sorticon.gif" alt="Sort Icon" border="0"
align="left"></a>
```

```
</th><th>
<a href="http://www.somesite.com/app_name/page_name&
sort=col1">Column 1<img src="http://www.somesite.com/images/sorticon.gif"
alt="Sort Icon" border="0" align="left"></a></th>
</tr>
<tr>
<td>Row Value 1-1</td>
<td>Row Value 1-2</td>
<td>Row Value 1-3</td>
<td>Row Value 1-4</td>
</tr>
<tr>
<td>Row Value 2-1</td>
<td>Row Value 2-2</td>
<td>Row Value 2-3</td>
<td>Row Value 2-4</td>
</tr>
<tr>
<td>Row Value 3-1</td>
<td>Row Value 3-2</td>
<td>Row Value 3-3</td>
<td>Row Value 3-4</td>
</tr>
<tr>
<td>Row Value 4-1</td>
<td>Row Value 4-2</td>
<td>Row Value 4-3</td>
<td>Row Value 4-4</td>
</tr>
</table>
</body>
</html>
```

In this simple example, the second page is about twice the size as the first one (753 versus 1,404 characters). Every feature decision you make for your application could have a detrimental impact on the user. In this case, the feature about doubled the size of the page delivered to the browser. For the mobile user, this would affect the amount of time it took to download and render the page and put a greater load on the battery and network utilization.

9.3 Building a Browser Application

This section describes how to use many of the standard features supported by the BlackBerry browser in web applications. The reason this is important is because, even though these technologies are supported in the BlackBerry browser, there are often limitations and other reasons why they should not be used or only used sparingly in the application.

Many browser limitations go away in BlackBerry Device Software 4.6, but there are still reasons to avoid potentially troublesome features unless you don't care about battery life, performance, and network utilization for the target users. When building the web application, decide whether it is being built for

- BlackBerry Device Software 4.6 and beyond
- BlackBerry Device Software up to and including version 4.5
- Any version of the BlackBerry Device Software

Beyond that, developers must also consider the network bandwidth available to target devices. How the user feels about the richness of the application varies depending on whether he or she is accessing the application on a second generation (2G) or third generation (3G) network connection. Even the availability of Wi-Fi enabled devices is spotty, so the faster connection cannot be relied on.

Penetration of 3G Networks

I recently read an article that indicated that, at the end of 2008, only 11 percent of mobile subscribers worldwide were running on a 3G network. The same article stated that only about 30 percent of wireless subscribers would be running on high-speed networks by the end of 2013. This means that, even though you want to build a web application with a bunch of bells and whistles, a majority of your audience is likely to be accessing your application across a 2G network connection.

9.3.1 Getting Started

When building a BlackBerry browser application, it doesn't matter what tool is used to create the application's pages. A developer can use Notepad, Dreamweaver, HomeSite+, or any tool he wants. The BlackBerry doesn't care, as long as the application consists of content that the BlackBerry browser can render.

Where the application is hosted also doesn't matter, except for two exceptions:

- For internal web applications, do not host the application on the BES; put it somewhere else, preferably on a web server running somewhere in your environment that MDS can access.
- Make sure that the server hosting the web application is accessible by the target users. The web server must be reachable by the mobile browser either inside the firewall via MDS (for BES connected users) or outside the firewall through an open firewall port (for BIS users).

9.3.2 Page Layout

When building web pages for a mobile device, developers should build pages in a vertical layout rather than the horizontal layout used for the desktop browser. The same information can still be displayed on the page, the mobile user just has to scroll down to view all of it on the limited screen real estate available on mobile devices.

The best practice is to use no more than two columns for the page. Additionally, too much vertical scrolling on a page can be cumbersome for mobile users; be sure long pages are split across multiple pages. Use a drop-down box (an HTML Select field) to allow the user to easily pick the portion of the page to which she wants to navigate.

9.3.3 Content

When building the mobile version of the application, focus attention on designing the pages so the user can quickly get to the data they are looking for. Keep the content brief and to the point because, for the mobile user, less is more. The pages should be set up so the mobile user does little or no scrolling to get to the beginning of the page's content. Put navigation, search, and other ancillary components of the page after the content or somewhere out of the way.

9.3.4 Images

When developing for BlackBerry Device Software 4.5 and earlier, use images as little as possible on pages. Use them where they're needed to provide information or highlight information that can only be shown using an image. Until the larger screen, faster processor and full featured browser found on BlackBerry smartphones running BlackBerry Device Software 4.6, images used for navigational components, graphical headers and just for eye candy on older browsers take up extra space on small screens and increase the time it takes to optimize then transfer the images to the mobile device.

Don't forget that MDS and the BIS carrier Internet gateways automatically optimize images before sending them to the browser. Images are converted to a limited set of file formats, resized to fit the screen resolution of the BlackBerry browser, and optimized for the fastest possible transmission. Even with this processing, the use of images makes the browser take longer to retrieve then render the page.

When showing images on web pages, crop them so that only the relevant portions of the images are displayed on mobile devices. To see an example of this, look at Figure 9.1; it shows my son (at an early age and a bad haircut) climbing into my lap. The photo has a lot of unused space, the main subjects of the photo are in the lower-right corner of the image—everything else is wasted space. On a mobile device with a small screen, when the image is first viewed, it is difficult to see the detail in the photo because of all the unused space. To view the photo most effectively on the mobile browser, the photos should be cropped so only the primary components are visible, as shown in Figure 9.2. This allows BlackBerry users to see the important part of the photo without having to zoom in manually. Many BlackBerry users also report that photos of groups of people do not render well when resized for the smaller screen.

Note: If the photo can't be cropped, the BlackBerry user can still zoom in to view the photo in its full resolution. The user has to pan around in the photo to see the full image.

Figure 9.1   Full sample image

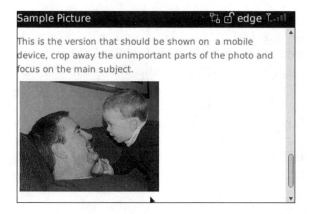

Figure 9.2 Cropped sample image

When resizing images, MDS takes into consideration the HTML `img` tag's `width=` parameter when resizing images. Because MDS resizes images proportionally, it ignores the `height=` parameter and scales the image to the specified width and keeps the same aspect ratio for the image. Using the following sample code as an example, MDS resizes image17.jpg to a width of 200 pixels while keeping the same aspect ratio and ignoring the `height="50"` parameter shown in the example:

```
<!DOCTYPE HTML PUBLIC "-//W3C//DTD HTML 4.01 Transitional//EN">
<html>
<head>
<title>Sample Picture</title>
</head>
<body>
<p>Sample image:</p>
<img src="http://www.someserver.com/images/image17.jpg"
  alt="Image 17" width="200" height="50" border="0">
</body>
</html>
```

Avoid images containing text. When components of the BlackBerry infrastructure resize images to make them fit more easily on the BlackBerry screen, the text scrunches up and could become unreadable.

9.3.5 Tables

Tables are a useful part of many web pages. It allows the developer to display tabular data on a web page in a clear and useful manner. For BlackBerry devices, however, tables can be problematic. First of all, before BlackBerry Device Software 4.5, tables were turned off by default in the BlackBerry browser's configuration. Because of this, although tables are supported, they might not display on the target device. Figure 9.3 shows the default BlackBerry Browser Options screen in BlackBerry Device Software version 4.1; notice that the Support HTML Tables is unchecked. There is currently no reliable way to ensure that tables remain enabled in the browser on devices prior to BlackBerry Device Software 4.5.

Figure 9.3   BlackBerry Browser Options screen

Another problem with tables is they just don't render well on small screens unless the entire table fits cleanly in the available screen space. When using a wide table on a small screen, the browser wraps the contents of the table when it reaches the right side of the screen. To see an example of this, look at Figure 9.4. It shows a simple table with four columns displayed in the desktop browser. When you look at the same page on the BlackBerry browser in Column View, it looks like the screen shown in Figure 9.5. When the BlackBerry browser tries to render the columns, it runs out of room width-wise and wraps the rows to fit the page. After the mobile user starts scrolling down the page, he loses context and is not able to tell which cells are for which table column.

BlackBerry Device Specifications

	BlackBerry Bold 9000	BlackBerry Storm 9500	BlackBerry Curve 8900
Device Software	4.6	4.7	4.6.1
Screen Resolution	480 x 320	480 x 360	480 x 360
Camera Mega Pixel	2.0 MP	3.2 MP	3.2 MP
Wi-Fi	Yes	No	Yes

Figure 9.4   Sample HTML table

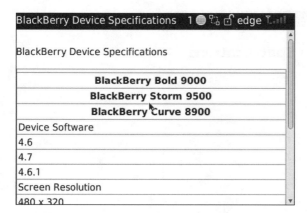

Figure 9.5 Wide table rendered in the BlackBerry browser

The recommended approach to take with tables is to use the HTML Horizontal Rule (<HR> tag) wherever possible to mimic the functionality of tables. As an example, look at the same page content formatted vertically using horizontal rules instead of tables, as shown in Figure 9.6.

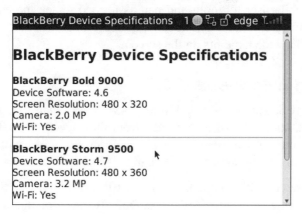

Figure 9.6 Wide table replaced with horizontal rules

Another option to use is an HTML Select tag to put a drop-down list on the page for the user to select the item (a particular table column) that he's interested in and load the information for the selected item only, as shown in Figure 9.7. This likely causes more trips to and from the web server, however, so developers need to weigh the benefits of this option against this drawback.

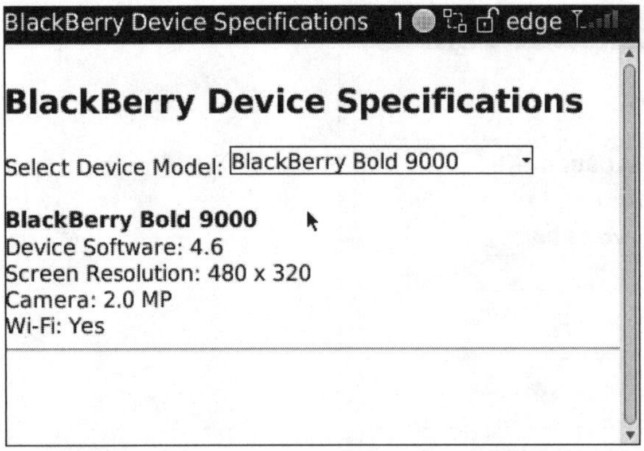

Figure 9.7   Using the Select tag instead of tables

If the target device is running BlackBerry Device Software 4.6 and higher, most of this does not matter. The 4.6 browser does not even have an option to enable HTML Tables—they're on by default and always available. If the browser is operating in Page View (described in Chapter 8), the browser renders the full page and allows the mobile user to zoom and pan as needed to see the entire page. For this device software version and beyond, the developer does not need to worry about how well a wide table fits on the screen.

9.3.6 Cascading Style Sheets (CSS)

Cascading Style Sheets (CSS) provides web developers with the means to isolate the layout, fonts, colors, and styles of a web page from the page content. This gives them tremendous control over exactly how a page or site looks without having to update every single page when a style change is made.

For the BlackBerry browser, CSS is supported, but in BlackBerry Device Software version 4.5 and earlier, it's turned off by default. Because of this, even through CSS is supported, it might not apply to the page on the target device. It's still OK to use CSS for your pages, but web designers must ensure that the page still renders reasonably well if support for CSS is turned off in browser options. If the target device is running BlackBerry Device Software 4.6 or higher, developers can relax a little; the option for enabling or disabling CSS is no longer available; it's enabled by default.

There is another reason why developers should be careful with CSS: It adds network traffic and drains battery life. The style control provided by CSS requires that additional style information be delivered with the web page. Depending on how this is implemented, the application could be dragging a bunch of extra data down to the device. If style information is included inline (included in the HTML content on the page) all of it is delivered to the device with the page. If using features of CSS that select different style information depending on the target device (mobile versus desktop, for example) or what's being done on the page (reading or printing for example), the application could be delivering style information to the device that is never used (style information for desktop browsers for example would be downloaded but not used). On the other hand, the site could be sending less data using external CSS files if multiple pages are downloaded and they all used the same style sheet.

Be careful using CSS to define positioning of page elements on the screen. As explained in Chapter 8, forcing the position of page elements on a small screen usually doesn't make sense. The application ends up with the page element exactly where it was told to be, but it might cause the rest of the page to be less readable. This is especially important for devices running BlackBerry Device Software 4.5 and below.

The best practice is to use CSS to format the font, color, and size of the application's content, but don't try to use layout and more advanced features, because it's usually wasted on a small screened, mobile device. When implementing CSS, be sure to test performance with either inline style information or storing it in an external style sheet file. When the style information is stored in an external file, MDS or the carrier's BIS gateway has to retrieve and process an additional file for each request. Depending on the size of the pages and the performance of the web server, the user might have better performance from using style information inline.

Keep in mind that using CSS places an additional load on the browser, network, and battery. When the browser renders a page using CSS, it has to perform extra steps to download the style sheet information and render the page. To prove this, try viewing a modern web page with CSS turned on and with it off; the page should load and render faster with CSS disabled.

9.3.7 JavaScript Support

JavaScript provides web developers with the means to create more dynamic web pages. The technology is used to perform field validation, implement menu systems, request portions of the screen to be updated in the background, and more. Support for JavaScript was added to the BlackBerry browser in BlackBerry Device Software 3.8, but as mentioned in Chapter 8, there are some limitations:

- **JavaScript could be disabled:** Support for JavaScript is a configuration option for the BlackBerry browser. JavaScript was disabled in the browser by default for many versions of the BlackBerry Device Software. Because of this, pages must be able to function without JavaScript.

- **Read-Only DOM:** Prior to BlackBerry Device Software 4.6, the browser Document Object Model (DOM) was read-only; a script couldn't modify the contents of the page in real-time. Because of this limitation, older BlackBerry browsers were not capable of running many of the scripts developers would use to create menu systems and interact with the user.

- **Background execution disabled:** In older BlackBerry browsers, Java-Script code would run on the page, but only in certain places. For example, the event-driven code behind buttons and drop-down boxes would execute, but any dynamic actions, such as mouseovers, hovers, and key-press events, would not work. Refer to the BlackBerry browser documentation for additional information on what would and would not function.

To ensure that JavaScript is enabled on a device requesting a page from the application, the application can query the HTTP `Accept` header and look for `application/x-javascript` in its contents. If the string is present in the header (as shown in Figure 9.8), JavaScript enabled pages execute in the browser.

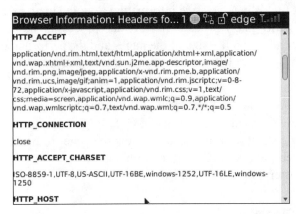

Figure 9.8   BlackBerry browser HTTP ACCEPT header

Beginning with BlackBerry Device Software 4.2.1, RIM added a feature to browser options that allowed it to prompt the user to enable JavaScript when a containing JavaScript code loaded. This at least allowed pages containing Java-Script to run even if the capability was disabled in the browser's configuration. The setting only appears when JavaScript support is disabled, as shown in Figure 9.9.

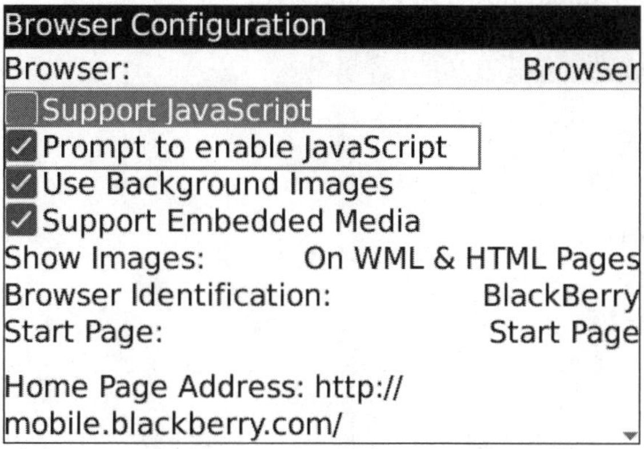

```
Browser Configuration
Browser:                          Browser
  Support JavaScript
✓ Prompt to enable JavaScript
✓ Use Background Images
✓ Support Embedded Media
Show Images:         On WML & HTML Pages
Browser Identification:          BlackBerry
Start Page:                      Start Page

Home Page Address: http://
mobile.blackberry.com/
```

Figure 9.9   BlackBerry Browser Configuration screen

A developer can actually enable JavaScript support programmatically on devices running BlackBerry Device Software 4.2.1 and higher. It's an obscure hack and isn't documented in RIM's documentation, but it works in situations where JavaScript support is turned off in the browser, but the Prompt to Enable JavaScript option shown in Figure 9.9 is enabled.

To make this work, add a call to a fake JavaScript function in the <noscript> section of a page, as shown in the following example:

```
<!DOCTYPE html public "-//W3C//DTD HTML 4.01 Transitional//EN">
<HTML>
<HEAD>
<TITLE>JavaScript Test</TITLE>
</HEAD>
</HEAD>
<BODY>
<H1>JavaScript Test</H1>
<SCRIPT type="text/javascript">
  document.write("JavaScript is enabled!")
</SCRIPT>
<NOSCRIPT>
JavaScript is disabled!<br />
Please <A href="javascript:void()">click here</A>
 to enable JavaScript.
</NOSCRIPT>
</BODY>
</HTML>
```

When the browser renders the page, the contents of the `<noscript>` tag display because JavaScript is disabled, as shown in Figure 9.10.

Figure 9.10 JavaScript Test NoScript page

When the user clicks the link, even though there's a call to invalid JavaScript behind it, the browser prompts the user to enable JavaScript, as shown in Figure 9.11.

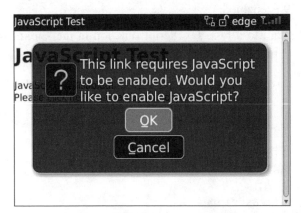

Figure 9.11 BlackBerry Browser JavaScript Confirmation dialog

If the user clicks the OK button, the browser enables JavaScript (for this session only) and reloads the page. At this point, because JavaScript is enabled, the contents of the `<script>` tag are processed (and the contents of the `<noscript>` tag ignored), and the user sees the page shown in Figure 9.12.

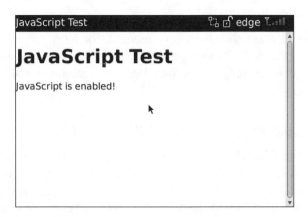

Figure 9.12   JavaScript Test Script page

If you remember from Chapter 4, you were told that MDS stripped out any unneeded or unrecognized content from the page before sending it to the Black-Berry browser. What's happening here is that MDS is still doing that, but it ignores the contents of the `<noscript>` tag because it isn't expecting there to be any JavaScript code there.

Don't forget that, prior to BlackBerry Device Software 4.6, the browser DOM was read-only; there's no sense in sending custom JavaScript code to a device if the code won't be able to manipulate the contents of the page client-side. Refer to the section, "Detecting the BlackBerry Browser," for information on how to determine the BlackBerry Device Software version the device is running.

The developer must be careful and only use JavaScript on a page where it adds value. For an example of this, look at the following input field samples. Both lines do the same thing, but the first line (using JavaScript) delivers more than twice the content to the browser than the second line:

```
<input type="button" value="Submit" onClick="submit()">
<input type="submit">
```

Every line of JavaScript code is additional stuff that must be downloaded to the mobile device across the wireless network. This extra data affects the battery life of the device, how long the page takes to download and render, plus impacts how much data is charged against the user's monthly data plan usage. Where Java-Script is useful on a page is where the price the mobile user pays to download the JavaScript code is worth the extra wait and drain on the battery. Use it for field validation (making sure that the value the mobile user has entered matches the required format, such as email address, phone number, order number, and so on) and other important client-side tasks.

The *BlackBerry Browser Content Developer's Guide* and, for more recent versions of the BlackBerry Device Software, the *BlackBerry Browser JavaScript Reference Guide* contain detailed information on all of the capabilities available to the browser via JavaScript.

9.3.8 Asynchronous JavaScript and XML (AJAX)

AJAX is supported on the BlackBerry browser, but only on devices running BlackBerry Device Software 4.6 and higher. As mentioned previously, prior to this version, the browser Document Object Model (DOM) was read-only and JavaScript didn't run in the background. Refer to the section, "Browser Detection," for information on how to determine the BlackBerry Device Software version the device is running.

9.3.9 Frames

Do not use frames in a mobile web applications unless absolutely necessary. As mentioned in Chapter 8, support for frames in the BlackBerry browser has changed dramatically over time and, until BlackBerry Device Software 4.6, it wasn't a pleasant experience for the mobile user. With today's modern web capabilities, it is usually possible to provide the experience needed to the application without resorting to the use of frames.

9.3.10 Navigation

For many users, the mobile browsing experience will never match the performance and capabilities of the desktop browser. To make it as easy as possible for mobile users to find what they want on slower devices or on slower networks, give them an easy way to get to any part of your application/site as quickly as possible.

For some types of web applications, it might be possible to provide users with a search box; they can use it to search for a particular part number or model and quickly get to the information they need without having to navigate through the application's menus. Be sure to put the search link or search box toward the bottom of the page to allow the user to focus on the content. They can always use the b keyboard shortcut (bottom) to get to the bottom of the page to use the search box.

Figure 9.13 shows a sample search form in the BlackBerry browser. Because one of IBM Lotus Domino's strengths is its built-in search capabilities, it only took a few minutes to create, and it gave the application's users an easy way to find anything they needed on the site.

Figure 9.13 Mobile Search Form sample

Some applications use a Site Map to give users a way to quickly get to the part of the web application that they're looking for.

9.3.11 Links

Beginning with BlackBerry Device Software 4.3, the BlackBerry browser was enhanced to allow the mobile user to use the trackball to scroll through the page more easily. In prior versions, when scrolling through a page using the trackball or the scroll wheel (on devices up through the BlackBerry 8700 smartphone), the cursor would pause (highlight) on every link encountered along the way. If the page contained a lot of links, the cursor had to stop on every one of them. The browser did this to provide the user with the ability to click on the link or just continue scrolling.

When building web applications for older devices, be careful how links are used on the page. It's best to focus pages on the content and put navigational and reference links near the bottom of the page. That way, the user can view all of the content via simple scrolling and jump to other pages within the application when they get to the bottom of the content.

With newer BlackBerry browsers, this is not as important. The mouse-like cursor provided in BlackBerry Device Software 4.3 and higher allows the user to click anywhere they want on a page.

9.3.12 Automatic Links

The BlackBerry browser turns certain types of data into links that can be clicked to perform specific actions. Many developers believe they need to code these links on their pages, but in reality it's done automatically by the browser. It turns

- Phone numbers into links the user can click to place a call or send an SMS message to the number
- Email addresses into links the user can click to compose an email to the selected address
- Web addresses (URL) into links the user can click to open the page, even if not inside an anchor tag

The BlackBerry PIN is treated a little differently. Because the PIN really looks like any other eight character string, developers must tell the browser it's a PIN by putting a PIN: (or pin:) in front of the PIN on the page. With this, mobile users can click on the PIN to compose a PIN to PIN message to the specified device.

The following sample web page demonstrates this feature:

```
<!DOCTYPE HTML PUBLIC "-//W3C//DTD HTML 4.01 Transitional//EN">
<html>
<head>
<title>Automatic Links Demo</title>
</head>
<body>
<h1>Automatic Links</h1>
<p>Device: pin:2086db43</p>
<p>Device: 2086db43</p>
<p>231.456.7890</p>
<p>someguy@someserver.com</p>
</body>
</html>
```

The BlackBerry browser displays a screen similar to the one shown in Figure 9.14. The first PIN displays on the page as a hot link while the second one is just treated like text. You can tell they're links because of the dotted line below the text.

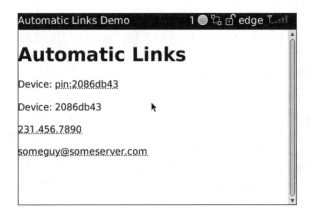

Figure 9.14 Automatic links sample

9.4 Detecting the BlackBerry Browser

Chapter 8 discussed how to use the HTTP USER-AGENT header to detect whether the requesting agent was a BlackBerry device. It also covered how to tell if the agent is a BlackBerry impersonating another browser. Based on what has been covered in this chapter, it's clear that there is often real value in knowing exactly which BlackBerry browser is being used.

The first thing to cover here is where browser detection should be performed: Applications should do it on the server, never on the device. Many developers, when first presented with this concept, often implement the browser detection inside the browser rather than on the web server. The problem with this approach is that, because client-side browser detection is performed in Java-Script and Java Script might be disabled in the browser, it just might not work.

The other problem with this approach is that, when browser detection is performed on the device, a lot of extra content is delivered to the browser but never used. With this approach, chances are that the application uses different chunks of JavaScript code that executes depending on whether the device is running BlackBerry Device Software 4.6 and higher or some other version. Any content downloaded that is never executed or displayed based on which browser is running is code that never should have been transmitted to the device at all.

There are two ways to detect the version of the browser from the server. One way is to parse the HTTP User-Agent header to retrieve the BlackBerry Device Software version. As shown in the following example, everything between the first forward slash and the first space represents the BlackBerry Device Software version running on the device:

```
BlackBerry9000/4.6.0.92 Profile/MIDP-2.0 Configuration/
CLDC-1.1VendorID/1
```

What the browser detection script needs to do is look for the word BlackBerry in the HTTP USER-AGENT header and then parse the string further to locate the BlackBerry Device Software version.

If the USER-AGENT header doesn't contain the word BlackBerry, the target device might be impersonating another agent (browser). To determine the BlackBerry Device Software version in this example, the application must parse the PROFILE header. As shown in Chapter 8, the PROFILE header contains a URL pointing to the Resource Description Framework (RDF) file describing the capabilities of the device. The URL follows a standard format and looks similar to the example shown here:

```
http://www.blackberry.net/go/mobile/profiles/uaprof/9000_edge/
4.6.0.rdf
```

To determine the BlackBerry Device Software version, the application must parse the URL and grab everything between the last forward slash and the .rdf that ends the string. After the BlackBerry Device Software version has been determined, the application can determine what features are supported on the device browser and return the appropriate content to the agent.

9.5 Location-Based Applications

BlackBerry web applications can be easily made location aware. The core of this functionality is provided through the JavaScript blackberry.location object available since BlackBerry Device Software 4.1. Table 9.1 lists the supported properties and Table 9.2 lists the available methods for the object.

Table 9.1 BlackBerry JavaScript blackberry.location Object Properties

Property	Description
GPSSupported	Boolean value. Indicates whether the device supports providing location information.
Latitude	Double value. Returns the latitude component of the current location.
Longitude	Double value. Returns the longitude component of the current location.
Timestamp	Unsigned Long value. Returns the time when the location object was last updated. The time is returned in milliseconds since the last epoch. Your application will need to do some conversion before you can really use this value. This property was added with BlackBerry Device Software 4.6.

Table 9.2 BlackBerry JavaScript blackberry.location Methods

Method	Description
onLocationUpdate()	Registers a callback method that is called whenever the device location is updated.
refreshLocation()	Manually refreshes the location object. Your application can call this to ensure that the most recent location information is available when not using onLocationUpdate.
removeLocationUpdate()	Removes a callback method that was previously registered. This method is only available on BlackBerry Device Software 4.6 and beyond.
setAidMode()	Specifies the method that the device uses to obtain GPS location information. In general, you can usually leave this alone because the BlackBerry has special tricks it uses to capture GPS signal if available.

The following code sample illustrates how to determine the device's location through JavaScript running on a web page:

```
<!DOCTYPE HTML PUBLIC "-//W3C//DTD HTML 4.01 Transitional//EN">
<HTML>
<HEAD>
</HEAD>
<BODY>
<SCRIPT type="text/javascript">
<!--
if(blackberry.location.GPSSupported) {
  blackberry.location.refreshLocation();
  document.write("The client BlackBerry device is currently
  located at " + blackberry.location.latitude +
  " degrees latitude and " +
  blackberry.location.longitude +
  " degrees longitude.");
}
//-->
</SCRIPT>
<NOSCRIPT>Sorry, this browser does not support JavaScript!</
NOSCRIPT>
</BODY>
</HTML>
```

Because this is all done through JavaScript, the target device, of course, has to have JavaScript enabled in the browser. In general, the application should check to see whether GPS is supported on the device by checking the value for blackberry.location.GPSSupported. After it's determined that the device can support GPS, the next step is to refresh the current location by executing a call to blackberry.location.refreshLocation(). After the application has completed those steps, it can retrieve values from blackberry.location. longitude and blackberry.location.latitude to determine the current location of the device. The example shows writing the location information to the page, but the application could easily use it to include position information in forms submitted from the device or to calculate variables passed in URLs opened from the script.

Beginning with BlackBerry Device Software 4.6, a function can be passed as the operator for a location listener, as shown in the following web page code. In this example, the onLocationUpdate executes the code passed to it whenever the device's location changes:

```
<!DOCTYPE HTML PUBLIC "-//W3C//DTD HTML 4.01 Transitional//EN">
<HTML>
<HEAD>
</HEAD>
<BODY>
<SCRIPT type="text/javascript">
<!--
if(blackberry.location.GPSSupported) {
  document.write("GPS is supported on this device!");
    blackberry.location.onLocationUpdate("window.alert(
    'Your new position is ' +
    blackberry.location.latitude + ' degrees latitude and ' +
    blackberry.location.longitude + ' degrees longitude.')");
  blackberry.location.refreshLocation();
}else{
  document.write("GPS is not supported on this device!");
}
//-->
</SCRIPT>
<NOSCRIPT>Your browser does not support JavaScript!</NOSCRIPT>
</BODY>
</HTML>
```

Although the BlackBerry browser on a GPS-enabled BlackBerry device supports providing location information through the JavaScript object, the feature is turned off by default. Before a web application can access GPS information in the browser, the BlackBerry user must turn it on by opening the browser, pressing the BlackBerry menu button, and selecting Options from the menu that appears. From the Options menu, select General Properties, and click the trackball. On the General Properties screen, enable the option labeled Enable JavaScript Location Support, as shown in Figure 9.15, and save the changes. With this enabled, the script is then able to access GPS location information.

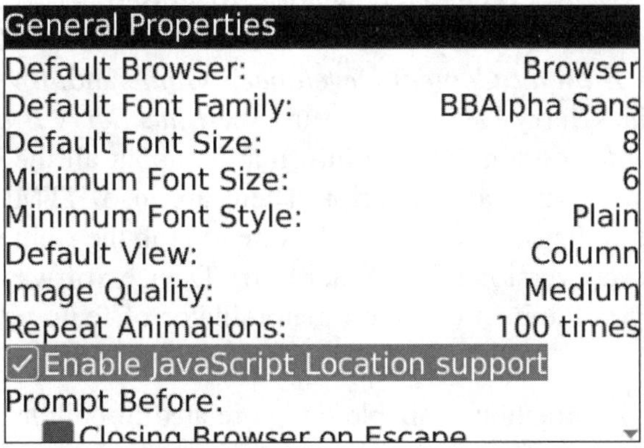

Figure 9.15   BlackBerry Browser General Properties

Save Hours of Troubleshooting Time

The first time I worked with the `blackberry.location` object, I wrote some code similar to the code shown previously, and I couldn't figure out why it didn't work. It was only after a lot of time and frustration that a colleague pointed out that the feature was disabled in the browser's configuration.

Be sure to make checking that GPS support is enabled in the browser is the first step that every support analyst performs when troubleshooting a location-aware web application.

9.6 Additional Resources

A complete listing of links to these resources is available online at www. bbdevfundamentals.com.

The BlackBerry Developers website (www.blackberry.com/developers) contains a lot of information about how to build web applications for the BlackBerry browser and other articles that cover the topics in this chapter in detail.

Look for the Developer Knowledge Base article DB-00435 called "How To: Retrieve Information About the BlackBerry Browser," and article DB-00698 called, "How To: Verify That the BlackBerry Browser Data Remains Encrypted at All Points Between the BlackBerry Smartphone and the BlackBerry Enterprise Server."

The BlackBerry Browser documentation site (http://na.blackberry.com/eng/support/docs/subcategories/?userType=21&category=BlackBerry+Browser) contains detailed information on every possible feature of the BlackBerry browser. The *BlackBerry Browser Content Developer's Guide* and, for more recent versions of the BlackBerry Device Software, the *BlackBerry Browser JavaScript Reference Guide* contain detailed information about all the capabilities available to the browser via JavaScript. There are also HTML and CSS references available in the same location. Be sure to grab the right set of documentation for the lowest version of the BlackBerry Device Software you will support; that gives you the best common denominator of features your applications can support.

There is also a wealth of information available online related to building web applications for mobile devices. The World Wide Web Consortium (W3C) has published some interesting guidelines for mobile web development: "Mobile Web Application Best Practices" (www.w3.org/TR/mwabp) and "Mobile Web Best Practices" (www.w3.org/TR/mobile-bp).

dotMobi is an organization that provides everything related to the .mobi Internet top-level domain (TLD). It has published a "dotMobi Mobile Web Development Guide," available from http://dev.mobi.

It also offers a free site-testing application called ready.mobi, which can be found at http://ready.mobi. It offers a product called Instant Mobilizer, which allows an organization to automatically convert existing websites into a mobile optimized version. For more information, check out www.instantmobilizer.com and www.instantmobilizer.com/test-your-site.htm.

Through a related organization called mobiThinking, dotMobi offers a free eBook called *Marketing Your Small Business on the Mobile Web*, located at www.mobithinking.com/white-papers/free-ebook-marketing-your-small-business-mobile-web.

Many mobile browser detection scripts are available online. MobiForge, another organization related to dotMobi, has several. There is a sample browser detection script in PHP located at http://mobiforge.com/developing/story/lightweight-device-detection-php and a sample ASP version located at http://mobiforge.com/developing/story/lightweight-device-detection-asp. You can also try http://detectmobilebrowsers.mobi for another version.

There is even an open source project called PhoneGap (www.phonegap.com) that is building a cross-platform framework for device-neutral mobile development using JavaScript. Their tools are supposed to support BlackBerry, Apple iPhone, and Google Android.

10

Testing/Debugging BlackBerry Browser Applications

After browser applications are coded, it's time to test the application on each of the client browsers that will be accessing the site. This chapter outlines the options available to developers for testing and debugging their browser applications on BlackBerry devices or the BlackBerry device simulator. It includes information on testing on BlackBerry devices and the BlackBerry device simulators, plus how to use the BlackBerry Web Tools: the BlackBerry Plug-in for Visual Studio and the BlackBerry Web Development Plug-in for Eclipse.

10.1 Testing on Devices

One of the easiest ways to test web applications for the BlackBerry platform is to access the application from one or more BlackBerry devices. Open the appropriate browser on a device, paste in the URL, and navigate through the application. Using this method, developers can easily validate the layout and format of the application's pages on multiple devices. It is also easy to determine whether the performance of the application is suitable for the application's audience. You will know which pages load quickly and which pages take a while to download and render.

Carefully choosing devices and network types (GPRS, EDGE, 3G, CDMA, and so on) based on the application's target audience allows you to test the application and understand what the application's users experience with the application. The drawback with this approach is that you must have access to each device your target audience will be using, and each device will need to be activated with a data plan so the browser can access the site. Another drawback of this approach is that, from a testing standpoint, you will not be able to perform real-time debugging of any scripts running within the application; the BlackBerry device has limited capabilities in this area (which is why the BlackBerry Web Tools were created).

If needed, third-party companies can provide access to real devices for testing. If you don't have access to a specific device and need to test on it, you can turn to companies like Device Anywhere (www.deviceanywhere.com) or Perfecto Mobile (www.perfectomobile.com) and test on any of the hundreds of mobile devices they have available online. With these services, you don't get to physically hold the devices you're testing on—the devices are accessed through a web interface—but you can test your web application on devices you don't have access to otherwise.

10.2   Testing on BlackBerry Simulators

Another option for testing BlackBerry browser applications is to test the application in one or more BlackBerry simulators. For testing web applications, the BlackBerry simulator is an almost exact representation of the corresponding BlackBerry device.

The BlackBerry simulators are free downloads from the RIM Developer's website and developers or testers can install the simulator for any BlackBerry device. If the BlackBerry Device Software for a particular device has been upgraded since release, it might be possible to install multiple Device Software versions of the simulator for testing. You can download the latest BlackBerry device simulators at the BlackBerry Developer's tools download site (http://na.blackberry.com/eng/developers/resources/simulators.jsp).

The BlackBerry device simulator does not need a carrier data plan; it can use the host system's network connection to access network resources. There is, however, a limitation to this: the device simulator cannot make direct connections to network resources; it can only connect to web servers or other systems through MDS. To make this easy for developers, RIM offers for download a free, standalone MDS simulator that can be installed along side the device simulators. Refer to Chapter 4, "The BlackBerry Mobile Data System (MDS)," for information on how to download, install, and run the BlackBerry MDS simulator.

When testing a BlackBerry browser application using the MDS simulator and BlackBerry device simulators, a few restrictions apply:

- The MDS simulator must run on the same system running the BlackBerry device simulators.
- The MDS simulator must be started before a BlackBerry device simulator is launched.
- Only one BlackBerry device simulator can run on a PC at a time. The simulators use the same port to communicate with the MDS simulator, so you will receive an error when a second simulator is started.
- The web server hosting the application must be visible (network accessible) to the system running the MDS simulator.

When you're ready to begin testing your BlackBerry browser application, follow these steps:

1. Launch the MDS simulator.
2. Launch the appropriate BlackBerry device simulator.
3. Open the browser on the BlackBerry device simulator.
4. Enter the URL for your application. (Save time by copying it from somewhere and pasting it into the browser's URL field.)
5. Test and refresh (the page after you make changes to the source pages).

For information on how to operate the BlackBerry device simulators, see Appendix A, "Using the BlackBerry Device Simulators," which is available online at www.bbdevfundamentals.com.

If the web page being tested is hosted on a web server external to the system running the BlackBerry device simulator, the URL for the application is the full URL to the page on the server. If the page is hosted on a web server running on the same system as the BlackBerry device simulator, the URL can point to the page via the IP address or machine name for the system; you cannot use the localhost hostname. Don't forget that any network resource that the system running MDS can see, the BlackBerry device simulator can also see.

10.3 Testing within Integrated Development Environments (IDE)

As you can see from the previous section, testing browser applications on a BlackBerry requires some work, and it doesn't integrate directly with the tools used to develop an application. RIM recently released web-development plug-ins for both Microsoft Visual Studio and the Eclipse IDE that simplify this process. The tools allow you to build your web application and integrate directly with the BlackBerry device simulator for testing and debugging. Developers can

- Launch the BlackBerry device and MDS simulators directly from within the IDE
- Set, remove, and/or disable breakpoints and step through JavaScript code being executed in the BlackBerry browser
- Add watches and view the values of variables while the page is running
- View XMLHTTPRequest requests and responses plus HTTP header information
- Leverage the additional debugging tools available in the IDE

The following sections describe how to install and use the BlackBerry Web Tools.

10.3.1 Installing the BlackBerry Plug-In for Visual Studio

The BlackBerry Plug-In for Visual Studio is a free tool that can be downloaded from the BlackBerry Developer's website (www.blackberry.com/developers). Look for the section labeled BlackBerry Web Development; the tool will be available there.

The requirements for the tool are

- Microsoft Windows XP or Windows Vista (32-bit)
- Microsoft Visual Studio 2008 (Service Pack 1) Standard Edition (minimum)

It is distributed as a standard Windows installation executable and installs just like any other Windows application. To complete the installation, launch the downloaded installation file and follow the prompts (agreeing with the license agreements and accepting all default options).

10.3.2 Debugging Web Applications Using the BlackBerry Plug-in for Visual Studio

If you're a Visual Studio developer, you probably know that you can right-click a web project and select View in Browser to view the site in the browser. You can also debug a site by starting the debugger; Visual Studio launches the debug server, opens the browser, displays the site, and connects the debugger with the application running in the browser so the site can be debugged in an interactive manner.

It takes some time for the BlackBerry simulator to start up the first time. To make things easier for debugging multiple iterations of an application, don't close the simulator between sessions. Stop the debug session in Visual Studio, but keep the simulator open. When beginning a new session, launch the debug session, switch over to the BlackBerry browser running on the simulator, and refresh the page to see the latest version.

With the BlackBerry Plug-in for Visual Studio installed, the options for debugging are enhanced by BlackBerry-specific options in the IDE. To see these options in action, right-click a web project and select Browse With. Visual Studio opens a dialog listing all the possible target browsers that can test the application, as shown in Figure 10.1. Notice that an option for the BlackBerry browser has been added to the list. When beginning a BlackBerry browser debugging session, set the BlackBerry browser as the default browser by clicking the Set as Default button.

Figure 10.1 Visual Studio Browse With dialog

With the BlackBerry browser set as the default browser, begin a debugging session the same way you would begin any debugging session in Visual Studio. (Click the Debug button in the toolbar, press the F5 key, or select Start Debugging from the Debug menu.) Visual Studio launches the BlackBerry development tools and then connects its debugger to the browser session running on the device.

When all the tools load, the BlackBerry simulator opens and displays the start page for the web application. At this point, switch back to Visual Studio and look at the Solution Explorer panel shown in Figure 10.2. Notice that there's a new section called Script Documents, which contains each of the page and script components from the project being debugged.

You can now open any of the files in this section and set breakpoints (the same way you would for any other Visual Studio project) that will hit when the BlackBerry browser executes the code lines. After the breakpoints are set, return to the application running in the BlackBerry simulator and interact with the site. When a line of code executes that is marked as a breakpoint, Visual Studio stops the application and opens a debug window similar to Figure 10.2.

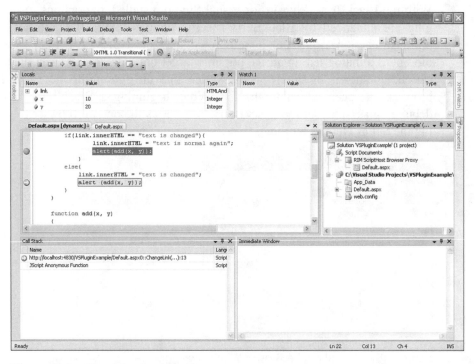

Figure 10.2   Visual Studio debug layout

The current source file is displayed in the IDE with the breakpoint highlighted. Any other breakpoints in the code are also displayed. At this point, the debugging of the application would proceed in the same manner it would for any other Visual Studio project. You can step through the code and use the additional debugging windows shown in Figure 10.2 to view the status of local variables, define watches, view the call stack, and more.

The plug-in can even display the contents of any XMLHttp request and XMLHttp response, which allows the complete interaction between a web application and a remote data source to be monitored. Developers can use this functionality to watch, in real time, the entire conversation performed by the web application as it retrieves information from the web server using XMLHttpRequest. To access this feature while debugging a web application on BlackBerry, open the Debug menu, expand the Windows submenu, and select BlackBerry XHR Watch from the menu that appears. Visual Studio opens the panel shown in Figure 10.3. The panel provides access to XMLHttpRequest properties, represented as separate tabs in the panel:

- **Parameters:** Displays the parameters passed to the XMLHttpRequest (usually an HTTP Put or Get)
- **Header:** Displays the HTTP header values for both the request and the response from the web server
- **Response:** Displays the body of the response message

The panel can display the properties for multiple transactions; the panel contains subpanels that can be expanded and collapsed by clicking the plus and minus buttons on the left side of each transaction.

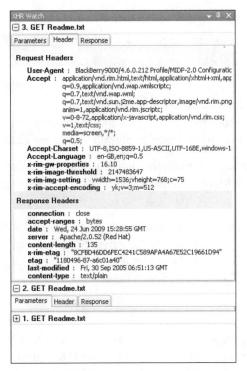

Figure 10.3   Visual Studio BlackBerry XHR Watch panel

Refer to the Visual Studio and BlackBerry Plug-in for Microsoft Visual Studio online help for additional information on the capabilities available during a debug session.

10.3.3 Installing the BlackBerry Web Development Plug-In for Eclipse

The BlackBerry Web Development plug-in for Eclipse is a free tool that can be downloaded from the BlackBerry Developer's website (www.blackberry.com/developers). On the developer's site, look for the section labeled BlackBerry Web Development; the tool should be available there. It is available as a full download, including a full Eclipse installation or as a plug-in used to install the tools into an existing implementation of Eclipse.

The requirements for the tool are

- Microsoft Windows XP or Windows Vista (32 bit)
- Eclipse IDE for Java EE Developers version 3.4.1 (requires the Java EE tools, EMF 2.4.1, and WTP 3.0.3)
- Java 1.6 SDK

Be sure that the Eclipse environment is configured with the appropriate local web server for the application and setup for web application debugging. Refer to the Eclipse documentation for information on how to complete this installation.

To install the complete Eclipse package, launch the downloaded installation file and follow the prompts (agreeing with the license agreements and accepting all default options).

To install the plug-in into an existing Eclipse installation, extract the files from the download to a temporary folder on your local hard drive. Start Eclipse, open the Help menu, and select the Software Updates menu item. Eclipse displays a screen similar to the one shown in Figure 10.4. Select the Available Software tab and click the Add Site button.

Eclipse displays a dialog similar to the one shown in Figure 10.5. Click the Local button. In the standard Windows Browse for Folder dialog that appears, navigate to the folder where the plug-in files were extracted and click the OK button. Click the OK button in the Add Site dialog to continue with the installation.

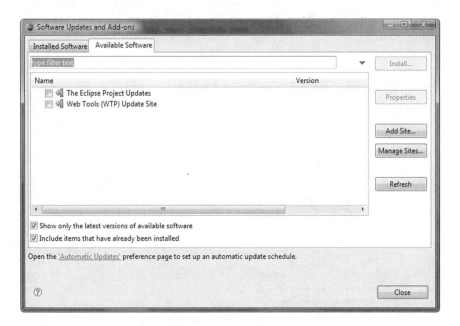

Figure 10.4   Eclipse software updates and add-ons window

Figure 10.5   Eclipse Add Site dialog

Eclipse returns to the screen shown in Figure 10.6. From here, enable the check-box next to the BlackBerry Browser Tools for Eclipse Category, and click the Install button.

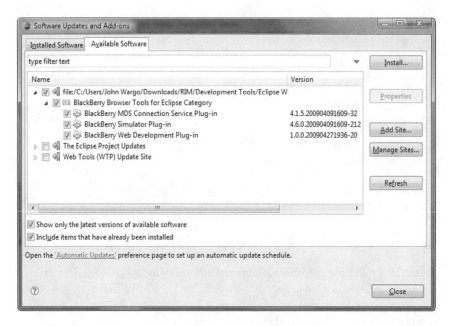

Figure 10.6   Eclipse software updates and add-ons window with the BlackBerry browser tools

Eclipse prompts you for confirmation on the components to be installed, as shown in Figure 10.7; click the Next button to continue the installation.

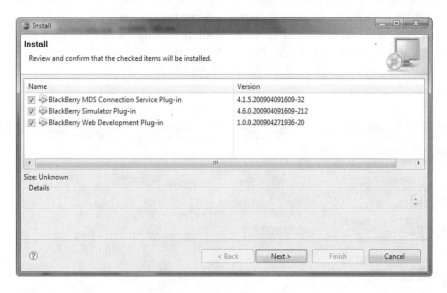

Figure 10.7   Eclipse component installation confirmation

Eclipse then prompts for acceptance of the BlackBerry SDK license agreement before allowing the installation to continue. After you accept the terms, click the Finish button to complete the installation. At this point, Eclipse churns away, completes the software installation, and suggests that you restart Eclipse.

10.3.4 Configuring the BlackBerry Web Development Plug-In for Eclipse

Before you can debug web applications using the BlackBerry web tools, you must first configure the Eclipse environment. To begin, click the Debug toolbar drop-down, shown in Figure 10.8, and select Debug Configurations from the menu that appears.

Figure 10.8   Eclipse Debug menu

In the Debug Configurations window, right-click the BlackBerry Web option and select New from the menu that appears. In the options panel that appears (shown in Figure 10.9), enter a name for the Debug Configuration and then enter the URL to the site being tested. Next, select any simulator configuration options (on the Simulator tab), click Apply and then Close.

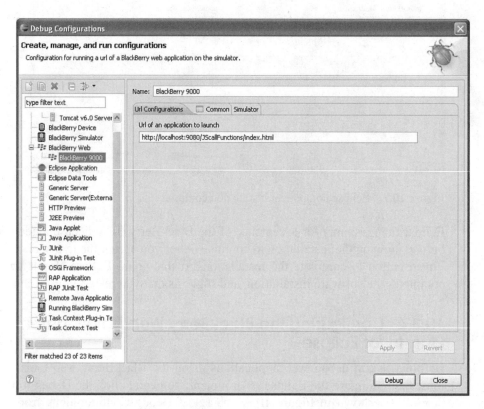

Figure 10.9   Eclipse Debug Configuration options

10.3.5 Debugging Web Applications Using the BlackBerry Web Development Plug-In for Eclipse

For Eclipse developers, the BlackBerry is just another debug target for the IDE; BlackBerry applications are debugged using the same tools used for debugging other web applications. To test a web application on the BlackBerry simulator, the web server installed with the plug-in must be started. In the Eclipse Servers window, shown in Figure 10.10, select the web server and click the button highlighted in the figure.

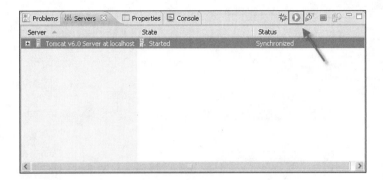

Figure 10.10 Eclipse Servers window

To begin debugging a web application in the BlackBerry simulator, open the debug menu and select one of the BlackBerry configurations defined in Eclipse, as shown in Figure 10.8. When the debugging session begins, Eclipse launches the MDS simulator, then the BlackBerry device simulator, and connects the debug server to the device simulator. When the simulator opens and renders the page, you can switch back to Eclipse and set breakpoints in any of the code being executed. It takes some time for the BlackBerry simulator to start up for the first time. To make things easier for debugging multiple iterations of an application, don't close the simulator between sessions. Stop the debug session in Eclipse, but keep the simulator open. When beginning a new session, launch the debug session and then switch over to the BlackBerry browser running on the simulator and refresh the page to see the latest version.

When debugging sites, the standard Eclipse debugging tools can be used, including stepping through JavaScript code, accessing local variables, setting watches, and more, as shown in Figure 10.11.

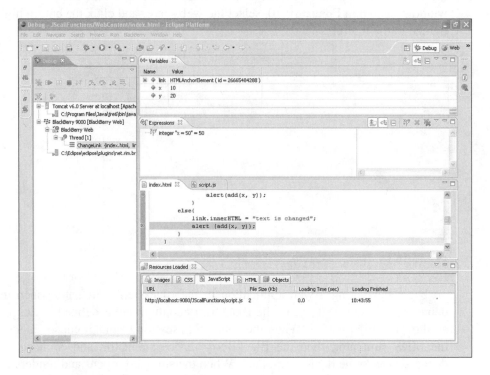

Figure 10.11 Eclipse debug perspective

When accessing a remote site, the Resources Loaded panel lists all the resources that were loaded into the simulator's browser when the site was accessed.

The plug-in can even display the contents of any XMLHttp request and XMLHttp response, which allows the complete interaction between a web application and a remote data source to be monitored. Developers can use this functionality to watch, in real time, the entire conversation performed by the web application as it retrieves information from the web server using XMLHttpRequest. To access this feature, open the Eclipse Window menu, select Show View, and then select Other. Eclipse opens a dialog similar to the one shown in Figure 10.12; expand the BlackBerry Web option, select XMLHttpView, and click OK.

Figure 10.12   Eclipse Show View dialog

Eclipse opens a panel similar to the one shown in Figure 10.13. The XmlHttp Request tab (shown in the figure) contains an expandable tree view, which, for each request, provides access to the contents of the HTML header, the method that was called and the request URL.

When the XmlHttp Response tab is selected (as shown in Figure 10.14), the panel displays options for viewing, for each response, the Header values, the Status Code, and the Response contents.

Refer to the BlackBerry Web Development plug-in for Eclipse and the Eclipse online help for additional information on the capabilities available during a debug session.

Figure 10.13   Eclipse XmlHttpView Panel—Highlighting XmlHttpRequest

Figure 10.14　Eclipse XmlHttpView Panel—Highlighting XmlHttpResponse

10.4　Viewing Browser Source

While the BlackBerry web-development tools described in the previous sections provide the ability to view everything happening on the device when accessing a website, there are times when you're not working in the development tools and need to troubleshoot a problem with a web page or site on a physical BlackBerry device.

The BlackBerry browser supports a feature that allows a user to view the source for the page being rendered in the browser. To access this feature, open the page, hold the Alt key on the BlackBerry, and type rbvs. When you release the Alt key, the current page's source code opens in a viewer, as shown in Figure 10.15. Using this feature, you can see exactly what is being delivered to the browser rather than guessing based on what's displayed on the screen.

```
Source Viewer
<html xmlns="http://
www.w3.org/1999/xhtml">
 <head>
  <meta http-
equiv="Content-Type"
content="application/xhtml
+xml; charset=UTF-8"/>
  <meta name="viewport"
content="width=440; initial-
```

Figure 10.15　BlackBerry browser source viewer

Unlike some browser tools (such as FireBug, for example), it's not possible to modify the code in the viewer and have it displayed in the browser in real-time. All this tool was designed to do was give developers a way to view the source for the content delivered to the browser.

The viewer supports some additional options that allow the developer to work with the page source outside of the BlackBerry browser. With the page open in the viewer, click the BlackBerry menu button to display a menu of available options. The options available from this menu are

- **Send:** Sends the page source to a contact defined in the BlackBerry Contacts application on the device. With this option, you do not have the ability to modify anything but the subject before the message is sent. If the source for the page you are viewing is large, you might want to use the Select option to copy only the portion of the source that is needed.

- **Copy to Clipboard:** Copies the contents of the source viewer window to the device's clipboard. Once it is on the clipboard, the content can be pasted into another device application.

- **Select:** Selects a portion of the page source to be copied to the clipboard. Position the cursor at the beginning of the source code segment you want to copy and choose the Select option from the menu. While in select mode (the cursor changes to indicate select mode is active), drag the cursor to select the code. After the selection is complete, press the BlackBerry menu and select Copy to copy the selected text to the clipboard.

- **Save:** Saves the browser page source to a file on the device. The page source can be saved to device memory or a media card. Once saved, it can then be emailed to a developer or support person for analysis.

10.5 Additional Resources

A complete listing of links to these resources is available online at www. bbdevfundamentals.com.

Each tool described in this chapter is available as a free download from the BlackBerry Developer's website, located at www.blackberry.com/developers. The MDS simulator can be downloaded from http://na.blackberry.com/eng/ developers/browserdev/devtoolsdownloads.jsp, and the BlackBerry device simulators can be downloaded from http://na.blackberry.com/eng/developers/ resources/simulators.jsp.

11

Building BlackBerry Java Applications

BlackBerry applications written in Java provide the most capabilities to the BlackBerry user. Developers who want to provide the best possible performance and experience for their end users will likely want to build their applications using Java. This chapter provides the information a developer needs to begin building Java applications for BlackBerry.

RIM provides extensive documentation for the BlackBerry Java platform, so do not expect this chapter to tell you everything you need to know about writing applications in Java. To cover every aspect of BlackBerry Java development could easily consume a book twice the size of this one. Instead, this chapter focuses on some of the BlackBerry-specific tasks to get you started rather than to dig deep into every application programming interface (API) available to BlackBerry developers.

This chapter covers

- Differences between MIDP, CLDC, and BlackBerry applications
- Building your first BlackBerry application
- Using the BlackBerry-specific APIs
- Using location-based capabilities of a BlackBerry device
- How an application can work within security restrictions placed on a device

11.1 Understanding the BlackBerry Java Developer's Options

The Java developer has several options at his disposal for building Java applications that run on a BlackBerry device. A developer must understand these options and know when to select one over another. The following sections describe these options and explain when each should be used.

11.1.1 CLDC and MIDP

A BlackBerry device includes a Java runtime environment based on two standards for mobile device platforms: Connected Limited Device Configuration (CLDC) and Mobile Information Device Profile (MIDP). Both standards are part of Sun Microsystems Java Micro Edition (JME) framework. Current BlackBerry devices support the CLDC 1.1 and MIDP 2.0 specifications.

CLDC is a specification targeted at devices with limited resources and capabilities; it defines several low-level libraries required by any mobile application. It includes streamlined versions of the standard Java libraries `java.io`, `java.lang` and `java.util`. Developers would build CLDC applications when targeting low power devices, such as regular old (non-smart) phones. For additional information on CLDC and the capabilities it provides, refer to http://java.sun.com/products/cldc.

MIDP is a specification published by Sun Microsystems for the use of Java on embedded devices, such as BlackBerry devices, smartphones, and PDAs. MIDP sits on top of CLDC and provides higher level libraries used to build JME applications on more capable devices. The core libraries available to MIDP applications are based on the version of CLDC the device supports. The MIDP specification includes additional libraries, such as `javax.microedition.io`, `javax.microedition.lcdui`, `javax.microedition.rms`, and `javax.microedition.midlet`. The application built to these specifications is called a MIDlet.

Building pure MIDlets is all about compatibility—compatibility with other Java-capable devices. You can build an application using the MIDP specification and the application runs on most devices that support JME. For additional information on the MIDP specification, go to http://java.sun.com/products/midp.

11.1.2 BlackBerry APIs

To support special hardware and software capabilities of the BlackBerry device, RIM has created BlackBerry-specific Java libraries. These libraries allow BlackBerry developers to build applications that look and feel like other BlackBerry applications and make use of the special features of the BlackBerry platform, such as special user interface components, integrating with PIM and messages applications, invoking applications (like BlackBerry Maps), and more. Without these extensions, developers would not be able to build applications that leverage the things that make BlackBerry devices special. Many of these options are described in later sections. Figure 11.1 provides an illustration of the library structure available to BlackBerry Java.

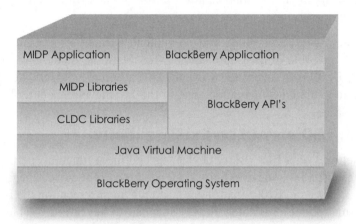

Figure 11.1   BlackBerry application architecture

The most common option for BlackBerry developers is to build CLDC applications using the RIM libraries; any application built using these libraries only runs on a BlackBerry, it does not run on any other platform. The sample applications included with the BlackBerry Java development tools and the standard applications provided on a BlackBerry device are all CLDC applications. A CLDC-based application that uses BlackBerry-specific APIs is called a RIMlet.

Except for the restriction on UI libraries described next, developers can use whichever libraries they want in their applications. BlackBerry Java applications can use MIDP, CLDC, and the BlackBerry-specific libraries as needed in their applications.

If you're not sure what the ultimate audience for the application will be, know that if you write a pure MIDlet, it will run on most JME-compatible devices, but the application won't feel like a BlackBerry application when executed on a BlackBerry. If you write a RIMlet and later learn that the application must also run on other JME platforms, work likely needs to be done before it will run on anything but a BlackBerry. A developer can mitigate some of that work by separating out the BlackBerry-specific code into libraries that would only be used on the BlackBerry version of an application.

11.1.3 Java Application Fundamentals Guide

This chapter covers the fundamentals a developer needs to know to begin developing applications for BlackBerry. There are many tricks and coding styles a BlackBerry Java developer can implement to optimize an application for the best possible performance, code size, and code efficiency. To support developers and help them take their applications to the next level, RIM regularly publishes the *BlackBerry Java Application Fundamentals Guide* for each BlackBerry Device Software version.

Developers should study this guide and implement as many of the suggested optimizations as possible in their applications. To obtain the guide, navigate to the BlackBerry Developer's website (www.blackberry.com/developers) and look for the document in the Documentation area for the Java development tools.

11.1.4 How MIDlets Act on the BlackBerry

When a MIDlet runs on a BlackBerry device, special input functions performed by the trackwheel (on older devices), trackball (on all current devices beginning with the BlackBerry Pearl 8100 smartphone), and the touchscreen (on the BlackBerry Storm smartphone) are automatically mapped to key events. Table 11.1 provides a list of the methods fired when the trackball or trackwheel are used within the application.

Table 11.1 Mapping BlackBerry Input Actions to MIDlet Methods

Action	Procedure	MIDP Methods
Scroll down	Roll the trackwheel clockwise or roll the trackball down.	Invokes the `keyPressed()` and `keyReleased()` methods of the current Canvas object with `keyCode` parameters set to `Canvas.DOWN`.
Scroll right	Press the Alt key and roll the trackwheel clockwise or roll the trackball to the right.	Invokes the `keyPressed()` and `keyReleased()` methods of the current Canvas object with the `keyCode` parameter set to `Canvas.RIGHT`.
Scroll up	Roll the trackwheel counter-clockwise or roll the trackball up.	Invokes the `keyPressed()` and `keyReleased()` methods of the current Canvas object with `keyCode` parameters set to `Canvas.UP`.
Scroll left	Press the Alt key and roll the trackwheel counter-clockwise or roll the trackball left.	Invokes the `keyPressed()` and `keyReleased()` methods of the current Canvas object with the `keyCode` parameter set to `Canvas.LEFT`.

This means that a MIDlet will not only run on a BlackBerry, but the navigational capabilities provided by the trackwheel, trackball, and touchscreen will still function.

A MIDlet can override the `Canvas.pointerPressed()`, `Canvas.pointer Released()`, and `Canvas.pointerDragged()` methods to respond to touch screen input events.

For devices with a touch screen interface, a MIDlet can override the `touch Event(TouchEvent message)` method in any of the BlackBerry specific MIDP classes: `BlackBerryCanvas`, `BlackBerryGameCanvas`, and `BlackBerry Custom-Item` to respond to touch screen input events.

11.1.5 Important Differences Between MIDlets and RIMlets

There are several places where the functionality available to MIDlets and RIMlets differs. When building MIDlets, developers must take these differences into account and plan accordingly.

User Interface

In general, BlackBerry developers can use the CLDC, MIDP, and BlackBerry APIs in the same application. The only exception to this is related to User Interface Libraries. The BlackBerry UI APIs provide more functionality and greater control over the layout of screen elements than the corresponding MIDP libraries. If an application uses the BlackBerry APIs for UI, it must use only the BlackBerry UI APIs. An application must not use both the `javax.microedition.lcdui` (MIDP library) and `net.rim.device.api.ui` (RIM library) packages in the same application.

Persisting Data (Persistence)

The MIDP includes functionality that allows MIDlets to store data persistently and retrieve it later. The functionality is implemented through `javax.microedition.rms` and contains a record store implemented through the `RecordStore` class and its supporting methods. A record store is a collection of records that remain persistent between executions of a MIDlet. For additional information on this capability, refer to the online documentation for the library (http://java.sun.com/javame/reference/apis/jsr118/).

The BlackBerry platform supports the MIDP standard for persistence described above plus a BlackBerry Persistent Store API implemented through `net.rim.device.api.system.PersistentStore`. A RIMlet developer would likely prefer the BlackBerry persistence model, because it's easier to use than `javax.microedition.rms`. Developers would use rms when forced to by the limitations of MIDP portability.

BlackBerry devices running Device Software 4.2 can write persistent data to the file system using the capabilities provided by JSR 75. Examples for both of these options are provided in the BlackBerry Java Development Guides appropriate for the target version of the BlackBerry Device Software being used.

Beginning with BlackBerry Device Software 5.0, RIM added support for the open source SQLite database. Developers can use this capability to implement local databases that can be queried using Structured Query Language (SQL).

Signing Code

Signing code is detailed later in this chapter, but it's also important here for the comparison between MIDlets and RIMlets.

MIDP 2.0 has the concept of untrusted and trusted applications. A signed application is considered to be trusted, and unsigned applications are untrusted. Untrusted applications work on a device, but the user is prompted for permission before the application performs sensitive functions. When a user downloads an untrusted MIDlet, she is notified of the status of the application and prompted to confirm the application should be installed.

To make a MIDlet trusted, the application must be signed by a signing authority trusted by the device. In some cases, a device will already contain certificates from the major players in the market (like Verisign and Thawte). In other cases, a carrier will not deploy standard certificates to a device but will instead require that an application is signed with one of their proprietary keys.

Where this becomes interesting for BlackBerry developers is that RIM has its own signing process (which you'll find out about later and in the following chapters) and an application can only have one signature. When an application is signed by RIM, it cannot also be signed by any other signing authority. Where this is an issue is when a carrier requires their signature on an application before it can be deployed, you will not be able to comply if the application needs to be signed by RIM.

In the BlackBerry case, trusted means something completely different than the trusted status of MIDlets. The BlackBerry platform has built-in security features that give administrators fine-grained control over what an application can do on a device. This is explained in detail later this chapter.

11.2 Supporting Industry Standards

Wherever possible, RIM has leveraged existing standards for JME development. Wherever a relevant standard exists, the BlackBerry platform will use it rather than create its own. Standards for the Java platform are described in Java Specification Requests (JSR) and are approved through the Java Community Process. JSRs are referred to by number, and the BlackBerry platform supports a robust number of them.

Support for individual JSRs is added to the platform in different versions of the BlackBerry Device Software. When building an application that leverages the capabilities of a particular JSR, be sure that the target devices are running at a minimum the version of BlackBerry Device Software that added support for the feature.

The following list shows the standards that the BlackBerry platform supports:

- **JSR 30:** Connected Limited Device Configuration Version 1.0 (supported on BlackBerry devices running Device Software version 4.0 or earlier)
- **JSR 37:** Mobile Information Device Profile Version 1.0 (supported on BlackBerry devices running Device Software Version 4.0 or earlier)
- **JSR 75:** PDA optional packages, provides developers with access to the PIM and File Connection APIs
- **JSR 82:** Java APIs for Bluetooth
- **JSR 118:** Mobile Information Device Profile Version 2.0
- **JSR 120:** Wireless Messaging API (WMA) Version 1.1
- **JSR 135:** Mobile Media APIs (MM API) Version 1.1
- **JSR 139:** Connected Limited Device Configuration Version 1.1
- **JSR 172:** J2ME Web Services
- **JSR 177:** Security and Trust Services API for J2ME (SATSA)
- **JSR 179:** Location API for Java ME
- **JSR 185:** Java Technology for the Wireless Industry (JTWI)
- **JSR 205:** Wireless Messaging API 2.0
- **JSR 211:** Content Handler API
- **JSR 226:** Scalable 2D Vector Graphics API for Java ME
- **JSR 238:** Mobile Internationalization API

The JSRs have been implemented at different times, and the only version of the BlackBerry Device Software supporting all of them will be the most recent version. In general, when a JSR is added to the platform, it remains available for all future devices. Refer to the documentation for the particular BlackBerry Java development environment you are using for your applications to determine which JSRs are supported on the platform you have selected.

When building a BlackBerry application that leverages a particular type of technology (whether it be Bluetooth, Web Services, or any other standard) verify whether the standard is already supported by the BlackBerry platform before looking to implement special libraries for the feature. The easiest way to do this is to look up a particular standard's package in the BlackBerry API documentation installed with the BlackBerry development tools.

11.3 Writing Your First BlackBerry Java Application

The entry point into any RIMlet is the `main()` method just like other Java applications. An application with a user interface will use a main class that extends `net.rim.system.UiApplication`. For a background application or an application that does not have a user interface, the application's main class will extend `net.rim.system.Application`.

A `UiApplication` typically creates one or more screens that contains labels, edit fields, and other components and displays them on the BlackBerry screen (detailed later in this chapter). The screen on top of the stack of screens is the one visible to the user. To display a screen, the application pushes it onto the display stack using `pushScreen()`. Applications can remove a screen from the stack by calling `popScreen()`.

Let's look at a simple BlackBerry CLDC (a RIMlet) application. The application is a variant of the standard Hello World application that's used to educate programmers on the structure of a typical program in any development language. The BlackBerry version of this application is shown here:

```
1  package com.bbdevfundamentals.helloworld;
2
3  import net.rim.device.api.ui.*;
4  import net.rim.device.api.ui.component.*;
5  import net.rim.device.api.ui.container.*;
6
7  //Create the HelloWorld class
8  public class HelloWorld extends UiApplication {
9
10    public static void main(String[] args) {
11      //Instantiate the HelloWorld object
12      HelloWorld hw = new HelloWorld();
13      //Enter the Event Dispatcher
```

```
14        hw.enterEventDispatcher();
15    }
16
17    public HelloWorld() {
18        //Create the HelloWorldScreen and open it
19        pushScreen(new HelloWorldScreen());
20    }
21 }
22
23 final class HelloWorldScreen extends MainScreen {
24    public HelloWorldScreen() {
25      super();
26      //Create the screen's title
27      LabelField lblTitle = new LabelField(
          "BlackBerry Development Fundamentals",
          LabelField.ELLIPSIS | LabelField.USE_ALL_WIDTH);
28      //Add the title to the form
29      setTitle(lblTitle);
30      // add the text to the screen
31      add(new LabelField("Hello readers!"));
32    }
33}
```

The application sets the package name in line 1. It is important to note that packages that begin with com.rim or net.rim will not run on devices. What many developers do for their first applications is grab one of RIM's samples and modify it to suit their needs without changing the package name. You must change this to something else before attempting to run the application on a device. The application will run just fine on a simulator, but it will fail when executed on a device.

In lines 3 through 5, the program imports the packages used by the application (in this case, the RIM UI libraries).

In line 8, the application creates the HelloWorld class by extending the UIApplication class. This gives the application the standard user interface capabilities found in any BlackBerry application.

Lines 10 through 15 define the main() method for the application; this is the starting point for the application. Line 12 creates the reference to the HelloWorld class (where the application creates the screen and places the content on it). The program then calls enterEventDispatcher(). At this point, the application's main thread becomes the event-dispatching thread, which will execute all drawing and event-handling code for the application. The program will not be able to respond to user activity until the Event Dispatcher is entered by the application.

Note: The BlackBerry event dispatcher handles all user input and must be called by any BlackBerry application that expects to be able to process user input. If your application opens any network connections or performs any activities that might take some time to complete, the code must be executed after the call to enter EventDispatcher() and should run on its own thread. If you don't, the application will appear unresponsive, and any prompts the device displays to allow restricted actions (described later in this chapter) never appear for the user to acknowledge. A developer can use invokeLater() to schedule initialization events to run after the call to enterEventDispatcher().

Line 19 creates the HelloWorldScreen class and immediately pushes it on to the top of the screen stack on the device.

Line 23 begins the process of building the application screen. The Hello WorldScreen extends the BlackBerry MainScreen class, which is responsible for providing features common to standard RIM device applications.

Line 24 creates the HelloWorldScreen, and line 25 calls the constructor for the MainScreen class. After that, the application builds the screen elements and adds them to the screen.

Line 27 creates the LabelField that displays the application's title at the top of the screen, which is then added to the screen in line 29. The additional parameters passed to the LabelField constructor (LabelField.ELLIPSIS | LabelField.USE _ALL_WIDTH) instruct the field to use all width of the screen to display the label and use of ellipsis for text that is too long to draw in the available space.

Line 31 creates another LabelField that displays the message, "Hello readers!" on the screen.[1]

When this application is built and deployed to an older BlackBerry device, it appears directly on the BlackBerry Home Screen, as shown in Figure 11.2. The

---

1. I know, it's supposed to say "Hello World," but I decided to be a little different and limit the scope of the application to you rather than the entire world.

application doesn't have an icon associated with it yet; the steps required to assign an application icon are covered in Chapters 13 and 14.

Figure 11.2   Hello World application on the BlackBerry 8800 smartphone

On some devices (depending on the theme used on the device), the application appears in the device's downloads folder, as shown on the BlackBerry Bold smartphone in Figure 11.3.

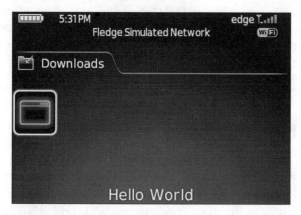

Figure 11.3   Hello World application on the BlackBerry Bold smartphone

When the application is opened, it displays a screen similar to the one shown in Figure 11.4. The title bar contains the text defined in line 27, and the main body of the screen contains the text defined in line 31.

> **BlackBerry Development Fundamentals**
> Hello readers!

Figure 11.4   BlackBerry Hello World application screen

 Note: Subsequent chapters demonstrate how to use the BlackBerry Java development tools to build the application. Chapter 12, "Getting Started with the Black-Berry Java Development Tools," contains information on how to get started with the different development tools; then Chapters 13, 14, and 15 provide information on how to use each of the tools. Chapter 16, "Deploying Java Applications," describes the ways a BlackBerry Java application can be deployed to BlackBerry devices.

11.4 Digging into the BlackBerry APIs

Now that we know about the different application types for BlackBerry and how to build a simple Hello World application, it's time to discuss the BlackBerry-specific libraries available to developers. The following sections deal with the extensions to Java RIM created to support additional capabilities provided by the BlackBerry platform. These extensions take the form of additional packages and associated classes, methods and properties a developer can use when creating applications targeted specifically at the BlackBerry platform. The extensions fit into the following categories:

- **User Interface APIs:** Create screens, menu items, and all the components of the application's user interface.

- **Persistent Data Storage APIs:** Store custom application data locally within an application.

- **Networking and I/O APIs:** Establish network connections to read or write data to a server-side application.

- **Event Listeners:** Respond to BlackBerry device user or system initiated events on a BlackBerry device.

- **Application Integration APIs:** Integrate with the existing BlackBerry applications, such as email, phone, calendar, contacts, browser, camera, media player, and task list applications.

- **Additional Utilities:** Provide access to Service Books, device information, data encryption and compression capabilities, XML parsing, Bluetooth connectivity, location-based services, and more.

In some cases, RIM has added libraries that provide additional capabilities beyond a specific JSR. For example, for Bluetooth, a developer can use the `javax.bluetooth` package for standard Bluetooth support, but can also use `net.rim.device.api.bluetooth` to add serial communication support for Bluetooth connections. For Location support, an application can use the services provided by JSR 179 (`javax.microedition.location`) but also the RIM extension `net.rim.device.api.gps` to access the GPS receiver settings.

To access detailed information about each of these libraries, refer to the BlackBerry JDE API Reference installed with the BlackBerry JDE. A sample of the content included in the API reference is shown in Figure 11.5. The upper-left window lists each of the packages included with the particular BlackBerry Device Software version. With a package selected, the lower-left window highlights the different classes included in the package. When you select a package or a class from the lower-left window, the documentation for the selected item appears in the window on the right.

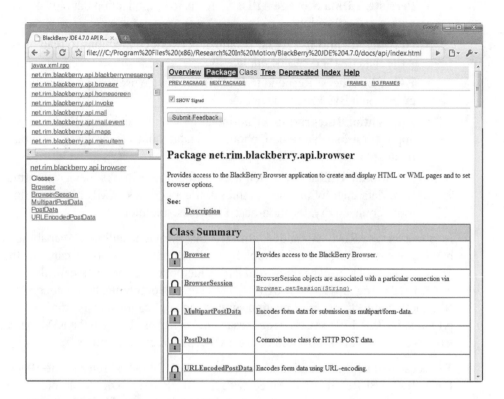

Figure 11.5   BlackBerry Java API reference

11.4.1 Building a User interface

Most BlackBerry applications have a user interface that the user can use to inter-act with the application. While the MIDP specification has libraries for user interface components, the BlackBerry platform has more flexible libraries, which is better suited to take advantage of the BlackBerry device. In general, an application's interface is typically built using fields, layout managers, and menus.

Figure 11.6 shows a subset of the BlackBerry Java object hierarchy. As is normal with Java, everything derives, either directly or indirectly, from the Object class. For the majority of the UI classes, the components you use to build screens for your application derive (directly or indirectly) from the Field class. What this means, essentially, is that the different field types, layout managers, and screen types all extend from Field.

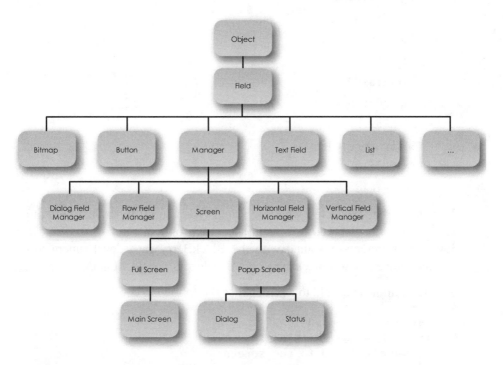

Figure 11.6   BlackBerry Java object hierarchy

Fields

Fields are the basic building blocks of any user interface, and if you look at the BlackBerry Java API reference, you see that both `Manager` and `Screen` descend from `Field`. The `Field` Class provides the fundamental properties and methods used by each of the Field types, Field Managers, and Screens (because they derive from Field Manager).

The default types of fields provided in the BlackBerry platform are as follows:

- `ActiveRichTextField`
- `BitmapField`
- `ButtonField`
- `CheckboxField`
- `ChoiceField`
- `DateField`
- `EditField`
- `GaugeField`

- LabelField
- ListField
- Manager
- MapField
- NullField
- RadioButtonField
- RichTextField
- SeparatorField
- TextField
- TreeField

You should be able to tell what each field type is used for by the field object's class name. For detailed information on each option, refer to the BlackBerry Java API Reference installed with the BlackBerry Java development tools or located online at www.blackberry.com/developers/docs/4.7.0api/index.html.

To add a simple text field to a screen, use the following code:

```
EditField lastName;
lastName = new EditField();
// add the field to the screen
add(tmpField);
```

You can also place a label to the left of the field using the following simplified version of the code:

```
EditField lastName = new EditField("Last Name: ", "");
// add the field to the screen
add(tmpField);
```

You can create a filtered field, a field that only accepts a certain type of data, using the following code:

```
BasicEditField editParts
editParts = new BasicEditField("Participants: ", "10", 3,
  EditField.FILTER_INTEGER);
// add the field to the screen
add(editParts);
```

In this example, "10" specifies the initial value for the field and the maximum number of characters allowed in the field is 3. The EditField.FILTER_INTEGER parameter specifies that the field can only contain Integer values.

The `RichTextField` class can be used to add fields to a screen that render richly formatted text. An extension of this is the `ActiveRichTextField`, which scans through the field's contents and picks out "active" regions. Active regions are underlined and supply additional actions when the user clicks on them. You would use this field type when you want to have your program make content within the field active (so the user can click them and perform actions) within the application. A BlackBerry automatically creates menu items for the standard web URLs, email addresses, phone numbers, and PIN. Developers can create custom string patterns (for order or part numbers, for example) and make them active within an application. The fields are added to a screen just like the other field types; you can also configure the field to be read-only, as shown in the following example:

```
// Allocate space for a temporary field
 ActiveRichTextField tmpField;
// Create the field and specify the contents value
tmpField = new ActiveRichTextField(strValue);
// Make the field read-only
tmpField.setEditable(false);
// add the field to the Screen
add(tmpField);
```

Another UI component available to BlackBerry Java developers is the Browser Field. The Browser Field isn't a field in that it derives from `Field`; it's a package that can be treated like a field. The Browser Field is implemented through `net.rim.device.api.browser.field` and can render web content within a Java application. For more information, refer to the `BrowserField` sample application included in the JDE and eJDE Samples workspace.

BlackBerry Widgets use the new BrowserField2 added to BlackBerry Device Software 5.0 to enhance the capabilities of the Browser Field.

Field Managers

Field Managers descend from `Manager` (which itself descends from `Field`) and control the layout of objects on a screen. Available options are

- `DialogFieldManager`
- `FlowFieldManager`
- `HorizontalFieldManager`
- `Screen`[2]
- `VerticalFieldManager`

---

2. Yes, a BlackBerry Screen is a type of layout manager; this is discussed in a later section.

By default, a BlackBerry application screen uses a Vertical Field Manager. When building a screen, you can nest Field Managers within other Field Managers and create some interesting interfaces. Figure 11.7 shows a simple example of how nested Field Managers can be used within an application.

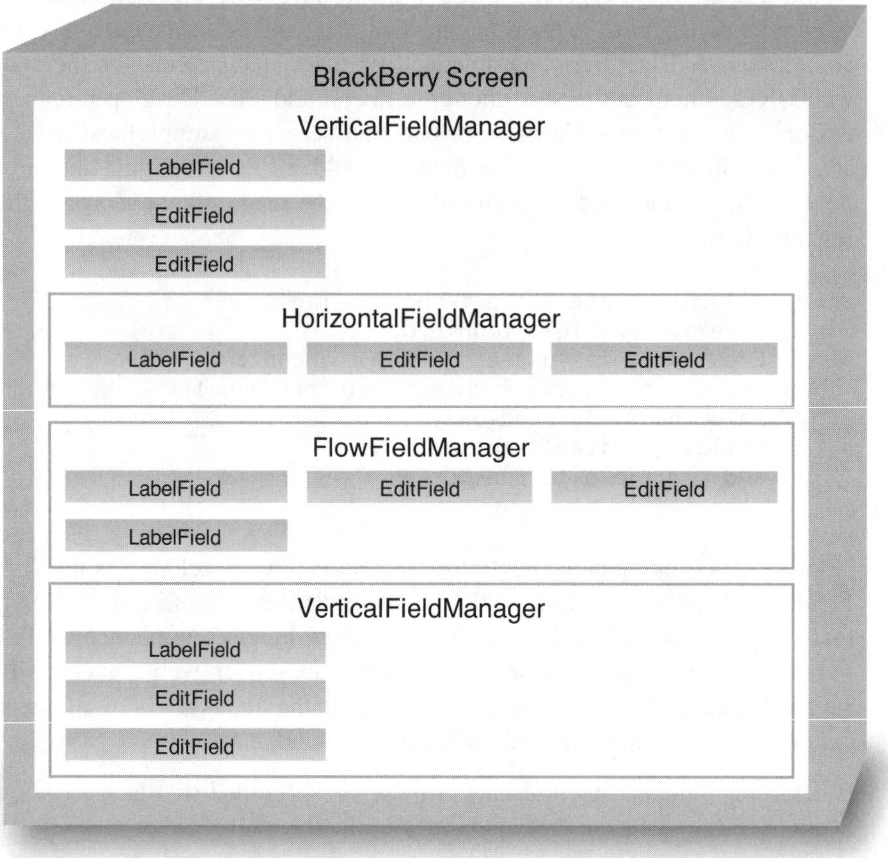

Figure 11.7   BlackBerry screen architecture

The following sample application illustrates how to build an application screen using multiple Field and Field Manager types:

```
1 package com.bbdevfundamentals.ScreenLayout;
2
3 import net.rim.device.api.ui.UiApplication;
4 import net.rim.device.api.ui.component.ButtonField;
5 import net.rim.device.api.ui.component.EditField;
6 import net.rim.device.api.ui.component.LabelField;
7 import net.rim.device.api.ui.component.RichTextField;
8 import net.rim.device.api.ui.component.SeparatorField;
9 import net.rim.device.api.ui.container.FlowFieldManager;
```

```
10   import
         net.rim.device.api.ui.container.HorizontalFieldManager;
11   import net.rim.device.api.ui.container.MainScreen;
12
13   //Create the HelloWorld class
14   public class ScreenLayout extends UiApplication {
15
16      public static void main(String[] args) {
17         // Instantiate the HelloWorld object
18         ScreenLayout sl = new ScreenLayout();
19       · // Enter the Event Dispatcher
20         sl.enterEventDispatcher();
21   }
22
23   public ScreenLayout() {
24      pushScreen(new ScreenLayoutScreen());
25   }
26   }
27
28   final class ScreenLayoutScreen extends MainScreen {
29   public ScreenLayoutScreen() {
30      super();
31      // By default the BlackBerry screen uses a
32      // Vertical Flow Manager
33      LabelField lblTitle = new
            LabelField("Screen Layout Sample",
            LabelField.ELLIPSIS | LabelField.USE_ALL_WIDTH);
34      setTitle(lblTitle);
35      add(new LabelField("Field 1"));
36      add(new LabelField("Field 2"));
37      add(new LabelField("Field 3"));
38
39      // Now lets switch to a Horizontal flow manager
40      HorizontalFieldManager hfm =
            new HorizontalFieldManager();
41      this.add(hfm);
42      hfm.add(new LabelField("Label Field 4"));
43      hfm.add(new LabelField("Label Field 5"));
44      hfm.add(new EditField("Edit Field", "1"));
45      hfm.add(new EditField("Edit Field", "2"));
46
47      // Now a flow field manager
48      FlowFieldManager flowManager = new FlowFieldManager();
49      this.add(flowManager);
50      ButtonField button1 = new ButtonField("Button 1");
51      ButtonField button2 = new ButtonField("Button 2");
52      ButtonField button3 = new ButtonField("Button 3");
53      ButtonField button4 = new ButtonField("Button 4");
```

```
54      flowManager.add(button1);
55      flowManager.add(button2);
56      flowManager.add(button3);
57      flowManager.add(button4);
58
59      // Back to using the default vertical flow manager
60      this.add(new SeparatorField());
61      this.add(new
           RichTextField("Let's add some more edit fields:"));
62      add(new EditField("Edit Field", "3"));
63      add(new EditField("Edit Field", "4"));
64   }
65 }
```

Figure 11.8 shows what the application looks like when executed on the Black-Berry simulator. Notice that the second edit field (defined in line 45) doesn't appear on the screen; that's because it was added to a Horizontal Field Manager and there wasn't enough room to display it in the available horizontal space. The user would have to scroll the screen horizontally to see the field.

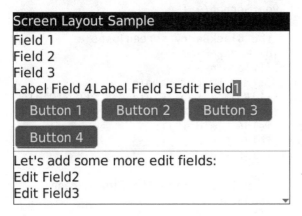

Figure 11.8   Screen layout sample

In lines 50 through 57, the application adds the buttons to the screen. Because there is usually more you want to do with buttons, they're created as individual objects (lines 50 through 53) so that code can be added later to execute when the button is clicked. Normally, you would create edit field objects and add them individually (so they can be manipulated later), but that was left out of the sample to make the code simpler.

Button 4 wraps around to the next line on the screen, because it was added to a Flow Field Manager and it knows how to deal with the available screen space.

Screens

In a BlackBerry Java application, a `Screen` is just a special kind of layout manager. The difference between a `Screen` and the other layout managers is the extra application functionality that's included automatically when the screen is created. A BlackBerry Java Application can display more than one screen at a time, but can have only one screen active at any time.

As shown in the HelloWorld example, after you create a screen, you can add fields to the screen and display it by pushing the screen onto the display stack. Here is a brief summary of the `Screen` types:

- **Screen:** Base class for all screens.
- **FullScreen:** Contains a single vertical field manager. You can create a `FullScreen` for your application to provide an empty screen that the application can add UI components to using a vertical layout.
- **MainScreen:** The standard screen for any BlackBerry Java application. This screen type contains a title section, a separator, and a main scrollable section consisting of a `VerticalFieldManager`. It also inherits the default menu and menu items for the application.
- **PopupScreen:** Provides features for building dialog and status screens.
- **Dialog:** Displays a dialog box with predefined configurations. This type of screen is displayed when the application executes `alert(java.lang.String)`, `ask(int)`, or `inform(java.lang.String)`. The screen displays and waits for user input.
- **Status:** Displays a simple dialog to show the status of a process.

For an example of how to create an application screen, refer to the HelloWorld sample application shown earlier.

11.4.2 Adding Menu Items

An application uses menu items to add contextual actions to an application in a way that does not take up any of the limited screen real estate available to the application. A `Menu` object has associated menu items that are created as `Runnable` objects executed when the menu item is selected. Menu items can be added to a custom application, but RIM also provides the means to add menu items to other applications on the device.

Adding Items to the BlackBerry Menu

An application can also add menu items to the BlackBerry menu. Menus are created by overriding the `UiApplication` class `makeMenu()` method and adding the code to execute when the menu item is selected, as shown in the following sample:

```
public MenuItem mnuAbout = new MenuItem("About", 150, 10) {
  public void run() {
    Status.show("Created by John M. Wargo,
      www.bbdevfundamentals.com");
  }
};

public void makeMenu(Menu menu, int instance) {
  menu.add(mnuAbout);
}
```

When the menu item is selected, the program briefly displays a message for the user. To implement this menu in the Hello World application, just add the code to the HelloWorld class (beginning after line 8 in the sample application).

After you have the code added that executes when the menu item is selected, it's time to build the list of menu options available to the user. This is accomplished by overriding the MainScreen class' makeMenu() method and adding the appropriate items as needed, as shown in the following example:

```
public void makeMenu(Menu menu, int instance) {
  //disable this menu item when there are no results to email
  if (myList.getSize() > 0) {
    menu.add(mnuEmail);
  }
  menu.add(mnuAbout);
  menu.add(mnuClose);
}
```

An application can also add menu items conditionally. In the sample code, the mnuEmail menu item is added to the menu only if at least one item is displayed in the myList ListBox.

To ensure that the default menu items provided by the MainScreen class are available to your program, add the following code to the constructor for the class that extends MainScreen in the application:

```
super(DEFAULT_MENU | DEFAULT_CLOSE);
```

Adding Menu Items to Other Applications

The BlackBerry platform allows Java applications to register menu items in other applications on the device. You can't add menu items to any application, just to the System menu (available to any application) and to specific, RIM-supplied device applications. The functionality is provided in the net.rim.blackberry.api.menuitem.* libraries.

To register the menu item, an application must run code similar to the example shown here:

```
class examplePluginMain{

    public static void main(String[] args){
        new examplePluginMain();
    }

    //Constructor called by main, to register the plugin.
    examplePluginMain(){
        registerPlugin();
    }

    void registerPlugin(){
        ApplicationMenuItemRepository repository =
            ApplicationMenuItemRepository.getInstance();
        repository.addMenuItem(
            ApplicationMenuItemRepository.MENUITEM_SYSTEM,
            new GetExampleMenuItem());
    }
}
```

In this example, the call to `repository.addMenuItem` is where the menu item is registered. The `ApplicationMenuItemRepository.MENUITEM_SYSTEM` parameter passed to the method tells the BlackBerry Application Manager to add the menu item to the System menu. To add the menu item to the list of email messages shown in the Messages application, the application would use the `ApplicationMenuItemRepository.MENUITEM_EMAIL_VIEW` field instead. For a complete list of the available locations where menu items can be added, refer to the API documentation for the `net.rim.blackberry.api.menuitem.ApplicationMenuItemRepository`.

The second parameter passed to `addMenuItem()` is the class that contains the code that is executed when the menu item is selected, as shown in the following example:

```
class GetExampleMenuItem extends ApplicationMenuItem {

    public GetExampleMenuItem(){
        // Controls the relative menu position
        super(1000);
    }

    public Object run(){
        //Do some stuff here
```

```
        }

    }
```

11.4.3 Local Data Storage

As mentioned previously, a BlackBerry Java application can use the BlackBerry Persistent Store APIs and the MIDP RMS APIs to store data to persistent (non-volatile) memory.

Beginning with the BlackBerry Pearl Smartphone (the first BlackBerry device with expandable memory), RIM added support for JSR 75, which included support for the Personal Information Manager (PIM) API and the `FileConnection` API. The `FileConnection` API is implemented through the `javax.microedition.io.file` package and allows developers to read and write to the file system available on a microSD Memory card plugged into the device.

Because BlackBerry devices have limited device memory available for application data, developers should use the capabilities provided by the `FileConnection` API to write large amounts of application data to the memory card. The data can be written in any format deemed appropriate for the application. For performance and battery life conservation, developers should seek to find a happy balance between the amount of space taken up by the data versus the amount of work the application has to perform to put the data into a particular format and write it out. Also, don't forget that, with the SQLite capabilities added in BlackBerry Device Software 5.0, developers have another way to write data to a repository.

11.4.4 Connecting to Network Resources

The BlackBerry platform supports a robust collection of options for connecting to network-based resources. The options supported are the ones provided by the standard `javax.microedition.io` package. The package supports connections using

- HTTP
- HTTPS
- Sockets
- Datagrams
- USB
- Serial Port
- Bluetooth

Most network-connection options were discussed in Chapter 3, "The Connected BlackBerry." For additional information on those connections and more, refer to the *BlackBerry Java Development Environment Development Guide* available on the BlackBerry Developer's website (www.blackberry.com/developers).

11.4.5 Accessing Service Books

In Chapter 3, the discussion focused on making connections to servers from BlackBerry applications. One of the important points from that chapter was that, in many cases, developers had to retrieve the appropriate APN to use to open certain types of connections (non-MDS connections). This is accomplished by searching Service-Book information maintained on the device. The sample class shown here demonstrates how to retrieve the WAP Browser Service Book from a device and can be easily extended to be able to locate any Service Book:

```
1  import net.rim.device.api.system.*;
2  import net.rim.device.api.servicebook.*;
3
4  public class ServiceBookExample extends Application {
5  //Create a ServiceRecord array
6  ServiceRecord[] _sRecordsArray;  ServiceBook _servicebook;
7  //Creates a ServiceBook variable
8  String cidValue, sbName, sbAPN;
9
10   public static void main(String[] args)
11   {
12     // Create a new instance of the application and
13     // start the event thread.
14     ServiceBookExample app = new ServiceBookExample();
15     app.enterEventDispatcher();
16   }
17
18   public ServiceBookExample() {
19     // Returns a reference to the service book from the
       factory.
20     _servicebook = ServiceBook.getSB();
21     // Returns an array of all registered service records.
22     _sRecordsArray = _servicebook.getRecords();
23     // Loops through the service record array
24     // and obtains specific information relating
25     // to each item and prints it to the debugging output.
26     for(int i = 0; i < _sRecordsArray.length; i++) {
27       // Obtains the Service Book CID
28       cidValue = _sRecordsArray[i].getCid();
29       // Obtains the Name of the Service Book
30       sbName = _sRecordsArray[i].getName();
```

```
31      if(cidValue.equals("BrowserConfig")
        && sbName.startsWith("WAP Browser")) {
32        // Obtains the Service Book's APN
33        // (Associated Access Point Name)
34        String sbAPN = _sRecordsArray[i].getAPN();
35      }
36    }
37  }
38 }
```

The example was taken from the BlackBerry Development Knowledge Base article titled, "How To: Access and Obtain Service Books on a Device," and is used with permission. To locate the full article online, go to www.blackberry.com/developers and search for knowledge base article DB-00418.

When working with Service Books, the UID is the unique identifier for a Service Record and the CID is the Content ID, its group designation.

In line 20, the application retrieves the Service Book from the device and line 22 gets all Service Book records. After the program has access to all the records, it begins looping through all of them in line 26.

The application obtains the Service Book CID (line 28), and the Service Book name (line 30) then queries the values to determine whether it points to a BrowserConfig entry and begins with the Service Book name we're looking for (line 31). After it knows it has the right Service Book entry, it retrieves the APN name from the record. This is the value you pass as a parameter when opening a connection to a server using this particular APN. Refer to Chapter 3 for additional information on this option.

11.4.6 Working with Other BlackBerry Applications

The BlackBerry Java development environment includes libraries that a developer can use to integrate with other applications included on the device. The methods for integration differ, depending on which applications you're integrating with and the nature of the integration. A detailed discussion of the available options is beyond the scope of this book, but RIM has created a document dedicated to application integration called the *BlackBerry Java Application Integration Development Guide* available for later BlackBerry Device Software versions. The guide can be downloaded from the Java section of the documentation downloads area of the BlackBerry Developer's website (www.blackberry.com/developers). Some of the integration options are described in the following sections.

Invoking Applications

One of the most common application integrations is to create a data item in another application or to control another application's actions. On the Black-Berry platform, those capabilities are provided by the `Invoke` class defined in the `net.rim.blackberry.api.invoke.Invoke` package.

To use `Invoke`, an application creates the appropriate `net.rim.blackberry.api.invoke.ApplicationArguments` for the application being invoked then passes them in a call to the `Invoke` method with a field indicating the application being invoked. The `ApplicationArguments` object contains information being passed to the invoked application. For example, to invoke the Messages application, use the following code:

```
Invoke.invokeApplication(Invoke.APP_TYPE_MESSAGES,
    new MessageArguments(message));
```

This instructs the BlackBerry to open the Messages application to the default view. To open the Messages application to a different folder, or to invoke the Messages application and create a particular message, you can invoke Messages with different `MessageArgument` objects.

Using the Content Handler API

An application can use the Content Handler API (JSR 211) to register a handler for a particular content type (a particular file attachment type for example) on a BlackBerry device. When the particular content type is opened (whether from an email message, browser session, or from the local file system), the registered application is opened to process the content. For additional information, visit java.sun.com/products/chapi.

Manipulating Message Folders

A BlackBerry Java application can manipulate the contents of message folders by retrieving a list of the available message folders and opening the folder of interest. For example, to access the inbox, import the `net.rim.blackberry.api.mail.Store` and `net.rim.blackberry.api.mail.Folder` packages and then execute the following code:

```
Store store = Session.getStore();
Folder[] folders = store.list(Folder.INBOX);
Folder inbox = folders[0];
```

After the application has a handle to the folder, it can register a listener on the folder using the following code:

```
inbox.addFolderListener(this);
```

With the listener in place, the application can act whenever something happens in the folder. This includes when new messages are deposited in the folder, deleted from the folder, and more.

Integrating with the Phone

The Phone application can be invoked like other BlackBerry applications. In general, an application would invoke the phone to place a call using the phone number provided through a PhoneArguments object passed to the application. Applications can register Phone listeners and retrieve information about an active phone call.

Integrating with PIM Applications

Included with JSR 75 is an interface that Java applications can use to integrate with PIM applications on a device. The libraries included in the javax. microedition.pim.PIM package provide access to retrieve information from and manipulate calendar entries, contact list and tasks.

Launching the Browser

The first application many developers are asked to build is an application that opens a URL in the browser. The following application sample illustrates how to build a BlackBerry Java application that launches the default browser and opens a URL included in the application. It uses the default browser (rather than a specific browser), because this is the simplest example to show.

 Note: Browser Channels (described in Chapter 6, "Pushing Data to Internal (BES) Users") can be used for this, but they have limitations in that an application must be executed to push the icon to a device, and it only works with BES-connected devices. By creating an application in Java for this, organizations get something that can be easily deployed from the BES, controlled by Application Control Policies, and can even be deployed to external devices without needing to code a Web Signal (described in Chapter 7, "Pushing Data to External (BIS) Users").

```
1  /*
2   * urlLaunch.java
3   *
```

```
 4 * This application launches a specific URL using the
     device's
 5 * default browser. Refer to BlackBerry Developer Knowledge
 6 * Base article DB-00701 for information on how to launch a
 7 * particular browser.
 8 */
 9 package com.bbdevfundamentals.urlLaunch;
10
11 import net.rim.blackberry.api.browser.Browser;
12 import net.rim.blackberry.api.browser.BrowserSession;
13 import net.rim.device.api.system.Application;
14
15 public class urlLaunch extends Application {
16
17   // Put the URL you want launched here
18 private static String appURL =
       "http://www.bbdevfundamentals.com";
19
20   public static void main(String[] args) {
21     urlLaunch theApp = new urlLaunch();
22     theApp.enterEventDispatcher();
23   }
24
25   public urlLaunch() {
26     // Get the default browser session
27     BrowserSession browserSession =
         Browser.getDefaultSession();
29     // Then display the page using the browser session
29     browserSession.displayPage(appURL);
30     // Once the URL is launched, close this application
31     System.exit(0);
32   }
33}
```

The unique thing about this application is that it doesn't have a user interface. The application's class extends Application instead of UiApplication as most BlackBerry Java applications do.

Line 18 creates a String variable to hold the URL that the application will launch. Developers should, of course, change this to the appropriate URL for the site being accessed.

All the work of the application is done in lines 25 through 32. A new Browser Session is created in line 27, then set to the default Browser session through the call to the Browser.getDefaultSession() method. In line 29, the default browser is opened using the URL provided in the appURL constant. In line 31, the program exits leaving the browser open to the specified page.

Note: There was a bug in BlackBerry Device Software 4.2, where the browser would load but not move into the forefront on the BlackBerry screen. When running the application on BlackBerry Device Software 4.2, you need to add `browser Session.showBrowser();` between lines 30 and 31.

Chapter 12 covers how to use the conditional compilation capabilities of the Black-Berry Java development tools to build two versions of this application from a single source file. This allows you to accommodate most devices and make a version of the application specifically for BlackBerry Device Software 4.2.

To learn how to launch a specific browser, refer to the BlackBerry Developer Knowledge Base article titled, "How To: Invoke the Browser." This application is similar to the Web Icons users can download from the BlackBerry App Store that opens the browser to a company's home page; for information on this option, refer to "How To: Create a Web Icon" (BlackBerry Developer Knowledge Base article DB-00709).

11.4.7 Event Listening and System Interfaces

For a many applications, it's important to know when the status of the device changes. For example, an application that regularly sends or receives data from a server will need to know when the network connection is available. Because the device could be going in and out of coverage as it moves from place to place, it's more efficient to know when the network status changes rather than to query it periodically. The BlackBerry `net.rim.device.api.system` library provides developers with interfaces they can use to register listeners for many different types of events that occur on a BlackBerry device:

- `AccelerometerListener`
- `AlertListener`
- `AlertListener2`
- `AudioListener`
- `CoverageStatusListener`
- `GlobalEventListener`
- `IOPortListener`
- `KeyListener`
- `KeypadListener`
- `PersistentContentListener`
- `RadioListener`
- `RadioStatusListener`
- `RealtimeClockListener`

- SensorListener
- SystemListener
- SystemListener2
- USBPortListener
- WLANConnectionListener
- WLANListener

An application must register a listener for the particular interface it's interested in, then provide the appropriate methods that are called when the listener fires. To see an example of how this works, look at the following code. It illustrates how to create a listener using the SensorListener interface. In the example, the application registers a Sensor listener and identifies the specific sensor being monitored (in this case, the holster). In this example, the application displays an alert whenever the device goes in and out of the holster:

```
package com.bbdevfundamentals.SensorTest;

import net.rim.device.api.ui.UiApplication;
import net.rim.device.api.ui.component.Dialog;
import net.rim.device.api.ui.component.LabelField;
import net.rim.device.api.ui.container.MainScreen;
import net.rim.device.api.system.Application;
import net.rim.device.api.system.SensorListener;
import net.rim.device.api.system.Sensor;

public class SensorTest extends UiApplication
  implements SensorListener {

  public static void main(String[] args) {
  // Instantiate the HelloWorld object
  SensorTest st = new SensorTest();
  // Enter the Event Dispatcher
  st.enterEventDispatcher();
  }

  public SensorTest() {
    pushScreen(new SensorTestScreen());
    Sensor.addListener(Application.getApplication(), this,
      Sensor.HOLSTER);
  }

  public void onSensorUpdate(int sensorId, int update) {
    if (update == Sensor.STATE_IN_HOLSTER) {
      Dialog.alert("Device is holstered");
    } else {
      Dialog.alert("Device is not holstered");
    }
```

```
    }
}

final class SensorTestScreen extends MainScreen {
  public SensorTestScreen() {
    super();
    // Create the screen's title
    LabelField lblTitle = new LabelField("Sensor Test",
      LabelField.ELLIPSIS | LabelField.USE_ALL_WIDTH);
    setTitle(lblTitle);
  }
}
```

There is a wealth of information exposed through the `net.rim.device.`
`api.system` library. When you get a chance, spend some time poking through
the documentation for the library to see what else is available.

BlackBerry applications can send notifications to other applications using
`GlobalEvents`. When an application triggers a `GlobalEvent`, any application
that has registered a `GlobalEventListener` will receive the event notification.
The application triggering the event specifies an ID unique to the application
and includes it with the event. The listening application then looks at the ID to
determine whether the event should be dealt with or ignored. The `Global`
`Event` is triggered through a call to `postGlobalEvent()`, as shown in the following example:

```
ApplicationManager.getApplicationManager().
  postGlobalEvent(SomeUniqueID);
```

The event can even include data that the listening application retrieves and processes; a `GlobalEvent` can pass two integer variables and two objects to a listening application. A `GlobalEventListener` is registered the same way as the
`SensorListener`, shown in the provided SensorTest application.

11.4.8 Location-Based Services and BlackBerry Maps

Most BlackBerry devices released starting with the 8820 and beyond included hardware support for determining the location of the device using information received
from GPS satellites. As previously mentioned, the BlackBerry Java platform supports interacting with GPS location information using the JSR 179 standard. To use

this in an application, the application must create a LocationProvider, as shown in the following example. The Criteria object shown in the code defines parameters controlling how the location is determined:

```
import javax.microedition.location.*;

public LocationProvider lp;
Criteria cr = new Criteria();

cr.setAddressInfoRequired(false);
cr.setAltitudeRequired(false);
cr.setPreferredResponseTime(Criteria.NO_REQUIREMENT);
cr.setSpeedAndCourseRequired(false);
cr.setCostAllowed(true);
cr.setHorizontalAccuracy(Criteria.NO_REQUIREMENT);
cr.setPreferredPowerConsumption(Criteria.NO_REQUIREMENT);
cr.setVerticalAccuracy(Criteria.NO_REQUIREMENT);

try {
  // set up a location provider instance
  lp = LocationProvider.getInstance(cr);
  if ( lp == null ) {
      Dialog.alert("GPS is not supported, exiting...");
    }
  };
}
} catch (LocationException le) {
  System.err.println(le);
  System.exit(0);
}
```

After the application has access to a LocationProvider object, it can obtain the location using the following code:

```
// Get location, one minute timeout
Location loc = lp.getLocation(60);
if (loc.isValid()) {
  Coordinates c = loc.getQualifiedCoordinates();
  if (c != null) {
    // use coordinate information to update the screen
    double latitude = c.getLatitude();
    double longitude = c.getLongitude();
    float altitude = c.getAltitude();
  }
} else {
  //Notify the user that we could not retrieve the location
}
```

Applications can also use the Invoke class to launch the BlackBerry Maps application. As described earlier, an application is invoked and passed an ApplicationArguments object that's used to tell the invoked application what to do. In the case of the Maps application, an application would use a MapsArgument to pass location information or routes to the Maps application. Several different types of locations can be passed to the Maps application. In the following example, a Longitude and Latitude are written into a XML-based location document and passed to the Maps application. In this example, when the Maps application loads, it immediately highlights the specified location:

```
int mult = 100000;
float tmpLat = Float.parseFloat(latValue);
float tmpLong = Float.parseFloat(longValue());
//Build our location document using the long and lat values
String location = "<location-document><location x='" +
  Integer.toString((int)(tmpLong * mult)) +
  "' y='" +  Integer.toString((int)(tmpLat * mult)) +
  "' label='Current Location' description=
  'This is your current location.'/></location-document>";
//Create a MapsArguments object to hold location information
MapsArguments ma = new
  MapsArguments(MapsArguments.ARG_LOCATION_DOCUMENT,
  location);
try {
  //Launch the maps application
  Invoke.invokeApplication(Invoke.APP_TYPE_MAPS, ma);
} catch (IllegalArgumentException iaex) {
  System.err.println(iaex);
  Dialog.alert("Illegal Argument Exception: " + iaex);
}
```

For additional information on how a developer can use the GPS and Maps application capabilities, refer to the *BlackBerry Java Development Environment: GPS and BlackBerry Maps Development Guide* available on the BlackBerry Developer's website (www.blackberry.com/developers).

11.4.9 Rich Multimedia Features

BlackBerry applications can leverage the rich multimedia capabilities of the BlackBerry device. A BlackBerry Java application can

- Play media files in the BlackBerry browser
- Load and play media files using the BlackBerry Media application
- Record audio from the device microphone or Bluetooth headset

- Play audio through the device speaker, earpiece, or Bluetooth headset
- Play binary SVG content

For additional information on the rich media capabilities available to Java developers, refer to the *BlackBerry Java Development Environment: Multimedia Development Guide* available on the BlackBerry Developer's website (www.blackberry.com/developers). For information on the supported media types, visit www.blackberry.com/btsc/support and look for knowledge base article KB05482.

11.4.10 Newer Capabilities

RIM is constantly updating the capabilities of the BlackBerry platform. This section covers several of the more interesting features that have made it into the most recent versions of the BlackBerry Device Software.

Accelerometer

To support the dynamic horizontal and vertical orientation available on the BlackBerry Storm smartphone, RIM added an accelerometer to the device. The accelerometer senses the orientation and acceleration of a BlackBerry device (in three dimensions). Beginning with the 4.7 JDE, RIM added the `AccelerometerListener` interface to the `net.rim.device.api.system` package to allow an application to respond to the orientation and acceleration of a BlackBerry device.

When the listener is triggered, the listener's `onData()` method is fired and passed an `AccelerometerData` object that contains information about the device's current orientation and speed. A developer can use this information to create a game application that uses the device's orientation instead of the keyboard to control activities within the game.

Décor

The `net.rim.device.api.ui.decor` package added in BlackBerry Device Software 4.6 allows developers to

- Create custom backgrounds for screens
- Create custom backgrounds for fields
- Customize input field borders

In this case, a background is defined as an "unfocusable rectangular region contained within a screen or a field." An application cannot create a background directly; it must use a `BackgroundFactory` when creating custom backgrounds for a field or screen.

Spell Check

Beginning with BlackBerry Device Software 4.3.1, RIM provided developers with the means to perform a spell check on the UI fields within an application. The functionality is provided by the `net.rim.blackberry.api.spellcheck` package and gives the application user options for spelling corrections. An application can use the `SpellCheckUI` interface to provide the user with an interface for correcting spelling issues as they are found.

Touch Events

With the release of the BlackBerry Storm smartphone, RIM's first touch-screen device, new libraries were added to the BlackBerry Java development environment to allow developers to leverage the new touch and gesture-based interface. Support for touch screens began with BlackBerry Device Software 4.7 and the classes for interfacing with the touch interface were added to the `net.rim.device.api.ui` package. The package includes `TouchScreen`, `TouchEvent`, and `TouchGesture` classes that provide developers with the capabilities they need to detect and respond to touch screen events.

Because the device does not contain a physical keyboard, the platform was also enhanced to include support for a virtual keyboard which can be used for data input.

To run applications created for older versions of the BlackBerry Device Software (devices with trackwheels or trackballs), the device also supports a compatibility mode, which locks an application in portrait mode and simulates the input controls native to older devices. When an application runs in compatibility mode,

- Clicking a touch screen is equivalent to clicking the trackball.
- Touching a location on the touch screen is equivalent to rolling the trackball to the location.
- Clicking an object sets focus to the clicked object.

Any application built for a BlackBerry Device Software version earlier than 4.7 automatically runs in compatibility mode. For an application built for BlackBerry Device Software 4.7 and later, a developer can force compatibility mode by making a modification to the application's .alx file.

To help developers build touch capable applications, RIM created a special document called *BlackBerry Java Development Environment: Transitioning to Touch Screen Development*. The *BlackBerry Java Development Environment Version: 4.7.0 Development Guide* has also been updated to include sample code and additional information on how to leverage the touch screen classes. To obtain the guides, go to the BlackBerry Developer's website (www.blackberry.com/developers) and look for the document in the Documentation area for the 4.7 Java development tools.

11.5 Using Controlled BlackBerry APIs

The BlackBerry architecture has been designed from the ground up with security in mind. If you think about the different APIs available to developers, many of them are rather innocuous, but some of them, such as the networking or browser APIs, could be useful in building viruses and malware applications. In other cases, RIM might also need to restrict access to a particular API because of export controls or third-party licensing requirements for a particular library.

Because of this, RIM controls access to certain APIs. These APIs are identified in the online Java API Reference by the addition of a lock icon next to a restricted class or method (refer to Figure 11.6). When you use a restricted API in an application, the application runs in the BlackBerry simulator, but it will not run on a physical device without first being signed by RIM. (The application signing process is simple, and it's described in Chapters 13, 14 and 15.)

The BlackBerry development tools warn a developer that the application must be signed before it can execute in a physical BlackBerry device. Figure 11.9 shows a sample warning displayed when building an application that uses the BlackBerry Browser API.

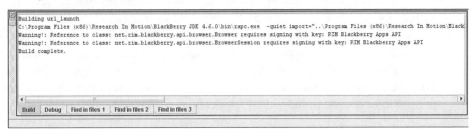

Figure 11.9 Signature warning in the BlackBerry JDE

The following list identifies the restricted packages available to BlackBerry developers in BlackBerry Device Software 4.7:

- `net.rim.blackberry.api.browser`
- `net.rim.blackberry.api.invoke`
- `net.rim.blackberry.api.mail`

- `net.rim.blackberry.api.mail.event`
- `net.rim.blackberry.api.menuitem`
- `net.rim.blackberry.api.options`
- `net.rim.blackberry.api.pdap`
- `net.rim.blackberry.api.phone`
- `net.rim.blackberry.api.phone.phonelogs`
- `net.rim.device.api.browser.field`
- `net.rim.device.api.browser.plugin`
- `net.rim.device.api.crypto`
- `net.rim.device.api.io.http`
- `net.rim.device.api.notification`
- `net.rim.device.api.servicebook`
- `net.rim.device.api.synchronization`
- `net.rim.device.api.system`

Refer to the BlackBerry Java API documentation included with the BlackBerry Java development tools for additional information on these APIs.

11.6 BlackBerry Application Control

When BlackBerry administrators deploy applications to a BlackBerry device, they have the option to define Application Control Policies that dictate what the application can and cannot do on the BlackBerry device. The administrator can apply application control policies only when the BlackBerry device is associated with a BlackBerry Enterprise Server. An administrator that didn't think an application should be using the Phone application could apply an Application Control Policy that blocks phone access for the application. Users can also control the permissions granted to individual applications deployed to their devices.

When building BlackBerry Java applications, developers must verify whether a particular activity is being restricted before attempting the activity. The APIs impacted by this are grouped into three categories:

- Connectivity and communication
  - Interprocess communication
  - Internal connections (through MDS)
  - External connections (through BIS, TCP, and WAP)
  - Local connections (through a USB connection)

- Third-party APIs with default access
  - Device key store
  - Bluetooth serial port profile (SPP)
  - Email API
  - PIM API
  - Phone API

- Third-party APIs without default access
  - Event injector API
  - Browser filters API

Beginning with BlackBerry Device Software 4.2.1, a security prompt was added that appears whenever an application attempts to access the following APIs:

- `Locale.setDefaultInputForSystem`
- `MIMETypeAssociations.registerMIMETypeMapping`
- `MIMETypeAssociations.registerType`
- `ApplicationDescriptor.setPowerOnBehavior`
- `ApplicationManager.lockSystem`
- `ApplicationManager.unlockSystem`
- `ApplicationManager.setCurrentPowerOnBehavior`
- `ApplicationManager.requestForeground`
- `ApplicationManager.requestForegroundForConsole`
- `Backlight.enable`
- `Backlight.setTimeout`
- `Backlight.setBrightness`
- `Device.requestPowerOff`
- `Device.requestStorageMode`
- `Device.setDateTime`
- `Display.setContrast`
- `EventLogger.setMinimumLevel`
- `EventLogger.clearLog`
- `Radio.activateWAFs`
- `Radio.deactivateWAFs`
- `Keypad.setMode`

The result of an application calling any of these methods is a security prompt: "Application <module name> is attempting to change device settings." The user can allow the action but can also deny the application access.

BlackBerry Java applications must always check for access to any restricted features before attempting to use them. If an application encounters a feature that is disabled by an Application Control Policy or denied by the user, the application throws a `ControlledAccessException`. The application should, therefore, wrap the method call in a `try/catch` block, as shown here:

```
try {
  Backlight.setTimeout(255);
} catch (ControlledAccessException cae) {
  //Execute code here to deal with the administrator or the
  //user denying access to the feature
}
```

Refer to the BlackBerry Java API reference to determine if a particular method an application is calling throws the `ControlledAccessException` and deal with it accordingly.

Beginning with BlackBerry Device Software 4.2.1, the Java APIs were enhanced to include an Application Control class (`net.rim.device.api.applicationcontrol`) that allowed developers to check for access to a particular feature before attempting to use it. Within the `ApplicationControl` class, `ApplicationPermissions` can be used to determine whether the application has permission to perform a specific action.

At a high level, an application can query `ApplicationPermissions` to determine whether a particular feature is enabled. If, for example, an application wants to use Phone APIs, it can check for access using something similar to this code sample:

```
public boolean isPhoneEnabled() {
  ApplicationPermissions original =
    ApplicationPermissionsManager.getInstance().
    getApplicationPermissions();
  if( original.getPermission(
    ApplicationPermissions.PERMISSION_PHONE )==
    ApplicationPermissions.VALUE_ALLOW )
  {
    return true;
  } else {
    return false;
  }
}
```

As shown in the example, the current application permissions can be compared to a particular type of permission (`ApplicationPermissions.PERMISSION_PHONE` in this example). The possible options for each permission are

- **VALUE_ALLOW:** Indicates that the application permission is set to Allow
- **VALUE_DENY:** Indicates that the application permission is set to Deny
- **VALUE_PROMPT:** Indicates that the application permission is set to Prompt

Another option is to code the application so it requests permission from the user using the following code:

```
ApplicationPermissions ap = new ApplicationPermissions();
ap.addPermission(
  ApplicationPermissions.PERMISSION_CHANGE_DEVICE_SETTINGS);
boolean result = ApplicationPermissionsManager.getInstance().
  invokePermissionsRequest(ap);
if(result == true) {
  //The user allowed the change
  Backlight.setTimeout(255);
}
```

Beginning with BlackBerry Device Software 4.5, RIM added the Application Control Reason Message API, which allows an application to display a custom message to a BlackBerry user whenever the Device Software displays an application control prompt.

11.7 Additional Resources

A complete listing of links to these resources is available online at www.bbdevfundamentals.com.

This chapter barely touched the tip of the iceberg called BlackBerry Java development. Chapters 12, 13, 14, and 15 cover using the Java development tools that RIM offers, and the following chapter covers how to test and debug BlackBerry Java applications.

In the meantime, there are a lot of resources available to help you understand every aspect of BlackBerry Java development. The complete API reference is installed along with the developer tools, but you can also find the same information available online at www.blackberry.com/developers/docs/4.7.0api/index.html. Because the APIs available to developers change with every version of the BlackBerry Device Software, there's a separate version released for each edition of the development tools.

The best place to go to get questions answered is the BlackBerry Developer Forums available at http://supportforums.blackberry.com/rim/?category.id= BlackBerryDevelopment. I'm up there almost every day answering questions, and you can also find many of the RIM product developers and other experienced BlackBerry developers there to help you. Be sure to mark your posts as complete when you receive the correct answer and give Kudos to those who help you.

A ton of information is available on the BlackBerry Developer's website (www.blackberry.com/developers). The most important place to look is the Developer's Resources section found at http://na.blackberry.com/eng/developers /resources/.

On the Resources page, you can find links to

- **Developer Video Library:** Video demonstrations of many developer topics.

- **Developer Documentation:** All the developer documentation.

- **Developer Tools & Downloads:** Free development tools and related downloads.

- **Online Forums:** Direct access to the Developer Forums.

- **Partner Services:** Information on the different RIM partners offering custom application development services, application testing services and more.

- **Developer Knowledge Base:** Searchable database containing articles written by the BlackBerry development team and developer support personnel.

- **Developer Labs:** Hands-on lab exercises designed to help any developer get started with BlackBerry development.

- **Developer Tutorials:** Step-by-step instructions on several developer topics.

- **BlackBerry Developer Newsletter:** Sign up for email updates from RIM on developer topics.

- **Developer Issue Tracker:** Access to a web application that allows developers to submit development-related issues and feature requests for consideration by the RIM product team.

- **BlackBerry Administration API:** Information on the new BlackBerry Administration API released with BES 5.0. Allows developers to write applications that interact with the BlackBerry Enterprise Solution.

For additional information on CLDC and the capabilities it provides, go to http://java.sun.com/products/cldc/ and http://wikipedia.org/wiki/CLDC.

For additional information on the MIDP specification, go to http://java.sun.com/products/midp/ and http://wikipedia.org/wiki/MIDP.

All the BlackBerry Java development tools can be downloaded from www.blackberry/developers.

RIM published the *BlackBerry Smartphones: User Interface Guidelines* to make it easier for developers to understand how BlackBerry applications should act. It can be downloaded from http://na.blackberry.com/eng/deliverables/4412/BlackBerry_Smartphones-2.0-US.pdf.

For information on how to leverage the GPS capabilities of a device or invoke the BlackBerry Maps application, refer to the *BlackBerry Java Development Environment: GPS and BlackBerry Maps Development Guide.* To locate the guide, navigate to the BlackBerry Developer's website (www.blackberry.com/developers) and look for the document in the Documentation area for the Java development tools.

Several interesting knowledge base articles are related to concepts in this chapter:

- How To: Invoke the Browser (Article # DB-00701)
- What Is: Global Events and Global Event Listeners (Article #DB-00145)
- How To: Access and Obtain Service Books (Article #DB-00418)

To access the articles, go to www.blackberry.com/developers and search for the relevant knowledge base article.

12

Getting Started with
the BlackBerry Java
Development Tools

This chapter provides the information developers need when beginning a
BlackBerry Java development project and trying to select the right development
tools to use. This chapter includes information on how to download and install
the RIM's Java development tools. Chapter topics are

- Understanding the BlackBerry Java Application files
- Selecting the right development platform for Java applications
- Installing the BlackBerry Java development tools
- Obtaining and installing the application signing keys needed to run appli-
  cations that use controlled application programming interfaces (APIs) on
  BlackBerry devices
- Using the Preprocessor to generate different versions of an application
  from a single set of source files

After the Java development platform is selected and the tools are installed, the
chapters that follow describe how to use the individual development tools to
build and debug Java applications for BlackBerry:

- Chapter 13, "Using the BlackBerry Java Development Environment
  (JDE)," covers the BlackBerry JDE.

- Chapter 14, "Using the BlackBerry JDE Plug-In for Eclipse (eJDE)," covers the BlackBerry eJDE.

- Chapter 15, "Using the BlackBerry JDE Component Package Tools," covers the BlackBerry JDE Component Package.

12.1   Understanding BlackBerry Java Application Files

The BlackBerry platform uses several types of files to contain application code and provide application deployment tools with the information they need about the application and its components. Developers must understand the role of each to be able to effectively build and deploy applications. The following sections describe each of the file types. Other files are used by development tools, but the files discussed here are only the ones deployed to devices or used when deploying applications to devices.

12.1.1   .cod Files

A BlackBerry .cod file is the compiled application file deployed to BlackBerry devices. The .cod file bundles together one or more compiled Java classes for use with the BlackBerry Java virtual machine. Unlike standard Java, which compiles individual Java classes into class files (with a .class extension) and aggregates compiled classes into JAR files (Java ARchives with a .jar extension), RIM uses this proprietary file format instead because it is optimized for the BlackBerry platform.

Each singleton .cod file contains one or more compiled Java classes (and is, therefore, roughly equivalent to the standard Java JAR file); however, it has a strict size limit of 64k of code and 64k of data. A sibling .cod file is an archive of multiple, separately built .cod files that help alleviate the size limit restriction of singleton .cod files. When an application approaches the .cod file size limit, a portion of the functionality of the application must be migrated off into separate modules (library projects in the JDE and eJDE), which are packaged by the development tools into a sibling .cod file for deployment.

A MIDlet application created for another platform (a .jar file) can be easily converted into a .cod file for deployment to a BlackBerry device; see the BlackBerry Developer's knowledge base article DB-00055 for additional information about this topic.

12.1.2 .alx Files

An application's .alx file is used by the BlackBerry Application Loader (through the BlackBerry desktop manager or the BlackBerry Enterprise Server), which is described in Chapter 16, "Deploying Java Applications," to deploy application .cod files to a BlackBerry device. The .alx file is a simple text file that

- Can be hand crafted (not really necessary, see next bullet)
- Is automatically generated by the BlackBerry JDE and eJDE
- Can reference multiple versions of an application (for deployment to different BlackBerry Device Software versions), device types, and capabilities

The file is in XML format and contains the information that the Application Loader needs to

- Describe the application (in dialogs displayed to users during installation and in the installed applications list on the BlackBerry device)
- Determine if the application is compatible with the target device
- Understand which files need to be deployed with the application (depending on BlackBerry Device Software version)

A portion of the application information defined in the file is populated from developer-entered application properties (application name, version, vendor, and copyright) defined in the JDE and eJDE. A developer generates or updates the .alx file and makes it available (along with the application .cod files) to anyone who will deploy the application using the BlackBerry Application Loader. The options for deploying BlackBerry Java applications are described in detail in Chapter 16.

A simple .alx file for the URL Launch application (described in Chapter 11, "Building BlackBerry Java Applications") is shown here:

```
<loader version="1.0">
<application id="URLLaunch">
  <name >
      URL Launch
  </name>
  <description>
    Launches the default browser and opens
    www.bbdevfundamentals.com
  </description>
  <version >
    1.0
  </version>
  <vendor >
    BlackBerry Development Fundamentals
```

```
12 MIDlet-Version: 1.0
13 MIDlet-Name: URLLaunch
14 MIDlet-Vendor: BlackBerry Development Fundamentals
15 MicroEdition-Profile: MIDP-2.0
16 RIM-MIDlet-Flags-1: 0
```

12.2 Selecting the Right Development Platform for Java Applications

Before digging into the development tools, it's important to talk about which development platform to select when building an application. Subsequent chapters cover the ins and outs of the different tools, but what most developers miss is which BlackBerry environment to start with when building their applications.

The features a BlackBerry application can leverage on a device vary greatly, depending on the version of the BlackBerry Device Software running on it. When RIM adds new features to a device, it usually adds a corresponding set of APIs a developer can use to take advantage of them. Any applications that make use of particular features (and corresponding APIs) will only run on a device that supports the feature. Everything is forward compatible, so the feature will be available in future versions of the BlackBerry Device Software; you wouldn't want the application breaking on a newer device. A BlackBerry Java application is tied to the minimum BlackBerry Device Software version for which it was created; it will not run on a device running any previous version of the BlackBerry Device Software.

When RIM releases a new version of the BlackBerry Device Software, the API libraries included with the corresponding version of the BlackBerry Java development tools are updated. This update also affects the online help and the code-completion capabilities in an Integrated Development Environment (IDE), the device simulators, and more.

 Note: You might actually get your application to run on an earlier version of the BlackBerry Device Software, but it probably won't. If it does work, don't get complacent; just because it works doesn't mean there won't be other problems later. Running an application crafted for a particular BlackBerry Device Software version on an earlier version is not supported and should not be attempted. Doing so could "brick" the device—make the device permanently unusable.

Because each version of the BlackBerry Device Software has its own special version of the development tools, if you are developing applications for multiple

BlackBerry Device Software versions, you have to install multiple versions of the tools.

12.3 Selecting the BlackBerry Java Development Environment

The BlackBerry Java development tools provide a complete set of APIs and tools that developers can use to develop Java applications that run on BlackBerry devices. RIM offers different development tools for Java developers, and the good news is that all of them are free. The only exception to this is the cost an organization incurs when purchasing a set of signing keys, as described later in this chapter.

Three types of Java development tools are available from the BlackBerry Developer's website (www.blackberry.com/developers). The one you select will vary, depending on your preference for IDE. The available options are

- **BlackBerry Java Development Environment (JDE):** A complete Java development environment for BlackBerry. Although not sophisticated as IDEs go, it is the tool RIM developers used for years to build the BlackBerry Device Software and associated applications. Developers might select this option if they didn't care which IDE they used to build BlackBerry applications or if they wanted to keep all BlackBerry development segregated to a separate development environment.
- **BlackBerry JDE Plug-in for Eclipse (eJDE):** Provides the same functionality as the JDE, but the tools are integrated as a plug-in to the Eclipse IDE. The benefit of this toolset is that developers get the development tools provided by the JDE along with all the other sophisticated features and plug-ins supported by the Eclipse platform. Developers might select this option if they were already familiar with Eclipse or if they were doing other types of development and wanted to use the same IDE for all. This is the development tool that RIM currently recommends developers use for Java development for the BlackBerry platform. Going forward, feature enhancements will only be made in the eJDE.
- **BlackBerry JDE Component Package:** A collection of the tools developers need when developing BlackBerry Java applications using a different IDE than the ones listed in the previous bullets. Developers might select this option if they were already familiar with another development environment and were unwilling or unable, for whatever reason, to switch to one of the integrated BlackBerry tools.

The tools are also useful to developers who want to build automated processes for building or manipulating applications outside of an IDE.

Each tool is described in subsequent chapters.

12.4 Getting the BlackBerry Java Development Tools

When you are ready to download some BlackBerry development tools, open a browser and navigate to www.blackberry.com/developers. The site might change by the time you read this, so look for a section called Java Application Development Tools & Downloads and click the downloads link, as shown in Figure 12.1. When the page opens, look for a section on Java Development Tools. There should be a link for downloading the BlackBerry JDE and the BlackBerry JDE plug-in for Eclipse. The link for the BlackBerry JDE should also contain links to download the BlackBerry JDE Component Package.

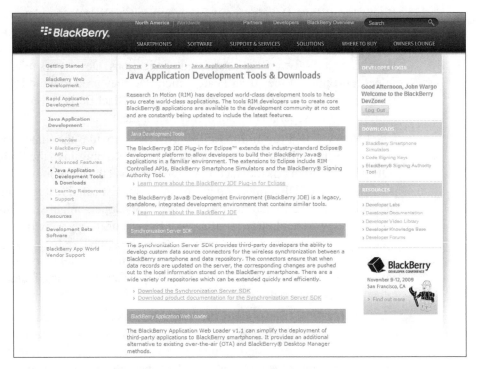

Figure 12.1   BlackBerry Development Tools & Downloads page

Depending on your selection, a different set of options appears. Pay special attention to the system requirements for each tool. Each requires that a version of the Sun Java Development Kit be installed on the system running the Black-Berry Java development tools.

12.4.1 Downloading and Installing the BlackBerry JDE or JDE Component Package

When downloading the JDE or BlackBerry JDE Component Package, scroll down the page until you locate a section of the page containing the links to download the specific versions of the tools. Select the appropriate downloads for your particular needs. If you're building applications for multiple BlackBerry Device Software versions, you need to download an installer for each version you will be using. If you're building for a single version or running a single application on multiple BlackBerry Device Software versions, you need to download the version that corresponds to the lowest BlackBerry Device Software version you will support.

To install the JDE or JDE Component Package, first make sure that a copy of the required Java SDK is installed on the system and launch the file you downloaded from the website. Follow the prompts to complete the installation, and you'll be ready to go. Depending on your Windows configuration, you might have to add the JDK bin folder to the Windows PATH environment variable before you can launch the development tools.

Note: The BlackBerry MDS simulator is required to test BlackBerry applications (using the device simulators) that make use of network connections to access a remote server. For some reason, the 4.2 and 4.2.1 JDE did not ship with the MDS simulator (all other versions since 4.1 did). If you exclusively work with either of those versions of the JDE, be sure to download and install the MDS simulator and then configure the affected JDE to use it.

If working in conjunction with other JDE versions, the 4.2 and 4.2.1 JDE can be configured to use the MDS simulator included within one of the other JDEs.

12.4.2 Downloading and Installing the BlackBerry JDE Plug-In for Eclipse

When downloading the BlackBerry JDE Plug-In for Eclipse, a different set of options appears on the downloads page. In this case, a full installer includes the editor components and associated files plus one of the eJDE Component Packs (version 4.5, at the time of this writing), which contain the libraries and simulators for a particular version of the BlackBerry Device Software. At a minimum, you must download the full installation; you won't be able to develop BlackBerry applications in Eclipse if you don't. If you need to support building or maintaining applications for additional BlackBerry Device Software versions, you will likely want to download additional eJDE Component Packages (one for each version of the BlackBerry Device Software being supported).

 Note: Because the eJDE components are installed as plug-ins to Eclipse, the Eclipse IDE must be installed in advance of the eJDE installation. You can download the latest version of Eclipse from www.eclipse.org.

The first step in the installation process is to install the BlackBerry Java development tools into the Eclipse IDE. Extract the eJDE full-installation package zip file to a local hard-drive folder; it doesn't matter where the files are placed, as long as the Eclipse installation has access to them. After the files are extracted, launch the Eclipse IDE and complete the following steps:[1]

1. With the program open, access the Help menu and select the menu item labeled Software Updates.

2. In the window that appears, select the Available Software tab and click the Add Site button.

3. In the Add Site dialog, click the Local button.

4. Using the standard Windows Open Folder dialog that appears, navigate to the folder where the installation files were extracted and open the folder.

5. Back at the Add Site dialog, click the OK button to continue.

6. Back at the Software Updates and Add-Ons window, ensure that the BlackBerry JDE Plug-In for Eclipse and BlackBerry Component Pack options are selected and then click the Install button. Eclipse prompts you to confirm the installation and finish the process, ultimately recommending that the IDE be restarted before continuing. At this point, the eJDE is installed and ready for use.

If you downloaded additional component packages, repeat the process for each of the additional component packages you want to use with this instance of Eclipse.

North American users can use the BlackBerry Eclipse update site to download and install component packages directly into an existing Eclipse installation. To do this, open the Software Updates and Add-Ons window and click the Add Site button. Instead of clicking Local to add a local reference, enter `http://www.blackberry.com/go/eclipseUpdate` in the Location field and click OK.

---

1. These same steps were documented in Chapter 10, "Testing/Debugging BlackBerry Browser Applications," in reference to the installation of the Black-Berry Web Development Plug-in for Eclipse. To see the screens associated with this process, refer to Chapter 10.

Eclipse connects to the BlackBerry Eclipse Update site and retrieves a list of the components available for installation, as shown in Figure 12.2. Select the component that you want to install and click the Install button to download and install the selected component(s).

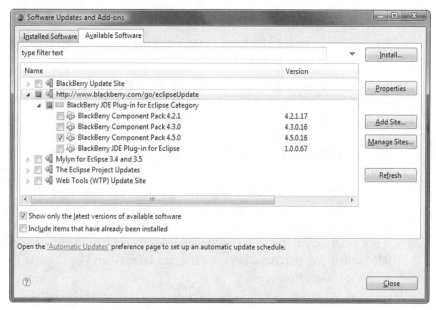

Figure 12.2   Completing the Component Package installation

12.5 Application Signing Keys

Chances are that most developer will find themselves needing to use one of the controlled APIs described in Chapter 11. Subsequent chapters show how to sign an application in the different Java development tools, but now, it seems to be a good time to discuss how to get a copy of the signing keys needed to sign an application.

BlackBerry applications that use controlled APIs do not run on BlackBerry devices until they are signed with the appropriate keys. The applications run in the BlackBerry simulators, so it is possible to build and test applications without the appropriate keys. This allows a developer to do all the work necessary to determine the best way to implement a programmatic feature and only purchase the keys if a controlled API is used and it's time to test on real devices.

Depending on the types of controlled APIs your application uses, you might need different sets of keys. Most controlled APIs can be used with the standard set of keys, which can be purchased for $20 from RIM directly. If your applications use any of the Certicom cryptography APIs, there is a separate process to secure a license from them. Considering that RIM recently completed a purchase of Certicom, it's likely that this restriction will disappear in the future.

Here are some important facts about signing keys:

- The keys must be installed on a system that has one of the BlackBerry Java Development tools installed.

- Each set of signing keys is associated with a specific PC. If you want to sign applications on multiple PCs, you must purchase a set of signing keys for each PC that will be used to sign applications. Some organizations set up a single signing PC and do all of their application signing on that PC. Other organizations purchase a set of keys for every developer workstation.

- Be prepared to associate a ten-digit personal identification number (PIN) with your signing key purchase. The PIN is needed when the keys are installed, so be sure to record it accurately and keep it in a safe place. This is not a device PIN; it's just a special key you create to identify yourself to RIM when you purchase keys, then again later when you register them after the order is processed.

- If you lose your keys or need to install them on a different PC, you must contact RIM Developer Support (devsupport@rim.com) to request a new set of keys.

- When you purchase a set of keys, you do not have to pay for each application you sign. They keys are configured to support a large number of signings (millions), so you should be OK.

- Keys are valid forever.

- The registered owner of the signing keys receives email messages from the RIM Signing Authority whenever the keys have been used. An email message will be sent for each type of library used in the application. The emails are sent for security purposes, so the owner of the keys will know if someone uses the keys to sign an application. Make sure the registered owner is someone who doesn't mind receiving a lot of emails. He can always use email filters to automatically redirect these messages to a folder or delete them automatically when they arrive.

Concerns About Signing Keys

One of the first questions most developers ask about the signing keys is, "Do I have to purchase a set of keys for each application I sign?" If you think about it, that would be a rather cumbersome process if it were true. No, you purchase one set of keys per PC, and you can sign as many applications as you want.

Actually, that's not true; there is a limit on the number of signings you can do, but it's such a huge number that you should be OK no matter what you do. In the set of keys installed to take the screen captures used in this chapter, the Signing Tool reports, "The client has 2,147,483,647 code signing request(s) left." That's more than enough signings for the normal developer's lifetime.

12.5.1 Purchasing Signing Keys

To purchase a set of signing keys, open the Microsoft Internet Explorer web browser and go to www.blackberry.com/developers. On the page that appears, navigate to the area of the site responsible for Java Development and look in the right-side navigation for an item labeled Code Signing Keys. When you click the link, a page opens where you can find information about the signing keys and how to purchase a set. You can use a web-based form and your credit card to purchase directly online or you can fill out a form and fax the information to RIM for processing.

Signing Keys Payment Options

When purchasing a set of signing keys, the keys must be purchased using a credit card. Because the keys are used partially for security purposes, RIM must ensure that it knows the identity of the entity requesting them.

If a set of keys were used to create an application considered dangerous or to be used for nefarious purposes, RIM wants to associate those keys with a person (name and billing address).

After you complete the purchase of the keys, it might take one to three business days to receive the signing keys from RIM. If you do not receive your keys within this timeframe, email devsupport@rim.com to request a status of the order. After RIM processes the order, you receive at least three separate email messages from the BlackBerry Application Development Support Team. The emails each contain a file attachment (a .csi file) and instructions on how to complete the installation of the keys.

12.5.2 Installing Signing Keys

Before installing the keys, make sure at least one of the BlackBerry Java development tools is installed on the PC where the keys will be installed. The installation process varies, depending on whether you are installing the keys into the JDE or into the eJDE. Additionally, if you will work with multiple versions of the JDE or JDE Component Package, or if you will be working with the JDE and the eJDE, an additional configuration step must be completed to make the signing keys available across multiple tools. All this is described in the following sections.

Installing Signing Keys into the JDE

To install the keys into the JDE, each key file must be launched individually to integrate the keys into the BlackBerry Java development tools. The key files can be launched directly from the email messages containing each key, or each file can be downloaded from a message and launched from Windows Explorer or My Computer.

When a key file launches, the BlackBerry Signature Tool opens and manages the process of installing the keys, which is described in the section, "Completing the Signing Key Installation." This process must be repeated for each signature key .csi file.

If you launch a .csi file and nothing happens, first ensure that a Java runtime environment and one of the BlackBerry JDE versions is installed on the system. In some cases, the Signing Tool will not launch automatically when the .csi files are launched. In that case, you need to register each .csi file manually from the command line. To start the manual installation, follow these steps:

1. Copy the .csi files to the JDE bin folder. (For the 4.7 JDE, the folder location should be C:\Program Files\Research In Motion\BlackBerry JDE 4.7.0\bin.)

2. Open a DOS command prompt in Windows and navigate to the folder containing the .csi files.

3. For each of the .csi files, execute the following command:

   ```
   javaw –jar SignatureTool.jar [CSI_File_Name].csi
   ```

   In this command, [CSI_FILE_NAME] refers to the filename for the .csi file.

At this point, follow the steps described in the section, "Completing the Signing Key Installation."

Installing Signing Keys into the eJDE

With the eJDE, the signature key file installation is integrated directly into Eclipse tools. To begin the process, access the BlackBerry menu in Eclipse, select the Install Signature Keys menu item, and follow the steps described next.

Completing the Signing Key Installation

When the first key installs, there are additional setup steps required to complete the process. The Signature Tool displays a dialog similar to the one shown in Figure 12.3, which indicates that the private key used to secure the signature keys cannot be located within the BlackBerry Java Tools installation. You must select Yes from the dialog to complete the installation, unless you believe this process has already been configured and you received the message in error. If you select No from the dialog, the installation process aborts.

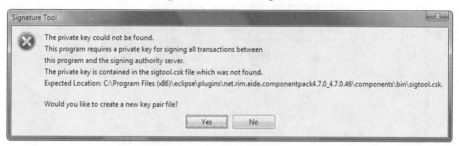

Figure 12.3 BlackBerry Signing Tool private key dialog

The Signature Tool then asks you to provide a password that will protect access to the signing keys on the PC, as shown in Figure 12.4. The password entered here is needed every time an application is signed using the keys. Select a password that is easy to remember when needed. If the password is lost, you need to obtain a new set of signature keys from RIM before you can sign Java applications. A replacement set of keys should be free; just send an email to devsupport @rim.com to request a replacement set.

Figure 12.4 BlackBerry Signing Tool private key password

The private key is generated using information generated through random mouse movement and keyboard entry, as shown in Figure 12.5. Move the mouse around and type random keys on the keyboard until the progress bar reaches 100 percent. At this point, the information the Signature Tool needs to manage and secure the signing keys has been generated, and you will not be prompted to complete the process again for the PC.

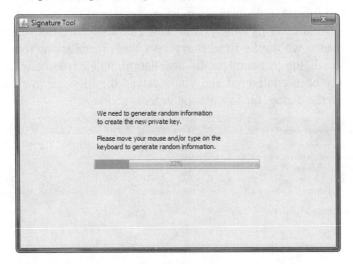

Figure 12.5   Generating random information for the private key

Because the signing keys are restricted to a single PC, the installation process includes a step where the key installation is registered with RIM.

The next step in the process must be repeated for each signing key. The Signing Tool prompts you to provide the PIN assigned to these keys during purchase and the private key password assigned in an earlier step, as shown in Figure 12.6. When the information is entered, click the Register button to register the signing key installation with RIM. Because the Signing Tool registers using an Internet connection, if the environment the keys are being installed into requires the use of a proxy server, you can provide the proxy server configuration settings after clicking the Configure Proxy button.

Figure 12.6   BlackBerry Signing Tool registration

If the registration process is successful, a dialog appears containing information about the key that was registered, including the number of signings supported by the key that was registered. If an error occurs in the process, search for the error in the Developer Knowledge Base at www.blackberry.com/developers and follow any appropriate instructions you find to resolve the problem.

Repeat this step for each key file you received. Because the private key has already been created, the only step in the process that must be completed is the registration of the additional keys with RIM.

Copying Signing Key Information

If you are using the eJDE exclusively, the signature information is installed with the plug-in and available across multiple versions of the eJDE Component Package. If using multiple versions of the JDE (one for each version of BlackBerry Device Software being supported) or the eJDE plus one or more versions of the JDE, there is an additional setup step required.

During the installation of the signing keys, the installation process creates two files containing information regarding your set of keys. These files must be available to each instance of the Signing Tool installed with the eJDE and JDE. The files are called `sigtool.csk` and `sigtool.db`, and they are created in the bin folder for the most recently installed version of the JDE or eJDE Component Package. To complete the installation, copy these two files into the same folder for each additional version of the JDE installed on the PC. For the JDE, the files are usually located in C:\Program Files\Research In Motion\BlackBerry JDE 4.7.0\bin (replacing the 4.7.0 with the version of the JDE you use). For the eJDE, the files are installed within the Eclipse installation, such as C:\Program Files\eclipse\plugins\net.rim.eide.componentpack4.7.0_4.7.0.46\components\bin.

Beginning with BlackBerry Device Software 4.3, the format of the signing key files was changed. To support signing applications using JDE versions prior to version 4.3, you must also copy the `SignatureTool.jar` file from the bin folder to the same folder in older versions of the JDE.

12.6 Conditional Compilation Using the Preprocessor

One of the issues that early BlackBerry Java developers faced was how to build Java applications for multiple versions of the BlackBerry Device Software. Say, for example, that a new feature became available in a newer Device Software version, and a developer wants to use it in his application. What the developer has to do is maintain separate source files for each version of the application: one that used the new feature and another for older versions of the BlackBerry Device Software. As an application gets more features and starts to support multiple devices, there might be more and more versions of the application being maintained. The developer could move the special code into libraries and link in the appropriate version when building, but this becomes complicated and requires some sophisticated configurations and special build tools.

It was only recently that RIM announced that the RIM Application Program Compiler (RAPC) supported preprocessing; a capability a developer can use to build multiple versions of an application from the same set of application source files.[2]

12.6.1 Preprocessor Defines

To enable this feature, a developer creates Preprocessor Defines in the project file or on the command line to RAPC and then places special Preprocessor Directives into the source files to instruct the preprocessor on how to manipulate the source code at build time. The Preprocessor Defines are like special variables used only by the Preprocessor. Because the Preprocessor Defines are configured differently depending on which BlackBerry Java development is being used, they are covered in the chapters that address each development tool.

12.6.2 Preprocessor Directives

RAPC supports only a limited suite of Preprocessor Directives, but they're enough to dramatically simplify the life of any developer building applications with multiple versions. The directives are placed into the application source files and instruct the Preprocessor on how to manipulate the code prior to compilation. This section describes the supported Preprocessor Directives available on the BlackBerry Java platform.

Enabling the Preprocessor

To enable the source file for preprocessing, the source file must contain the following directive. For readability and ease of use, it needs to be placed near the beginning of the source file. The proper syntax for the directive is

```
//#preprocess
```

---

2. Not only is this capability available in the most recent versions of the BlackBerry Java development tools, but it's been available for years and nobody outside of RIM knew it. This functionality has been present since RAPC version 4.0.

Using an If, Else, Endif Block

To execute different code branches depending on whether a particular Preprocessor Define value is defined, use the following structure:

```
//#ifdef <tag>
  [Code executed if the preprocessor define exists]
//#else
  [Code executed if the preprocessor define does not exist]
//#endif
```

In this case, the first block of code is executed if *<tag>* is defined as a Preprocessor Define within the project. If *<tag>* is not defined, the second block of code executes.

To see an example of this at work, look at the following code. In the URL Launch application described in Chapter 11, there was a special condition identified where the application would not work correctly on BlackBerry Device Software 4.2. To support BlackBerry Device Software 4.2, an additional line of code needed to be added to the application. In the following example, a Preprocessor Directive is defined that inserts the additional line of code only if the Preprocessor Define, called BBDS42, is defined for the project:

```
public urlLaunch() {
  // Get the default browser session
  BrowserSession browserSession = Browser.getDefaultSession();
  // Then display the page using the browser session
  browserSession.displayPage(appURL);
  //#ifdef BBDS42
  browserSession.showBrowser();
  //#endif
  // Once the URL is launched, close this application
  System.exit(0);
}
```

Using an If Not, Else, Endif Block

To execute different code branches depending on whether a particular Preprocessor Define value is not defined, use the following structure:

```
//#ifndef <tag>
  [Code to be executed if the preprocessor define exists]
//#else
  [Code executed if the preprocessor define does not exist]
//#endif
```

This example is the opposite of the previous one. The first block of code is executed if *<tag>* is not defined as a Preprocessor Define within the project. If *<tag>* is defined, the second block of code executes.

12.7 Additional Resources

A complete listing of links to these resources is available online at www.bbdevfundamentals.com.

The BlackBerry Java development tools can be downloaded from www.blackberry.com/developers.

Several interesting knowledge base articles are related to concepts in this chapter:

- How To: Create a Single .alx File to Install Multiple Versions of an Application (Article #DB-00028)
- How To: Compile a MIDlet into a COD File (Article #DB-00055)
- How to: Manually Register the CSI Files (Article #DB-00100)
- What Is: Signature Key Format Changes in BlackBerry JDE 4.3.0 (Article #DB-00639)
- Support: Unable to Register Keys or Sign a File While Behind a Proxy Server (Article #DB-00105)
- How To: Use the Preprocessor (Article #DB-00712)

To access the articles, go to www.blackberry.com/developers and search for the relevant knowledge base article.

The BlackBerry Developer's website hosts several tutorials related to content in this chapter:

- A60: How and When to Sign: http://na.blackberry.com/eng/developers/resources/A60_How_And_When_To_Sign_V2.pdf
- A70: How to Deploy and Distribute Applications: http://na.blackberry.com/eng/developers/resources/A70_How_to_Deploy_and_Distribute_Applications_V1.pdf

13

Using the BlackBerry
Java Development
Environment (JDE)

The BlackBerry Java Development Environment (JDE) is a complete Integrated Development Environment (IDE) for building BlackBerry Java applications. The tool has been around for quite a while and was the primary tool that Research In Motion (RIM) used to create BlackBerry software. It offers tight integration with the MDS simulator and BlackBerry device simulators, which allows developers to build and debug BlackBerry Java applications in the same tool.

This chapter helps BlackBerry developers understand how to get started using the tool and covers the following:

- Creating a workspace and project
- Adding source files to a project
- Adding an icon to the project
- Signing BlackBerry Java applications
- Creating the .alx, .cod, and .jad files for an application
- Using Conditional Compilation
- Debugging BlackBerry Java applications

13.1 Starting the BlackBerry JDE

When the JDE is installed, the installer creates Windows Start menu items for the JDE and other associated components. To start the JDE, launch the JDE entry under Start, Programs, Research In Motion, and select the version of the JDE you want to use. There's a folder in the Windows Start menu for every version of the JDE you have installed. When the selected folder opens, select the icon labeled JDE. When you open the JDE, you probably also want to open the BlackBerry Java API reference (which can be loaded from the same Start menu folder or from the Help menu in the JDE), because most developers find themselves regularly switching between those two applications.

If the appropriate Java Development Kit (JDK) is installed and accessible on the Windows PATH, the JDE loads and displays a screen similar to the one shown in Figure 13.1. On the left is the Files window, which shows all the folders and files in the current workspace (described later). On the right is the Code Editing window, and on the bottom is a tabbed panel that displays build results (and errors), debug information, and allows you to search through the source files for information.

The JDE groups Java projects together into workspaces. Workspaces are nothing more than a container holding references to multiple Java projects. In the file browser shown in Figure 13.1 is a workspace called Samples. It contains a reference to each of the sample applications included with the JDE. Rather than dig into detail on every API in the developer's guide, RIM creates a sample application that demonstrates the use of the API and adds it to the Samples workspace.

The key-like icon next to the Samples workspace (samples.jdw) can be clicked to expand the workspace to show all the individual projects. Figure 13.1 shows the workspace and one of the projects expanded (HelloWorldDemo) and a source file opened in the editor (HelloWorldDemo.java). Using this interface, a developer can work in multiple projects simultaneously.

Figure 13.1 Samples workspace expanded

13.2 Creating a Workspace

To create your first BlackBerry Java project using the JDE, you first need to create a workspace. Remember, a workspace is just a container that groups project files together. The projects contained within a workspace are usually all in the same folder tree, so you can generally think of the workspace as being a pointer to a particular file system directory.

To create a workspace, access the JDE File menu and select the New Workspace menu item. The program displays a dialog similar to the one shown in Figure 13.2. You need to provide a name for the workspace and specify the folder that will hold all the project files. If the folder does not exist, the program prompts you to create the folder before continuing.

Figure 13.2   Create Workspace dialog

13.3 Creating a Project

A project is a collection of related files that comprise a BlackBerry application or library. To create a BlackBerry Java project, access the JDE File menu and select the New menu item. The program displays a dialog similar to the one shown in Figure 13.3. Select the Projects tab and select the Empty project type. Enter a name for the project and specify the folder location where the project's files should be stored. When all the options are set, click the OK button to continue the process.

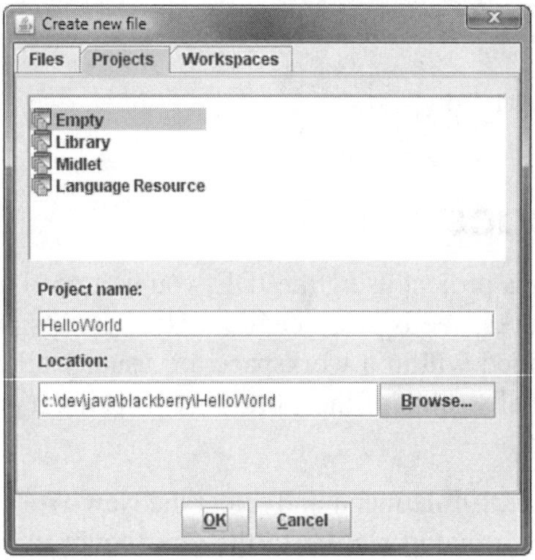

Figure 13.3   Create New File dialog

The JDE prompts you to set some properties for the project, as shown in Figure 13.4. You need to specify the output filename for the project and, at the same time, you can specify some additional settings for the project:

- **Always make project active:** Controls whether the application is automatically set as an active project in the JDE. It's only active projects that are built when selecting the Build menu option or running applications using Go from the JDE's Debug menu.

- **Exclude from Build All:** Excludes the project from being built when Build All is selected from the Build menu.

- **Auto-run on startup:** Allows the application to be loaded when the BlackBerry device starts. This option is used when creating an application that must always be running, such as a push listener application (described in Chapters 6 and 7).

- **System module:** Allows the application to run in the background without displaying an icon on the BlackBerry device Home Screen or ribbon.

When all the options are set, click the Finish button to create the project file.

Figure 13.4 New Application dialog

13.4 Creating Java Source Files

An application won't be able to run without some code behind it. There are several ways to create a new source file for the project. You can right-click the project and select Create New File in Project or you can open the Project menu and select the Create New File in Project Menu item. The JDE opens the dialog shown in Figure 13.5, prompting for the name of the source file and the destination folder where the file should be created. When all the information is entered, click the OK button to create the file.

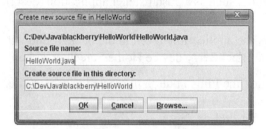

Figure 13.5 Create New Source File dialog

Another way to add a file to a project is to open the File menu and select the New menu item. The program prompts you to select the type of file to be added, plus the filename and destination folder, as shown in Figure 13.6. Using this option allows you to add Java source files to the project, but also other file types, as shown in the figure.

Figure 13.6 Create New File dialog

At the conclusion of either process, the BlackBerry JDE looks similar to what is shown in Figure 13.7. The source file is open and ready to be populated with Java code.

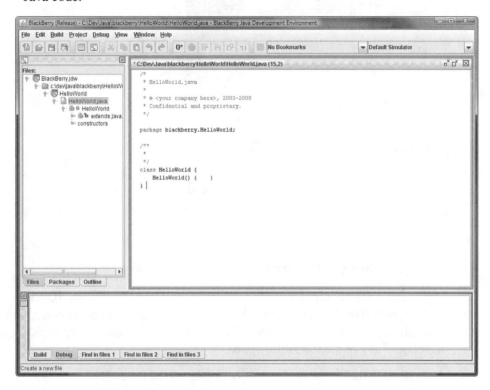

Figure 13.7   New Java source file

You can also import an existing source file into the project. To do this, right-click the project and select Add New File to *[Project-Name]*, where *[Project-Name]* is the name of the selected project. You can also access the Project menu and select the Add File to Project Menu item. The JDE opens the Java version of the standard Windows Open File dialog; select the file you want to add to the project and click the Open button.

13.5 Activating a Project

If you did not set Always Make Project Active when creating the project, you must make the project active before it can be built or run on a simulator from the JDE. To make a project active, open the JDE's Project menu and select the Set Active Projects menu item. The program displays a dialog similar to the one shown in Figure 13.8. Check the checkbox next to each project you want to activate and click OK to continue.

Figure 13.8 Active Projects dialog

13.6 Building a Project

Unlike the eJDE (described in Chapter 14, "Using the BlackBerry JDE Plug-In for Eclipse (eJDE)"), there is no automatic building of projects supported in the JDE. To build a project, press the F7 key. You can also access the Build menu and choose any of the following options:

- **Build:** Builds the current project being edited in the JDE.
- **Build All:** Builds all projects in the workspace.
- **Build Selected:** Builds the selected project when a project folder is selected in the workspace navigator.
- **Build All and Run:** Builds all applications in the workspace and then, if there are no build errors, launches the default BlackBerry device simulator and loads the built applications onto the simulated device.

You would build the application to identify errors within the source code and prepare the application for testing on the simulator or deploying to a device.

13.7 Setting Application Properties

A developer can configure many properties for a Java project. To access a project's properties, right-click the project in the JDE's file navigator (on the left side of the JDE) and select Properties. The JDE opens a window similar to the one shown in Figure 13.9.

The General tab sets the title for the application and other relevant information. The title is the string that appears at the bottom of the BlackBerry Home Screen or ribbon when the application is selected.

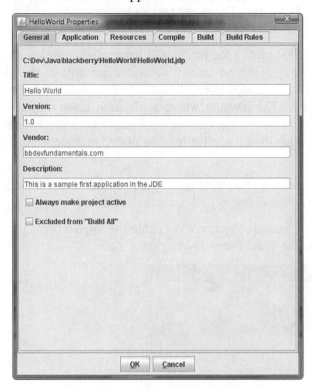

Figure 13.9   Application Properties—General tab

The Application tab, shown in Figure 13.10, allows you to set the project type. In the Project Type field, set one of the following options, depending on the needs for your application:

- **CLDC Application:** An application that can use the MIDP, CLDC, and BlackBerry APIs. This is the default application type for BlackBerry applications.

- **MIDlet:** An application that uses only MIDP APIs.

- **Library:** Instead of being a standalone application that runs on a device, it creates a library that other applications can use. Remember from Chapter 12, "Getting Started with the BlackBerry Java Development Tools," that moving code into a library is a way to deal with the size limitation for .cod files.

This is also where developers can set the entry point for the application. An example of this is the Push Listener application included with the BlackBerry ECL application that uses an alternate entry point other than the main user interface. Refer to the BlackBerry Java Development Guides for additional information on alternate entry points.

You can also specify the recommended position of the application's icon on the BlackBerry ribbon by specifying an integer value for priority in the Home Screen Position field. Use a value between 1 and 255; 1 is highest priority and 255 is the lowest priority. The location where application icons are placed is dependent on the theme in use on the device. On BlackBerry Device Software version 4.6 and higher, downloaded applications are placed in folders rather than on the Home Screen.

Check the System Module checkbox to enable the application to run in the background and not appear on the ribbon or task switcher application.

Check the Auto-Run on Startup checkbox to enable the application to launch automatically whenever the BlackBerry device starts.

Figure 13.10   Application Properties—Application tab

The Resources tab, shown in Figure 13.11, configures resource options for an application. Options on this tab are used by an application that uses resources to support Internationalization (I18N) of the application. (The discussion of I18N is beyond the scope of this book, but there are great tutorials available on the BlackBerry Developers website and in the Samples workspace.)

This is also where you can specify additional icon image files used by the application. Later versions of the BlackBerry Java development tools (version 4.7 and higher) can specify application icons and rollover icons associated with the application. Developers can specify one or more icon files to the project and manipulate them using the BlackBerry `net.rim.blackberry.api.homescreen.HomeScreen` libraries.

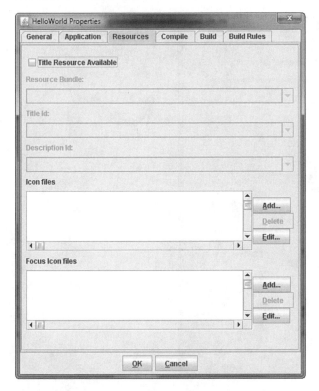

Figure 13.11   Application Properties—Resources tab

Refer to the JDE online help for information on the remaining application properties.

13.8 Adding an Icon to an Application

The application's icon is the user's entry point into the application. It needs to clearly identify the application and be visually appealing. The application can have one icon or separate icons for when the application is selected or not selected on the ribbon. The Project Properties dialog has options for defining icons, but there is also another way. To add an icon to an application, add the icon's image file to the project, right-click the file, and select Properties. In the dialog that appears (see Figure 13.12), check the appropriate checkbox to indicate whether the icon is the application and/or the application focus icon. The application focus icon is the icon that appears when the icon is selected on the device ribbon.

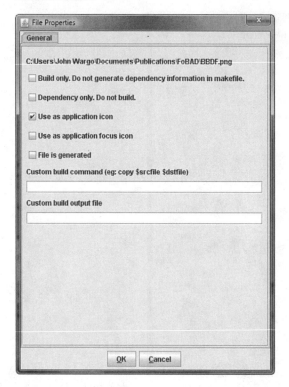

Figure 13.12   BlackBerry application icon properties

Information on how to create icons for your applications can be found in Appendix B, "Creating Application Icons," available at www.bbdevfundamentals.com.

13.9 Signing an Application

If an application uses any of the controlled APIs, the application must be signed before it runs on a BlackBerry device. It can run on a simulator, but not on a device; refer to Chapter 11 for additional information on this restriction.

When the JDE builds an application that uses restricted APIs, the Build window in the JDE indicates which signatures are required, as shown in Figure 13.13. When you see this warning, know that the application will not run on a device without the appropriate signatures. These warnings only appear for a build performed after a modification to the source code; if the application has not been modified since the last build, the warning will not appear.

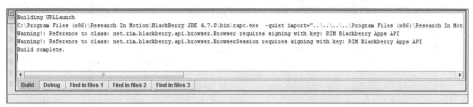

Figure 13.13 Build window

These warnings are controlled by Preferences Settings in the JDE; they can be enabled to remind you that the application needs to be signed or disabled to reduce the number of warnings seen when building an application.

Access JDE Preferences by opening the Edit menu and selecting the Preferences menu item. A sample Preferences window appears, which is similar to the one shown in Figure 13.14. Select the Code Signing tab and use the checkboxes at the bottom of the dialog to enable/disabling the warning messages.

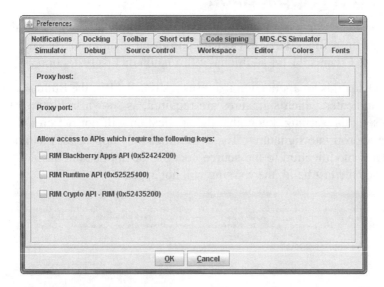

Figure 13.14   JDE Preferences dialog

The ability to sign applications is built into the JDE, so it's easy to do. In the JDE, open the Build menu and select the Request Signatures menu item. The JDE launches the Signature Tool, which is a Java application included with the JDE that manages the process of obtaining the necessary signatures for an application. When the Signature Tool opens, it displays a list of all the active applications in the project and identifies which signatures are required, as shown in Figure 13.15. To begin the signing process, click the Request button shown in the figure.

File	Status	Category	Signer...	Signer Name
URLLaunch.cod	Not Signed	Required	RBB	RIM Blackberry Apps API
URLLaunch.cod	Not Signed	Optional	RCR	RIM Crypto API - RIM
URLLaunch.cod	Not Required	Not Required	3	Not registered with optio...
URLLaunch.cod	Not Required	Not Required	RCI	Not registered with optio...
URLLaunch.cod	Not Required	Not Required	RCC	Not registered with optio...

Figure 13.15   Signature Tool

The Signature Tool prompts for the password used to secure the signing keys. This is the password that you created when you installed the keys in Chapter 12; if you lose the password, you cannot request signatures and need to secure a new set of signing keys from RIM. Enter the password and click the OK button.

When the Signature Tool requests a signature, the program creates a Secure Hash Algorithm (SHA-1) hash of the application code and sends it to RIM for processing. The RIM Signing Authority generates the necessary signature and returns it to the Signature Tool. The application code is not sent anywhere during this process; only a secure hashed version of the compiled code is sent. The RIM signing authority does not look at or validate the code in any way; it merely signs the hashed code and returns it to the Signature Tool. When the data is returned, the program appends the signature to the compiled application code; the application is now ready to be deployed to devices.

At this point, the Signature Tool displays a summary of the actions it performed. If there were any issues with the signing process, there would be additional information provided in this dialog identifying the problem.

When the RIM Signing Authority processes a signing request, for each key used, it sends a notification message to the owner of the keys used to sign the application. This is used partially as a security mechanism, so the owner of the keys knows then they've been used. This is why the keys should be purchased using the email address of the developer responsible for the keys; in many cases, a developer's manager purchases the keys and becomes inundated with email messages as the developer works through building and testing an application. What some developers do is set up a mailbox filter that automatically files these messages to a folder or deletes them when they come in.

13.10 Creating the Application Files Needed for Deployment

In the JDE, an application's .jad and .cod files are created for an application every time the project is built.

BlackBerry Java applications deployed via the BlackBerry Desktop Manager or the Application Loader on the BlackBerry Enterprise Server use an .alx file to describe the application being deployed. In the JDE, the .alx file must be created manually, but it is a simple procedure. To create the .alx file for an application, use one of the following options:

- Right-click the application's project in the JDE and select Generate ALX File from the menu that appears.
- Open the JDE Project menu and select the Generate ALX File menu item.

The JDE creates the .alx file in the project folder.

The options for deploying BlackBerry Java applications are described in Chapter 16, "Deploying Java Applications."

13.11 Configuring Projects to Use Preprocessing

Using the Preprocessor to build multiple versions of an application from a single set of source files was described in Chapter 12. This section describes how to configure a BlackBerry Java project with the Preprocessor Defines used to control the Preprocessing process.

The process for creating Preprocessor Defines differs depending on which version of the BlackBerry JDE is being used. Because the existence of the Preprocessor was announced around the time the BlackBerry Storm smartphone was released, only the JDE versions released since the announcement (4.7 and above) contain the user interface components necessary to assign Preprocessor Defines.

To manage the Preprocessor Defines associated with a project in the 4.7 JDE and above, right-click a project in the JDE and select Properties from the menu. In the dialog that appears, click the Compile tab (shown in Figure 13.16). Use the Add, Delete, and Edit buttons to manipulate the definitions.

For JDE versions prior to 4.7, the Preprocessor is enabled by manually editing the application's project file. The file is stored in the project folder associated with the application; the filename has a .jdp extension.

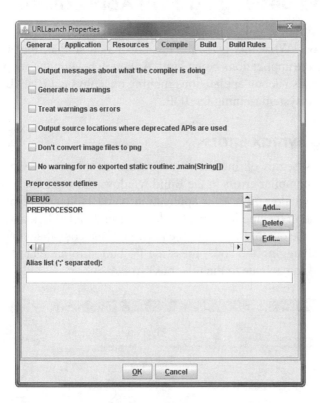

Figure 13.16 JDE project properties

 Warning: When using the Preprocessor, make sure that at least one definition is defined, typically PREPROCESSOR, or it will not engage.

To configure the file, complete the following steps:

1. Open the JDP file using a simple text editor.
2. Locate the line in the file that starts with Options.
3. At the end of the line, add the word -define followed by each of the Pre-processor Defines separated by semicolons (such as *<tag1>;<tag2>;…;<tagN>*), like this:

```
Options=-quiet -define=DEBUG;PREPROCESSOR
```

In this example, the contents of the Options line are passed as additional argument to the RAPC when the project is built within the JDE. This same mechanism can use used in command-line driven build processes discussed in Chapter 15, "Using the BlackBerry JDE Component Package Tools."

13.12 Testing and Debugging Java Applications

The BlackBerry JDE offers seamless integration with both the MDS and BlackBerry device simulators. What this gives the developer is a simple, integrated way to test and debug the applications being built. Although beyond the scope of this book, the JDE can also debug applications running on a physical BlackBerry device connected to the system running the JDE.

13.12.1 Finding Syntax Errors

The debugging process begins during the build process; at the conclusion of a build, the IDE lists all compiler errors in the Build window, shown at the bottom of Figure 13.17. The window lists each application being built and identifies each of the errors found in the application. Developers can double-click an error (1) and the IDE places the cursor in front of the portion of the code that contains the error (2). When debugging the code, press the F4 button to navigate to the next error and Shift-F4 to navigate to the previous error.

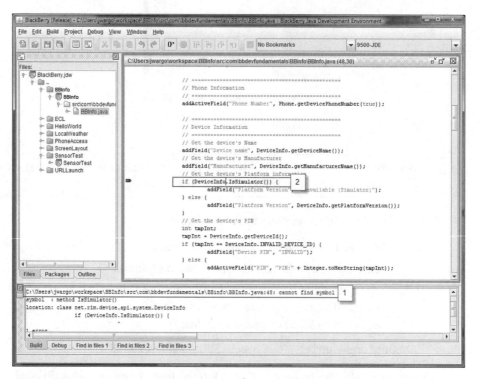

Figure 13.17   Navigating to source code errors

13.12.2 Managing Breakpoints

When the code compiles without error, it's ready to test. If you want to step through the code or look at variable contents at a particular point in the application, set one or more breakpoints in the code by placing the cursor on the line and pressing the F9 key or right-clicking and selecting Add Breakpoint from the menu. A red dot appears next to the line of code, indicating that a breakpoint is active. The breakpoint can be removed by selecting the line and pressing the F9 key again or, in the right-click menu, there are options for removing, disabling, and editing breakpoints.

By default, breakpoints trigger every time the marked line of code executes on the device simulator. The Edit Breakpoint option allows a developer or tester to fine tune how and when a breakpoint fires. When Edit Breakpoint is selected, a separate window opens that displays the list of all breakpoints in the application, as shown in Figure 13.18. For each breakpoint there are options that are evaluated whenever the breakpoint is reached. The available options are

- **Condition:** Populate with a Boolean expression, when the breakpoint is reached, execution stops if the expression evaluates to true.
- **Iteration:** Populate with an integer value and execution of the program stops at the breakpoint after the number of times through the breakpoint equals the value entered. Use this option to make program execution stop only after the breakpoint has been reached a certain number of times.
- **Execute when hit:** Populate with an expression that will execute when the breakpoint is reached. Can be used to place text in the JDE's output window by executing `System.Out.println("")` with an appropriate message.
- **Resume if true:** Populate with an expression, when the application reaches the breakpoint, program execution resumes if the expression evaluates to true.
- **Hits:** Determines the number of times application execution stops at a breakpoint when the Condition is true or if Condition is empty. Use this to only have program execution stop at the breakpoint for the first x times.

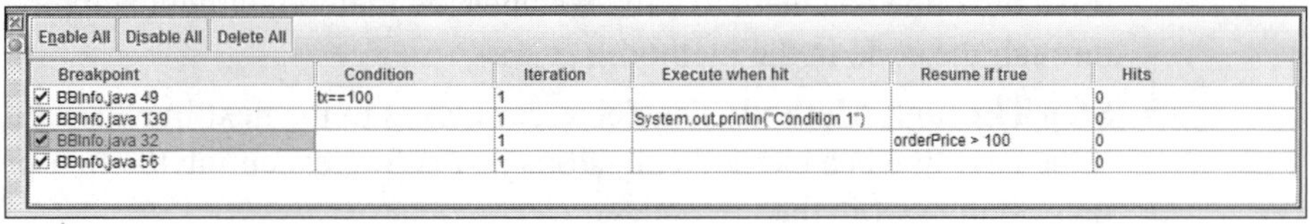

Breakpoint	Condition	Iteration	Execute when hit	Resume if true	Hits
✔ BBInfo.java 49	tx==100	1			0
✔ BBInfo.java 139		1	System.out.println("Condition 1")		0
✔ BBInfo.java 32		1		orderPrice > 100	0
✔ BBInfo.java 56		1			0

Enable All Disable All Delete All

Figure 13.18   Edit Breakpoint window

13.12.3 Starting the Debugging Process

When the application is ready to be tested on a device simulator, select the appropriate simulator from the drop-down list in the upper-right corner of the JDE, open the JDE Debug menu, and select the Go menu item (or use the short-cut key F5). The JDE prepares the environment for debugging and

1. Launches the MDS simulator (if configured to launch automatically during testing).

2. Launches the selected BlackBerry device simulator (for information on how to use the BlackBerry simulator, see Appendix A, "Using the Black-Berry Device Simulators," available at www.bbdevfundamentals.com).

3. Connects the JDE debugger to the BlackBerry simulator virtual machine.

4. Displays all output from the simulator to the Debug window in the JDE (see Figure 13.19).

Developers can use `System.out.println("");` to send information to the debug window to help simplify debugging. Rather than stepping through a bunch of code, the application can write messages to `System.Out` for analysis when the program is running or after it has been closed or stopped at a breakpoint.

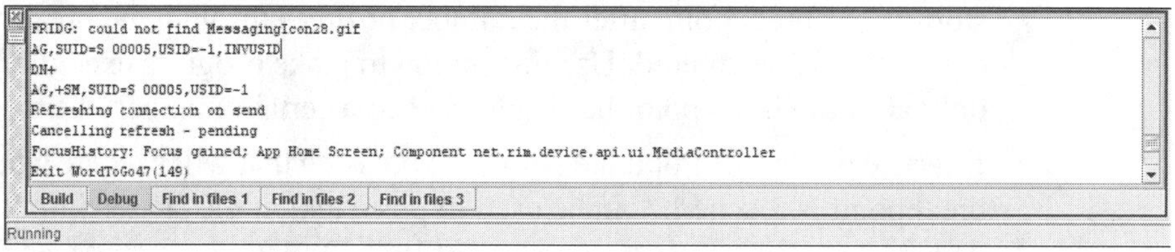

Figure 13.19 Debug window

Developers can force an application to execute to a particular part of the source code by selecting a line of code and opening the Debug menu and selecting the Run to Cursor menu item. Within the Debug menu are several options that developers can use to step through their code. The options are

- **Step Over Method Call:** The debugger moves to the next line of code or, if the next line is a method call, executes the method without stepping through the code in the method.

- **Step Through Method:** The debugger moves to the next line of code or, if the next line is a method call, stops just before executing the first program statement in the method.

- **Step Out of Method Instructions:** The debugger moves to the next line of code. If the next line is within a method call, it executes the remaining lines of code in the method and returns control to the code that called the method.

13.12.4 Interacting with an Application While It's Running

While an application is running in the debugger and stopped at a breakpoint, you can

- Hold the mouse cursor over a variable in the source code and the JDE will display the current value for the variable.
- Ctrl-click a variable name to open a window containing information about the variable.
- Select an expression and hold the mouse cursor over it to display the current value of the selected expression.

13.12.5 Using the View Menu

When the application is being executed in the debugger, the JDE's View menu offers additional features that enhance the debugging process. These options are shown in Figure 13.20 and described in the following section.

Figure 13.20 View menu

The first part of the View menu—Breakpoints, the Output window, the Workspace, and the list of bookmarks in the code—provides options for viewing components of the debug session.

Locals

The Locals menu option adds a panel to the JDE similar to the one shown in Figure 13.21. Click a tab in this panel to change scope:

- **Locals**: View all the local variables and their values in the current thread.
- **Auto**: View all local variable names and expressions at or around the currently executing line of code.
- **This**: View the values associated with the current object.
- **Watch**: View the value of expressions. Select an expression and right-click the selected expression to add a watch.

The values associated with the variables can be changed within this window.

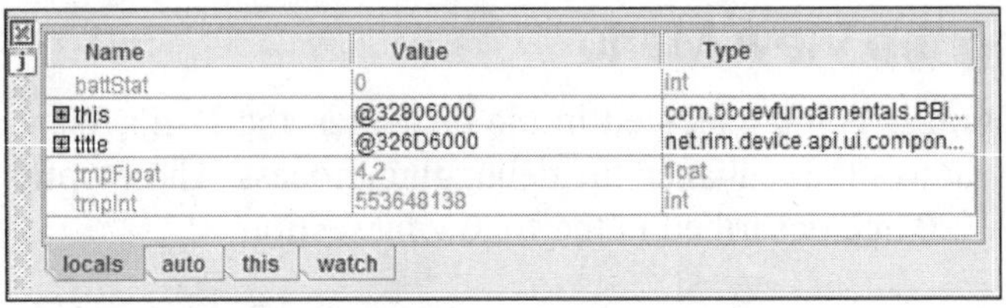

Name	Value	Type
battStat	0	int
⊞ this	@32806000	com.bbdevfundamentals.BBi...
⊞ title	@326D6000	net.rim.device.api.ui.compon...
tmpFloat	4.2	float
tmpInt	553648138	int

locals | auto | this | watch

Figure 13.21   Local variables panel

Static Data

To view all the static data members in the application, select the Static Data menu item. The JDE opens a panel similar to the one shown in Figure 13.22, which shows the static data member's name, value, and data type. In this panel, you can right-click an item and

- Change the display of the Value field.
- Set a watch on a variable.
- View the source code of a variable's defining class.
- Instruct the application to stop when an item is modified.

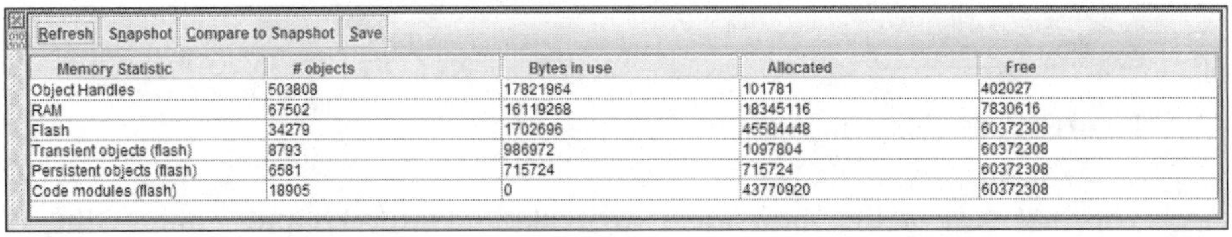

Refresh | Snapshot | Compare to Snapshot | Save

Memory Statistic	# objects	Bytes in use	Allocated	Free
Object Handles	503808	17821964	101781	402027
RAM	67502	16119268	18345116	7830616
Flash	34279	1702696	45584448	60372308
Transient objects (flash)	8793	986972	1097804	60372308
Persistent objects (flash)	6581	715724	715724	60372308
Code modules (flash)	18905	0	43770920	60372308

Figure 13.22   BlackBerry Static Data panel

Watch

The Watch menu item opens a panel in the JDE that displays three interactive Watch panels that allow the developer to evaluate expressions within the running application. In one of the watch panels, select a row and enter an expression; the JDE will evaluate the expression in real time and display the results.

Threads

The Threads menu option opens a panel in the JDE that displays a list of all of the threads running on the simulated BlackBerry device with the most recent thread highlighted, as shown in Figure 13.23. From this panel, you can double-click a thread to have the JDE open the source code and mark with an arrow the line that started the thread.

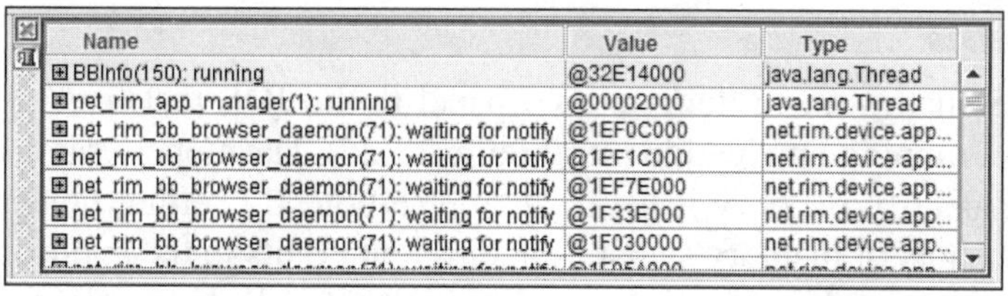

Name	Value	Type
⊞ BBInfo(150): running	@32E14000	java.lang.Thread
⊞ net_rim_app_manager(1): running	@00002000	java.lang.Thread
⊞ net_rim_bb_browser_daemon(71): waiting for notify	@1EF0C000	net.rim.device.app...
⊞ net_rim_bb_browser_daemon(71): waiting for notify	@1EF1C000	net.rim.device.app...
⊞ net_rim_bb_browser_daemon(71): waiting for notify	@1EF7E000	net.rim.device.app...
⊞ net_rim_bb_browser_daemon(71): waiting for notify	@1F33E000	net.rim.device.app...
⊞ net_rim_bb_browser_daemon(71): waiting for notify	@1F030000	net.rim.device.app...

Figure 13.23   JDE Threads panel

Locks

The Locks menu item opens a panel in the JDE that displays all objects that have active locks (when a thread is executing in a synchronized block for that object). Locks are beyond the scope of this book; refer to the JDE online help for information about the options available in the Locks window.

Processes

The Processes menu item opens a panel in the JDE that lists all the processes currently running in the simulator (see Figure 13.24). Each process can be expanded to view the data members associated with the process, and you can view the current CPU utilization and cumulative processing time for the process.

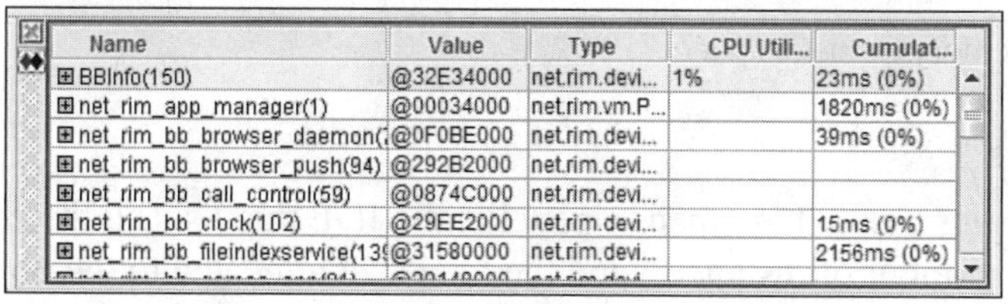

Name	Value	Type	CPU Utili...	Cumulat...
⊞ BBInfo(150)	@32E34000	net.rim.devi...	1%	23ms (0%)
⊞ net_rim_app_manager(1)	@00034000	net.rim.vm.P...		1820ms (0%)
⊞ net_rim_bb_browser_daemon(:	@0F0BE000	net.rim.devi...		39ms (0%)
⊞ net_rim_bb_browser_push(94)	@292B2000	net.rim.devi...		
⊞ net_rim_bb_call_control(59)	@0874C000	net.rim.devi...		
⊞ net_rim_bb_clock(102)	@29EE2000	net.rim.devi...		15ms (0%)
⊞ net_rim_bb_fileindexservice(13!	@31580000	net.rim.devi...		2156ms (0%)

Figure 13.24   Processes panel

Call Stack

The Call Stack menu item opens a panel in the JDE that lists the call stack for the current method (see Figure 13.25). This option helps a developer determine the execution hierarchy for the current method.

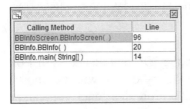

Figure 13.25   Call Stack panel

Memory Statistics

The Memory Statistics menu item opens a panel in the JDE that lists memory statistics for the running application (see Figure 13.26). Developers can use this option to help identify memory leaks in an application. By setting breakpoints and taking snapshots of memory statistics at different points in the application, a developer can pinpoint the area of the application that is leaking memory. The Memory Statistics panel has the following buttons:

- **Refresh:** Refreshes the contents of the Memory statistics panel
- **Snapshot:** Captures a snapshot of the current memory statistics
- **Compare to Snapshot**: Compares the current memory statistics against the previous snapshot
- **Save**: Saves the current memory statistics to a Comma Separated Value (.csv) file

Memory Statistic	# objects	Bytes in use	Allocated	Free
Object Handles	503808	22358432	150311	353497
RAM	113068	19603212	21069448	5104724
Flash	37243	2755220	46649476	59301648
Transient objects (flash)	10541	1025068	1103808	59301648
Persistent objects (flash)	7038	1730152	1730152	59301648
Code modules (flash)	19664	0	43815516	59301648

Figure 13.26   Memory Statistics panel

Object Statistics

The Object Statistics menu item opens a panel in the JDE that lists all the current objects, the total number of instances, and the total size allocated to the objects.

Event Log

The Event Log menu item opens a panel in the JDE that displays the contents of the simulator's event log. The event log displays all exception messages created by applications running on the simulator. Developers can use the Event Log to identify problems in the code; select a record in the log, right-click and select Show Source to view the line of code causing the exception.

Objects

Use the Objects menu item to open a panel in the JDE that displays the list of all Objects in memory on the simulator, as shown in Figure 13.27. Developers can troubleshoot Object and memory issues by taking snapshots at different points in the application and comparing snapshots to identify any objects that were created or destroyed since the previous snapshot. In the panel, click the Refresh button to refresh the contents of the panel and click the Snapshot button to take a snapshot. When the program stops at the next breakpoint, compare current Object information by selecting Compare to Snapshot from the drop-down list to the left of the Refresh button.

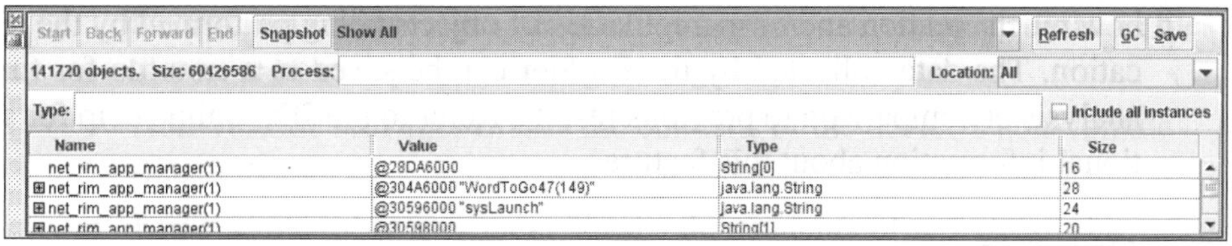

Figure 13.27   JDE Objects panel

Profile

Developers can use the JDE Profiler tool to analyze a running application to determine where the application is spending most of its time and how it is managing the Objects it is creating. To use the tool, follow these steps:

1. Place two breakpoints in the application being profiled; the Profiler profiles the application as it runs between the two breakpoints.

2. Run the application in the debugger.

3. When the application stops at the first breakpoint, open the Profiler application by selecting Profile from the JDE View menu.

4. In the Profiler application, click the Options button and set the options appropriate for the application being tested.

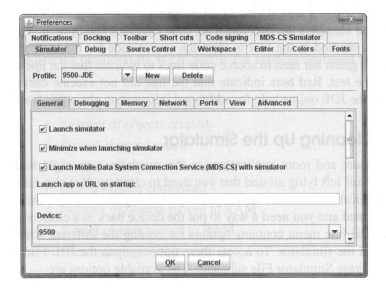

Figure 13.28 Preferences dialog

One important setting needs to be changed for anyone developing BlackBerry Java applications that access network-based resources. To test applications that access the network, you need to run the BlackBerry MDS simulator—described in Chapter 4, "The BlackBerry Mobile data System (MDS)"—before launching the device simulator. You can launch MDS manually from the Windows Start menu before you start any debugging sessions, but the easier solution is to configure the JDE to launch it for you automatically whenever a debug session is started. To configure this, open the Preferences dialog and complete the following steps:

1. Click the Simulator tab in the dialog.
2. Select the appropriate simulator model.
3. Enable the checkbox Launch Mobile Data System Connection Service (MDS-CS) with simulator.

With this enabled, MDS launches automatically with every debug session and enables the simulator to access the network resources it needs.

13.14 Additional Resources

A complete listing of links to these resources is available online at www.bbdevfundamentals.com.

The BlackBerry Java development tools can be downloaded from www.blackberry/developers.

To access sample applications that can help you learn BlackBerry development, refer to the BlackBerry Development Environment Labs at http://na.blackberry.com/eng/developers/resources/developer_labs.jsp.

To access online developer learning resources, go to http://na.blackberry.com/eng/developers/javaappdev/learningresources.

Several interesting knowledge base articles are related to concepts in this chapter:

- How To: Define a Rollover Icon for an Application (Article #DB-00467)
- How To: Use the Preprocessor (Article #DB-00712)
- How To: Run an Application in the BlackBerry Device Simulator (Article #DB-00044)
- How To: Debug an Application Running on a Live BlackBerry Smartphone (Article #DB-00038)

To access the articles, go to www.blackberry.com/developers and search for the relevant knowledge base article.

14

Using the BlackBerry JDE Plug-In for Eclipse (eJDE)

The BlackBerry JDE Plug-In for Eclipse (eJDE) enables developers to build BlackBerry Java applications using the Eclipse IDE. It offers the same tight integration with the MDS simulator and BlackBerry device simulators as the Black-Berry JDE, which allows developers to build and test BlackBerry Java applications in the same environment. This chapter helps BlackBerry developers understand how to get started using the eJDE and covers the following:

- Creating a BlackBerry project
- Adding source files to a project
- Adding an icon to the project
- Signing BlackBerry Java applications
- Creating the .alx, .cod and .jad files for an application
- Using Conditional Compilation
- Debugging BlackBerry Java applications

14.1   Starting the Eclipse JDE

Because the Eclipse installation doesn't create a Windows Start Menu item or any desktop or Quick Launch shortcuts, Eclipse needs to be launched using whichever shortcut or batch file you created to start the program. When Eclipse starts for the first time, it displays some introductory information and gives you an option to open the workbench. The workbench is where you spend most of your time working with Eclipse and contains all the tools a developer needs to build Java applications. The first time the workbench opens, you are prompted to specify the folder location for the workspace; use the default (c:\users\username \workspace on Windows Vista) if you are not sure where to place it.

When you launch the Eclipse IDE after installing the eJDE, there's not much to indicate that anything is different except for the addition of the BlackBerry menu to the IDE.

14.2   Importing the BlackBerry Sample Projects

The eJDE ships with a set of sample projects that demonstrate how to use many of the specific capabilities of the BlackBerry. Rather than detail every API in the developer's guide, RIM creates a sample application that demonstrates the use of the API and adds it to the Samples workspace. Unlike the JDE, the Samples workspace is not automatically loaded into the eJDE when it first opens. To access the projects, you need to import the projects into an existing workspace. During this process, you can import individual projects or the complete workspace.

To import the projects, open the File menu and select the Import menu item. Eclipse prompts you for the type of import being performed; click BlackBerry to expand the option, select Existing BlackBerry Projects into Workspace, and click Next.

Eclipse prompts you for the folder location where the project file is stored. During installation, the component package files, including the samples, are copied into the Eclipse plug-ins folder. Navigate to the Eclipse installation folder and drill down to the plug-ins folder. Select the samples workspace file (samples.jdw) file and click the Open button.

Eclipse imports all the projects from the workspace and presents the dialog shown in Figure 14.1. In the dialog, each project from the workspace is listed individually, and you can choose which projects will be imported or accept the default of all projects.

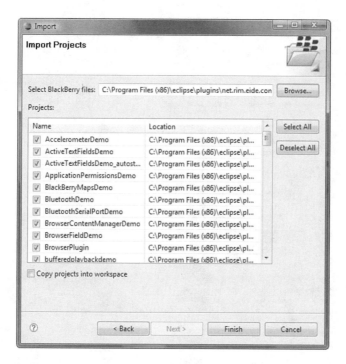

Figure 14.1   Import BlackBerry projects dialog

You can also have Eclipse copy the projects' files into the workspace by checking the Copy Projects into Workspace checkbox located under the project list. By default, Eclipse leaves the project files in their current location; it merely points to the project files in the Eclipse workspace. For the BlackBerry samples, it's probably a good idea to copy the files over if you think you might modify the samples and want an easy way to restore to the original version later.

Figure 14.2 shows the eJDE workspace with the imported Samples projects and the HelloWorldDemo project source files opened. Within the application's main screen are the standard components for most IDEs. On the left is the Package Explorer, which displays a hierarchical view of all the workspace's project files. The code editing panel is in the middle, and on the right is the outline area that shows the outline for an object being edited. At the bottom of the window is the Views area, which displays panels containing informational and debug information. Additional tools and views can be opened; refer to the Window and online help for additional information.

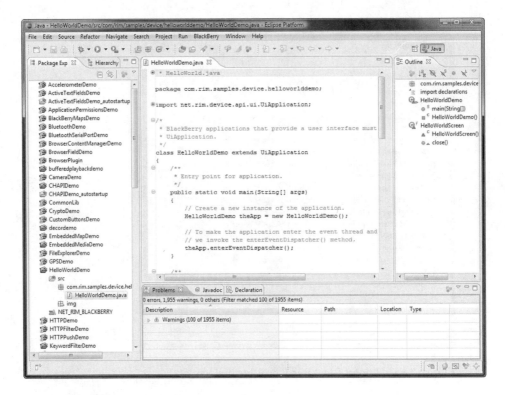

Figure 14.2 BlackBerry Samples workspace

The Package Explorer shows each project in the workspace and each can be expanded to show the files and resources associated with the project, including images and packages used by an application. Notice that the Outline area on the right displays a hierarchical representation of the variables, methods, and classes within the project.

14.3 Creating a Project

To create a new BlackBerry Java project in an existing workspace, open the Eclipse File menu, select the New menu item, and Project. Eclipse opens the New Project wizard (see Figure 14.3). Expand the BlackBerry option in the wizard, select BlackBerry Project, and click the Next button.

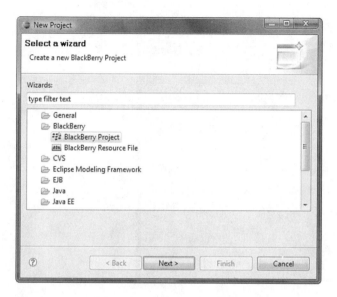

Figure 14.3   New project—Select a Wizard dialog

Eclipse then prompts for the name for the BlackBerry project, as shown in Figure 14.4. Enter the name for the new project and click the Finish button to create the project. Eclipse creates the the project files and associated folder structure in the default location defined within the Eclipse workspace. To specify a different location for the project, uncheck the Use Default Location checkbox and select a new location before finishing.

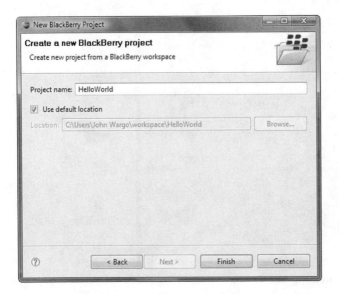

Figure 14.4   New BlackBerry—Create a New BlackBerry Project dialog

14.4 Creating a Java Source File

An application cannot run without some code behind it. There are several ways to create a new source file for the project. You can open the File menu and select New, or you can right-click the project and select New from the menu that appears. Eclipse displays a menu listing the different items that can be created. To add a new Java file to the project, select Class from the menu. Eclipse presents a dialog prompting for the options for the new file (shown in Figure 14.5). Enter the package name and class name for the file and click the Finish button to create the class file and open it in the code editor (shown in Figure 14.6).

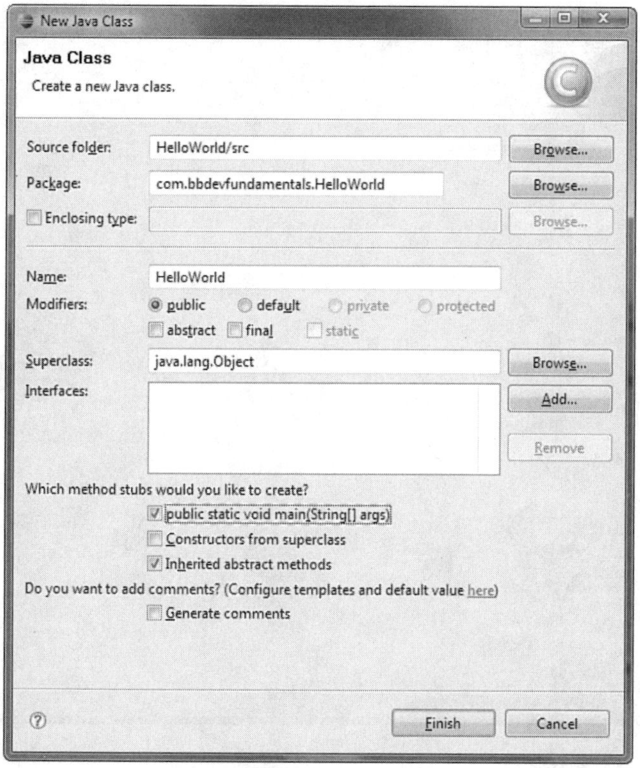

Figure 14.5 New Java Class dialog

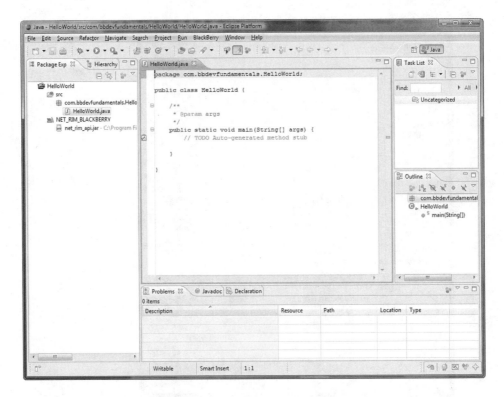

Figure 14.6   Empty HelloWorld application

At this point, you're ready to populate the project with code and begin testing.

14.5 Building a Project

You would build the application to identify errors within the source code and prepare an application for testing on the simulator or deployment to a device. By default, Eclipse builds applications automatically whenever changes are made to them. This option is controlled in the Eclipse Project menu. If you're working with a large project or you want manual control over the build process, uncheck the Build Automatically option.

14.6 Defining Build Configurations

The Eclipse JDE does not support the concept of activating projects like the JDE. Instead, it allows developers to define Build Configurations that control which applications are built and tested in the BlackBerry simulator. To access the build configurations, open the Eclipse BlackBerry menu and select Build Configurations. A submenu appears that lists the available build configurations.

To control which applications are included in a build, select Edit from the menu. Eclipse displays a dialog similar to the one shown in Figure 14.7. Select the build you want to modify from the list of options in the dialog and the list of projects appears. Place a checkmark next to each application you want included in the specified build and click OK to continue.

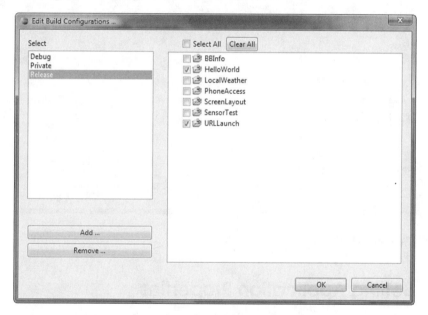

Figure 14.7   Edit Build Configuration dialog

You can also control which build is deployed when debugging BlackBerry applications. Open the Eclipse Run menu and select the Debug Configurations menu item. Eclipse opens a dialog similar to the one shown in Figure 14.8 where the options for debugging BlackBerry projects should be selected by default. In the Deployed Build Configurations tab, the selected build type is deployed to devices when testing in the debugger.

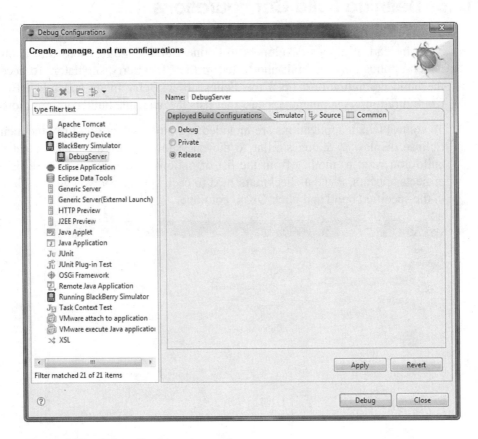

Figure 14.8   Debug Configuration settings

14.7 Setting Application Properties

There are many properties that a developer can configure for a Java project. To access a project's properties, right-click the project in the Package Explorer (on the left side of the eJDE), select Properties or select the file, open the File menu, and select the Properties menu item. Eclipse opens a dialog similar to the one shown in Figure 14.9. Providing a detailed description of each of the possible options in the properties dialog is beyond the scope of this book, but let's dig into the more fundamental options.

Options on the General tab define information about the application and the organization creating it. The Title is the string that appears at the bottom of the BlackBerry Home Screen when the application is selected. If a title is not specified, the BlackBerry uses the class filename for the application instead. On the

General tab, enter a title for the application and any additional information as needed. The version number identifies different versions of the application during installation.

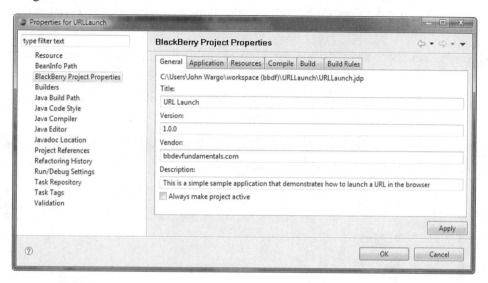

Figure 14.9   Application Properties—General tab

The Application tab, shown in Figure 14.10, allows you to set the project type for the application:

- **CLDC Application:** An application that can use the MIDP, CLDC, and BlackBerry APIs. This is the default application type for BlackBerry applications.

- **MIDlet:** An application that uses only MIDP APIs.

- **Library:** Instead of being a standalone application that runs on a device, it creates a library that other applications can use. Remember from Chapter 12, "Getting Started with the BlackBerry Java Development Tools," that moving code into a library is a way to deal with the size limitation for .cod files.

This is also where developers can set the entry point for the application. An example of this is the Push Listener application, included with the BlackBerry ECL application, that uses an alternate entry point other than the main User Interface. Refer to the BlackBerry Java Development Guides for additional information on alternate entry points.

You can also specify the recommended position of the application's icon on the BlackBerry ribbon by specifying an integer value for priority in the Home

Screen Position field. Use a value between 1 and 255; 1 is highest priority and 255 is the lowest priority. The location where application icons are placed depends on the theme in use on the device. On BlackBerry Device Software version 4.6 and higher, downloaded applications are placed in folders rather than on the Home Screen.

Check the System Module checkbox to enable the application to run in the background and not appear on the ribbon or task switcher application.

Check the Auto-Run on Startup checkbox to enable the application to launch automatically whenever the BlackBerry device starts.

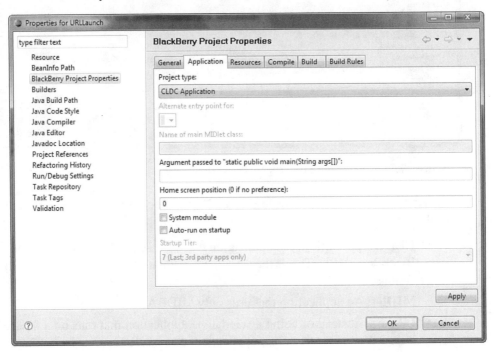

Figure 14.10 Application Properties—Application tab

The Resources tab, shown in Figure 14.11, configures resource options for the application. Options on this tab are used by an application that uses resources to support Internationalization (I18N) of the application. (The discussion of I18N is beyond the scope of this book, but there are great tutorials available on the BlackBerry Developers website and in the Samples workspace.)

This is also where you can specify additional icon image files used by the application. Later versions of the BlackBerry Java development tools (version 4.7 and higher) can specify application icons and rollover icons associated with the application. Developers can specify one or more icon files to the project and manipulate them using the BlackBerry `net.rim.blackberry.api.homescreen.HomeScreen` libraries.

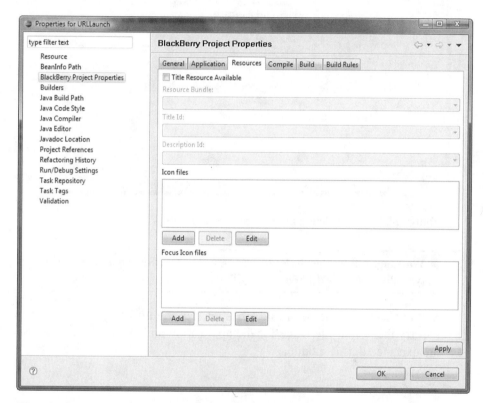

Figure 14.11   Application Properties—Resources tab

Settings on the Properties Compile tab (see Figure 14.12) allow you to configure options that are passed to the compiler when the application is built.

It's also where Preprocessor Defines are specified. Using the Preprocessor to build multiple versions of an application from a single set of source files was described in Chapter 12. Unlike the JDE, because the eJDE uses a single editor plug-in with multiple versions of the eJDE Component Packages, the way Preprocessor Defines are set is consistent no matter which version of the BlackBerry Device Software for which you are building. Use the Add, Delete, and Edit buttons on this tab to manipulate the Preprocessor Defines.

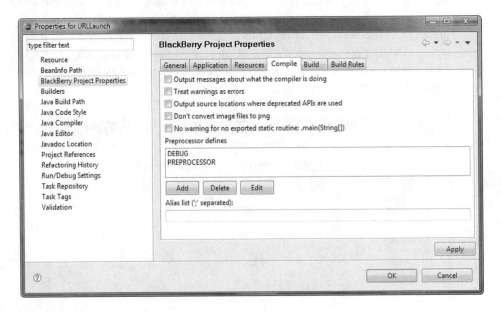

Figure 14.12 Application Properties—Compile tab

 Warning: When using the Preprocessor, make sure at least one definition is defined, typically PREPROCESSOR, or it will not engage.

Settings on the Properties Build tab, shown in Figure 14.13, allow developers to specify the output file name for the application and any external processes that are executed during a build.

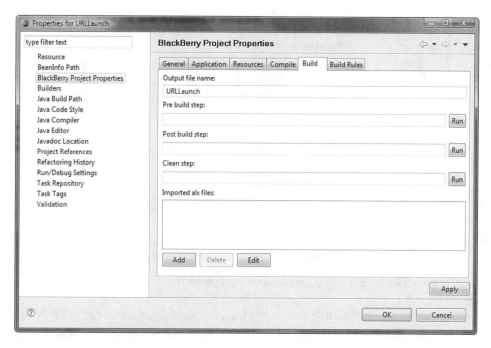

Figure 14.13   Application Properties—Build tab

14.8 Adding an Icon to an Application

The application's icon is the user's entry point into the application. It needs to clearly identify the application and be visually appealing. The application can have one icon or can have separate icons for when the application is selected or not selected on the ribbon. The project properties dialog has options for defining icons, but there is another way. To add an icon to an application, add the icon's image file to the project, right-click the file, and select Properties. In the dialog that appears (see Figure 14.14), check the appropriate checkbox to indicate whether the icon is the application and/or the application focus icon. The application focus icon is the icon that appears when the icon is selected on the device ribbon.

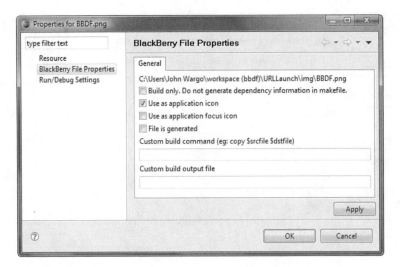

Figure 14.14   BlackBerry application icon properties

Information on how to create icons for your applications can be found in Appendix B, "Creating Application Icons," available at www.bbdevfundamentals.com.

14.9 Signing Applications

If an application uses any of the controlled APIs, the application must be signed before it runs on a BlackBerry device. It can run on a simulator just fine, but it won't run on a device. Refer to Chapter 11, "Building BlackBerry Java Applications," for additional information on this restriction.

When the Eclipse builds a BlackBerry application that uses restricted APIs, the IDE highlights restricted API calls in two ways, as shown in Figure 14.15. Each line of code that uses a controlled method is marked with a warning symbol (1); when the mouse is held over the symbol, a box appears describing the warning. Additionally, the Problems window in the IDE displays a list of warnings (2). These warnings are controlled by BlackBerry workspace settings in Eclipse; see the section, "Configuring the BlackBerry Workspace," for information on how to hide these warnings.

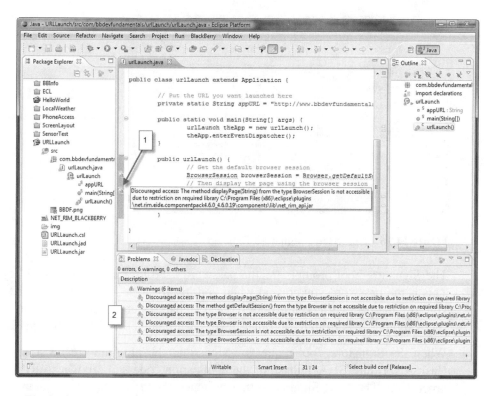

Figure 14.15 Problems window

The ability to sign applications is built directly into the eJDE, so it's easy to do. Open the BlackBerry menu and select the Request Signatures menu item. Eclipse launches the Signature Tool, which is a Java application included with the eJDE that manages the process of obtaining the necessary signatures for an application. When the Signature Tool opens, it displays a list of all the active applications in the project and identifies which signatures are required, as shown in Figure 14.16. To begin the signing process, click the Request button.

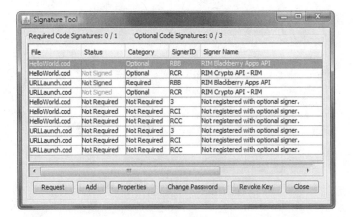

Figure 14.16   BlackBerry Signature Tool

The Signature Tool prompts for the password used to secure the signing keys. This is the password you created when you installed the keys in Chapter 12. If you lose the password, you cannot request signatures and need to secure a new set of signing keys from RIM. Enter the password and click the OK button.

When the Signature Tool requests a signature, the program creates a Secure Hash Algorithm (SHA-1) hash of the application code and sends it to RIM for processing. The RIM Signing Authority generates the necessary signature and returns it to the Signature Tool. The application code is not being sent anywhere during this process, only a secure hashed version of the compiled code is sent. The Signing Authority does not look at or validate the code in any way; it merely signs the hashed code and returns it to the Signature Tool. When the data is returned, the program appends the signature to the compiled application code; the application is now ready to be deployed to devices.

At this point, the Signature Tool displays a summary of the actions it performed. If there were any issues with the signing process, additional information is provided in this dialog identifying the problem.

When the Signing Authority processes a signing request, for each key used, it sends a notification message to the owner of the keys used to sign the application. This is used partially as a security mechanism, so the owner of the keys knows they've been used. This is why the keys should be purchased using the email address of the developer responsible for the keys; in many cases, a developer's manager purchases the keys and then becomes inundated with email messages as the developer works through building and testing an application. What some developers do is set up a mailbox filter that automatically files these messages to a folder or deletes them when they come in.

14.10 Creating the Application Files Needed for Deployment

Unlike the JDE, the .cod file is not created for an application every time the project is built. To create a .cod file for an application, open the Eclipse Project menu and select Build Active BlackBerry Configurations.

BlackBerry Java applications deployed via the BlackBerry Desktop Manager or the Application Loader on the BlackBerry Enterprise Server use an .alx file to describe the application being deployed. In the eJDE, the .alx file must be created manually. To create the .alx file for an application, right-click the application in the eJDE and select Generate ALX File from the menu that appears. The eJDE creates the .alx file in the project folder.

An application's .jad file is created automatically every time a project is built in the eJDE.

The options for deploying BlackBerry Java applications are described in Chapter 16, "Deploying Java Applications."

14.11 Configuring the BlackBerry Workspace

The BlackBerry eJDE offers configuration options to help developers write and test their code. To access the BlackBerry workspace configuration options, open the Eclipse BlackBerry menu and select the Configure BlackBerry Workspace menu item. Eclipse displays a dialog similar to the one shown in Figure 14.17. Complete coverage of every configuration option is beyond the scope of this book, but developers should spend some time looking through the available options and configuring the development environment to their personal tastes and development needs.

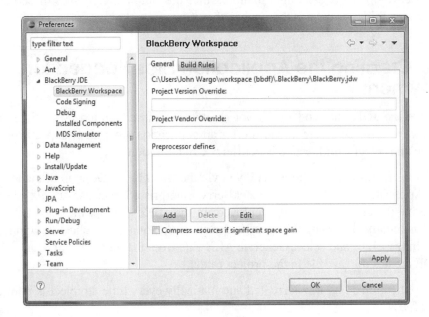

Figure 14.17   BlackBerry workspace configuration

14.11.1 BlackBerry Workspace Settings

The General tab contains configuration options that apply to every project in the workspace. Developers can set the following options:

- **Project Version Override:** Allows developers to apply a single version number to every project in the workspace. Developers would use this option if the applications in the workspace were all part of a single product or initiative and needed to all show the same version number.
- **Project Vendor Override:** Sets the same vendor name for every project in the workspace. Unless building applications for multiple customers, developers need to automatically set their company name in every workspace.
- **Preprocessor Defines:** Sets Preprocessor Defines that apply to every project in the workspace. Set Preprocessor Defines here that apply to each project, and then set individual Preprocessor Defines in project properties.

14.11.2 Code Signing Settings

Eclipse can be configured to ignore warnings for code that use controlled APIs. The default option for the eJDE is to warn whenever the APIs are used, but that can be easily changed. You might disable this to reduce the number of warnings you see after a build or if you were certain that the applications would always be signed if needed by your final build process.

In the Code Signing section of BlackBerry Preferences, shown in Figure 14.18, disable warnings for one or more controlled API types by checking the checkbox next to the item.

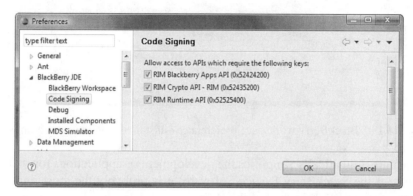

Figure 14.18   BlackBerry Workspace Preferences—Code Signing settings

14.11.3 Installed Components

Chapter 12 described how a developer had to install and use multiple versions of the BlackBerry JDE to create applications for multiple versions of the Black-Berry Device Software. With the eJDE, RIM separated the IDE components from the BlackBerry Device Software components and made it easy to use a single development environment (Eclipse) and switch between different Black-Berry Device Software configurations as needed.

The BlackBerry workspace Installed Components settings, shown in Figure 14.19, allow a developer to quickly switch the BlackBerry Java Component Package being used by Eclipse. In this dialog, use the Installed Components drop-down field to set the current environment in the IDE. After clicking the OK button, Eclipse rebuilds the workspace using the selected Components. All BlackBerry library references are reevaluated, and unsupported code in the workspace is flagged to indicate that it is not compatible (and must be rewritten).

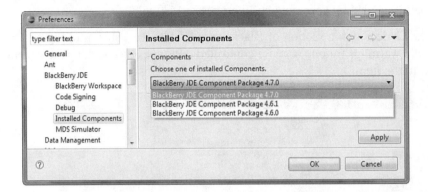

Figure 14.19 BlackBerry workspace preferences—Installed Components settings

This feature dramatically simplifies the development of applications for multiple versions of the BlackBerry Device Software; it is probably the most important reason to use the eJDE instead of the JDE.

14.11.4 MDS Simulator

The BlackBerry workspace MDS simulator settings allow a developer to specify the instance of the MDS simulator used when debugging. Because the eJDE ships with the appropriate version of the MDS simulator for the version of the BlackBerry Component Package being used, there is little need to change this setting.

One possible scenario where you might change the setting is if the target environment for the application was using an older or newer version of MDS and needed to be tested against that version. In this case, you enter the full path to the older version of the MDS simulator or use Browse to navigate to it and click the OK button to confirm the change.

14.12 Modifying Run and Debug Configurations

One important setting needs to be changed for anyone developing BlackBerry Java applications that access network-based resources. To test applications that access the network, you need to start the BlackBerry MDS simulator (described in Chapter 4, "The BlackBerry Mobile Data System (MDS)") before launching the device simulator.

Developers can launch MDS manually at the beginning of a coding session or before testing any applications, but the simpler solution is to configure the eJDE to launch it automatically whenever a test or debug session is started. To configure this option, open the Run menu and select either the Run Configurations or the Debug Configurations menu item, depending on the type of configuration you will use. A Run Configuration is used when simply testing an application in the simulator (discussed in the section, "Testing and Debugging BlackBerry Applications"). A Debug Configuration is used when using the integrated debugger in Eclipse to interact with the simulator while the application is running. After selecting the appropriate option, Eclipse displays a dialog similar to the one shown in Figure 14.20.

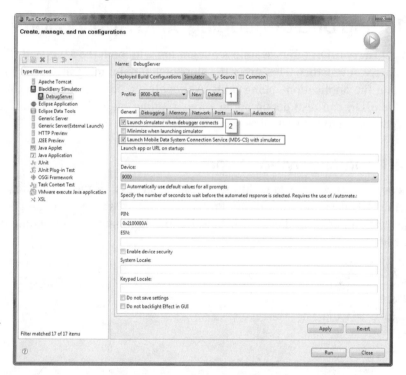

Figure 14.20   BlackBerry workspace Run Configurations options

There are many options configured in this dialog, but all that matters for now is the contents of the Simulator tab. In the tab, select General, click the Profile drop-down field, and select the specific device model being used (1). After the model is selected, the options for the simulator are enabled. Enable the checkbox labeled Launch Mobile Data System Connection Service (MDS-CS) with Simulator (2) and apply the changes. With this enabled, MDS launches automatically with every test or debug session (depending on which configuration you updated) and enables the simulator to access the network resources it needs.

Launch Simulator when Debugger Connects (2) is required for Eclipse to start the simulator when testing or debugging.

There are a lot of other interesting settings on this dialog; notice that you can set the PIN or the Electronic Serial Number (ESN) associated with the simulated device, control whether the simulator saves changes between sessions, and more. Take some time and investigate all the options on this dialog before you continue.

14.13 Testing and Debugging Java Applications

The BlackBerry eJDE offers seamless integration with both the MDS and BlackBerry device simulators. This gives developers a simple, integrated way to test and debug the applications being built. Although it's beyond the scope of this book, the eJDE can also debug applications running on a physical BlackBerry device connected to the system running the eJDE.

14.13.1 Finding Syntax Errors

The debugging process begins during the build process; at the conclusion of a build, the IDE lists all errors in the Problems window, shown in Figure 14.21. Double-click an error in the window and Eclipse highlights the offending code in the editor.

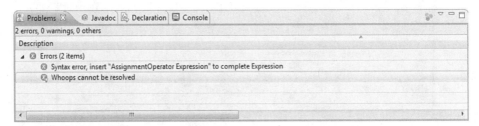

Figure 14.21 Navigating to source code errors

14.13.2 Testing Applications

To test one or more applications in Eclipse (to run applications in the simulator without debugging), use any of the following methods:

• Open the Eclipse Run menu and select Run.

- Use the keyboard shortcut Ctrl-F11.
- Click the debug icon (green arrow icon on the toolbar).

Depending on how you have your Run configurations set up, Eclipse

1. Launches the MDS simulator (if configured to launch automatically during debugging).
2. Launches the selected BlackBerry device simulator (for information on how to use the BlackBerry simulator, see Appendix A, "Using the Black-Berry Device Simulators," available at www.bbdevfundamentals.com).
3. Deploys the applications associated with the Run Configuration to the sim-ulator.

After the simulator launches, navigate to the application(s) being tested (depend-ing on your Run Configurations) and start testing. At any time, you can close the simulator and return to Eclipse to make changes to the code.

14.13.3 Debugging Applications

The Eclipse platform and the BlackBerry eJDE provide tools developers can use to manage the debugging process. This section describes the tools most likely to be used by the beginning BlackBerry Java developer.

Managing Breakpoints

After your application code compiles without error, it's ready to test. If you want to stop code execution at one or more places in the application, set breakpoints in the code by right-clicking in the gutter (the narrow margin on the left side of the editor) next to the line and selecting Toggle Breakpoint in the pop-up menu. You can also press the Ctrl-Shift-B key combination to toggle a breakpoint. A blue dot appears next to the line of code, which indicates that a breakpoint is active. Breakpoints trigger every time the marked line of code executes on the device simulator.

A developer can fine-tune how and when a breakpoint fires if needed. To do this, highlight a breakpoint in the editor, right-click it, and select Breakpoint Proper-ties from the pop-up menu. For each breakpoint, there are options that are evalu-ated whenever the breakpoint is reached. The available options in the dialog are

- **Enabled:** Toggles the checkmark to enable/disable the breakpoint.
- **Hit Count:** The breakpoint suspends execution the *n*th time the breakpoint is hit.

- **Enable Condition:** Populate with a Boolean expression. When the breakpoint is reached, execution stops if the expression evaluates to true or if the value of the condition changes depending on the status of the Suspend When radio button below the code window.

- **Method Entry:** Suspends execution when the method associated with the breakpoint is entered.

- **Method Exit:** Suspends execution when the method associated with the breakpoint is exited.

- **Suspend Policy:** Indicates whether the thread or the entire VM should be suspended when a breakpoint is hit.

To view a list of and manage all breakpoints, open the Window menu, select Show View, and then Other. Select Breakpoints and click the OK button. Eclipse opens a window listing all the breakpoints in the current application, as shown in Figure 14.22. The icons across the top of the window provide developers with options to use to modify or manage the breakpoints. Refer to the Eclipse online help for information on how to use these options.

Figure 14.22   Eclipse Breakpoints window

Starting the Debugger

If you find problems with the application during testing or if you skip testing all together and want to do everything in the debugger, you can

- Open the Eclipse Run menu and select Debug.
- Use the keyboard shortcut F11.
- Click the green "bug" icon on the debug toolbar.

By default, Eclipse wants to switch to a perspective more suitable for debugging. It is usually best to allow Eclipse to do this; it makes for a more pleasant debugging experience to use the correct layout.

Depending on how you have your Run Configurations set up, Eclipse

1. Launches the MDS simulator (if configured to launch automatically during debugging).

2. Launches the selected BlackBerry device simulator (for information on how to use the BlackBerry simulator, see Appendix A, available at www.bbdevfundamentals.com).

3. Deploys the applications associated with the debug configuration to the simulator.

4. Connects the Eclipse debug server to the BlackBerry simulator virtual machine.

Hopefully, you let Eclipse switch to the Debug Perspective, and you see what is shown in Figure 14.23. There's a lot going on here, so each section of the UI is described separately in the following sections.

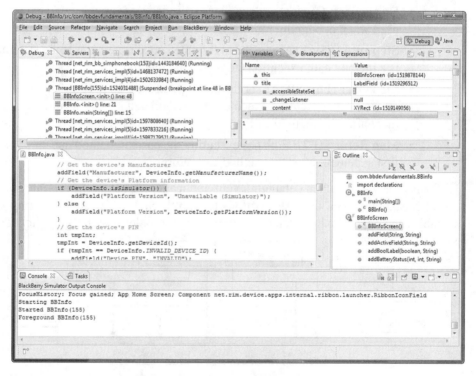

Figure 14.23   Eclipse IDE in Debug Perspective

If you didn't let Eclipse switch to the Debug Perspective, you can switch back and forth between the Debug and Java perspectives by using the buttons in the upper-right corner of Eclipse.

Using the Debug View

The Debug view (shown in the upper-left corner of Figure 14.23) displays the stack frame for the suspended threads running in the device simulator. Each thread in your program appears as a node in the tree; the node can be expanded to see the individual processes for the thread.

At the top of the Debug view are toolbar buttons that control the debug process; the purpose for each button is illustrated in Figure 14.24. For most developers, the important buttons are

- **Resume (F8)** Resumes a suspended thread. When the debugger stops on a breakpoint, Resume continues execution of the program.
- **Suspend**: Suspends the selected thread so the thread can be inspected in the debugger.
- **Terminate (Ctrl-F2):** Terminates the device simulator.
- **Disconnect:** Causes the debugger to disconnect from the debug target; it's used when debugging remotely.
- **Step Into (F5):** Executes the highlighted code statement. If the statement is a method call, execution steps into the method.
- **Step Over (F6):** Steps over the highlighted statement. If the statement is a method call, execution executes the method and highlights the next statement after the method call.
- **Step Return (F7):** Finishes executing the current method and stops on the first statement after the method call returns.

What you will do when debugging your applications is set an appropriate number of breakpoints then use these buttons to step through the code, inspecting variables and objects to help determine the cause of problems with the application.

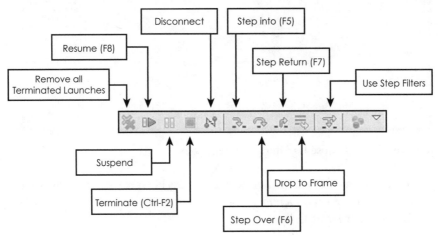

Figure 14.24   Debug toolbar buttons

Using the Variables View

The Variables view displays information about all the variables associated with the stack frame selected in the Debug view. Java objects can be expanded in the view to show the individual fields of the object. When a variable is selected, a details pane appears at the bottom of the view where values can be inspected. The Variables view allows developers to change the values associated with items in the view; while execution is paused, just highlight the value, change it as needed, and then resume program execution.

Using the Code Editor View During Debugging

The Editor view becomes active when a breakpoint is reached or a particular thread is suspended. It highlights the statement being executed and updates as the debugger steps through the application's code.

Using the Outline View

The Outline view displays an outline of the application source code file open in the editor. It lists the structural elements of the file (classes, fields, and methods). Use this view to more easily locate portions of the source file; when you double-click an element in the view, the editor automatically highlights the object in the source file.

Using the Console View

The Console view displays all output from the simulator. For applications that process a large amount of data or execute large loop structures, stepping through the code can be time consuming. To simplify debugging for this case, developers can use `System.out.println("")` within an application to write information directly to the Console view. When a breakpoint is hit or when the application terminates, the data written to the console can be analyzed to help determine the cause of a problem.

Using BlackBerry Specific Debugging Tools

The eJDE includes several debugging tools that are specific to BlackBerry development. To access these tools, open the Eclipse Window menu, open Show View, and then select the Other menu item. Eclipse displays a dialog similar to the one shown in Figure 14.25. Expand the BlackBerry item in the tree, as shown in the figure to see the available options. Each option is described in the following sections.

Figure 14.25   Show View dialog

Using the Memory Statistics View   The Memory Statistics view lists memory statistics for the running application, as shown in Figure 14.26. Use this option to help identify memory leaks in an application. By setting breakpoints and taking snapshots of memory statistics at different points in the application, a developer can pinpoint the area of the application that is leaking memory. The Memory Statistics panel has the following buttons:

- **Refresh:** Refreshes the contents of the Memory statistics window
- **Snapshot:** Captures a snapshot of the current memory statistics
- **Compare:** Compares the current memory statistics against the previous snapshot
- **Save:** Saves the current memory statistics to a Comma Separated Value (.csv) file

🖳 Console Tasks 🗋 BlackBerry Memory Statistics View ⌗ 🔍 BlackBerry Objects View 📄 BlackBerry Profiler View				⊟ ▢

Refresh Save Compare Snapshot

Memory Statistic	# objects	Bytes in use	Allocated	Free
Object Handles	524288	11917172	92381	431907
RAM	48693	11103660	12726416	19412460
Flash	43688	813512	44410324	52772920
Transient objects (flash)	2328	251876	384484	52772920
Persistent objects (flash)	5607	561636	561636	52772920
Code modules (flash)	35753	0	43464204	52772920

Figure 14.26   BlackBerry Memory Statistics view

Using the Objects View The Objects view displays the list of all Objects in memory on the simulator, as shown in Figure 14.27. Developers can troubleshoot Object and memory issues by taking snapshots at different points in the application and comparing snapshots to identify any objects created or destroyed since the previous snapshot. In the window, click the Refresh button to refresh the contents of the window then click the Snapshot button to take a snapshot. After you have two snapshots, you can click the Filter button the select Compare Snapshots from the drop-down list in the filter dialog to compare the snapshots.

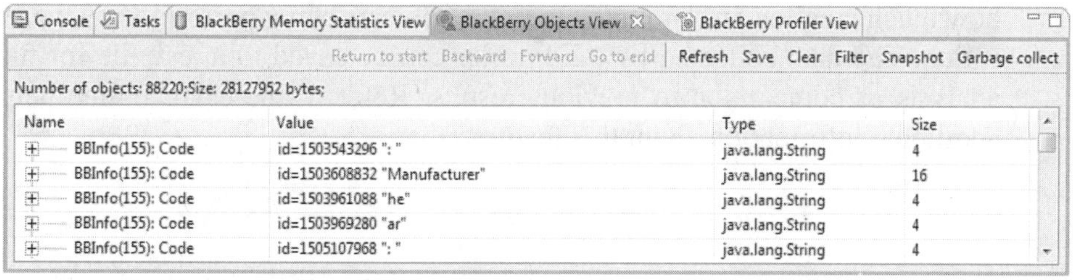
Console
Tasks
BlackBerry Memory Statistics View
BlackBerry Objects View
BlackBerry Profiler View
Return to start Backward Forward Go to end
Refresh Save Clear Filter Snapshot Garbage collect
Number of objects: 88220;Size: 28127952 bytes;
Name
Value
Type
Size
BBInfo(155): Code
id=1503543296 ": "
java.lang.String
4
BBInfo(155): Code
id=1503608832 "Manufacturer"
java.lang.String
16
BBInfo(155): Code
id=1503961088 "he"
java.lang.String
4
BBInfo(155): Code
id=1503969280 "ar"
java.lang.String
4
BBInfo(155): Code
id=1505107968 ": "
java.lang.String
4

Figure 14.27 BlackBerry Objects view

Using the Profiler View Use the Profiler view (shown in Figure 14.28) to analyze a running application to determine where the application is spending most of its time and how it is managing the objects it is creating. To use the tool, follow these steps:

1. Place two breakpoints in the application being profiled. The Profiler profiles the application as it runs between the two breakpoints.
2. Run the application in the debugger.
3. When the application stops at the first breakpoint, open the Profiler view.
4. In the Profiler application, click the Options button and set the options appropriate for the application being tested.
5. Continue running the application. When the second breakpoint is reached, open the Profiler, refresh the view contents by clicking the Refresh button, and view the information the Profiler collected about the application as it ran.

When the profiler runs, it can profile based on the following criteria:

- Time spent executing parts of the application
- Number of objects created
- Size of objects created

- Number of objects committed
- Size of objects committed
- Number of objects moved to RAM
- Size of objects moved to RAM
- User counting

Use the information provided by the Profiler to determine where to optimize the application's code, depending on how much time it spends on certain tasks or how much creation and/or manipulation of objects being performed by the application. The data collected by the Profiler can be saved to a .csv file for further analysis or comparison to previous results. Refer to the eJDE online help for additional information about this feature.

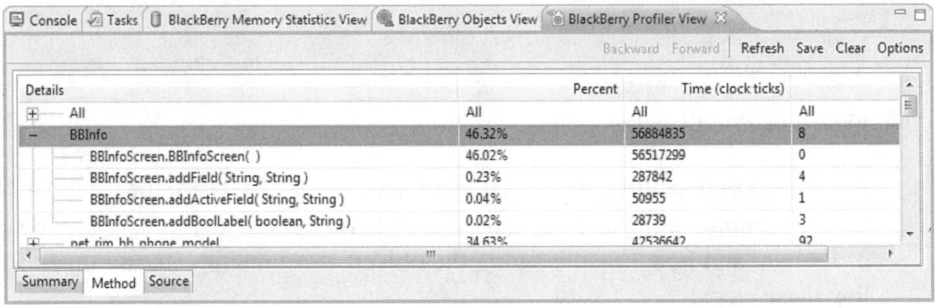

Figure 14.28   BlackBerry Profiler view

14.13.4 Cleaning Up the Simulator

As you test more and more applications in the simulator, you might find that extra stuff is lying around that you need to clean up. You also might be testing an application that does some special processing the first time the application is executed and you need a way to put the device back to a clean configuration. The Eclipse BlackBerry menu contains options for erasing simulator files; to access these options, open the BlackBerry menu and select the Erase Simulator File submenu. The available options are

- **All:** Performs each of the erasures listed here.
- **Erase Removable Memory:** Erases the contents of any removable memory (simulated SD Card) on the device.
- **Erase Non-Volatile Storage:** Erases the contents of the device's non-volatile (flash) memory.

- **Erase File System:** Erases the simulator file system, which includes all files that are not part of the core simulator. This option erases any application files that have been deployed during testing.

14.14 Additional Resources

A complete listing of links to these resources is available online at www.bbdevfundamentals.com.

The BlackBerry Java development tools can be downloaded from www.blackberry/developers.

To access sample applications that can help you learn BlackBerry development, refer to the BlackBerry Development Environment Labs at http://na.blackberry.com/eng/developers/resources/developer_labs.jsp.

To access online developer learning resources, go to http://na.blackberry.com/eng/developers/javaappdev/learningresources.

Several interesting knowledge base articles are related to concepts in this chapter:

- How To: Define a Rollover Icon for an Application (Article #DB-00467)
- How To: Use the Preprocessor (Article #KB-00712)
- How To: Run an Application in the BlackBerry Device Simulator (Article #DB-00044)
- How To: Debug an Application Running on a Live BlackBerry Smartphone (Article #DB-00038)

To access the articles, go to www.blackberry.com/developers and search for the relevant knowledge base article.

15

Using the BlackBerry JDE Component Package Tools

The BlackBerry JDE Component Package is a collection of tools that developers can use to build and debug BlackBerry Java applications outside of the BlackBerry JDE and eJDE. It consists of many of the tools behind the menus in the BlackBerry Java development environments. The package consists of the following tools:

- BlackBerry API documentation
- BlackBerry API library
- BlackBerry device simulator
- BlackBerry Java tools
- BlackBerry MDS simulator
- Email server simulator
- Sample Java applications

The tools are described in this chapter because developers often use them to build BlackBerry Java applications using third-party IDEs, such as NetBeans, IntelliJ, JCreator, and others or outside of an IDE as part of an automated build process.

15.1   BlackBerry API Documentation

The BlackBerry API documentation consists of the standard JavaDoc online help for the BlackBerry Java APIs. It contains information about the BlackBerry-specific APIs available to Java developers (see Figure 15.1). Although the API documentation is integrated into the help menu in both the JDE and eJDE, it must be opened manually or integrated manually with the online help of third-party IDEs. When using the JDE Component Package, it's probably a good idea to place a shortcut for the API documentation on the desktop or Windows Quick Launch bar for easy access. The API documentation is placed in the docs folder under the JDE Component Package installation folder.

The API documentation is not searchable unless you search the contents using a local file-system indexer, such as Google Desktop.

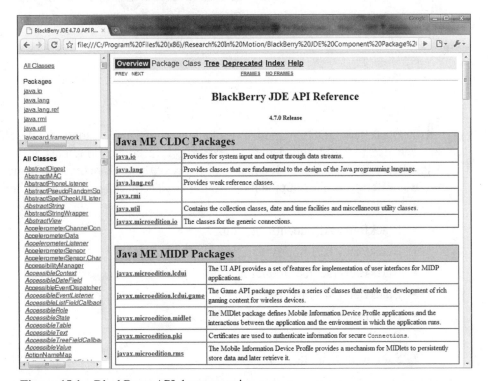

Figure 15.1   BlackBerry API documentation

15.2   BlackBerry API Library

The BlackBerry API library consists of a single .jar file called net_rim_api.jar located in the lib folder under the JDE Component Package installation. This file contains all of the class files for the RIM APIs and is used by RAPC to build BlackBerry applications.

When configuring third-party IDEs for BlackBerry development, you likely need to add the path pointing to the library to the `classpath` used by the IDE so that syntax checking and code completion works correctly.

15.3 Launching the BlackBerry Device Simulator

Each version of the JDE Component Package is linked to a particular version of the BlackBerry Device Software. The package includes the BlackBerry device simulators for the particular BlackBerry Device Software version being used. The JDE Component Package includes batch files for launching each of the simulators included with the package. The files are located in the simulator folder under the JDE Component Package installation folder. To start a simulator, launch the appropriate batch file manually or within an IDE.

The simulator supports many command-line options to tailor the simulator's configuration. The following sample is from the 9500.bat file installed with the 4.7 JDE Component Package. Notice that many parameters are passed to fledge.exe (the simulator engine); there are many more command-line options available for the simulator; visit the simulator's online help for a complete list of the command-line options:

```
@echo off
fledge.exe /app=Jvm.dll /handheld=9500 /session=9500
  /app-param=DisableRegistration
  /app-param=JvmAlxConfigFile:9500.xml /data-port=0x4d44
  /data-port=0x4d4e /pin=0x2100000A
```

 Note: Remember that the current device simulators will run on Windows Vista 64-bit, but, in most cases, do not close without being terminated using the Windows Task Manager. This is a known problem, and will hopefully be fixed in newer simulators.

15.4 Using the BlackBerry Java Tools

The BlackBerry JDE Component Package includes several command-line tools that are used to build, debug, and deploy Java applications. This section contains information on each tool included in the package.

Because each tool is executed from a command line, RIM includes a batch file in the Windows Start Menu to open a command prompt in the appropriate folder.

To execute this batch file, open the Start Menu, navigate to the folder where the JDE Component Package is installed, and launch JDE Components Command Prompt. With the command window open, you can directly execute any of the commands listed in this section.

15.4.1 JavaLoader.exe

In most environments, BlackBerry Java applications are deployed to devices via the BlackBerry Desktop Manager, Web Desktop Manager, or over the air (OTA) from a web server or the BES (described in detail in Chapter 16, "Deploying Java Applications"). The JavaLoader is a command-line utility that developers use to deploy Java applications directly to and retrieve application information from BlackBerry devices. Use this tool rather than the other options if you're testing an application and don't want to go through the hassles of using the end-user deployment tools, or if you are trying to troubleshoot a problem and need to retrieve specific information from a device.

JavaLoader supports a large number of options. The easiest way to learn what the options are is to execute JavaLoader without any parameters; the program lists all the command options to the console. The following is the default command line for the tool:

```
JavaLoader [-u] [-p<port>|<pin>] [-b<baud>] [-d0|-d1]
    [-w<password>] [-q] <command>
```

In this example, *<command>* is one of the supported options for the program, and the following list contains the additional supported options:

- -u uses USB to connect to the BlackBerry device (you likely need to use this every time because the default connection option is Serial, and all current devices use USB).
- -p*<port>* specifies the serial port used to connect to the device (used for serial handhelds only).
- -p*<pin>* specifies the handheld PIN being connected to (use for USB devices only); prefix hexadecimal PINs with an '0x'. This option allows a command to target a specific device when multiple devices are connected to the computer using different USB cables.
- -b*<baud>* specifies the baud rate used to communicate with serial devices.
- -d0 disables VM debug mode.
- -d1 enables VM debug mode.
- -w*<password>* connects to the device using the specified password.
- -q enables quiet mode.

Note: Because most modern devices connect to a PC using USB, the following examples use the –u parameter.

To list all the modules on the device, use the `dir` command in the form of

```
javaloader.exe –u dir [-d] [-s] [-1]
```

To retrieve information about a specific module on the device, use

```
javaloader.exe –u info [-d] [-s] [-v] codFileName.cod
```

Both examples use any of the following optional parameters:

- `-d` displays dependency information
- `-s` displays sibling information
- `-v` displays verbose module information

To retrieve device information from the device, use

```
javaloader.exe –u deviceinfo
```

To copy an application .cod file to the connected device, use

```
javaloader.exe –u load codFileName.cod
```

To copy multiple.cod files to the connected device, use

```
javaloader.exe –u load codFileName1.cod codFileName2.cod […]
```

To load all the modules specified in a .jad file, use

```
javaloader.exe –u load jadFileName.jad
```

To copy a module from the device to the local computer, use

```
javaloader.exe –u save codFileName.cod
```

To copy application .cod files listed in the same .jad file from the device to the local computer, use

```
javaloader.exe –u save jadFileName
```

To wipe the connected device, use

```
javaloader.exe –u wipe [-a|-f]
```

Using any of the following optional parameters:

- -a wipes applications only
- -f wipes the device file system only

To erase a particular module from the device, use

```
Javaloader.exe –u erase [-f] codFileName
```

The optional –f parameter forces the erasure of any in-use modules.

To take a screen shot of the active screen displayed on the device, use

```
javaloader.exe –u screenshot active outputFileName.bmp
```

To remove any IT policies from a device, use

```
javaloader.exe –u -resetToFactory
```

As you can probably see, JavaLoader provides many useful features beyond what the desktop manager and other application deployment tools provide.

15.4.2 Java Debug Wire Protocol (JDWP)

The Java Debug Wire Protocol (JDWP) manages communication between a debugger and the BlackBerry virtual machine. You can configure a third-party IDE to launch this utility when initiating a BlackBerry debug session. When the program runs, it prompts for the settings to use for the debugging session, as shown in Figure 15.2.[1] When all the settings are configured correctly, click the Launch Simulator button to launch the simulator and connect to the debug server running in the IDE.

 Note: If the application being tested requires access to network-based resources, be sure to enable launching the MDS simulator before launching the device simulator.

For information on how to integrate the JDWP application into an IDE, see the documentation for the IDE.

---

1. Figure 15.2 should look familiar; it's the same dialog used when configuring the simulator launch process in both the JDE and eJDE.

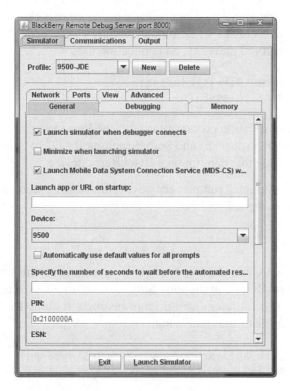

Figure 15.2   BlackBerry JDWP dialog

15.4.3 preverify.exe

Preverifying an application reduces the amount of work a BlackBerry device does when loading an application. Preverification is a multipass process where certain checks are performed on the application's Java bytecode before the application is deployed to a device. When the first pass completes without error, the preverifier annotates the Java class files with standard Java bytecode attributes. If the BlackBerry JVM sees these annotations in the class files, it knows that certain compile-time checks were completed, and it can perform its own verification and security checks much faster and then begin executing the application more quickly.

This application is useful when compiling third-party libraries that have not been compiled for the BlackBerry.

The preverification process is implemented using the preverify.exe utility included in the JDE Component Package. The preverify utility takes a class path as input and saves the verified classes in an output directory specified on the command line. To use this utility to preverify, an application uses

```
Preverify.exe [-d <outputDir>] -classpath
    <classDir1; classDir2; classDirN>
```

In the build process, the preverification process runs after the Java source code is compiled by the Java compiler (javac.exe) and before running RAPC to convert the compiled files into a .cod file that can run on a BlackBerry device.

For additional command-line options, run preverify.exe without any parameters. It returns usage information to the console.

15.4.4 rapc.exe

The RIM Application Program Compiler (rapc) compiles .java and .jar files into .cod files that run in the BlackBerry Smartphone Simulator or on a BlackBerry device. For example, the following command-prompt instruction compiles the myBBApp.jar file into a .cod file of the same name:

```
Rapc.exe import=net_rim_api.jar codename=samples\myBBApp -
midletsamples\myBBApp.jad samples\myBBApp.jar
```

The utility supports the following options:

- `import=` specifies the RIM APIs and other dependent libraries used by the application; when compiling any BlackBerry application, you must include the path to the `net_rim_api.jar` file.
- `codename=` specifies the name for the outputted .cod file.
- `-midlet` specifies that the application is a MIDlet.
- `jad=` specifies the name of the .jad file for the application.
- `<path>\filename_1.java <path>\filename_2.java` specifies the name of the Java source files if compiling from Java files.
- `<path>\JAR_filename.jar` specifies the name of the Java .jar files if compiling from a JAR file.

In an automated build process, rapc.exe would be executed after the Java source code has been compiled by the Java compiler javac.exe and after preverification using preverify.exe.

The rapc utility is highly optimized for the BlackBerry platform with the goal to minimize the size of the resulting application. It provides a significant amount of obfuscation-like services by removing the following items from a COD file:

- All debug information
- Local variable names
- Source line numbers
- Private method and members names

15.4.5 SignatureTool.jar

SignatureTool.jar is the same utility used in both the JDE and eJDE to request signatures from the RIM Signing Authority. The only difference is that, in the other tools, the execution of the signing tool is built into the IDE. To sign applications in a third-party IDE or as part of an automated build process, you must launch the signing tool with the correct command line. Executing the Signature Tool directly from the command line allows you to use additional parameters on the command line to speed up and automate the signing process.

BlackBerry Java development tools version 4.3 and higher can use the -p <password> flag (with -a -C) to automate the processes. If you don't use these automation flags, the signature tool dialogs prompting for the password and for requesting signatures are displayed, which interrupts any automated process being performed.

To run the signing tool, use the following command:

```
java.exe -jar SignatureTool.jar [-p <password>][-a][-c][-C]
    [-f [-d] inputFile][-r directory ][-help]
    ( codFile (codFile) ... | csiFile )
```

The supported command line options are as follows:

- -a instructs the program to automatically request signatures.
- -c instructs the program to close after requesting signatures if no errors have occurred.
- -C instructs the program to close after requesting signatures regardless of the results of the request.
- -d, when used in conjunction with the -f option, instructs the program to delete the temporary file specified using the -f option.
- -f specifies the name of a text file containing a list of .cod files rather than passing the .cod filenames on the command line.

- `-p password` passes the private key password (described in Chapter 12, "Getting Started with the BlackBerry Java Development Tools") to the signing tool when automatically requesting signatures. This option is only available with BlackBerry Java development tools version 4.3 and higher.
- `-r` instructs the program to recurse through a directory and request signatures for all .cod files in the directory and subdirectories.
- `-s` instructs the program to print code signing statistics on the number of signatures received and the number of signatures requested.

The signature tool command line can also register the .csi signature files received when a set of signing keys is purchased from RIM. See Chapter 12 for additional information about this feature.

15.4.6 UpdateJad.exe

When an application file is modified using RAPC or the signing tool, the .jad file used by the application must be updated with information about the application. The JDE Component Package includes a utility called UpdateJad.exe that can perform that update. The utility can also update a .jad file to reference multiple .cod files.

 Note: The utility can only be used on .jad files created or updated using the BlackBerry Java development tools (the JDE, eJDE, and RAPC).

To execute the utility, use

```
updatejad.exe -q -n inputFile.jad [additionalFile.jad]
```

The supported command-line options are

- `-q` suppresses output messages for successful .jad file processing; the program returns a nonzero return code if an error occurred during processing.
- `-n` suppresses the backup of the original .jad file.
- `inputFile.jad` specifies the filename for the .jad file being updated.
- `additionalFile.jad` specifies additional .jad files to be added to the `inputFile.jad`.

To update the .cod file sizes listed in myApp.jad file, use

```
Updatejad.exe myApp.jad
```

15.5 Launching the BlackBerry MDS Simulator

To support testing applications directly and debugging applications using JDWP, both the BlackBerry device simulators and the BlackBerry Mobile Data System (MDS) simulator are included with the JDE Component Package. Configuration options for the JDWP allow the MDS simulator to be launched automatically with the simulator, but it can also be launched manually by executing the run.bat file in the MDS folder under the JDE Component Package installation folder.

Use this option if you know that you are going to do a lot of testing and hopping in and out of the device simulator as you work. Launching the MDS simulator in advance reduces the amount of time needed to begin each debugging session.

15.6 Using the Email Server Simulator

Some BlackBerry applications send outgoing messages and process incoming email messages. To test these applications, the device simulator needs to be able to send and receive email messages. A developer can activate the simulator against the BES and associate it with a real email account or can use the email simulator capabilities of MDS to perform this function. Another option is to use the BlackBerry Email Server Simulator (ESS) included with the JDE Component Package.

Note: Because the ESS and MDS provide the same email simulation functionality, you cannot run both when testing messaging applications in the simulator. Only use the ESS when testing BlackBerry Java applications that do not need the network connectivity provided by the MDS simulator.

The ESS is accessed from the Windows Start Menu; the application's shortcut is installed with the other applications in the JDE Component Package. When the program launches, it displays a dialog similar to the one shown in Figure 15.3.

Figure 15.3 BlackBerry Email Server Simulator

To configure the program, populate the fields at the bottom of the dialog with the appropriate values for name, email, and PIN. The PIN shown in Figure 15.3 is the default PIN used for the device simulators shipped with the JDE Component Package; only change the value here if the PIN passed on the command line to the simulator has been changed. Refer to the section, "Launching the BlackBerry Device Simulator," for additional information.

As shown in Figure 15.3, the ESS runs in two modes, each of which are described in the following sections.

15.6.1 Standalone Mode

In Standalone mode, the ESS communicates directly with the desktop email client. The program acts as a gateway between the BlackBerry Messages application and the desktop mail client. Any message sent from the desktop mail client is delivered to the device, and any messages sent by the BlackBerry Messages application are delivered to the desktop mail client.

You must configure the desktop mail client to use localhost for both of its mail servers (POP3 on port 110 and SMTP on port 25). If the desktop account needs to use different port numbers for these protocols, make the appropriate changes to the POP3 Port and SMTP Port fields on the dialog. When all the settings are configured, click the Clean FS button to clear out any old messages and click the Launch button to start the email simulator.

15.6.2 Connected Mode

In Connected mode, the ESS communicates with a server-based mail account using settings provided in the dialog. To configure this option, populate the server names and credentials (username and password) in the Connected Mode section of the dialog and click the Launch button to launch the simulator.

The beauty of Connected mode is that, because it's using a real mail account, the device application being tested can work with real messages sent or received from users outside of the test environment.

15.7 Accessing Sample Java Applications

The JDE Component Package includes the same sample Java applications included in the JDE and eJDE. The sample applications are installed in the samples folder under the JDE Component Package installation folder.

Unfortunately, unless the third-party IDE you are using to build your applications can read BlackBerry Java Project files, you have to import the Java source files into new projects within the IDE.

15.8 Additional Resources

A complete listing of links to these resources is available online at www. bbdevfundamentals.com.

The BlackBerry Java development tools can be downloaded from www.blackberry. com/developers.

To access sample applications that can help you learn BlackBerry development, visit the BlackBerry Development Environment Labs at http://na.blackberry. com/eng/developers/resources/developer_labs.jsp.

To access online developer learning resources, go to http://na.blackberry.com/ eng/developers/javaappdev/learningresources.

Several interesting knowledge base articles relate to concepts in this chapter:

- How To: Use the Preprocessor (Article #DB-00712)
- How To: Use the BlackBerry Signature Tool from a Command Line (Article #DB-00098)
- How To: Manually Register the CSI Files (Article #DB-00100)
- How To: Use JavaLoader to Take a Screen Shot (Article #DB-00484)

- How To: Use the RAPC Compiler (Article #DB-00066)
- How To: Obfuscate Code in a BlackBerry Application (Article #DB-00438)
- How To: Load Applications onto a BlackBerry Smartphone (Article #DB-00041)
- How To: Configure Email Simulation Support in the BlackBerry MDS Simulator (Article #DB-00651)

To access the articles, go to www.blackberry.com/developers and search for the relevant knowledge base article.

For information on how to build BlackBerry applications in NetBeans, visit www.netbeans.org/kb/55/blackberry.html and http://docs.sun.com/app/docs/doc/820-3753/ghjjt?a=view.

For information on MIDlet preverification, visit http://en.wikibooks.org/wiki/J2ME_Programming/MIDlet_Preverify.

16

Deploying Java Applications

After an application is tested, debugged, and certified for distribution, the next thing a developer must worry about is how to deploy the application to its users. The BlackBerry platform supports several ways to deploy applications, including the following:

- Wired deployment using BlackBerry Desktop Manager
- Wired deployment using the BlackBerry Application Web Loader
- Wired deployment using JavaLoader.exe
- OTA Pull using the BlackBerry Browser
- OTA Push via the BES
- Deploying applications through the BlackBerry App World

This chapter covers each deployment method and highlights the strengths and weaknesses of each option. This topic affects both developers and administrators, and many will argue that it's a BlackBerry administrator's job to manage application deployment. Developers still need to know about the available options and how they affect users of their applications.

With the available application deployment options, it's important to understand the differences between them. Table 16.1 lists the available options and highlights the differences.

Table 16.1 Summary of Deployment Options

Deployment Type	Deployment Method	Deployment Initiation	Deployment Descriptor	Additional Software
Desktop Manager	Wired	User	.alx file	BlackBerry Desktop Manager
Application Web Loader	Wired	User	.jad file	ActiveX control (automatic installation)
JavaLoader	Wired	User	.jad file (optional)	javaloader.exe
OTA Pull (BlackBerry Browser)	OTA	User	.jad file	
OTA Push (BES)	OTA	Server	.alx file	
BlackBerry App World	OTA	User	Release.xml	BlackBerry App World client

Each of the options, requirements, and components are described in the following sections.

 Note: Because this is a book for developers, this chapter does not describe the BlackBerry IT Policies or Application Control Policies that an administrator uses to secure his BlackBerry environment. Refer to the BlackBerry Enterprise Server Administration Guide and security information available online (www. blackberry.com/security) for additional information on these topics.

16.1　Deploying Applications via a Wired Connection

Using a wired connection to deploy BlackBerry applications is useful when deploying to a small subset of an organization's devices or when the target user is external to the organization and OTA pull is not available. It is also useful for users who have restricted data plans and don't want to waste kilobytes on application loading. Three types of wired deployment are supported by the BlackBerry platform: the BlackBerry Desktop Manager, the BlackBerry Application Web Loader, and the JavaLoader. Each option is described in this section.

16.1.1　Using the BlackBerry Desktop Manager

The BlackBerry Desktop Manager (BDM) is an application BlackBerry users can install on their PCs to manage their BlackBerry devices. The BDM uses the

Application Loader utility to deploy applications to BlackBerry devices. The software can be downloaded from the BlackBerry Downloads page at http://na.blackberry.com/eng/services/desktop.

In the early days of BlackBerry, the BDM was required to

- Synchronize PIM and other data to a BlackBerry device
- Backup and restore data on the device
- Manage which mail folders were synchronized with the device
- Upgrade the BlackBerry Device Software
- Deploy applications

With the additional capabilities added to the BlackBerry Enterprise Server (BES) over the years and an organization's reluctance to deploy additional applications on a PC, the BDM is becoming less important to BlackBerry users. Much, but not all of, the functionality provided by this application has been replaced by the BlackBerry Web Desktop Manager (BWDM). Because the BWDM does not support deployment of applications to a connected device, it is not covered in this book.

To deploy Java applications to BlackBerry devices using this option, the user must first install the BDM on the computer system being used to deploy applications. After the application is installed, the user can use it to add and remove BlackBerry applications. To deploy an application using the BDM, the user needs the .cod and .alx files for the application. Administrators or developers can distribute the files by

- Emailing the files to the user
- Placing the files on a network share to which the user has access
- Packaging the files into an installer that the user runs to place the files on her local hard drive and (optionally) updating the BDM configuration so it knows where the files are[1]

---

1. This topic is beyond the scope of this book. For additional information, refer to BlackBerry Developer Knowledge Base article DB-00061, "How To: Update the Registry to Deploy Java Applications Using Desktop Manager."

After the application files are in place, connect a device to the computer using a USB cable and launch the Desktop Manager to begin the process. When the Desktop Manager launches, it displays a screen similar to the one shown in Figure 16.1. It will process for a while as it recognizes the device and validates software versions on the device.

Figure 16.1   BlackBerry Desktop Manager

To start the Application Loader, click the appropriately named Application Loader link on the Desktop Manager Home page. In the Add/Remove Applications area, click the Start button. The Desktop Manager displays a dialog that prompts you to select the target device to use for the add/remove process, as shown. If a password is assigned to the device, it must be entered here before the application-loading process can continue.

At this point, the Desktop Manager connects to the device and retrieves a list of applications installed on the device, as shown in Figure 16.2. From here, the user can delete applications (by unchecking them in the list) or add new applications.

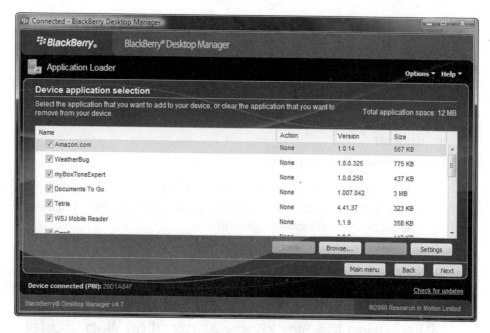

Figure 16.2 BlackBerry Desktop Manager device application selection

To add a new application, click the Browse button. The Desktop Manager presents the standard Windows Open dialog. Navigate to the folder where the .cod and .alx files for the application are located, select the .alx file, and click the Open button. Back in the Desktop Manager, the application is added to the list of device applications and enabled by default. Click the Next button to continue.

The Desktop Manager displays a summary of the actions being performed in this session. It displays a list of all applications being installed and removed from the device. Click the Finish button to complete the installation. When the process completes, click the Main Menu button to leave the Application Loader. At this point, the application is installed and ready to go. Depending on the version of the BlackBerry Device Software running on the target device, the application is placed on the BlackBerry Home Screen or either the Applications or Downloads folder.

Administrators can use the Application Loader in standalone mode to automate installation of a BlackBerry application from a local folder or network file share. Refer to the BlackBerry Deploying Java Applications' white paper for additional information   (http://na.blackberry.com/eng/deliverables/2733/Deploying_Java_Applications.pdf).

Strengths

The strengths of this approach are

- Provides an easy way for BlackBerry users to manage the applications installed on a device.
- Installation can be performed (or not performed) at the user's discretion.
- No over the air (OTA) data usage.

Weaknesses

The weaknesses of this approach are

- Users must install additional software on a PC to use this option.
- This type of installation can only be performed on a system running the BlackBerry Desktop Manager software.
- Requires that the user perform the installation.
- Requires a wired connection to a PC running the installation process.
- Can be more difficult than what many BlackBerry users can handle.

16.1.2 Using the BlackBerry Application Web Loader

In response to customers' reluctance to install additional software on a PC for wired installation of BlackBerry applications, Research In Motion (RIM) created the BlackBerry Application Web Loader (BAWL). The BAWL provides over-the-wire deployment of BlackBerry applications using a web browser. For this option, the Web Loader software (an ActiveX control) is placed on a web server with the BlackBerry application files (the .cod and .alx files) and a web page. BlackBerry users who want to install the application connect their BlackBerry device to the PC using a USB cable and point their desktop browser to the web page to begin the installation.

The first step in implementing this solution is to download the BAWL application from http://na.blackberry.com/eng/developers/resources/devtools.jsp. When you install the application, the only files installed are the ActiveX control (AxLoader.cab) and a folder containing a sample BlackBerry application and installation HTML file.

After you have access to the files, perform the following steps to set up the installation of your application:

1. Configure the web server so it knows how to process .cod and .jad files (.cod files: application/vnd.rim.cod and .jad files: text/vnd.sun.j2me. app-descriptor). For information on how to configure web servers to recognize the BlackBerry application MIME types, see the section, "Configuring the Web Server."

2. Create a folder on the local hard drive or network share to hold all the installation files for the BlackBerry application.

3. Copy the AxLoader.cab and sample HTML file (helloworld_sample.html) from the installation folder to the folder that was just created.

4. Change the filename for the HTML file to something more appropriate for the application being installed. Because most web servers automatically load the index.html file when a folder is accessed from a browser, this is likely the best filename to use here.

5. Modify the HTML file to remove references to the HelloWorld application and replace with references to the application being deployed. Adjust the content and style information on the page to suit the needs of the hosting organization.

6. Copy the folder to a web server and set the appropriate permissions to grant users access to the files.

After the files are installed on the appropriate web server, the installation can be tested and deployed to users. The link to the application's installation page has to be distributed to users or placed on an intranet portal or another website where the users have access.

When the user accesses the page, he sees a page similar to the one shown in Figure 16.3. If the user's device has a password assigned to it, a password prompt displays before the page appears.

 Note: This process only works on a browser that supports ActiveX controls. If the user receives errors when accessing the site, be sure that he's instructed to use Microsoft Internet Explorer or another browser that supports ActiveX controls and that he has the device connected to the computer using a USB cable.

If the device is password protected, enter the password and click the Enter button to continue. If the device is not password protected or after the password has been entered, the page shown in Figure 16.3 appears. Click the Load button to continue with the installation.

Figure 16.3 BlackBerry Application Web Loader Start

At the conclusion of the installation, the browser opens a page displaying the results for the process. Any errors encountered during installation are displayed on the page. If there are no errors, the device can be disconnected from the computer and the application is available for use.

Digging into the Sample HTML File

Normally for this book, I would paste in the sample installation file (helloworld_sample.html) and explain the different parts of the page. In this case, the file is rather large, so it's easy to get lost in it, and RIM does a good job of describing how to use the code within the file and in the documentation available online.

RIM has built this particular tool with the full understanding that every user will take what it has provided and modify it for their particular application. Because of this, there is no need to create the HTML file from scratch; everything the developer needs to know about how to use this technology is included in the sample page. At a minimum, every page created to use this technology is going to contain the information already in the sample; any additional information added will probably relate to page formatting, additional content, or navigation.

To access instructions on how to use this technology, see "Deploying Java Applications," located at http://na.blackberry.com/eng/deliverables/2733/Deploying_Java_Applications.pdf and the "BlackBerry Application Web Loader–Developer Guide," located at http://na. blackberry.com/eng/deliverables/1079/_BlackBerry_Application_Web_Loader_Developer_ Guide.pdf.

Strengths

The strengths of this approach are

- Provides an easy way for BlackBerry users to manage the applications installed on a device.
- Installation can be performed (or not performed) at the user's discretion.
- Does not require that any additional software be installed on the user's PC in advance. (The ActiveX control used by this process is deployed as needed in real time.)
- Multiple applications can be installed from the same page—a developer could create a menu or dynamic website containing all available applications and let users install as many as they want.
- No OTA data usage.

Weaknesses

The weaknesses of this approach are

- Requires Microsoft Internet Explorer.
- The user must perform the installation.
- Only works with a single browser—organizations that have adopted a different browser cannot use this technology.
- Requires a wired connection to a PC running the installation process.

16.1.3 Using the JavaLoader

JavaLoader is a command-line tool that deploys applications to a BlackBerry device. Although it can deploy applications, it's not really an end-user tool. JavaLoader was designed to allow developers to

- Quickly deploy a .cod file to a device (either a .cod file directly or one or more .cod files listed in a .jad file)
- Remove one or more .cod files from a device
- Retrieve information about a device or the applications running on a device

For additional information about this tool, see Chapter 15, "Using the BlackBerry JDE Component Package Tools."

Strengths

The strengths of this approach are

- Quickly deploys any .cod file or the applications listed in a .jad file to a device.
- Does more than just deploy applications.

Weaknesses

The weakness of this approach is

- The tool was not meant to be used by end users.

16.2 Deploying Applications Over the Air (OTA)

Over the air (OTA) deployment of BlackBerry Java applications benefits users because the application can be deployed (in the case of push) or installed (in the case of pull) no matter where the user is or what the user is doing. As long as the device has wireless network access and the application is available, it can be deployed to the device.

16.2.1 Using OTA Pull

OTA Pull is by far the easiest OTA deployment mechanism for BlackBerry applications, and it is useful for both internal (enterprise) and external (consumer) applications and users. With this deployment option, the application files (.cod and .jad files) are placed on a web server and the user installs the application by clicking a link to the .jad file from his BlackBerry device (either through the browser directly, a link in an email, or even as an action inside a custom application).

 Note: For an example of what this looks like, point your BlackBerry browser to www.google.com/gmm; this is Google's site for installing Google Maps. The link on this page points to the .jad file for the application.

As shown in Figure 16.4, when the user activates the link on the device, the browser connects to the web server and retrieves the application's .jad file. When the .jad file arrives on the device, the browser (or some software loaded by the browser) parses the .jad file to determine which .cod files are needed to install the application. The browser then requests the .cod file(s) and completes the installation.

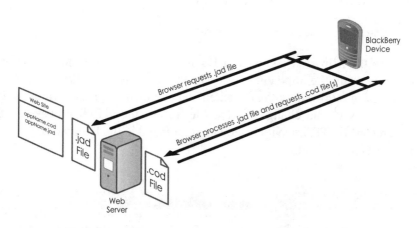

Figure 16.4   BlackBerry Application OTA Pull process

To implement this deployment option, the following steps must be performed by an administrator or developer:

1. Configure the web server to recognize the BlackBerry file types. Information on how to configure web servers to recognize the BlackBerry application MIME types, see the section, "Configuring the Web Server."

2. (Optional) Create a web page the user can open to view information about the application and include a link to the application's .jad file.

3. Copy the web page and application files to the web server.

4. Provide users with access to the page or a link to the .jad file with the appropriate instructions for its use.

Configuring the Web Server

To allow the BlackBerry browser or BAWL to manage the installation of the application, the web server must be configured to ignore the file types involved used by this process (.cod and .jad) and pass them unmodified to the browser. This is accomplished by defining the appropriate MIME types for the files. This is accomplished differently depending on the web server being used; examples are provided here for IBM Lotus Domino and Microsoft Internet Information Server (IIS). Check the web server's documentation for instructions if you're not using one of these servers.

The .cod MIME type must be defined as follows:

```
application/vnd.rim.cod
```

The .jad MIME type must be defined as follows:

```
text/vnd.sun.j2me.app-descriptor
```

To configure the MIME types in IBM Lotus Domino, navigate to the Domino Data folder and edit the httpd.cnf file, as shown in Figure 16.5. Each line begins with an AddType followed by the file extension and file type, as shown in the figure. After you save the changes to the file, restart the HTTP process on the server. To restart HTTP, issue the following command in the Domino server console: tell http restart.

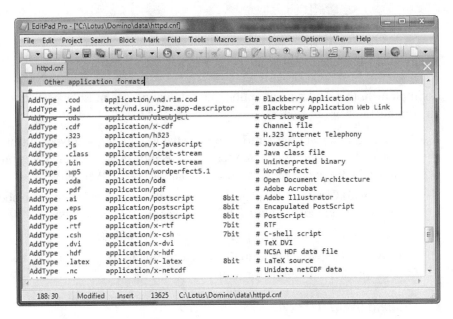

Figure 16.5   Updating the Domino HTTPD.CNF file

To configure the file types in Microsoft IIS, open the Internet Information Services Manager application, as shown in Figure 16.6. If configuring the file types for a single website, right-click the site and select Properties from the menu that appears. If configuring the MIME types for all websites on the server, right-click the Web Sites entry in the tree view (as shown in the figure) and select Properties. If configuring for a particular site, right-click the site's folder and follow the instructions.

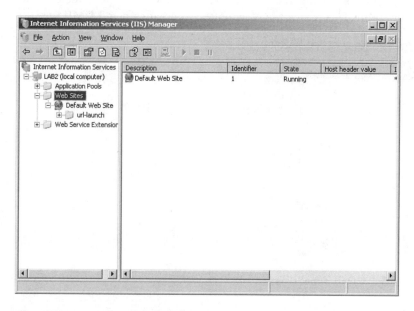

Figure 16.6   Microsoft Internet Information Services Manager

In the dialog that appears, click the HTTP Headers tab (1), shown in Figure 16.7, and click the MIME Types button (2).

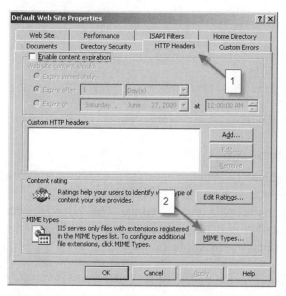

Figure 16.7   Microsoft Internet Information Services Manager default website properties

A dialog appears, listing the MIME types defined for the selected folder, as shown in Figure 16.8. Click the New button to create a new MIME type.

Figure 16.8   MIME Types dialog

In the dialog that appears (see Figure 16.9), enter the file extension and the appropriate MIME type for the file. Click the OK button to continue. The example shows the process for the .jad file; repeat the process for the .cod file MIME type.

Figure 16.9   Defining a MIME type

Creating an Installation Web Page

The web page used to manage the installation doesn't have to be complicated; all that is needed is some information about the application (perhaps some installation instructions) and a link to the application's .jad file. The following code was created to facilitate the installation of the URL Launch utility highlighted in Chapter 11, "Building BlackBerry Java Applications."

```
<!DOCTYPE html public "-//W3C//DTD HTML 4.01 Transitional//EN">
<HTML>
<HEAD>
<TITLE>URL Launch</TITLE>
<LINK href="std.css" rel="stylesheet" type="text/css">
```

```
</HEAD>
<BODY>
<H1>URL Launch</H1>
<P>Thank you for your interest in the URL Launch utility.
When the application is opened, it will launch the default
browser on the BlackBerry and open the <A
href="http://www.bbdevfundamentals.com">
www.bbdevfundamentals.com</A> web site.</P>
<A href="urllaunch.jad">Click here to begin the installation.</
A>
</BODY>
</HTML>
```

Installing an Application

Now, let's look at what the user's experience is with this installation process. When a user accesses the web page shown in the previous section, she is presented with a screen similar to the one shown in Figure 16.10. This is just the browser rendering the HTML content shown in the sample page.

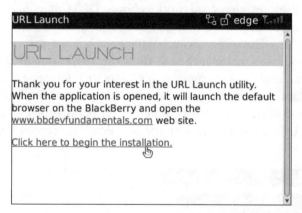

Figure 16.10   URL Launch installation page

To install the application, the user must click the Click Here to Begin the Installation link on the page. The browser retrieves information about the application and displays the screen shown in Figure 16.11. At this point, the application is ready to be installed, but the user has to click the Download button to start the installation.

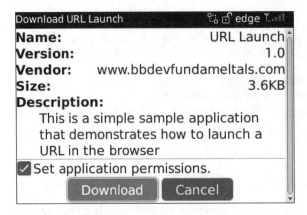

Figure 16.11 Installation Download screen

In the figure, the Set Application Permissions checkbox has been checked by the user. If an application uses resources (network, phone, GPS) that might be restricted on the device, some additional configuration steps must be performed to complete the installation. These steps can be skipped, but the user is still prompted when an application is first launched to allow the application to access the resources it needs, so doing this now removes a prompt that will appear later. The user can just click the Download button to start the download of the application for installation on the device. If the user wants to set permissions first, he can check the checkbox before continuing with the download; the screen shown in Figure 16.12 appears.

Figure 16.12 Changes to application permissions

The user can ignore this prompt and continue with the installation, or he can click the View button to access the screen shown in Figure 16.13. From here, the user can enable the permissions that he believes the application needs. In this case, the figure shows that the user has enabled access to the internal network, the Internet, and the use of Wi-Fi connections (not needed for this particular application but shown for example purposes).

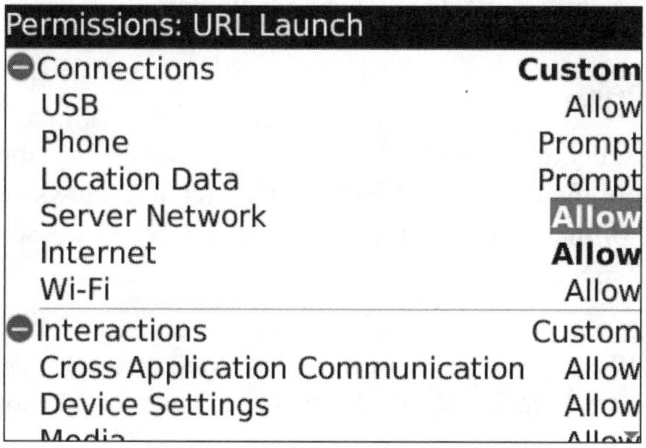

```
Permissions: URL Launch
●Connections                          Custom
 USB                                   Allow
 Phone                                 Prompt
 Location Data                         Prompt
 Server Network                        Allow
 Internet                             Allow
 Wi-Fi                                 Allow
●Interactions                         Custom
 Cross Application Communication       Allow
 Device Settings                       Allow
 Media                                 Allow
```

Figure 16.13   Application Permissions screen

After the application downloads and installs, the user is notified that the process has completed. If the application requires that the device be restarted, the user is prompted to confirm the restart.

Deploying Application Versions Based on BlackBerry Device Software Version

When dealing with an application that has different versions depending on which version of the BlackBerry Device Software the application will be running on, a developer can build logic into the web page to automatically link to the correct version. The page would parse the HTTP USER-AGENT or PROFILE header values (described in Chapter 8, "The BlackBerry Browser") to determine the BlackBerry Device Software version, and then provide the link to the right .jad file for the device.

Strengths

The strengths of this approach are

- Anybody can install the application, as long as he has access to the correct URL.

- Easy to set up.

- Can easily create a menu or dynamic website for installation of many applications.

Weaknesses

The weaknesses of this approach are

- Anybody can install the application, as long as he has access to the correct URL.[2]
- The user must perform the installation.
- Requires wireless network connectivity during installation.

16.2.2   Using OTA Push

BlackBerry administrators can configure the BES to deploy BlackBerry applications to devices OTA without the user's involvement. This feature allows central control and administration of the application deployment process and is suitable for organizations large and small.

Note: This section covers BES 5.0. If your organization is running an older version of the software, refer to the appropriate BES Administrator Guide for additional information.

The application deployment capabilities of the BES support:

- Deployment of applications to users or groups of users
- Application Whitelists: A list of applications that are allowed to run on devices
- Application Blacklists: A list of applications that are not allowed to run on devices
- Application Control Policies that control what an application can and cannot do on a device
- Deployment of different versions of applications to different groups of users
- Application upgrades

Beginning with BES 5.0, a user can be a member of multiple groups. When an application is associated with a group, the application is available (and optionally deployed) to all members of the group. Because the user can be a member of multiple groups, she receives access to applications through the groups she

---

2. The ability for anyone to deploy the application is both a strength and weakness. It's a strength because people can easily forward the installation URL to anyone they think should use the application. It's a weakness because people will be able to install the application who really shouldn't have access to it.

belongs to. This is a much better scenario than what was available previously with BES 4.1.

In BES 4.1, a user could only be assigned a single Software Configuration Policy. This meant that, if an administrator had to support multiple applications distributed across multiple types of users, he would have to create a large number of Software Configurations on the BES and carefully manage them.

Before an administrator can deploy BlackBerry Java applications through the BES, he must first create a network share (a shared folder on a network server) accessible by any BES that will deploy the application. After the network share is created, the BlackBerry Administration Service (BAS) must be configured with the location of the shared folder. For additional information on setting up the share and configuring the BAS, refer to BlackBerry Enterprise Server Administration Guide. After the BAS is configured, a BlackBerry Java application can be pushed to devices over the air by performing the following tasks:

1. Publish the BlackBerry Java application to the application repository (the shared folder).
2. Create a Software Configuration.
3. Assign the Software Configuration to a users or groups of users.

After the software configuration is assigned to a user or a group that the user belongs to, the BES begins the process of deploying the application or applications for the user. The deployment does not happen immediately; the BES has a lot to do and delivering mail and synchronizing PIM data will likely take precedence. Expect at least 15 minutes to pass before the application is deployed to target devices.

All the configuration steps for this type of deployment are performed in the web-based BAS console accessed by using the following URL and the resolvable hostname for the system running the BAS for *<server-name>*:

```
https://<server-name>/webconsole/login
```

Publishing an Application

Before the application can be published on the BAS, the application files (the .jad file and any associated .cod files) must be compressed into a .zip archive file.

The first step in the process involves publishing the application files on the BAS. When the zip archive for the application is ready, open the BAS URL in Microsoft Internet Explorer (the BAS uses ActiveX controls and will only run in

Internet Explorer) and log in using the credentials provided by the BES administrator. Ultimately, the browser shows a page similar to Figure 16.14.

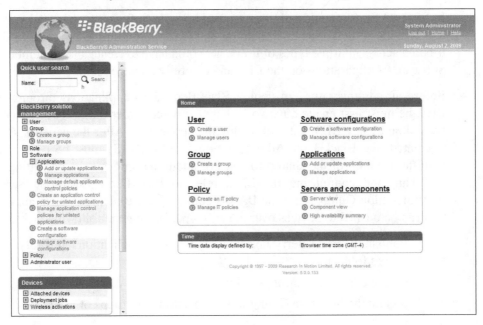

Figure 16.14 BAS Console: Manage Applications

There are two places in the interface that provide access to the publishing function. In the navigator on the left is a section called BlackBerry Solution Management. Expand the Software option, then Applications, and you will see the options for managing applications. You can also find the same options in the primary content area of the page labeled Home in the figure. Click one of the Add or Update Applications links on the page. The browser returns a page with the same header and navigation as Figure 16.14, plus the content shown in Figure 16.15. To add an application to the repository, add the full path pointing to the file in the field or click the Browse button, navigate to the folder where the application archive was created, and select the file. When the field is populated with the archive filename, click the Next link to continue the process.

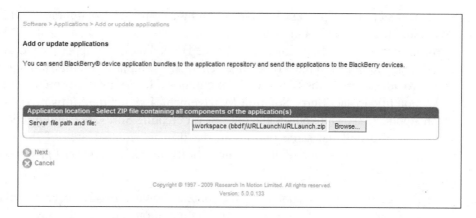

Figure 16.15   BAS Add or Update Applications page

The BAS processes the archive and displays summary information about the application, as shown in Figure 16.16. Click the Publish Application link to complete the process.

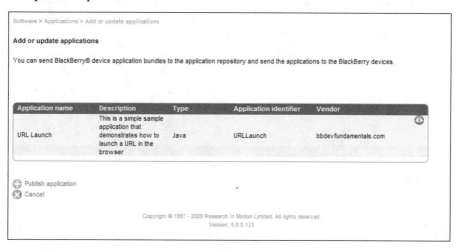

Figure 16.16   BAS Application Summary page

At this point, the BAS displays a page indicating that the application has been published, and the first step in the process is complete. Repeat this process for any additional applications ready to be published.

Creating a Software Configuration

The next step in the process involves defining a Software Configuration which contains information about one or more applications published on the BAS. From any page in the BAS console, click the Home link in the upper-right corner of the page to return to the Home page. There are two places on the Home page that provide access to the Software Configurations. In the navigator on the left is a section titled BlackBerry Solution Management. Expand the Software option, then Applications, and you see the options for creating Software Configurations. You can also find the same options in the primary content area of the page labeled Home. Click one of the Create a Software Configuration links on the page.

The BAS displays a page containing the content shown in Figure 16.17. Populate the form with the name for the Software Configuration and click the Save button to continue. The description field can store a brief description of the Software Configuration. (The other fields on the form are beyond the scope of this book.)

Note: The BAS does not allow you to create resources and populate them at the same time (in this case, creating a Software Configuration and populating it with applications). You must create a resource, then go back and edit it to define additional properties for the resource.

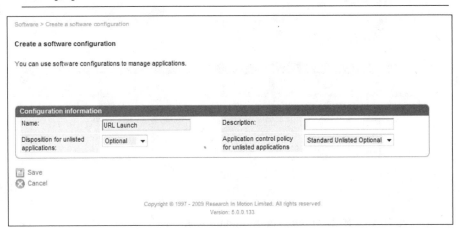

Figure 16.17   BAS Create a software configuration page

At this point, the BAS confirms that the Software Configuration has been created. On the page that appears, click the Software Configuration's name to begin the process of assigning applications to the Software Configuration. The BAS displays a page showing detailed information about the Software Configuration, shown in Figure 16.18. Click the Applications tab (1), and then click the Edit Software Configuration link (2).

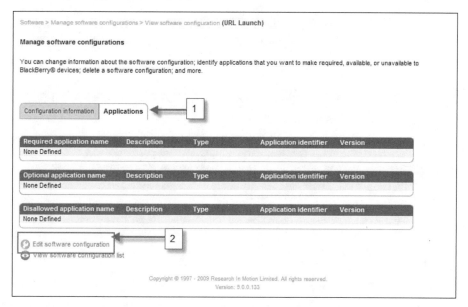

Figure 16.18   BAS Manage Software Configuration page

The BAS displays a page containing a list of all the applications associated with the selected Software Configuration. Make sure that the Applications tab is selected (it should be from the previous step) and click the Add Applications to Software Configuration link on the page.

The BAS opens the page shown in Figure 16.19; use the search feature to locate the application(s) to be added to this Software Configuration. The search can be refined by providing a little information about the application, such as the partial application name (URL) shown in the figure (1). Click the Search button (2) to execute the search.

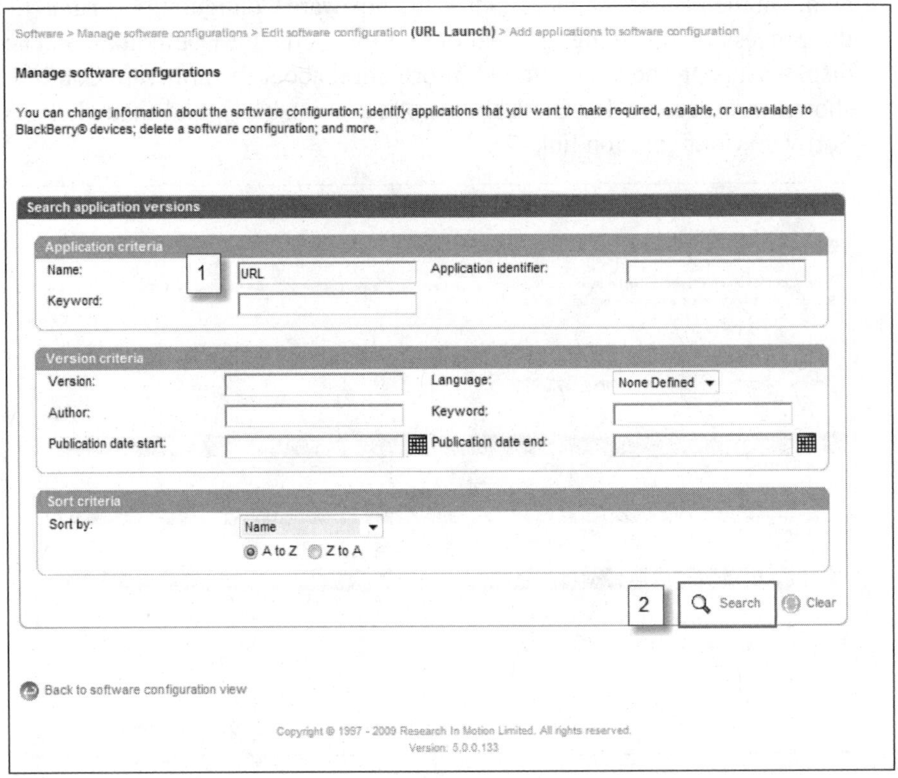

Figure 16.19 BAS Search application versions page

The BAS searches its repository of applications and returns the list of applications that matched the search criteria. Select the application(s) that will be added to the Software Configuration and the contents of the page expand to expose deployment options for the selected application shown in Figure 16.20.

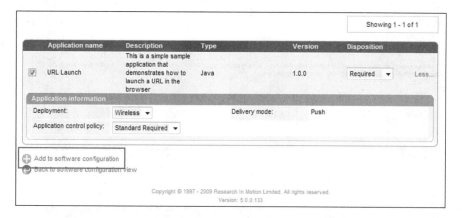

Figure 16.20   BAS application deployment options

On the page, the options for deployment are

- **Wired:** Indicates that the application will be deployed over a wired connection (via the BlackBerry Desktop Manager or Application Web Loader)
- **Wireless:** Indicates that the application will be pushed to the device OTA

The options for Application Control Policy vary depending on the BAS configuration. This field allows assignment of a policy that defines the actions and activities the application is allowed to perform on the device. (Further discussion of this option is beyond the scope of this book.)

Click the Add to Software Configuration button to add the application to the Software Configuration.

 Note: In this example, only one application is being added to the Software Configuration, but there's no reason a Software Configuration can't include multiple applications.

After the application is added to the Software Configuration, the BAS displays the summary page shown in Figure 16.21. You must click the Save All link (highlighted in the figure) to save the changes to the Software Configuration.

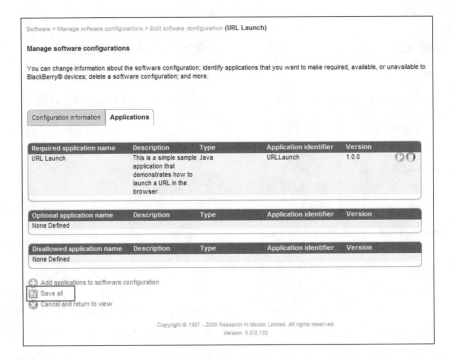

Figure 16.21   BAS updated software configuration

The BAS opens a page containing information about the updated Software Configuration. At this point, the Software Configuration is ready to go, and step 2 has been completed. Now, it's time to associate the Software Configuration with users or groups.

Assigning a Software Configuration to a User

The last step in the process involves assigning the Software Configuration to one or more users (described in this section) or to one or more groups (described in the next section). Click the Home link in the upper-right corner of any page to return to the BAS Home Screen.

Two places on the Home page provide access to the managing users. In the navigator on the left is a section titled Users, and you can find the same options in the primary content area of the page labeled Home. Click one of the Manage Users links on the page to begin the process.

The BAS displays the Search page shown in Figure 16.22. Enter a partial user-name to search for a particular user or leave the form blank. Click the Search button to search for all users.

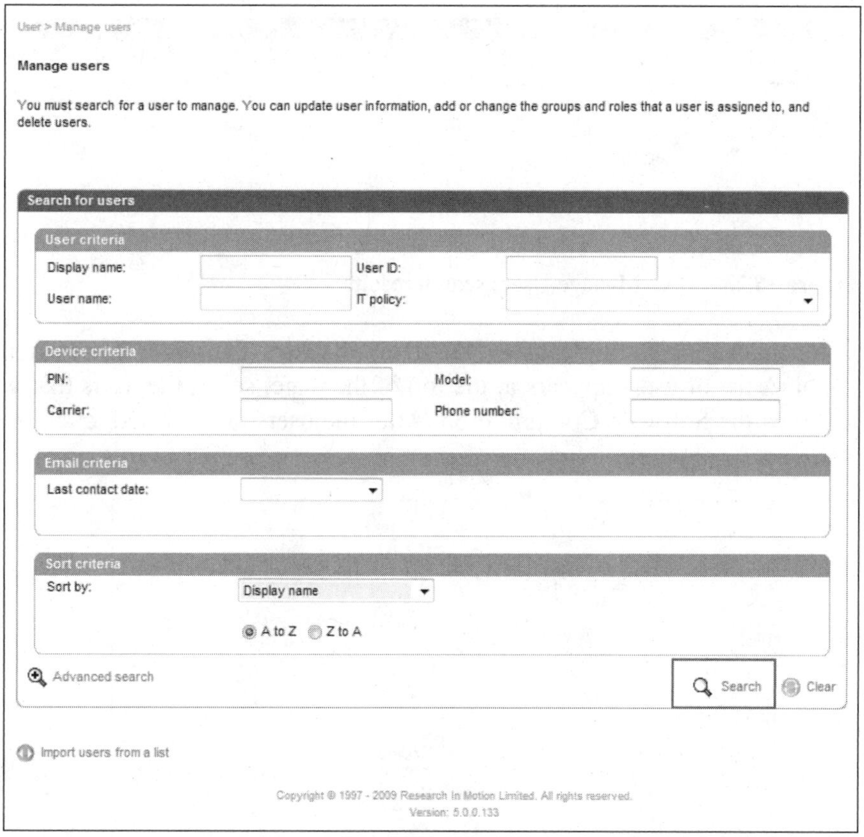

Figure 16.22 BAS Manage Users Search form

The BAS displays a page listing the results of the search, shown in Figure 16.23. To assign a Software Configuration to a single user, click a user's name to continue. To assign a Software Configuration to multiple users, click the Manage Multiple Users link at the bottom of the page. At this point, the discussion splits to cover assigning to multiple users (next) or a single user (later in this section).

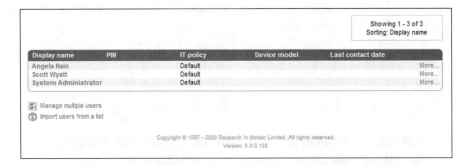

Figure 16.23   BAS Manage Users search results

When managing multiple users, the BAS displays the page shown in Figure 16.24. A list of users appears at the top of the page; select the users that will be assigned the Software Configuration. After the users are selected, click the Add Software Configuration link.

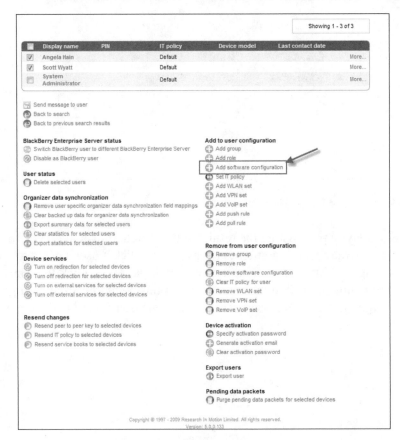

Figure 16.24   BAS Managing Multiple Users page

The BAS displays the page shown in Figure 16.25. Select one or more Software Configurations to be assigned to the selected users (1), click the Add button (2), and then click the Save button (3) to complete the assignment.

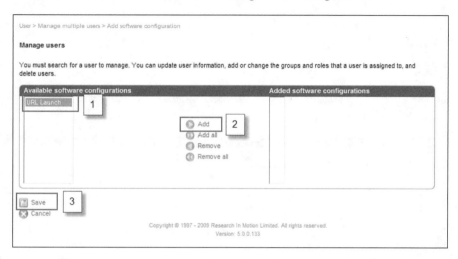

Figure 16.25 BAS Manage Software Configuration Assignment to Multiple Users page

When a single user is clicked on the results page shown in Figure 16.23, the BAS will display the page shown in Figure 16.26. Click the 'Software Configuration' tab then click the 'Edit User' button.

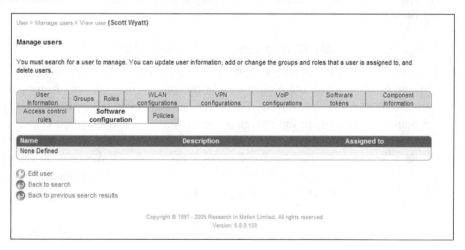

Figure 16.26 BAS Manage User page

The BAS will display the page shown in Figure 16.27. Select one or more Software Configurations to be assigned to the selected user (1), click the 'Add' button (2) then click the 'Save all' link (3) to complete the assignment.

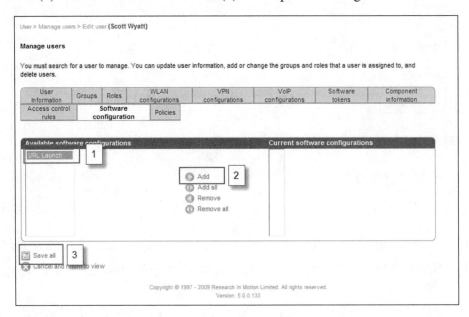

Figure 16.27   BAS Assign Software Configurations to User page

At this point, the BAS displays a summary page to indicate that the assignment has been made.

Assigning a Software Configuration to a Group of Users

This section describes how to assign one or more Software Configurations to one or more groups. Click the Home link in the upper-right corner of any page to return to the BAS Home Screen. Two places on the Home page provide access to the managing groups. In the navigator on the left is a section titled Groups, and you can find the same options in the primary content area of the page labeled Home. Click one of the Manage Groups links on the Home page to continue. The BAS displays the page shown in Figure 16.28. Click the name of the group that will receive the Software Configuration assignment.

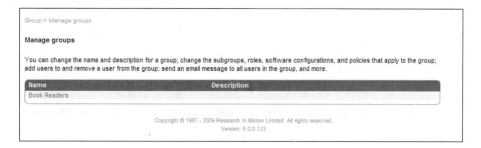

Figure 16.28 BAS Group Management page

On the page that appears (shown in Figure 16.29), select the Software Configurations tab and click the Edit Group link.

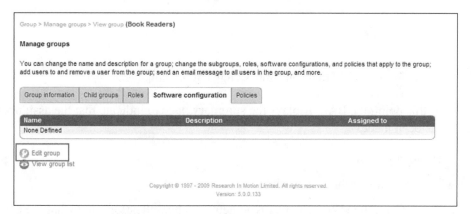

Figure 16.29 BAS Group Software Configuration page

The BAS displays the page shown in Figure 16.30. Select one or more Software Configurations to be assigned to the group (1), click the Add button (2), and then click the Save All link (3) to complete the assignment.

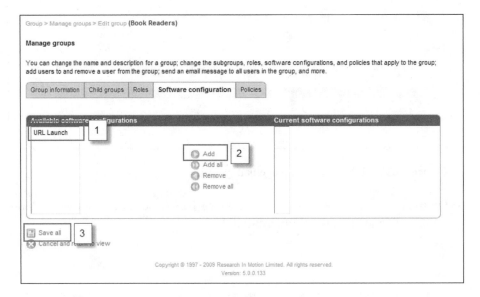

Figure 16.30   BAS Group Software Configuration Assignment page

At this point, the BAS displays the summary page to indicate that the assignment has been made.

Strengths

The strengths of this approach are

- Centralized control over who gets which applications and what the applications are allowed to do.
- Applications are deployed without the user's involvement.
- Easy to manage deploying different applications to different groups of users.

Weaknesses

The weakness of this approach is

- Places additional load on BES administrators.

16.3 Deploying Applications Through BlackBerry App World

A recent trend among smartphone companies and carriers is to create portals where users can purchase or download, for fee or free, applications for mobile devices. In 2009, RIM opened BlackBerry App World, where people can download free BlackBerry applications or purchase and install applications directly to their devices. This section provides some information on the program and its capabilities. For additional information, go to the BlackBerry App World website, located at http://na.blackberry.com/eng/developers/appworld.jsp.

16.3.1 Joining the Program

To join the App World program, a developer must complete a registration process and pay a $200 U.S. developer administration fee. (The fee covers the cost of up to 10 application submissions and is refundable if you are not accepted into the program.) To participate in the program, you must have a PayPal account; this account pays any fees and is where any profits are deposited.

If charging a fee for your application, you have to agree to Digital River's license agreement. Digital River is the world's premier digital distribution company—many name-brand companies use this service to process purchases of software and other media online.

Developers can control which devices are supported by the application, which carrier's customers can download the application, and more.

16.3.2 Managing Applications

Developer must submit applications and allocate time for RIM to review and test the application before users can purchase and/or download them from App World. You manage your interaction with the App World through a web interface. From this interface, you will be able to

- Add applications
- Set availability for applications
- Configure application settings
- Set pricing for your applications

 Note: For App World, RIM has set a minimum price for all applications ($2.99 U.S.) and defines pricing tiers for all applications. The result is that you can't set any price you want for your application.

When submitting applications, there are many options available to make the deployment process as seamless as possible. The App World supports multiple bundles of .cod files to target multiple versions of BlackBerry Device Software and allows you to provide additional information users will need to help decide whether they want to download or purchase your application.

The App World also supports flexible licensing options that allow you to control who can and cannot use your application. Refer to the App World website for additional information on all options.

Strengths

The strengths of this approach are

- Access for your application to a much wider audience.
- Simple way to deploy and periodically update applications.
- Easy access to statistics on application downloads and user reviews.

Weaknesses

The weaknesses of this approach are

- Costs $200 to get into the program.
- Only supports specific BlackBerry device models (running BlackBerry Device Software 4.2.0 and higher).
- Only supports trackball and SurePress™ devices.
- RIM controls pricing tiers; you cannot charge whatever you want for your application.

16.4 Additional Resources

A complete listing of links to these resources is available online at www.bbdevfundamentals.com.

The BlackBerry Device Manager software can be downloaded from http://na.blackberry.com/eng/services/desktop.

A great summary of the deployment options can be found in "Deploying Java Applications," located at http://na.blackberry.com/eng/deliverables/2733/Deploying_Java_Applications.pdf.

For additional information on how to use the BlackBerry Application Web Loader, refer to the "BlackBerry Application Web Loader - Developer Guide," located at http://na.blackberry.com/eng/deliverables/1079/_ BlackBerry_Application_Web_Loader_Developer_Guide.pdf and the "BlackBerry Application Web Loader - Release Notes and Known Issues List," located at http://na.blackberry.com/eng/deliverables/1129/BlackBerry_ Application_Web_Loader_Release_Notes.pdf.

Several interesting knowledge base articles are related to concepts in this chapter:

- How To: Update the Registry to Deploy Java Applications Using Desktop Manager (Article # DB-00061).
- How To: Create a Single .alx File to Install Multiple Versions of an Application (Article # DB-00028).

To access the articles, go to www.blackberry.com/developers and search for the relevant knowledge base article.

For additional information on the BlackBerry App World, visit http://na. blackberry.com/eng/developers/appworld.jsp.

17

Using Additional BlackBerry Application Technologies

This chapter is for BlackBerry application development topics that didn't fit within the other chapters. These topics are not covered in great detail; they're included to explain the additional capabilities they provide. You need to refer to the documentation available online for additional information on these topics. The following topics are included:

- Plazmic Content Development Kit
- e-Commerce Content Optimization Engine
- Supporting the BlackBerry Wallet in web applications
- Sync Server SDK

17.1 Creating Rich Content Using the Plazmic Content Development Kit

Many years ago, RIM purchased Plazmic, a company that sold tools for creating content for mobile devices. The result of this acquisition is the availability of the free Plazmic Content Development Kit (CDK) for BlackBerry smartphones. The kit allows developers or designers to create different types of rich content optimized for use on a BlackBerry smartphone. Content types include splash screens, graphics, animated content, and device themes. The CDK and associated documentation can be downloaded from www.plazmic.com, and it consists of two components: the Plazmic Theme Builder and Plazmic Composer.

The Theme Builder is used to create themes for BlackBerry smartphones, and Composer is used to create rich content for BlackBerry smartphones. These tools are described in the following sections. You must download and install the CDK before you can use the applications.

17.1.1 Using the Plazmic Theme Builder Application

The Plazmic Theme Builder application customizes the BlackBerry smartphone user interface. It's used by Research In Motion (RIM), carriers, and designers to create customized BlackBerry interfaces. Themes define many aspects of the user interface displayed on a BlackBerry smartphone; application interface components are usually rendered deep within the BlackBerry Java application programming interfaces (API), but much of what a user interacts with outside of applications is customized using Theme Builder. The exceptions to this are the theme components that can be created for the BlackBerry Messages and Phone applications.

You need to have created the appropriately sized and styled graphics for each theme element controlled in Theme Builder. You can create these images using any graphical design tool, including the Plazmic Composer (described later). All that matters is that the images conform to the size constraints dictated by the target device's capabilities.

When you launch the Plazmic Theme Builder, you are prompted to create a new theme, as shown in Figure 17.1. A theme is tightly bound to the device family for which it was created, because the screen resolution can vary between families. You need to provide a name for the new theme, select the screen resolution for the theme, and select the theme type being used. Theme types vary, depending on which device is being targeted. The Bold, for example, shipped with the new Precision theme, while the BlackBerry Curve 8300 smartphone supported the Icon, Today, and Zen theme types. Because of this, you need to know a bit about the target device before you create a new theme.

Figure 17.1   Creating a new theme in the Plazmic Theme Builder

After you create the new theme, you are presented with an image for the device selected as the target for the current theme, as shown in Figure 17.2. The right half of the screen (the Inspector) defines the options for different visual components of the selected device.

Figure 17.2   Defining Banners for the Device Home Screen in Theme Builder

In Figure 17.2, the selected Inspector option defines options for the different banners associated with the theme. There are two Banner types: Home Screen and Application. The Home Screen banner is displayed on the top of the device's home screen and when the screen is locked. The Application banner is displayed at the top of several BlackBerry applications, such as the Messages application, Phone application, and more. These banners display relevant device information, such as network connectivity information, data, time and message notification icons (phone, email, Facebook, SMS) and more.

With this item selected, you have the ability to change any of the graphical elements associated with the two banners. This includes graphics to display for background, alerts and indicators, plus the font and font attributes used. Click any of the images to open the Windows File Open dialog to select the image file you want to use for the resource.

If you click the Next button on the Inspector (shown in Figure 17.3), you can define the icons that appear on the device's Home Screen. You can select which applications appear on the screen and can rearrange them to suit the needs of the theme.

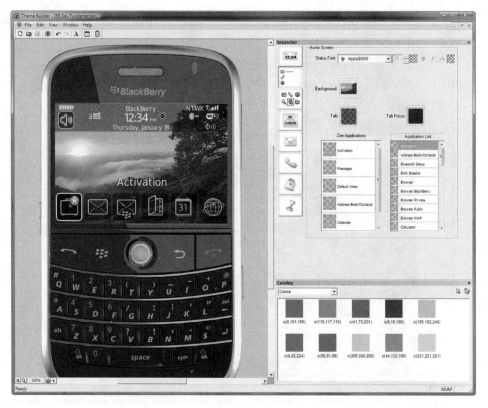

Figure 17.3 Defining Home Screen Options in Theme Builder

The Next button on the Inspector allows you to define which applications appear on the Applications screen and how they are ordered, as shown in Figure 17.4. You can define the background graphic, the image used to indicate new items for an application, and even how an icon appears when it is being moved.

Figure 17.4 Defining Applications screen options in Theme Builder

To change the order of applications on the screen, click the Edit Application Hierarchy button, as shown in Figure 17.4. You are presented with the list of applications displayed in the order in which they are shown in the screen. To move an application, select the application with the mouse and, while holding the mouse button, drag the application to the correct location in the application hierarchy.

The next button on the Inspector allows you to control the look and feel of menus and dialogs, as shown in Figure 17.5. From here, you can select which font is used for the screen, menus, and dialogs, plus select images that will be used for each type of dialog box.

Figure 17.5   Defining menu and button options in Theme Builder

The look and feel of the Messages application is controlled by the options defined behind the next Inspector button, as shown in Figure 17.6. From here, you can control the font used within the application, which background is displayed and which icons are used for email messages and web pages pushed to the messages application (described in Chapter 6, "Pushing Data to Internal (BES) Users").

Figure 17.6 Defining options for the Messages application in Theme Builder

Figure 17.7 shows the options for configuring the Phone application. From here, you can configure options for the Call Log screen, the Active Call screen, and the Incoming Call screens.

Figure 17.7   Defining options for the Phone application in Theme Builder

Figure 17.8 shows the options for the Lock Screen. From here, you can define the background image to use when the device is locked, plus the font used to display owner information.

Figure 17.8 Defining options for the Lock Screen in Theme Builder

Figure 17.9 shows the options for configuring global options for the theme. In this area of the application, you define all the remaining icons and images displayed within the theme. You can select images to use for network transmission icons, key modifiers (Alt, Caps Lock, Num Lock, multitap), navigation icons (up and down), hourglass cursors, and progress bar colors. Click an image file to open the Windows File Open dialog to select the file you want to use for the selected resource.

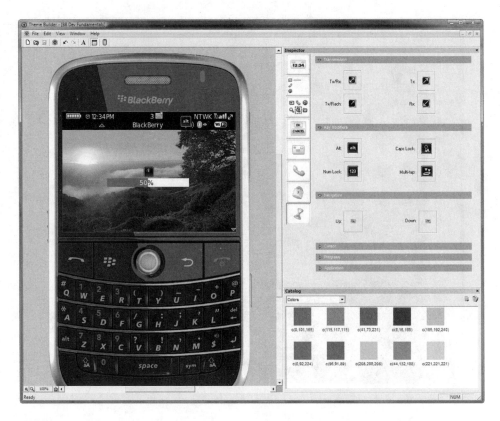

Figure 17.9 Defining global theme options in Theme Builder

After you customize your theme, it's time to get it ready to be deployed to a device. Open the application's File menu and select Export. The program displays a screen like the one shown in Figure 17.10. Specify the parameters for your theme, such as target device, targeted BlackBerry Device Software version, and the output folder. You also want to select whether you want to export an .alx or a .jad file for your theme. Select the option that works best for how you will deploy your theme to devices.

Figure 17.10   Plazmic Theme Builder Export dialog

When you have all the settings set correctly, click the OK button, and the application exports your theme. After the export process, you have two new files in the destination folder: .cod and .alx files. The .alx file tells the BlackBerry Desktop Manager or the BES how to deploy the theme. The .cod file is the compiled version of all the theme information. After you have these files, you can deploy the theme using any of the methods described in Chapter 16, "Deploying Java Applications."

17.1.2 Using the Plazmic Composer Application

Designers use the Plazmic Composer application to create content. It creates things such as splash screens, web graphics, and icons for BlackBerry smartphone themes. It can also create animations for animated themes. Composer is a graphical design tool, just like many available on the market today. The difference is that this tool can export content (both static and animated) in formats optimized for viewing on a BlackBerry smartphone.

Figure 17.11 shows an animated Home Screen being edited. There is a tool palette and different layers, objects, and a timeline that can be manipulated. This is similar to how Adobe Flash or Microsoft Silverlight works. Because this book is for developers, not designers, you have to refer to the Plazmic Composer documentation for information about how to create content using the application.

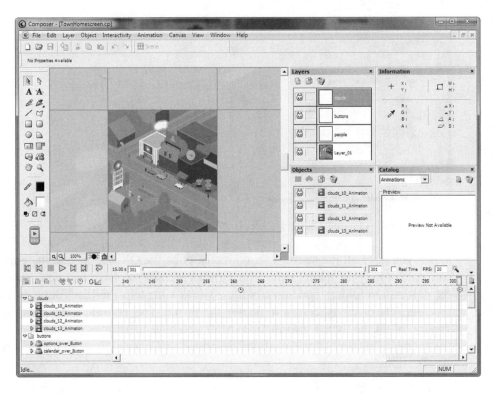

Figure 17.11   Editing content in the Plazmic Composer application

17.2 e-Commerce Content Optimization Engine

The BlackBerry e-Commerce Content Optimization Engine (ECOE) is a system that Internet retailers can use to give BlackBerry customers easier access to their sites. It allows for optimized viewing of e-Commerce websites through preprocessing of the site's data by the BlackBerry Infrastructure before sending it to a BlackBerry device. The system cannot work with any site without first being analyzed and configured for the BlackBerry infrastructure. When the site is accessed, it's viewed through a special version of the BlackBerry browser, called the Client for the e-Commerce Content Optimization Engine (CECOE), which must be deployed to target devices.

Here's how it works.

An organization selling products through a website contacts RIM to begin the process of analyzing its online store for use with the ECOE. RIM ECOE specialists work with the customer to build a conversion rules file that the BlackBerry infrastructure uses to convert the store's pages into a format more easily rendered on the device. The process involves analyzing the site to determine what content is displayed, how it is displayed, and what content is deemed nonessential and won't be delivered to target devices.

Additionally, any relevant site navigation is converted so it appears in the browser's application menu rather than within the site's content. This means that instead of selecting a navigation item on the site's pages, the user of an ECOE optimized site presses the BlackBerry menu button and selects the navigation elements from there. This allows the application to not take up any screen space for navigational elements.

The checkout process is even optimized, and the application can use the BlackBerry Wallet capabilities described later in this chapter.

The engine dramatically improves the end user's experience with the site because much of the time spent delivering layout and navigational content is removed from the equation; when the user requests the page from the site, mostly data (not markup) is delivered across the network.

With the conversion rules file in place, the customized version of the BlackBerry browser can be posted to the company's website for download by visitors using BlackBerry devices. After the user installs the special ECOE optimized browser, the site is no longer accessible from the BlackBerry browser. When the site's URL is launched on the device, processing of the site's pages automatically switches over to the optimized browser.

To use this system, the site's content cannot be static; it must be generated content, using such technologies as Cold Fusion, PHP, Java Server Pages (JSP), Active Server Pages (ASP), and others. If the layout or content on the site changes, the conversion rules file must be updated before BlackBerry devices can access the updated site. Organizations must work very closely with RIM whenever changes are planned for the site.

Figure 17.12 illustrates this process, which differs depending on whether the connection to the server is performed over an HTTP or an HTTPS connection.

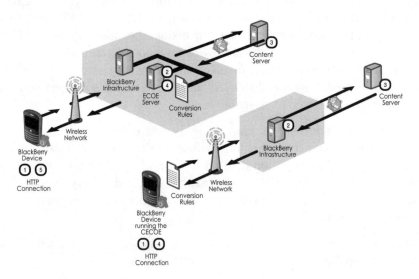

Figure 17.12 BlackBerry e-Commerce Content Optimization Engine process

For an HTTP connection to the content server, the request for content is submitted by the user from the CECOE (1). The request travels across the carrier's network to the BlackBerry infrastructure to the ECOE server (2). The ECOE server requests the data from the content server (3) and applies the conversion rules to the content (4) before sending the optimized content to the requesting device. The CECOE receives the optimized content (5) and renders it for the user.

For an HTTPS connection to the content server, the request for content is handled by the CECOE (1). The application requests the conversion rules from the BlackBerry infrastructure (2) and the content from content server (3). When the content and rules are received, the CECOE applies the conversion rules to the content client-side and renders the optimized data for the user (4).

 Note: Because of the difference between how HTTP and HTTPS connections are handled, from a performance and battery life standpoint, it's better to use HTTP connections to retrieve data.

17.3 Supporting the BlackBerry Wallet in Web Applications

The BlackBerry Wallet is an application that allows BlackBerry users to store personal information on their device in a secure manner. Web developers can make slight modifications to their site to allow BlackBerry Wallet users to populate credit card and other information into online order forms without typing the information—it comes directly from the wallet.

To get BlackBerry Wallet on a device, download the latest version from www.blackberry.com/wallet. When the application is first opened on a device, the user must provide a password before any personal information can be stored or retrieved. Whenever the application is opened, the program displays a screen showing the different types of information that can be maintained in the wallet, as shown in Figure 17.13.

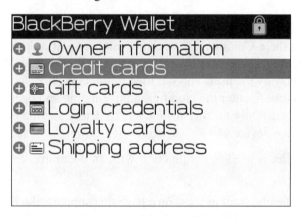

Figure 17.13   BlackBerry Wallet main screen

To create a new credit card, click the Credit Cards item on the screen and click New Credit Card. The program opens a screen similar to the one shown in Figure 17.14. Enter your credit-card information, press the Menu button, and save the information you entered.

Figure 17.14 BlackBerry Wallet: adding a new credit card

Because entering data using the BlackBerry Wallet changes how input forms are configured, when creating the e-Commerce site, the developer must prepare two different input forms: one for automated data entry using the BlackBerry Wallet and another for manual entry by the user. The site then prompts the user to select which method he wants to use to enter the credit-card information and opens the appropriate form. There is currently no way for the site to detect that the Black-Berry Wallet is installed on a device.

When the BlackBerry Wallet is used in conjunction with an e-Commerce website,

1. As the user begins the checkout process on a page that supports the Black-Berry Wallet, the user presses the BlackBerry menu button and selects Open Wallet from the menu.

2. The BlackBerry Wallet opens and the user is prompted to enter the Wallet password.

3. The user selects the data set (credit card, shipping address, and so on) from the Wallet.

4. The information is passed to the browser and populated in the appropriate fields on the input form.

Many different types of data can be populated into web forms, but for this discussion, only entering credit-card information is covered. For information on the other data sets supported by the BlackBerry Wallet, see the *BlackBerry Wallet Web Integration Guide* found on the BlackBerry Wallet documentation site (www.blackberry.com/wallet).

The first thing a developer must do is enable the web page for integration with the BlackBerry Wallet. To do this, the content type for the page must be set to

```
Content-type: application/x-vnd.rim.bb.wallet charset=""
```

In PHP, the value is set with the following code:

```
header('Content-type: application/x-vnd.rim.bb.wallet
charset=""');
```

In Perl, it can be set with the following code:

```
print "Content-type: application/x-vnd.rim.bb.wallet
charset="";
```

After the page is set up, the type of wallet data set being entered on the form must be defined. To enable the form for entering credit-card information, add the following hidden input field to the form:

```
<input type="hidden" id="bbwallet:cardType:creditCard" />
```

After the form is set up for the BlackBerry Wallet, it's time to start defining the input fields that will hold the credit-card information. The first thing the user must do when entering credit-card information is select the credit card type being used:

```
<select name="creditcard_type"
id="bbwallet:creditCard:creditCardType">
<option value=""></option>
<option value="mastercard">MasterCard</option>
<option value="visa">Visa</option>
<option value="amex">American Express</option>
<option value="diner">Diners Club</option>
</select>
```

Next, an input field must be provided to hold the credit-card number:

```
<input name="creditcard_number"
id="bbwallet:creditCard:creditCardNumberFull" value=""
type="text">
```

The form will need a field for storing the credit card expiration month:

```
<select name="expire_month"
id="bbwallet:creditCard:expiryMonth">
```

```
<option value=""></option>
<option value="01">01</option>
<option value="02">02</option>
<option value="03">03</option>
<option value="04">04</option>
<option value="05">05</option>
<option value="06">06</option>
<option value="07">07</option>
<option value="08">08</option>
<option value="09">09</option>
<option value="10">10</option>
<option value="11">11</option>
<option value="12">12</option>
</select>
```

And a place to store the credit card expiration year:

```
<select name="expire_year"
id="bbwallet:creditCard:expiryYear">
<option value=""></option>
<option value="2009">2009</option>
<option value="2010">2010</option>
<option value="2011">2011</option>
<option value="2012">2012</option>
<option value="2013">2013</option>
<option value="2014">2014</option>
</select>
```

That's all there is to it. After the form is completed and all the other content added to the page, it's ready to be tested.

17.4 Sync Server SDK

The BlackBerry Synchronization Server is a component of the BES that manages the synchronization of data between the device and backend servers. On the BES, the Synchronization Service works with other BES components and is responsible for synchronizing changes to PIM data between the device and the mail server over the wireless network. The BlackBerry Sync Server SDK allows developers to build a connector DLL that acts as an interface between a backend application server and the BlackBerry Synchronization Server running on the BES.

When a connector detects a change in the server database, it packages up the changes and delivers them to the Synchronization Server. The Synchronization Server then makes sure the data is delivered across the wireless network to the destination device and device application database. Using the same mechanism, when a device application updates data in the device-side application, the Synchronization Server delivers the updated data to the connector so the server database can be updated.

Figure 17.15 highlights how data is synchronized between the application server and the device application. When data is delivered to the Synchronization Server, the data is sent in a compact format to the BlackBerry Dispatcher (another component of the BES) for delivery. The dispatcher sends the data to the BlackBerry router, and then to the device either through the Internet and the BlackBerry infrastructure for wireless delivery (1) or using Serial Bypass (described in Chapter 3, "The Connected BlackBerry") for a local Wi-Fi (2) connected device or through the desktop for wired delivery (3).

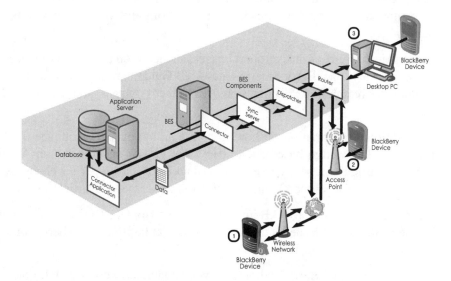

Figure 17.15   Sync Server SDK data flow

The connector provides the Synchronization Server with XML-based mapping files that define the server and device database schemas. The Synchronization Server uses these files to translate the database fields while synchronizing the data between data sources. The mapping files are called `appnameConnector Mapping.xml` and `appnameDeviceConnectorMapping.xml`, where `appname` refers to the name of the application being synchronized. Additionally, all data passed between the connector and the Synchronization Server are passed in XML format.

The easiest way to understand how the Synchronization Server SDK works is to dig through the client-side sample application included with the BlackBerry Java Development tools. Information on how to build a Synchronization Server connector is provided in the *Sync Server SDK Development Guide*. A link to the development guide is provided in the section, "Additional Resources."

17.5 Additional Resources

A complete listing of links to these resources is available online at www. bbdevfundamentals.com.

Download the Plazmic Content Development Kit from www.plazmic.com.

BlackBerry themes can be purchased or downloaded from www.pinstack.com, www.rimarkable.com, www.blackberyforums.com, www.crackberry.com, and many other sites.

Dimensions for screens, background images, and icons on BlackBerry devices can be found in the BlackBerry Smartphones – UI Guidelines at http://na.blackberry. com/eng/deliverables/6625/Dimensions_for_screens_images_and_icons_476251 _11.jsp.

For additional information on how to create an application icon, see the RIM developers knowledge base article "How To: Create an Icon for an Application." The article can be accessed at the BlackBerry developer's website (www. blackberry.com/developers), and search for knowledge base article DB-00126.

For information on the BlackBerry e-Commerce Content Optimization Engine, see the Features and Benefits document located at http://na.blackberry.com/eng/ deliverables/2594/Ecoe_FTO_434376_11.pdf.

Download the BlackBerry Wallet from www.blackberry.com/wallet. For information on how to use the BlackBerry Wallet in your applications, go to http:// na.blackberry.com/eng/support/docs/subcategories/?userType=21&category= BlackBerry+Wallet. For information about how to use the BlackBerry Wallet, go to http://na.blackberry.com/eng/devices/features/browser/wallet.jsp.

Information on the BlackBerry Sync Server SDK can be found at http://na.blackberry.com/eng/support/docs/subcategories/?userType=21&category=BlackBerry+Java+Application+Development&subCategory=Synchronization+Server+SDK.

Index

FREE Online Edition

Your purchase of **BlackBerry Development Fundamentals** includes access to a free online edition for 45 days through the Safari Books Online subscription service. Nearly every Addison-Wesley Professional book is available online through Safari Books Online, along with more than 5,000 other technical books and videos from publishers such as Cisco Press, Exam Cram, IBM Press, O'Reilly, Prentice Hall, Que, and Sams.

SAFARI BOOKS ONLINE allows you to search for a specific answer, cut and paste code, download chapters, and stay current with emerging technologies.

Activate your FREE Online Edition at
www.informit.com/safarifree

> **STEP 1:** Enter the coupon code: XKFJAZG.

> **STEP 2:** New Safari users, complete the brief registration form.
> Safari subscribers, just log in.

If you have difficulty registering on Safari or accessing the online edition, please e-mail customer-service@safaribooksonline.com